The Play of Ideas in

RUSSIAN
ENLIGHTENMENT
THEATER

The Play of Ideas in

RUSSIAN
ENLIGHTENMENT
THEATER

Elise Kimerling Wirtschafter

NORTHERN

ILLINOIS

UNIVERSITY

PRESS

DeKalb

Library of Congress Cataloging-in-Publication Data

Wirtschafter, Elise Kimerling.

The play of ideas in Russian Enlightenment theater / Elise Kimerling Wirtschafter.

p.   cm.

includes bibliographical references and index.

ISBN 0-87580-310-5 (alk.paper)

1. Russian drama—18th century—History and criticism. 2. Theater—Russia—

History—18th century. 3. Theater and society—Russia—History—18th century.

4. Enlightenment—Russia. 5. Social ethics in literature.

6. Social Justice in Literature. I. Title.

PG3076 .W57 2003

891.72'209—dc21

To Gary, Eric, Carla, and Valerie—

whose names also belong on the cover of this book

CONTENTS

PREFACE

• This book began with a simple problem. For roughly two decades I had studied the organization of Russian imperial society, yet still I knew relatively little about how the empire's subjects understood the social relationships that defined their lives. Armed with a belief in the efficacy of archival research, I had engaged in a search for evidence of social consciousness, but instead of giving voice to real people, I had given voice to the legal-administrative categories of official society. Although I had moved beyond the barrier of obtaining appropriate archival sources and selecting appropriate methodologies, I had hit the even mightier barrier of historical subjects who did not express themselves in writing. Petitions, judicial proceedings, and instructions to legislative commissions offered important insights into social attitudes, but the people who spoke in these sources did so in a framework and through categories provided by the state. To break through the silence, I needed sources in which Russians self-consciously reflected on their own social experience. For this reason I turned to the relatively unexplored corpus of eighteenth-century Russian plays, which while mediated through the prisms of literary formula and publicly permissible discourse, nonetheless expressed the ideas of educated people who self-consciously sought to create a Russian literary product for a Russian imperial theater.

On the face of it, the eighteenth-century plays seem merely to reproduce the plots, social conflicts, and moral dilemmas of earlier European or classical models. But while filled with clichés, the plays also express the problems and solutions that inhered in the self-definitions and perceptions of various groups and individuals in contemporary Russian society. For this reason, they provided a tool for reconstructing the social thinking of the past. My work in social and institutional history prepared me to read the plays not for their aesthetic contribution, but rather as a source from which to understand how educated Russians conceptualized "society," or a social way of life, beyond the immediate spheres of household and locality. The educated classes of the eighteenth century, being predominantly noble, not only wrote poems and plays, they also governed the enormous Russian Empire. As servicemen, they advocated civic engagement and built civic institutions, yet the "civic society" they envisioned did not add up to a politically organized "civil society" independent of the state. When eighteenth-century playwrights advocated civic engagement for the good of society, they assumed not that the autonomy of society needed to be protected from the state, but rather that the power of the state needed to be enhanced through the mobilization of society. To emphasize the important distinction between the conception of civic engagement in eighteenth-century Russia and the modern European conception of civil society, I have used the term "civic society" rather than "civil society."

My interest in how educated Russians came to identify with a larger "society" emerged from the straightforward desire to understand what people thought about social experience and how their thoughts related to social relationships. I was attracted to the later eighteenth century, particularly the reign of Catherine II, because of the cosmopolitan Enlightenment orientation of its elite culture—its grounding in universalistic principles and humanistic concerns, its deep sense of duty and commitment to moral education, its religious sensibility and deference to God-given natural order, and finally, its belief in earthly progress despite recognition of human shortcomings and despite keen awareness of the frailty of human life. Literary and intellectual historians have done much to elucidate the development and dissemination of specific Enlightenment ideas and thinkers in various national contexts, including eighteenth-century Russia. More recently, cultural historians have turned their attention to the practices of the Enlightenment as it was lived in specific social contexts. Throughout this book, the reader will find implicit and direct engagement with this massive body of research. If I have devoted little attention to concrete historiographic analysis or to situating "the Russian Enlightenment" within trends found elsewhere in Europe, this is because even in its Russian variant, the Enlightenment was far too diverse and diffuse a phenomenon to permit precise and consistent definition. What drew my attention to Enlightenment Russia was not the lineage of specific ideas or the emergence of distinct and distinguished Enlightenment thinkers and movements, but rather *the problematic pursuit of enlightenment* among the educated nobles who formulated policy, governed the country, and served the monarchy.

Given that the empire's educated service classes professed Enlightenment principles of natural equality and human goodness, I felt compelled to consider how in the face of Russian social reality—a reality filled with inequity and injustice—they remained reconciled to hierarchy and authority. How, in a society organized around serfdom and governed by absolute monarchy, did educated Russians confront the social questions posed by Enlightenment thinking? How did their reconciliation with reality occur in cognitive moral and philosophical terms? How, in other words, did they live with themselves? One can argue about the extent to which members of the educated service classes understood or internalized Enlightenment belief in the underlying equality and moral worth of all human beings, the efficacy of properly cultivated human reason, and the ability of people and government to reform and improve society. There can be no doubt, however, that they consistently articulated these principles in literary and legal-administrative sources.

That I would turn to plays as an embodiment of social and political ideas reflects the limited market for commercially produced culture in eighteenth-century Russia. Further west in Europe, historians have at their disposal a wider range of sources, from books to broadsheets to the records of parliamentary debates, out of which to extract the self-understanding and characteristic dilemmas of social groups. In Russia, where constituted political bodies—bodies such as guilds, diets, *parlements,* provincial estates, estates general, and the English parliament—did not exist, and where the periodical press was in its infancy, plays offered a unique forum for the debate of civic issues. Because plays were staged at court, in private homes and sheds, in seminaries and schools, and in commercial as well as state-sponsored settings, they were accessible to a socially diverse audience. Eighteenth-century performers came from all age groups and a variety of social statuses ranging from serfs to monarchs. Nor were playwrights necessarily professional men of letters. On the contrary, their ranks included obscure noblemen and noblewomen, civil servants, military officers, courtiers, churchmen, educators, the lowly serf M. A. Matinskii, and the illustrious empress Catherine II. Lacking pretensions to the calling of poet, these amateur authors wrote to educate children, honor patrons, entertain family and friends, influence society, serve the fatherland, promote knowledge, and express feelings. In their works, the strains of social and political life found vivid expression.

Because the primary purpose of this study is to explain how Russia's educated service classes understood social and political relationships, the analysis is limited to original Russian plays. But what was an "original Russian play" in the pan-European context of eighteenth-century Enlightenment culture? I define as Russian those plays *presented* as original Russian works or as adaptations of foreign plays to Russian mores. Across Europe, Enlightenment culture was cosmopolitan and imitative, plagiarism and piracy were rampant, authorial attribution was erratic, and literary classics of the highest value— Shakespeare immediately comes to mind—were appropriated and reworked without regard for origins, ownership, or creative integrity. Copyright laws were vague or nonexistent, and those that did apply only partially protected the proprietary claims of authors and publishers. Despite the threat of censorship, literary culture in the eighteenth century constituted a freewheeling, relatively unregulated, and unstandardized public arena where high and low forms of artistic expression overlapped and intermingled. In such a context— one where authors borrowed freely from existing works, where almost any educated person could claim the calling of writer, and where romantic notions of individual genius and originality were in gestation—an idea or a story did not have to originate in Russia in order to express a genuinely Russian point of view. Whether original, imitative, or plagiarized, a play associated with a Russian author or identified as a Russian work represented the articulation of ideas, attitudes, and beliefs embraced by an educated Russian. Precisely because the plays depict stock situations and operate within formulaic terms of morality and personal worth, it is important to examine their specifically Russian implications.

NOTE ON SOURCES

I began my research with a "database" of more than 650 plays, published or performed in Russia between 1672 (the year that theater based on literary texts began to be staged at court) and 1825 (the year of the Decembrist uprising, the first attempt to overthrow the monarchy by members of the educated service classes). Subsequently, I focused on 260 secular plays written and for the most part also published from the 1740s to the 1790s, the period when Russian theater achieved national self-consciousness and European recognition. A. P. Sumarokov's earliest published play, *Khorev*, a five-act tragedy in verse, appeared in 1747; it was performed at the Noble Cadet Corps in St. Petersburg in 1749, at court in 1750, and reportedly also by the Volkov troupe in Iaroslavl at about the same time. The late 1790s provide a logical terminus, because before the reign of Paul (1796–1801), there was little effort to impose systematic censorship on literature or the periodical press. In terms of literary movements, this was an era of neoclassical ascendancy, with the incorporation of sentimentalism and preromanticism in the last third of the century and the eventual rise of romanticism proper in the first decades of the nineteenth century. Intensive foreign borrowing characterized the entire eighteenth century, though by 1800 the European cultural models had become so thoroughly Russianized that they cohered as something identifiably Russian in language, content, and meaning.

To the best of my ability, I thoroughly surveyed the surviving corpus of plays *published* in the second half of the eighteenth century. In selecting specific plays for study, I chose—to repeat—those *presented* as Russian originals or adaptations, even though some of these actually may be translations. For purposes of economy, I relied on the main genres of tragedy, comedy, comic opera, and drama—thereby excluding ceremonial spectacle, prologue, epilogue, dialogue, interlude, ballet, pantomime, pastoral, foreign opera, commedia dell'arte, translation, and free translation. On occasion, I incorporated a "free translation" either because of its content or because it seemed closer to an adaptation. I also tried to consult the earliest available version of each play, unless it was rejected by the author. Thus, in 1768 Sumarokov reworked almost every play he had written since 1747, and it is the later versions that entered the literary canon. In another example, M. A. Matinskii disowned the 1791 version of his comic opera *The St. Petersburg Bazaar*, published, according to the author, without his permission and with errors.

The 260 plays examined in the course of writing this book represent the work of 78 known authors; 45 of the plays remain without authorial attribution. For authorial attributions—many plays were published anonymously or pseudonymously—I relied on published anthologies and the *Svodnyi katalog russkoi knigi grazhdanskoi pechati XVIII veka, 1725–1800*. In addition, because so many eighteenth-century authors are unknown outside a narrow circle of specialists, I provided brief biographies in the appendix. Together with scholarly monographs and anthologies, the main sources for the biographical data include encyclopedias and biographical dictionaries.

NOTE ON DATING, SPELLING, AND TRANSLITERATION

Although throughout this book I followed the Library of Congress system of transliteration, I also anglicized the names of rulers and on occasion a widely known author. In transliterating titles and names from the Russian, I preserved the original eighteenth-century spelling. In the citations provided in the endnotes, I likewise followed the original publication information. This can and did produce inconsistencies that the reader will notice in the endnotes and bibliography. The spelling of foreign names (primarily in chapter 1) posed another problem. I have tried to confirm the correct spelling of foreign names, but when this proved impossible I generally provided a foreign equivalent for the Russian spelling found in my sources. In some cases I also included the transliterated spelling in parentheses, and in others I gave only the transliterated Russian spelling. In cases where I have only initials, I likewise transliterated from the Russian. Thus, for example, I.-K. Ekkenberg appears as I.-K. Eckenberg.

The dates given in the text to identify individual plays generally refer to the year of original publication. If publication did not occur in the eighteenth century, I provided the year the play was written or first performed. In every case, the reader may consult the endnotes for details on the publication and performance of a particular play. Information on performances comes primarily from *Istoriia russkogo dramaticheskogo teatra* published under the editorship of E. G. Kholodov. For the period from the late seventeenth century until 1750, *Istoriia russkogo dramaticheskogo teatra* lists all known Russian theatrical performances, except for the productions of ambulatory troupes. By contrast, the repertoire lists for the period 1750–1825 cover only "permanent, professional, public theater" in Moscow and St. Petersburg. Court and state theaters fall under the rubric of "professional dramatic troupes," whereas ambulatory or seasonal troupes, school performances, domestic (usually noble) productions, and private serf troupes do not. On rare occasions information about specific amateur productions is culled from secondary sources, memoirs, and archives, but by no means have I attempted to reconstruct repertoire in any systematic fashion. The information provided about performances is therefore incomplete and subject to revision.

ACKNOWLEDGMENTS

This book has benefited from the support of numerous colleagues and institutions. James Melton read the entire manuscript, some of it more than once, and shared his knowledge of European history during hours of

"Enlightenment conversation." Gail Lenhoff likewise shared hours of conversation, commented on individual chapters at various points, and in general gave me the courage to face literary sources. Marc Raeff, with his rare gift for accepting the work of another on its own terms, offered stimulating criticism and generous encouragement that helped to bring this book to gestation and completion. James Cracraft brought a keen eye for detail and coherence to the book's final revision. Mary Lincoln and the late Bruce Lincoln posed tough questions that needed to be answered early on in the project, and several other colleagues offered thoughtful and productive criticisms of individual chapters along the way: Jane Burbank, Gary Hamburg, Daniel Kaiser, Valerie Kivelson, and Nancy Kollmann. Finally, Jerry Muller patiently responded to questions about European intellectual history and used his intelligence and moral sense to encourage precision and clarity. I am grateful to all these people for the good energy they so consistently provided.

A fellowship awarded by the John Simon Guggenheim Memorial Foundation and a sabbatical leave granted by California State Polytechnic University, Pomona, allowed me to devote two years to full-time research and writing. Mini-grants from the Faculty Center for Professional Development and released time from the College of Letters, Arts, and Social Sciences, both at California State Polytechnic University, facilitated the acquisition of research materials and the completion of final revisions. Sue Benney and the Document Delivery staff at the University Library filled a steady stream of interlibrary loan requests, always with efficiency and good humor. Also in southern California, Leon Ferder of the Young Research Library at UCLA kept me apprised of the most recent additions to that library's extensive microfilm collection of eighteenth-century Russian publications.

Further afield, Edward Kasinec and his staff at the New York Public Library offered generous access to their rich Russian holdings and patiently endured repeated requests for copies, microfilms, and extra hours. My sister, Leslie Kimerling, welcomed repeated intrusions into her already crowded Manhattan dwellings. Ekaterina Gerasimova of the Russian State Historical Archive of Ancient Acts (RGADA) in Moscow provided crucial research assistance, without which this book could not have been written, and my brother, Michael Kimerling, took time from his very busy schedule as an international tuberculosis expert to act as transatlantic courier. In Milan, Maria Di Salvo tracked down the correct names of Italian impresarios in eighteenth-century Russia.

At various stages in the research and writing of this book, foreign and domestic universities provided the opportunity to engage in serious discussion of this work's progress: the University of Leiden, the University of Milan, the University of Michigan at Ann Arbor, the University of Notre Dame, Stanford University, Harvard University, UCLA, and Arizona State University. Material I adapted from my essay "The Common Soldier in Eighteenth-Century Russian Drama," published in *Reflections on Russia in the Eighteenth Century,* ed. Joachim Klein, Simon Dixon, and Maarten Fraanje (Cologne: Böhlau, 2001), has been used with permission. Finally, I continue to marvel at the careful and able eye that the editorial staff at Northern Illinois University Press invariably brings to my "laserscripts."

On a more personal note, my parents, Rita and Sol Kimerling, continue to keep their grandchildren happy while I attend conferences and visit research facilities. My mother also performed editorial labor with the insertion of commas and the correction of word choices that only a mother would bother to notice. I owe a deep debt to my husband, Gary, and to our children—Eric, Carla, and Valerie—for the love, exhilaration, and sense of serenity that only they can provide. My life with them is a gift from heaven.

The Play of Ideas in

RUSSIAN

ENLIGHTENMENT

THEATER

Theater is always a sensitive seismograph of an era,
perhaps the most sensitive one there is; it's a sponge
that quickly soaks up important ingredients in the
atmosphere around it.

—*Václav Havel*

A true poet does not avoid influences or continuities
but frequently nurtures them, and emphasizes them
in every possible way. . . . Fear of influence, fear of
dependence, is the fear—the affliction—of a savage,
but not of culture, which is all continuity, all echo.

—*Joseph Brodsky*

1

THEATER AND SOCIETY

• Scholars and other observers have long debated the impact of the broad-ranging reforms initiated by Tsar Peter I in the first quarter of the eighteenth century. Although the persistent image of Peter as the creator of modern Russia borders on myth, historians of the imperial period would be hard-pressed to identify a significant social, political, or cultural institution left untouched by his actions. To be sure, important precedents for Peter's policies can be traced back to the sixteenth and seventeenth centuries, but the changes of the Petrine era were quantitatively and qualitatively different.[1] Never before had so many legal-administrative innovations been introduced in so brief a time. Never had the monarchy made such a concerted effort to import European learning and technology. The results were particularly striking in the state's ability to command resources and maintain military forces on a heretofore unprecedented scale. Equally noteworthy, though less effective, was the prescriptive legislation that penetrated local communities and everyday life in ways previously unimaginable. Despite the existence of Muscovite models for many of the changes associated with Peter, the sheer magnitude and concrete institutionalization of his reforms represented a substantive departure from earlier experience. It would not be an exaggeration to say that from Peter's death in 1725 until the Great Reforms of the 1860s, no major policy initiative seriously challenged the Petrine vision.

But while generations of rulers and officials embraced the military and administrative goals of the Petrine state, social and cultural change—Europeanization, education, technical progress, and the organization of civic society—followed a more tortuous course. The transformation wrought by Peter proved to be uneven and erratic, as heavy fiscal and service obligations disrupted household relationships and generated popular resistance. Opposition also arose among courtiers and in the educated classes, though in general the servicemen who administered the new institutions acquired European learning and internalized the cameralist Petrine outlook with amazing rapidity.[2] Several generations would pass before provincial nobles embraced the reforms begun by Peter, yet within decades, the Europeanization of elite culture and sociability took hold in the capitals of Moscow and St. Petersburg. As educated Russians assimilated the Petrine reforms, they also developed a new social and political language—a language that would define the terms of policymaking and political opposition for much of the imperial period. An eclectic combination of cameralism, civic humanism, natural law theory, classicism, Enlightenment principles, and Christian morality, this new language arose in a variety of organized public spaces. Theater represented just one of these spaces, and its corpus of literary plays effectively articulated the broader process of social and cultural change.

Historians have long recognized that political authority can be "essentially a matter of linguistic authority," and Tsar Peter I certainly understood the power of language to promote change.[3] Thus, together with the importation of European learning, technology, and bureaucratic organization, the tsar-reformer also introduced foreign terminology and etiquette to define the institutional and social relationships he hoped to create. Legislative measures such as the decree on assemblies (1718) and the General Regulation (1720) called for changes in the patterns of thought and behavior that elite nobles and high-level officials exhibited in civic life. Introduction of the civil script and the use of reasoned argumentation to explain legal prescriptions likewise bespoke an awareness that language could serve the cause of reform. In this context, Peter's early effort to establish permanent public theater based on a literary repertoire can be seen as a tool of social and cultural transformation. Theater not only served as the institutional locus for a new brand of public sociability, it also articulated social ideas and provided models of social behavior.

THE EMERGENCE OF RUSSIAN PUBLIC THEATER

The emergence of Russian public theater cannot be detached from the long history of popular and court entertainment, or religious and political ceremony, but neither can improvisational and ceremonial performance be equated with literary theater. Fairground entertainers, clergy, and political leaders performed theater without self-consciously creating a literary product.[4] In Russia, the beginnings of theater based on written plays, though not necessarily in the form of self-conscious literary creations, can be traced to the Orthodox churchmen who in the second half of the seventeenth century brought Jesuit-style school drama to Moscow from Kiev and

Polotsk. School drama aimed primarily to provide religious instruction to clergy and laity, but it also introduced staging techniques that could be incorporated into public theater and a literary product that on occasion represented the work of identifiable authors.

Already in the late sixteenth century, Orthodox brotherhoods in Ukraine maintained schools in which students performed religious plays and panegyrical declamations. Of particular importance for the development of theater in Russia was the Kiev Collegium founded by Metropolitan Petro Mohyla in the 1630s and elevated to an academy in 1701.[5] By the early eighteenth century, students at the Kiev Academy staged religious plays for a public consisting of Orthodox clergy, nobles, and townspeople. Professors composed and directed the plays, which were derived from Bible stories and saints' lives, while students served as actors, technicians, and stagehands.[6] The reach of these performances extended well beyond the Orthodox educational institutions. During holidays and leaves, student troupes put on plays for the general public, and semi-professional companies incorporated elements of the school repertoire into their secular performances. Public theater, understood as theatrical performances open to the general population and staged in public spaces, easily assimilated material from religious, literary, and oral sources. Nor were the influences unidirectional: in the school setting, short comic interludes depicting scenes from everyday life, presumably familiar from fairground theater, were performed between the acts of serious dramas.[7]

For Russia proper, there is no evidence that Kievan school drama was staged before the early years of the eighteenth century. A Jesuit school reportedly performed mystery plays for the Moscow public from 1699 to 1701, and from 1701 until the 1740s, school drama flourished at the Slavonic-Greek-Latin Academy, the product of Kievan-style Latin studies brought to Russia by Ukrainian teachers and students. During the 1710s, the school tradition found a second home at the surgical school of the Moscow hospital established by the Dutch doctor Nicolaas Bidloo in 1706. In both Moscow settings panegyrical plays with political themes assumed a prominent position alongside the traditional religious stories.[8] Polish-Ukrainian school drama also spread to the Russian provinces, remaining influential into the 1760s and 1770s and providing a foundation for the public theaters that Catherine II's governors began to establish in the 1780s. In Rostov and Iaroslavl, performances began as early as 1702 under the supervision of Metropolitan (and later Saint) Dimitrii Rostovskii (D. C. Tuptalo, 1651–1709), a luminary of the Kievan Orthodox schools. Among the plays performed, several were written by the metropolitan himself toward the end of the seventeenth century: *The Christmas Drama* (or *The Comedy on the Birth of Christ*), *The Dormition Drama* (or *The Comedy on the Falling Asleep of Theotokos*), and *The Repentant Sinner*. The latter play entered the repertoire of the Iaroslavl troupe of F. G. Volkov, which in the early 1750s was brought to St. Petersburg to help found the Russian Theater.[9]

That the impact of school drama also spread beyond the Muscovite center is evident from the activities of Metropolitan Filofei Leshchinskii. In 1702, Leshchinskii arrived in Tobol'sk from Kiev and established a Slavonic-Russian school for the children of clergy and recently Christianized Siberian natives. The Tobol'sk school became a seminary in 1743, and school drama continued to be performed there into the 1760s. Already in 1721 the student actors began to receive payment for their performances, and in the 1740s the seminarians added secular plays and puppet shows to the repertoire. Although for a time the nonreligious programs were closed to the general public, by the 1760s the seminarians functioned as semi-professional performers, allowed to keep all the earnings from their "theater." The status of theatrical productions at the seminary in Vologda is less certain, though according to an historical and topographical description published in 1782, regular evening performances took place during the 1770s.[10] In the absence of permanent Russian theater for a paying audience, school drama easily acquired public significance.

Equally important, even though school drama did not achieve visibility in Moscow before the beginning of the eighteenth century, already in the 1670s it contributed to the performance of written plays at court. A second stimulus, also the product of ties with Europe, came from Russian ambassadors who traveled abroad, Europeans living in Moscow's German settlement, and boyars involved with the foreign community. Historians possess limited information concerning the decision of Tsar Aleksei Mikhailovich (ruled 1645–1676) to establish a court theater, though clearly he lived among individuals who had experienced the pleasures of dramatic spectacles. Fairground and court entertainment had long histories, and the English ambassador reported seeing a comedy in the German settlement as early as 1664. In 1660 and again in 1672, the tsar personally initiated efforts to bring foreign actors to the Russian court, unfortunately to no avail. Then in 1672, with the encouragement and assistance of the powerful favorite A. S. Matveev, Aleksei Mikhailovich enlisted a Lutheran pastor living in Moscow, Johann Gottfried Gregorii, to write a play based on the biblical story of Esther and to stage it with actors chosen from among the residents of the German settlement.

Written in German and rendered into Russian by translators in the Foreign Affairs Office, *The Artaxerxes Play (Artakserksovo deistvo)* was performed on October 17 in a specially built theater *(komediinaia khoromina)* at the tsar's Preobrazhenskoe residence outside Moscow. The success of the spectacle led to the creation of a second theater inside the Kremlin palace, a school to train actors, and a Russian troupe that performed until the tsar's death in 1676. This first court theater employed about two hundred persons including actors and craftsmen, and its repertoire treated biblical, hagiographical, historical, and mythological themes. Although close to the school tradition in its preference for edifying and panegyrical subject matter, the main purpose of the theater was neither pedagogical nor religious.

Designed to entertain the tsar, his family, and courtiers, the theater based its repertoire on the "English tragedies and comedies" popular in the Germanies from the end of the sixteenth century.[11]

The initial flowering of court theater withered under Tsar Fedor Alekseevich (ruled 1676–1682), who did not share the dramatic interests of his father. But while the Preobrazhenskoe and Moscow theaters fell silent, the memory of court theater remained, even giving rise to legend. Persistent stories that the regent Sophia (ruled 1682–1689) personally participated in theater both as actress (along with her sisters) and playwright have not been substantiated; however, it is known that in 1686 Ukrainian singers performed in the private palace of her confidant Prince V. V. Golitsyn.[12] The Russian theater historian L. M. Starikova, generally a trustworthy source, accepts the account of Sophia's theatrical activities, and also claims that the regent attended a performance in Golitsyn's palace of *The Comedy of the Parable of the Prodigal Son* written by the monk Simeon Polotskii (1629–1680) in the early 1670s.[13] Whatever the facts, and in the absence of new documentation the skeptics seem more reliable here, the stories about Sophia in no way challenge the conclusion that, at the seventeenth-century court, theater constituted domestic entertainment for the ruler's inner circle.

It may be possible to trace the "origins" of Russian public theater to the school and court performances of the late seventeenth century, but the protracted and complicated process of creating theater in a permanent public space became a self-conscious enterprise only in the reign of Tsar Peter I. In 1701–1702, the tsar's emissaries visited Gdansk and arranged to bring to Moscow a troupe of nine German actors, headed by Johann Kunst and including his wife. By December 1702, the German troupe, and a Russian troupe trained by Kunst, began to stage comedies before paying audiences in the Lefort palace. The performances, which alternated between German and Russian, included adaptations of seventeenth-century French, German, Spanish, and Italian plays—including works by Giacinto Andrea Cicognini, Thomas Corneille (younger brother of Pierre), Andreas Gryphius, Daniel Casper von Lohenstein, Molière, and Tirso de Molina (Fray Gabriel Téllez). Both troupes survived the death of Kunst in early 1703. Otto Fürst soon replaced him, and at the end of the year the performances moved to Russia's first public state theater *(komedial'naia khramina)*, erected outside the Kremlin walls on Red Square. The new wooden theater operated until 1706, when for reasons unknown the tsar dismissed the German actors. Partially dismantled the following year to allow for the improvement of Kremlin fortifications, the structure remained standing at the end of 1713. No further performances are recorded, and the timing of the theater's final demise is unclear; possibly, it was destroyed in 1722 to make way for the arsenal, and certainly, it was gone by the end of 1730, when Empress Anna (ruled 1730–1740) ordered the construction of a larger theater at precisely the same location.[14]

So much for the actual building, but what became of the Russian actors after the departure of their German colleagues? It is possible they were transferred from the jurisdiction of the Foreign Affairs Office to the Preo-brazhenskoe household of Peter's sister, Natal'ia Alekseevna. Although there is no concrete information about the actors, it is known that props, costumes, and scenery from the Moscow theater, as well as copies of plays performed by the Kunst-Fürst troupe, were handed over to the tsarevna. Reputed herself to be the author of several plays, Natal'ia presided over theaters in Preobrazhenskoe (1707–1710) and St. Petersburg (1711–1716), but only for the years 1715–1717 does the archival record supply specific data showing the salaries paid to actors, singers, musicians, craftsmen, and other personnel.[15] Judging from the registry of expenditures and equipment, the theater staged substantial productions taken from the court, school, and foreign repertoires. Yet, to equate Natal'ia's theater with the continuation of state-supported public theater, as some historians would like to do, is problematic. There was no paid entry to the performances, and attendance by foreign diplomats is not proof of publicness.[16] Natal'ia's theater, like that of her father, was a domestic institution open to courtiers and invited guests. It can be called public only in the sense that any social appearance by a member of the royal family, outside his or her personal rooms, constituted a public event.

Although the theater of Natal'ia Alekseevna remained domestic, it nonetheless contributed to the development of permanent public theater by preserving a foreign literary repertoire alongside the better known school plays.[17] At court, where European troupes operated continuously from 1731 onward, imported foreign theater became especially influential. Efforts to engage an "Italian ensemble" of musicians and singers began in the reign of Peter II (ruled 1727–1730), and in 1731 Empress Anna, assisted by Augustus II of Poland and Saxony, brought commedia dell'arte to Moscow.[18] An improvisational brand of comedy that incorporated pantomime, acrobatics, juggling, music, and song, commedia dell'arte was not tied to a literary text, and thus could appeal to audiences unable to understand Italian. The first Italian troupe left Russia at the end of 1731; however, performances by a small group of Italian actors, musicians, and singers (male and female) continued. The court then moved back to St. Petersburg in 1732, and the next year a second Italian troupe arrived for a two-year stay. Finally, in 1735 a large Italian ensemble of comedy, opera, and ballet artists came to Russia, and from that moment until the mid–1760s, the "Italian company," though not purely Italian in composition, functioned as the production center for court theater.[19]

Over the years the Italian company included a variety of foreign acting troupes engaged by the court, as well as musicians, singers, dancers, ballet masters, composers, set designers, scenery decorators, and machinists. Intermittent court theater, which in the past had depended for its success on the personal involvement of an Aleksei Mikhailovich, Peter I, or Natal'ia Alekseevna, now had become a permanent conduit for the dissemination of foreign theatrical models. Equally significant, the new theater entered the

realm of Russian print culture. Beginning in 1733, the translation and publication of the Italian comedies and intermezzos *(intermedii)* allowed people
to read or hear descriptions of the plays even if they could not view actual
performances.[20] In this environment, educated Russians quickly began to
assimilate the foreign theatrical models into their own forms of literary
self-expression.

Whether one looks at school, court, or public theater in the early eighteenth century, it is difficult to maintain distinctions between the foreign
and Russian cultural lineages. The Russian court housed foreign theater
throughout the century: German troupes performed in 1738 and 1740,
French comedy arrived in 1742, and Italian opera continued. The court's
1766 table of organization *(shtat)* assigned revenues from the salt tax to pay
for the French and Italian troupes, and published data show that in the
1780s and 1790s the imperial theaters regularly staged French and German
plays along with Italian operas.[21] In addition, beginning in the reign of
Anna, the staging of Russian comedies also began to revive. The court did
not yet maintain an organized Russian troupe comparable to those established by Aleksei Mikhailovich or Peter I, but at least twice in 1734 and
1735 court entertainers, pages, and students from the Noble Cadet Corps
performed *The Comedy on Joseph.* Royal domestic theaters likewise provided
a home for Russian comedy. The future empress Elizabeth continued practices established in the Izmailovo household of Ivan V's widow Praskov'ia
Fedorovna and her daughter Catherine during the years 1713–1723. At
both courts, courtiers, entertainers, and servants put on plays, as yet
unidentified, except for *The Comedy on Princess Lavra,* written by Elizabeth's
maid of honor, M. E. Shepeleva.[22] Designed to amuse royal personages and
their close associates, none of these productions aspired to the Petrine vision of Russian public theater—a vision that Empress Elizabeth (ruled
1741–1761) brought to fruition only in the late 1750s.

Between the closing of Peter's wooden theater on Red Square and the
opening of Elizabeth's Russian Theater in the Opera House beside the Winter Palace, court theater remained a source of domestic entertainment for a
highly select company. At the same time, however, foreign and Russian impresarios consistently and with ever greater frequency produced public theater for paying audiences. During the reign of Peter I, a steady stream of
foreign troupes, some closer to circus acts than literary theater, began to entertain the Russian public. Independent of the court, these troupes depended on ticket sales but lacked the benefit of regular seasons or permanent quarters. One of the first foreign entertainers on record is I.-K.
Eckenberg, who in 1719 received a privilege *(privilegiia)* allowing him to
perform throughout the Russian state. An Italian troupe of "masters of cu-
riosities" *(kunstmeistery)* followed in 1721. Sources from the early eighteenth century do not necessarily distinguish mechanical, musical, dramatic, circus, and puppet artists. The literary repertoire did not yet define
theater in Russia, and actors tended to mix a variety of performance skills.

Even so, documents from the 1720s onward record the arrival in Russia of troupes that performed "comedies": the German troupe *(banda)* of I.-G. Mann (1723–1725), the troupe of "Hungarian native" Johann Grieg (1725), the French troupe of Peter Ishotur (1726), the troupe of English actor William Durham (1726), the German troupe of K.-L. Hoffmann (1726–1727), a French troupe directed by Jacques Renault (Renol't [1727–1728]), a troupe of Parisian actors that arrived from Amsterdam under the management of Jacob Riu/Riol (1728), and yet another company of French actors, also from Amsterdam, headed by Gemei Vili (1728).[23]

Little is known about the repertoires or productions of these troupes. The *St. Petersburg News* announced a performance for 17 September 1729 by French actors, probably the troupe of Jacques Renault, which remained in Russia until 1731. The troupe also performed in Moscow, including an appearance before Peter II in the German settlement. Johann Grieg first visited Russia in 1725, and when he returned from Sweden in 1734, he tended to a theater in Riga before moving on to St. Petersburg to perform comedies. In 1733, the tightrope-walker and actor Johann Christoph Siegmund (Iogann Khristofor Zigmund), attested in St. Petersburg already in 1727, staged a puppet comedy in the quarters of Empress Anna. Siegmund traveled back and forth between Russia and other European countries before receiving in 1742 a privilege from Empress Elizabeth that allowed him to establish German comedy in Moscow, St. Petersburg, Riga, Narva, Reval, and Vyborg. In the two capitals, Siegmund also received access to plots of land upon which to build actual theater structures. When Siegmund died in 1747, Peter Hilferding took over operation of the German theaters, and the performances before paying audiences continued until 1754 in Moscow and until 1761 in St. Petersburg.[24]

Except for language, the German comedy came close to realizing Peter I's idea of permanent public theater. Siegmund's theaters, housed in appropriately equipped permanent quarters and operated throughout the year, admitted spectators who bought tickets. Nor was their German-language repertoire a barrier to publicness. The German actors performed short plays and improvised scenes in the spirit of commedia dell'arte; occasionally they delivered dramatic episodes and songs in Russian, and when they staged more complicated productions, spectators received printed brochures with translations. But within a decade, German theater for a paying Russian audience began to fade, partly due to circumstances but also because Russian impresarios had begun to attract public attention. In Moscow, the German comedy remained active until a fire required demolition of the building in 1754. When a new comedy building opened in 1757, the Hilferding troupe was gone.[25] Instead, the English tightrope-walker Michael Stewart displayed his artistry, and the following year the English acrobat Berger staged comedy in a theater he had built.[26] Although new German troupes emerged in subsequent decades, they lacked the visibility of Siegmund's company.[27] In 1762 Johann Neihof (Iogan F. Neigof) received permission to stage German comedies in St. Petersburg, Moscow, Riga, and Reval. Nei-hof died in 1765, and Giuseppe Scolari (I. Skoliari) took over his privilege.[28] The German troupe of I. F. Mende performed in St. Petersburg in 1769–1770, and in 1799, Joseph Miré's German Theater opened its doors. Miré's company combined the troupes of actress L.-K. Tilly and impresario Karl Rundthaler, becoming in 1800 an imperial theater under the direction of August von Kotzebue.[29]

Despite individual setbacks, foreign impresarios remained prominent in Russian theatrical life throughout the eighteenth century. After the creation of the Russian Theater in 1756, they increasingly entered into direct relations with the imperial court and local officials. In return for a subsidy the Italian impresario Giovanni-Battista Locatelli (Dzhovanni-Batista Lokatelli) put on free performances for the St. Petersburg court, but also produced operas and ballets for the paying public. In 1757 performances began in St. Petersburg, and in 1759 Locatelli began to stage comic operas in Moscow, where he also built an opera house. Attendance fell off after the first few months, forcing the impresario to place his theater under the protection of Moscow University. As part of this arrangement, he organized a Russian troupe of student actors to stage translations of contemporary European plays alongside the tragedies and comedies of Russia's first celebrated playwright, A. P. Sumarokov. But unfortunately, Russianness failed to ensure financial stability. Empress Elizabeth died in December 1761, theaters closed for a period of official mourning, and in 1762 Locatelli declared bankruptcy.[30]

Although the early economic difficulties of Locatelli seem to have resulted from insufficient audience interest, the continuing receptiveness of the eighteenth-century court and urban theater-going public to foreign-language theater can only be called striking. A privilege of 1770 allowed the French merchant I. A. Pochet (Poshe) to stage Italian and French comic operas and ballets in St. Petersburg. Detailed information is lacking, but the privilege granted Pochet use of the Wooden Theater near the Summer Palace.[31] An Italian troupe followed in 1778–1781 with performances of comic operas in the theater of the Noble Cadet Corps, and before Gennaro Astarita's Italian opera became a court troupe in 1796, it gave public performances in Moscow and St. Petersburg.[32] Even English theater made a brief appearance beyond the amateur theatricals performed by members of the British community in the late 1760s. Toward the end of 1770 the company of a Mr. Fisher reached the Russian capital, and performances soon began in a shed on the property of the merchant F. G. Wulf. In November, Catherine II granted Fisher permission to construct a theater in the Tsaritsyn meadow, where his company performed until early 1772. The repertoire was entirely English—Shakespeare's *Othello* was performed in January 1772—but the theater attracted an audience of British, German, and Russian playgoers, among them the empress on two separate occasions.[33] Throughout the century Russian audiences remained interested in foreign plays, and Russian playwrights continued to work with recognizable European models.

By the 1730s, however, Russian public theater had also revived under the leadership of native impresarios.[34] As noted above, the school tradition engendered public performances for a fee beginning no later than 1721 in Russia and already in the seventeenth century in the Polish-Ukrainian lands. But where school drama ended and public theater began is difficult to determine. During the 1730s students and administrative clerks (prikaznye sluzhiteli) in Moscow and St. Petersburg put on popular plays (igrishcha) at Christmastide (sviatki) and Shrovetide (maslenitsa). The Moscow actors were students from the Slavonic-Greek-Latin Academy, and their St. Petersburg counterparts were "soldiers' children," studying at the Artillery School, and grooms from the imperial stable.[35] Students from the Noble Cadet Corps participated in plays at court in the 1730s and began to perform in their own theater in the 1740s. Throughout the century, they gave "public" performances for invited guests—relatives, courtiers, and other interested parties. At the theater of the Academy of Arts (established in 1757), students staged plays from 1764 until 1798, and at the Smol'nyi Institute for Noble Girls (established in 1764), exclusive theatricals for invited guests, some given in French, began in 1771.[36] Although the state schools did not open their theaters to paying audiences, student actors contributed to the development of Russian public theater in significant ways. Performances of Sumarokov's tragedies and comedies at the Noble Cadet Corps in 1750–1751 led directly to the creation of the Russian Theater in 1756, and when the Moscow University theater was revived in 1777, it also served as a laboratory for Russian playwrights and actors.[37]

More genuinely public were the Moscow productions of Russian "enthusiasts" (okhotniki) and impresarios. Judging from petitions addressed to the office of the Moscow police master, the enthusiasts who performed episodically in makeshift premises during the 1730s gave way to impresarios in charge of organized troupes by the late 1740s. Initially, the Moscow authorities viewed the public theatricals with suspicion and responded to unruly audiences by levying fines, punishing offenders, and using the public gatherings to identify illegal residents. But by 1750 they had devised procedures for policing the productions, which also received legal sanction in an imperial decree.[38] Incomplete data for the years 1749–1771 show that 50 managers of 46 troupes requested permission to stage Russian comedies (in six instances "puppet comedies"). The impresarios rented quarters for the performances, usually buildings owned by nobles and merchants or the theater of the German comedy. Because they were able to occupy the same premises year after year, it became possible to equip the structures for theatrical use. The productions also tended to follow a seasonal cycle, extending from December to March (Christmas to Lent) but sometimes lasting an entire year.[39] Finally, while there is no precise information on repertoire, surviving manuscripts reveal significant overlap with school drama: the plays performed in the Russian public theaters reproduced Bible stories, European chivalrous romances, and social comedies inspired by everyday life.[40]

Except for the absence of permanent theater buildings, the productions of the Moscow impresarios constituted Russian public theater in the fullest sense. The troupes supported themselves through ticket receipts, and their audiences and organizers were socially diverse. Merchants of the second and third guilds, administrative clerks and copyists, students of various church schools (primarily the Slavonic-Greek-Latin Academy), private employees, serfs, lower military ranks, and artisans—these were the groups from which the Russian impresarios came. Their audiences were even more broadly representative of urban society and would have included the masters of the serf managers as well as the nobles and merchants in whose homes the plays were staged. Social hierarchy and hereditary inequality were unavoidable facts of life in eighteenth-century Russia, but at the public theater society was not understood in socially exclusive terms. In contrast to court and school productions, theater for paying audiences created a sphere of civic activity, defined by culture and sociability, that temporarily transcended traditional social affiliations.

During the 1750s and 1760s, it appeared that impresarios had set Russian public theater on the road to commercial development independent of the government. Russia's prepolitical literary public sphere seemed poised to become a genuine public sphere, grounded in autonomous social and economic relationships.[41] But before long, state-supported and increasingly state-managed public theater began to overshadow the self-sustaining commercial trajectory. The public theaters suffered a financial blow when legislation establishing the Moscow Foundling Home in 1763 required that a quarter of the admission receipts collected from public entertainments—including comedies, operas, and balls—be handed over to the orphanage.[42] A more serious crisis hit in 1771, when plague decimated Moscow, and public social life temporarily came to a halt. Although the city began to recover in 1773, the independent impresarios did not return. By that time, moreover, Russian public theater under the protection of the court had become firmly established.

The founding of the Russian Theater in 1756 combined the public and school traditions with state financial support. Soon after the establishment of the Noble Cadet Corps in 1731, students had participated in plays at court. But when in 1750 student actors again appeared at court, it was to perform a new kind of Russian literary play: A. P. Sumarokov's neoclassical tragedies *Khorev*, staged in St. Petersburg, and *Sinav and Truvor*, staged at Peterhof. In these productions the traditions of school and court theater combined with the self-conscious creation of a Russian literary product.[43] Meanwhile, in provincial Iaroslavl, the public theater of independent impresarios had joined forces with the older tradition of school drama no later than 1750. Among the dramatic performances put on in merchant homes, those directed by F. G. Volkov (1728–1763) attracted the attention of St. Petersburg. By birth the son of a merchant and by occupation a factory owner, Volkov had acquired some education in Moscow during the

1740s, and on repeated visits to both Moscow and St. Petersburg could have attended the theater. In addition, two of Volkov's collaborators were sacristans *(tserkovniki)* from Rostov, an important site of church-sponsored school drama in the early eighteenth century. Tellingly, the only play known to have been part of the troupe's repertoire was Dmitrii Rostovskii's *The Repentant Sinner.* The eclectic influences that produced the Volkov troupe typified the development of theater in eighteenth-century Russia.

Information is sparse, but in 1752 authorities summoned the Iaroslavl actors to St. Petersburg to give performances. For the next few years they intermittently appeared in plays and studied at the Noble Cadet Corps. Then in 1756 an imperial decree ordered them to join the "Russian theater for the production of tragedies and comedies," newly established under the direction of A. P. Sumarokov in "the Golovin [Golovkin] stone house, which is on Vasil'evskii Island near the Cadet house." Empress Elizabeth allocated five thousand rubles to support the theater, one thousand of which went to cover the personal expenses of Sumarokov. In February 1757 the Russian troupe performed Sumarokov's tragedy *Semira* before the empress in the Winter Palace's Little (Malyi) Theater. A few days later a second performance took place in the Opera House before a paying audience, and a couple of days after that, the troupe performed Sumarokov's *Sinav and Truvor.* The Russian Theater soon closed for Lent, and when it reopened in May, regular performances were given on Mondays and Thursdays. Toward the end of the year, the new Opera House beside the Winter Palace began operations with a performance of *Semira* and a Russian translation of Molière's *Le mariage forcé* (1664).[44]

It took some time, however, to establish the Russian Theater on a firm institutional and financial footing. Although conceived as a public theater for paying audiences, the theater housed in the new St. Petersburg Opera House actually represented the founding of the Russian Imperial Theater. In 1759, the Russian Theater, which by now included actresses, became a professional court theater under court administration. Sumarokov stayed on as director until 1761, when he asked to be relieved of his duties. Not only did Empress Elizabeth grant Sumarokov's request, she continued to pay his salary, expressing the wish that he devote more time to literary compositions, "which bring such honor to him and such satisfaction to all who love reading."[45] Sumarokov had become a court poet, and the Russian Theater, now a court institution, ceased to be public: attendance by private invitation replaced open paid entry. Still, the court had committed itself to maintaining a permanent Russian troupe alongside the already existing French and Italian troupes, and the idea of Russian theater for the general public remained.

Indeed, whenever the court left the capital, the imperial theaters could stage performances for the St. Petersburg public. During the years 1767–1783, 555 of the 1,261 performances given by the imperial theaters were open to "private viewers" *("partikuliarnye smotriteli").*[46] The government also promoted public access to theater by providing financial assistance to impresarios. Locatelli's Russian theater at Moscow University could be called a state theater because of its reliance on the university's patronage, but Locatelli also functioned as an independent entrepreneur dependent on ticket receipts to finance his operations. Catherine II moved well beyond the irregular support offered to individual impresarios and tried to promote publicness by creating public theaters that did not charge an entry fee. It is unclear whether the empress intended these theaters to be permanent, or if they merely represented a continuation of coronation festivities in Moscow that had included an elaborate three-day street masquerade depicting Catherine as Minerva, goddess of wisdom and the arts.[47] Be that as it may, beginning in 1765, Moscow's open-air theater on the Devich'e field operated with state funds, and true to its public mission, served a socially diverse audience of nobles and commoners.[48] No list of performances has survived, but documents describing the wardrobe suggest a broad repertoire. Like other impresarios, the theater's directors promised that the content of the comedies staged would be "neither indecent nor abusive to society, neither impious nor opposed to the law."[49]

Historians have less information about the theater on Brumberg Square in St. Petersburg. According to V. I. Lukin, who attended the theater in 1765, the troupe performed plays by Molière, Marc Antoine Legrand, Philippe Néricault Destouches, Ludvig Holberg, Robert Dodsley, and A. A. Volkov.[50] The directors of both the Moscow and St. Petersburg public theaters fit the profile of contemporary Russian impresarios who served the general public on a commercial basis. Second-guild merchant Semeon Posnikov, head of the theater on the Devich'e field in 1765 and again in 1771, had staged comedies with a troupe of enthusiasts in Prince A. F. Viazemskii's home in 1750. During the years 1766–1769, chancery clerk *(kantseliarist)* Il'ia Skorniakov directed the theater. In St. Petersburg, at the time of Lukin's visit, a compositor from the Academy of Sciences publishing house managed the theater on Brumberg Square.[51] Theater at no charge to spectators surely increased public accessibility and, if Lukin's experience is indicative, encouraged potential playwrights to pen literary compositions.[52]

But the monarchy could not long maintain public theaters that generated no revenues through ticket sales. Throughout Catherine's reign, financial problems plagued court and public theater, as productions became more elaborate, acting troupes more professional, and the monarchy more budget-minded. A 1773 decree reviving the theater on Brumberg Square did not mention unpaid entry but did order the construction of an appropriate building.[53] The monarchy's dealings with Locatelli and other foreign impresarios seemed to offer a more viable model for promoting public theater. The government long had granted privileges to individuals who agreed to stage theater for the public, and in 1766, Colonel N. S. Titov established a Russian theater in Moscow to perform operas, tragedies, and comedies. His actors included sacristans and students from the university. Housed in the

Opera House of the Golovin Palace, the theater quickly ran into economic difficulties. Neither a loan from the empress nor a privilege to produce masquerades solved the problem. By March of 1769, Titov was fleeing creditors and unpaid employees. His theater closed when I. P. Elagin, director of the imperial theaters, refused to place it under court administration.[54] Instead, the Italians Giovanni Belmonti (Dzhiovanni Bel'monti) and Giuseppe Cinti (Dzhuzeppe Chinti), who also had been putting on masquerades and concerts, took over the Russian theater from Titov.[55]

The Italian impresarios received a five-year privilege authorizing them to build a wooden theater inside the city, a task accomplished in the home of Count R. L. Vorontsov on Znamenskaia Street. The privilege also specified that only Russian comedy and tragedy would be staged during the first year, after which comic opera, ballet, and pantomime could be added. In what appear to have been regularized professional dealings, Belmonti concluded contracts with actors and agreed in writing with Sumarokov not to stage the author's plays without his permission. These promising developments ended prematurely, however, after plague hit Moscow in 1771. Belmonti died, Cinti returned to Italy, and beginning in 1772 a parade of managers assumed responsibility for the Russian theater. First, Tereza Demota, the guardian of Belmonti's son, took charge and established a partnership with the provisioner *(proviantmeister)* M. G. Akulov. In 1773, Demota sold her share to Provincial Procurator Prince P. V. Urusov, and Akulov's share, due to his departure, went to second-guild Moscow merchant I. A. Gutkov. Between 1774 and 1776, Urusov managed the theater with the Italian, Melchior Groti (Mel'khior Groti), and after Groti fled without settling accounts, Urusov formed a partnership with the English impresario and tightrope-walker Michael Maddox. Finally, following the destruction of the Znamenskii Theater in a 1780 fire, Maddox became sole proprietor of the privilege.[56]

In taking over Urusov's privilege, Michael Maddox acquired a monopoly on theatrical performances in Moscow along with the obligation to pay the Foundling Home 3,100 rubles annually. Maddox also was in need of a theater: the Znamenskii Theater was supposed to be temporary, and the Urusov privilege had specified that a new stone theater would be built. Assisted by Moscow officials, Maddox built the Petrovskii Theater with 1,500 seats, but not without going into debt. In order to obtain financing, he mortgaged the privilege and the projected theater (that the loan would be used to build) to the Board of Guardians *(Opekunskii Sovet)* of the Moscow Foundling Home. In addition, although Maddox was able to extend his privilege to 1796, he also had to contend with the establishment of a competing theater at the Foundling Home itself. In a 1784 agreement reached with the Board of Guardians, Maddox preserved a monopoly on public theater in Moscow on condition that at his own expense he incorporate wards of the Foundling Home (and their teachers) into the Petrovskii troupe. For roughly two decades the Englishman put on plays and various entertainments for the Moscow public, but he never managed to get out of debt or ensure the economic viability of the Petrovskii Theater. Eventually, Tsar Paul ordered the Board of Guardians to take over both the theater and Maddox's debts. The impresario stayed on as vice director until 1801, when he was granted a pension and removed entirely from the theater's operations. Nor did the Petrovskii long outlive Maddox's tenure: in 1805 it burned to the ground, and in 1806 the Directorate of Imperial Theaters in St. Petersburg took over the management of Moscow public theater.[57]

Fire, plague, and debt—such were the obstacles to the consolidation of permanent public theater in Moscow and elsewhere. Yet despite Maddox's chronic financial problems, his arrangement with the Foundling Home sustained public theater for a relatively long period. More importantly, local officials and patrons supported the theater, even if inadequately, regardless of ticket sales. When the new Arbatskii Theater opened in 1808, it was not a public theater under private management, but a state theater controlled by the Russian government. Indeed, Michael Maddox himself could hardly be called an independent impresario, given his economic dependence on the Foundling Home. From the outset, it can be said, his public theater approximated a state theater. But neither was he a state serviceman, and there is no evidence that the government closely regulated his programming. Maddox managed the Petrovskii Theater based on a privilege, and his relationship with the Foundling Home was contractual. Unlike the impresarios who staged theater productions while also holding other jobs, and whose productions received no financial support from the state, Maddox was economically dependent yet worked on a full-time professional basis. Although his was not an autonomous professionalism, his operations were regularized in a manner that would have been unfamiliar to the Russian impresarios of the 1740s–1760s. Similar "professional" arrangements had characterized foreign theater in Russia since the 1740s; now Russian theater had reached the same degree of complexity in organization.

In contrast to the situation in Moscow, Russian public theater in St. Petersburg depended almost entirely on state support.[58] The court of Catherine II spent lavishly on entertainment, and cost overruns failed to constrain the empress's pleasure, but the empress's officials did try to bring fiscal stability and accountability to the administration of the imperial theaters. The effort to define a budget began with the 1766 table of organization, which covered ballet, chamber music, Italian opera, French and Russian theater, balls, actors, and craftsmen.[59] By 1783 German theater also had been incorporated into the court budget, and after Prince N. B. Iusupov became director of the imperial theaters in 1791 officials finally brought expenditures under control.[60] Amidst enormous financial pressures, the government also supported Russian public theater in St. Petersburg. Legislation of 1783 designated two "city theaters" for the paying public: the theater between the Moika [river] and Ekaterininskii canal near Kolomna (the Stone or Bol'shoi Theater) and the theater on the Tsaritsyn meadow [also Mars Field] by the Summer Garden (the Wooden or Malyi Theater).[61] Although the 1783 legislation forbade the Directorate of Imperial Theaters "to appropriate for itself the exclusive right to [produce] shows"—and thus upheld the practice of granting privileges and leasing theaters to impresarios—Russian Imperial Theater increasingly became the provenance of permanent public theater.[62] By 1800 the imperial theaters in St. Petersburg and its environs included the Stone (Bol'shoi) Theater, the Hermitage Theater, the theater on Stone Island, the theater on Nevskii Prospect near the Admiralty, the theater in the home of Kushelev (Miré's German Theater), and suburban theaters in Gatchina, Oranienbaum, Pavlovsk, Peterhof, and Tsarskoe Selo.[63]

During the reign of Catherine II, the network of state-supported imperial theaters that would bring such glory and international acclaim to Russian arts began to take shape. But in a land as vast as Russia, the court could not on its own carry theater to the entire country. Nor did the emergence of public theater outside the capitals of St. Petersburg and Moscow necessarily depend on the transfer of a cultural product from the center to the periphery. On the contrary, the establishment of the Russian Theater in St. Petersburg required the importation of actors from provincial Iaroslavl, and school drama, which repeatedly gave rise to acting troupes headed by Russian impresarios, also reached Moscow from "peripheral" areas. There was no single trajectory of development or lineage of cultural transmission that accounts for the appearance of permanent public theater in the Russian capitals or provincial cities. There was, however, a literary repertoire, part of a larger Russian and broadly European print culture, that connected various publics. A common literary culture is not equivalent to a conscious social or political identity, but in the absence of translocal constituted bodies and parliamentary politics, one could argue that the shared experience of Russian theater helped to institutionalize civic society.[64]

Catherine II's reform of local administration also contributed to the institutionalization of civic society, and the consequent appointment of educated governors and governors-general gave an unprecedented boost to provincial theater. Kaluga became the center of a governor-generalship *(namestnichestvo)* in 1776, and Governor-General *(namestnik)* M. N. Krechetnikov immediately set about establishing a theater with actors recruited from St. Petersburg. The Kaluga Social Welfare Board *(prikaz obshchestvennogo prizreniia)* administered and financed the theater, which in 1777 opened in a building acquired from a local merchant. The board also collected the revenues generated from ticket sales, and as in the capitals, a portion of the receipts went to support the local foundling home.[65]

In Tobol'sk, as discussed above, religious school drama had evolved into public theater for a paying audience already in the first half of the eighteenth century. Dominated in the 1760s by seminarians, public theater became city theater, likewise administered by the Social Welfare Board, under A. B. Aliab'ev, governor of Tobol'sk province from 1787 to 1795. When A. N. Radishchev attended the Tobol'sk theater in the spring of 1791, he was one of only 40 spectators in a hall reportedly built for 560. But in subsequent years, public support must have increased: a 1799 contract reveals the presence of a self-supporting, self-managed theater troupe—an actors' collective or *artel'* in the language of the nineteenth century. Although the theater's equipment and costumes belonged to the local state authorities, the actors' salaries came from ticket sales, and their contract specified that for the year 1800, they would stage 42 shows, including 11 new plays—6 dramas, 1 opera, and 4 comedies. There is no detailed description of the Tobol'sk performances, but the repertoire definitely included literary plays (Russian and foreign) from the late eighteenth century.[66]

Catherinean officials in need of entertainment also brought literary theater to Vologda, Tambov, Riazan, and Voronezh. Theatrical performances marked the opening of the Vologda governor-generalship in 1780, and when Governor-General A. P. Mel'gunov was reappointed in December 1786, performances took place in the theater in his home.[67] The actors included performers from Iaroslavl, local civil servants, and Mel'gunov's own daughter. During the summer of 1787, the Vologda governor and noble society requested and received permission to establish a public theater in the governor-general's home, and in 1791 a traveler recorded the presence in the city of a stone theater maintained by the Social Welfare Board.[68]

When the poet G. R. Derzhavin became governor of Tambov province in 1786, he organized balls, concerts, and theatrical productions—the latter performed by young nobles, civil servants, and students. Although the Tambov theater appears to have been the domain of local enthusiasts and amateur actors, rather than a truly public theater for paying audiences, its opening was a public event announced in the *St. Petersburg News*.[69] After the governor-general of Tambov and Riazan, I. V. Gudovich, got wind of the new cultural amenities, he insisted that the Tambov ballet master, scene-shifter, and painter be sent to Riazan. There, in 1787, a wooden theater opened, financed by the Social Welfare Board, which also collected the receipts.[70]

In Voronezh, V. A. Chertkov became governor-general in 1782 and had established a noble theater in the home of a superior by 1787.[71] The troupe included the children of Chertkov, amateurs from the local nobility, and in the role of director and leading actor, the vice governor, Prince R. I. Ukhtomskii. Entry to the Voronezh performances was by invitation, and while the audiences were not exclusively noble, the theater remained a domestic noble institution throughout the eighteenth century. But as in Tambov, the creation of the Voronezh theater was a public event, even though the governor-general did not establish a public theater.

The same can be said of the noble theaters created in Tver, Khar'kov, and Penza. In 1787 students at the Tver Noble School performed a drama with ballet before Grand Prince Alexander Pavlovich (the future Alexander I) and his brother Constantine, and in 1789 Khar'kov's governor, I. F. Kishenskii, organized a domestic theater with young actors from local schools, administrative offices, and noble families. Khar'kov also was home to public performances produced by impresarios—first among them, the military deserter

Sergeant Dmitrii Moskvichev, and in 1795–1796, court actor T. V. Konstanti-nov. By 1799 the noble and public theaters reportedly had merged.[72] In Penza, yet another provincial governor, I. M. Dolgorukov, took the initiative in establishing a theater on the property of a local nobleman. Built to ac-commodate up to one hundred spectators, the theater began to give weekly performances in 1793. The actors of the Penza theater were local nobles in search of useful entertainment. There was nothing public or commercial about their activities, yet the Penza theater clearly played a public role. When Governor-General *(general-gubernator)* Prince P. A. Viazemskii visited in 1796, a troupe of Simbirsk actors performed for him there.[73]

Because in the provinces noble theaters frequently represented the only show in town, their public significance was greater than one might expect. Even when confined to a socially exclusive circle, the theaters encouraged identification with translocal civic society by disseminating European forms of sociability and a shared literary culture. After A. T. Bolotov settled in Bogoroditsk (Tula province), he organized and wrote plays for a chil-dren's theater that—from 1779 until 1781—entertained the families of landowners and officials from the surrounding area. Although Bolotov's goals were primarily pedagogical, and although the children of Bogoroditsk officials already had been performing poetic declamations and excerpts from plays, to produce theatricals in a specially adapted structure consti-tuted a public event. The children's theater not only served a pedagogical purpose but also gave shape to a local public, defined through culture and social intercourse.[74]

Amateur domestic theater played a similarly public role at court and in the capitals even after professional performances became regularly avail-able. In 1765, at the St. Petersburg home of P. B. Sheremetev, Empress Catherine II attended an amateur theatrical in which the actors and ac-tresses came from some of Russia's most illustrious families.[75] Tsarevich Paul appeared in a Sheremetev production the following year and hosted his own amateur theatricals before ascending the throne.[76] Among aristo-crats and courtiers, domestic performances continued throughout the cen-tury. The 1774 staging of a French tragedy at court brought together a cast from the Gagarin, Golitsyn, Kurakin, Neledinskii, Razumovskii, Saltykov, Sheremetev, and Shuvalov families.[77] Two decades later, these practices con-tinued.[78] In 1794, Princess K. F. Dolgorukaia and Countess Golovkina man-aged competing amateur troupes in which foreign diplomats and the cream of St. Petersburg society acted.[79] Long after court and public theater became institutionalized, Russia's governing classes expressed their continuing iden-tification with the social experience of theater by staging rival domestic pro-ductions. More than an art form, an instructional tool, or a source of enter-tainment, theater represented a public space where the individual participated in a broader, though at times highly exclusive, civic society.

If even domestic theater could encourage identification with civic soci-ety by blurring the distinction between performer and audience, it did so primarily by placing actors in social roles other than those they occupied in real life. Noble serfowners appeared as commoners and servants in amateur productions, and serfs appeared as monarchs and magnates in the theaters of their masters. In these settings, concrete reality could be set aside, social hierarchy ignored, and moral truths revealed without disturbing good order. Historians identify a total of 155 serf theaters that operated from the 1760s to the 1840s, and contemporary reports of another 18 remain unsubstantiated. A significant majority of the serf theaters (103) were located in 14 towns, and of these, 40 existed in the eighteenth century, 31 in eighteenth-century Moscow. The 53 serf theaters located on rural estates in 23 provinces included 24 that also can be dated to the eighteenth century.[80] The Sheremetevs established the most famous serf theater, which from 1779 until 1797 gave performances in Moscow, Kuskovo, Markovo, and Ostankino. In the manner of monarchs, P. B. and N. P. Sheremetev (father and son) maintained a "court" troupe of professionally trained serf actors and musicians. The Sheremetevs also engaged an international array of artists, masters, architects, and composers, and their theater produced a varied repertoire of French, Italian, German, and Russian works—including operas, comedies, and ballets.[81] For this regal family, serf theater represented the means both to entertain the master and to cultivate the arts in Russia.

But few masters of serf theaters could compete with the Sheremetevs in terms of resources, elaborateness, and artistic sophistication. Thus in its most exploitative form, serf theater also could become public theater organized on a commercial basis. In Nizhnii Novgorod, local amateurs held center stage until the wealthy serfowner Prince N. G. Shakhovskoi arrived in 1798. Shakhovskoi, who spent winters in Moscow and summers on his estate in Nizhnii Novgorod province, reportedly maintained a troupe of close to 300 serf musicians, singers, and actors (male and female). With financial assistance from the local nobility, he transformed his domestic theater into the Nizhnii Novgorod public theater. The theater remained the family's property until 1827, when it was purchased by Provincial Secretary I. A. Rasputin and first-guild merchant M. S. Klimov on condition that the serf actors and actresses—96 persons, including children—be freed.[82] Well before the end of serfdom, Shakhovskoi's commercialized serf theater became a commercially operated public theater where salaried actors entertained a paying public. Thus, while neither serf theaters nor amateur noble productions can be equated with permanent public theater, both contributed to the creation of a theatrical life in the capitals and provincial cities of Russia.

• In European terms, permanent public theater came late to Russia. France, Spain, and England all possessed non-ambulatory public theater companies by the last quarter of the sixteenth century. These companies "performed on a regular basis before paying patrons," and their existence indicated that a "critical mass" of educated theatergoers had been reached.[83] In Russia, permanent public theater devoted to the performance of Russian and foreign literary plays did not begin to take hold until the 1750s. Decades would pass, moreover, before sufficient resources had been marshaled to create a Russian repertoire or to secure continual public access to permanent standing institutions. One cannot say that Russian theater arose primarily from oral culture, from liturgical or school drama, from the domestic theaters of the nobility and court, or from the importation of foreign models. To the contrary, Russian public theater, based on a literary repertoire, incorporated elements from all these settings. To trace the intricate social, institutional, and artistic relationships produced by the intermingling of multiple cultural traditions lies beyond the scope of this book. One point is certain, however: the central task for scholars is not to determine whether the sources of cultural development were original or derivative, foreign or Russian, popular or elite. Long before the age of Enlightenment cosmopolitanism, European theater culture had become far too mobile to sustain notions of indigenous origins or national theater. Distinctive national histories surely produced identifiable theatrical forms, but these "original" elements were quickly absorbed, transmitted, adapted, and retransmitted across political boundaries. What emerges from the historical record so briefly described above is a picture of individuals from all segments of society—individuals, not social classes or ethnic nations—carrying cultural forms and practices from one context to another, and in the process transforming human experience and perception.[84]

PUBLIC EXPRESSION AND SOCIAL CONTROL

At the same time that permanent theater for paying audiences began to encourage artistic creativity and public expression in Russia, it also increased the problems of social control associated with urban sociability. In contrast to religious processions, carnivalesque merriment, and fairground entertainment, Russian theaters crowded hundreds—sometimes thousands—of people into a confined space.[85] Across Europe, moreover, eighteenth-century audiences were notoriously rambunctious and irreverent. A. P. Sumarokov erroneously asserts in the published introduction to *Dmitrii the Pretender* that theatergoers in London and Paris did not crack nuts, converse loudly, or engage in fisticuffs.[86] In fact, the seasoned spectators of western Europe did more than eat, drink, talk, steal, fight, and deposit bodily excretions during performances; in London and Paris, they sometimes erupted into full-scale riot to protest ticket prices and unpopular productions.[87] Across Europe, long after public theater productions became tied to set literary texts, audiences and actors continued to engage in impromptu interaction during the course of performances.

In recent decades historians of early modern Europe have begun to associate Enlightenment sociability, including rowdy audience behavior, with the emergence of a self-conscious public opinion. Although theatergoers

were demonstrative and potentially volatile long before public opinion acquired political significance, it was eighteenth-century policymakers and
social critics who explicitly accepted the legitimacy of spontaneous audience judgment. Defenders of the audience's right to judge—early Enlightenment critics such as Joseph Addison in England, Abbé Jean-Baptiste Du-
bos in France, and Johann Mattheson in Germany—rejected strict
neoclassical aesthetics in favor of the idea that art should be evaluated as
much by public reception as by conformity to specific rules of
composition.[88] Such thinking at once heralded commercialization and recognized audiences as courts of public opinion. Sumarokov, by contrast, un-
forgivingly subordinated audience reception and hence public opinion to
his own neoclassical criteria of literary achievement. From his towering position as the father of Russian theater, to evaluate a play in terms of public
appeal would have been tantamount to accepting baseness over taste, unless of course the public's taste corresponded to his own.[89]

Accustomed to the ceremonial etiquette of the court and the discipline
of the school, Sumarokov decried the behavior of audiences at Moscow's
public theater. His position surely promoted the dignity of literature and
underscored the literary significance of theater, but it also ignored a crucial
requirement of public theater: the need to engage and satisfy paying audiences. Sumarokov's fellow playwright V. A. Lukin, the son of a court lackey,
appeared more willing to accept performers and theatergoers on their own
terms. But Lukin also reacted to public theater audiences with aloofness
and repugnance. After visiting the St. Petersburg theater on Brumberg
Square in 1765, Lukin emphasized the slovenliness of the spectators. Two
men with whom he spoke smelled unpleasantly of liquor, and the audience
at a Russian performance of Molière's L'Avare (1688) consisted "almost entirely of lower-class people (chern'), merchants, unranked administrative
clerks (pod'iachie) and others similar to them." His own humble origins
notwithstanding, Lukin openly disdained the common people. Only as an
afterthought did he give modest credit to the audience, adding that it also
included "eminent gentlemen and people of middle ranks who attend out
of curiosity."[90] As if to reiterate his repugnance for public theater audiences,
Lukin's account of a 1765 court production of his comedy, The Spendthrift
Reformed by Love, contained no derisive social commentary. Lukin praised
the actors and took no offense at the spectators who talked, coughed, blew
their noses, and smoked during the first act. By the second act they began
to pay attention and for the duration of the performance remained quiet.
For Lukin, whose enemies had been spreading the rumor that his patron
Elagin was the real author of the play, the audience's silence brought validation and proof of success.[91]

Whatever the nuances in their reactions to audiences, Sumarokov and
Lukin both belonged to an educated service class that identified with the
civilizing mission of Enlightenment culture. Both agreed, therefore, that
theater represented a tool of moral instruction and that audience behavior

indicated whether spectators were being properly instructed.[92] The satirical journal *All Sorts of Things*, founded by Catherine II in 1769, mused that while Russian nobles regarded themselves as lovers of the theater, they exhibited more interest in the personal lives and quarrels of the actors than in the characters developed on stage. Attentive solely during dances, audiences ignored the moral questions set before them.[93] The periodical *Evenings* concurred, noting that spectators failed to learn anything sensible from tragedy and comedy because instead of listening, they attended the theater "to show themselves and look at others." Echoing Sumarokov, the *Evenings* commentator expressed dismay at the drinking, eating, and loud laughing that went on in the theaters. The behavior, moreover, could not be explained by the social composition of the parterre (the general theater audience in the pit), which at the imperial theater included only nobles.[94]

The *Evenings* correspondent seemed to suggest that nobles who attended court theaters should behave differently from the audiences at public theaters. But based on the Russian sources examined to date, it is impossible to explain audience rowdiness in terms of social origins. Nor do accounts of contemporary European theaters indicate that social composition determined comportment. A circus atmosphere pervaded many theatrical venues, and however one explains audience unruliness, the growing popularity of public theater exacerbated longstanding problems of urban social control. In 1750, the general police master of Moscow, A. D. Tatishchev, sought guidance from Empress Elizabeth, asking her to give legal sanction to the theatricals already being staged by impresarios. The resulting decree permitted the performance of Russian comedies at evening parties *(vecherinki)* as long as "no disorders, illegal acts, noise, and fighting occur." In addition, it forbade performers to don clothing associated with the clergy or to go about town in costume. Already prior to the decree, entrepreneurs interested in putting on parties, concerts, and comedies registered with the police, and the police in turn routinely forbade noise, shouting, fighting, gambling, obscenities, and plays that displayed impious behavior, depicted priests and monks, or opposed the laws. The decree of 1750 confirmed these practices, and by year's end local directives also specified that police units, pickets, or guards—at times reinforced by soldiers—be present during performances.[95]

The coming together of a crowd at the theater created the potential for disorder that both officials and impresarios hoped to prevent by posting guards and punishing violence. Disturbances continued, however, and sometimes resulted from the behavior of the police. During the 1750s and 1760s, guards sent to protect the Moscow theaters bullied their way into performances or admitted spectators in return for a pawn. In general, however, the police identified serfs and servants waiting outside the theaters as the main troublemakers. In 1758, one foreign performer received permission to build a hut so that the servants who accompanied their masters to his shows could keep warm during performances. Otherwise, they would continue to break planks and build fires to provide heating. Servants also reportedly threw bricks at theater windows, got into fights, and committed assaults. In a case from 1761, a soldier even went undercover dressed as a serf in order to determine who was responsible for recent acts of vandalism at the Moscow Opera House. Repeatedly, the authorities admonished serf-owners to control and punish their people yet also intervened, without regard for seignorial rights (or perhaps at the seignior's urging). Public whippings, which could be followed by assignment to the army, bolstered the master's disciplinary powers.[96] Consistent with broader policies designed to expand the administrative reach of the state, the policing of theaters focused more on the public setting than on the actual content of the shows.

But the regulation of content lay only a stone's throw away in the concept of good taste. The makers of Russian literary theater generally condemned what they regarded as audience inattention and in the name of enlightened pedagogy presented themselves as the rightful arbiters of good taste.[97] Long before "regulative censorship" became enshrined in legal-administrative institutions, "social censorship"—defined as constraints on expression imposed by dominant discourses—policed the written word.[98] Good taste even functioned as a juridical concept backed by the monarchy and the law. Authors who aroused the Russian monarch's displeasure found their works banned and their persons imprisoned or exiled. Under the legal principle of "the Sovereign's word and deed" ("slovo i delo Gosudarevo"), any unauthorized discussion of the ruler could be punished as treason. Although the practice was abolished by Peter III, "word and deed" represented an early form of censorship that would be supplemented and eventually replaced by more elaborate social controls and administrative mechanisms. The threat of criminal prosecution for the written or spoken word always loomed on the Russian horizon, even though in contrast to the situation in the nineteenth and twentieth centuries, for much of the eighteenth century, the empire lacked a bureaucratized censorship apparatus.[99]

Indeed, the small number of presses in eighteenth-century Russia made bureaucratic censorship unnecessary. At the end of Peter I's reign, the Moscow Printing Office under the authority of the Holy Synod of the Orthodox Church published religious and secular books, while presses at the Senate and St. Petersburg Naval Academy published only secular books.[100] In addition, the Synod operated religious presses in St. Petersburg, Kiev, and Chernigov, as well as a fourth religious press at the Aleksandr Nevskii Monastery in St. Petersburg. Beginning in 1727, the Supreme Privy Council took measures to centralize publishing under its supervision, though in practice censorship remained concentrated in the hands of either the Synod or the Senate. Religious publishing under synodal control moved to Moscow, while secular publishing remained in St. Petersburg, carried out by the Senate through the recently created Academy of Sciences.[101] Full codification of this arrangement came in 1743 with the Synod assuming explicit responsibility for religious publishing and the Senate for secular. Subsequent decades brought additional modifications as the number of official and semi-official presses multiplied: Moscow University (1756), the Noble Cadet Corps (1757), the School of Artillery and Fortification (1759), and the War Department (1762). Although the institutions engaged in publishing continued to fall under the broad authority of either the Synod or the Senate, the principle of internal censorship generally became decisive. Censors appointed from within the relevant institutions reviewed proposed publications, including submissions by authors and publishers who were permitted to rent the state presses for private ventures. During the 1770s, a handful of foreign publishers also received permission to operate private presses under similar restrictions. In all cases, the in-house censors were supposed to ensure that the works published not be opposed to existing laws, the government, the church, or standards of decency and good manners.[102]

In practice, at the institutional presses and at court, the everyday exercise of censorship appeared barely distinguishable from the need to preserve good taste through earnest editing. In 1769, Catherine personally "suggested" that A. P. Sumarokov eliminate from his comedy *The Usurer* any references to the church, Christ, and the Legislative Commission.[103] As long as authors, editors, publishers, and censors worked within the same institutions and possessed personal knowledge of each other, censorship could be "voluntary." But once private printing presses became legal in 1783, police supervision of publishing also became necessary. The police already regulated the activities of impresarios who staged public theatricals, though there is no evidence that the plays being staged were subject to prior censorship. By contrast, the law of 1783 required private publishers to register their presses with the local police *(uprava blagochiniia)*, who then became responsible for guaranteeing that nothing inimical to church, government, or decency would be published.[104] As before, the presses at state institutions remained subject to internal censors, and of course the ruler could ban any publication at any time. In general, however, the fragmentation of censorial authority continued to produce relatively mild controls. During the reigns of Elizabeth and Catherine II, most historians agree, the censorship of books, periodicals, and the theater remained intermittent and unintrusive.

Until the 1790s, Catherine II's cultural policies focused more on encouraging than on controlling artistic and philosophical expression. But conditions changed in 1796, when the empress ordered the closure of private printing presses and the establishment of local censorship committees in the capitals and port cities. Henceforth three local censors—chosen respectively by the Senate, Synod, and Academy of Sciences or Moscow University—presided over the publication of religious and secular literature.[105] It seemed as if the enlightened empress suddenly had embraced repression, although in fact, Catherine had been expressing impatience with Russian intellectuals for some time. Her criticism of Freemasonry in the 1780s followed by the arrests of A. N. Radishchev and N. I. Novikov in the early 1790s revealed the limits to her toleration. If early in her reign Catherine felt the need to cultivate educated cadres, by the 1790s she could conclude that the empire possessed an adequate supply of writers, translators, and purveyors of print culture. Nor can the impact of the French Revolution on repression in Russia be ignored. Developments abroad—the abolition of the French monarchy, bloody popular regicide, and revolutionary war— brought home the dangers of too much free expression.

The changes of 1796 surely represented a watershed, but in important respects the regulative censorship decreed by Catherine did not depart radically from the haphazard controls of the past. Since 1785 the publications of private presses in Moscow had been subject to examination by two state and two church censors. Under the new system the major institutions previously responsible for censorship, with the exception of local police, retained authority over publishing. The decree of 1796 also preserved the focus on imported and foreign-language books, censored as early as 1763.[106] The real significance of the Catherinean legislation lay in the creation of an administrative apparatus specifically designated to impose censorship. Fragmented authority gave way to standardized regulation, and the banning of private presses made clear Catherine's intention to impose effective control over the written word. The church remained responsible for religious publications, and even though periodicals were not subject to prepublication censorship, postal officials were expected to examine their contents based on the same criteria applied to books—to wit, that church, government, and decency not be challenged.[107]

Catherine II's censorship legislation also laid the foundation for further centralization under her successors. Emperor Paul reaffirmed his mother's decree and created a special committee attached to the Imperial Council to oversee the decisions of local censors. By 1800 censorship offices had been established in every port through which imported publications passed. Alexander I (ruled 1801–1825) lifted the prohibition on private presses and subsequent restrictions on foreign books imposed by Paul, but also implemented Russia's first systematic censorship law requiring prepublication review of all books by the government.[108] Censorship of the theater likewise became bureaucratized in the reign of Paul. Previously, the local police, censors at Moscow University, and—since the time of Elagin—the director of the imperial theaters had exercised authority over the staging of plays. In general, however, there was little official interference in theater productions. The impresario, official, artist, or serfowner in charge of a particular troupe decided what would be performed—assuming of course that the content of the productions did not threaten church, government, or public morals.[109] By contrast, Paul ordered that theaters in private homes stage only plays already approved by the censors, and in 1799 he established the post of censor of the Russian troupe under the office of the theater directorate. From then on, before any imperial theater produced a play, it had to be examined and corrected by the censor.[110] Again, it was the centralized bureaucratic form rather than the fact of oversight that represented the significant departure. For although in practice censorship appeared mild during the second half of the eighteenth century, the principle of regulative control over the written word had a long history.

The impact of censorship and, perhaps more importantly, self-censorship in eighteenth-century Russia is difficult to gauge. Censorship and repression were omnipresent but also erratic and unsystematic. In response to one critic of the Russian stage, Catherine II's *All Sorts of Things* argued that given the condition of the sciences *(nauki)* in Russia, it was necessary to encourage rather than criticize writers and translators.[111] That was 1769, and Catherine's thinking clearly had changed by 1796. But in the world of print culture tight regulation also would have been redundant, given the small size of the Russian reading public and the small number of potential patrons, royalty included, whose cultural needs literary figures labored to meet. Compared to Britain, France, and Germany, eighteenth-century Russia possessed a small though not insignificant number of books, literary journals, and readers. Nor is there good evidence for a broad-based readership in social terms. Clergy and merchants did indeed appear among the subscribers to books and literary journals, but the reading public remained overwhelmingly noble.[112] Theater audiences tended to be more diverse; the playwrights whose works appeared on stage, however, also belonged to the largely noble reading public. There was, then, little need for formal censorship at a time when the makers of literary culture basically talked among themselves. The absence of cultural pluralism, not the presence of pluralistic thinking, accounts for the "liberal" censorship of the eighteenth century.

2

THE SOCIAL MEANING OF PLAYS

• A civic institution outside kinship and patronage networks, eighteenth-century Russian theater provided a public forum for the expression of social and political ideas. Designed to entertain, educate, and inform, it at once communicated social criticism and encouraged social control. Precisely because playwrights represented issues in idealized literary terms, they can appear to have challenged authority by drawing attention to the gap between idea and reality. For this reason, scholars often identify in eighteenth-century Russian literature the seeds of disaffection leading to organized political opposition in the first quarter of the nineteenth century. What has received considerably less comment is the extent to which literature also served an integrative function by supplying cognitive resolution to the challenges raised. Although the gap between idea and reality invariably pushed some people in the direction of resistance or reform, it encouraged others to seek accommodation. When read as a body of self-conscious literary expression, eighteenth-century plays actually reveal less about the emergence of political opposition and more about how educated Russians, imbued with Enlightenment ideas, avoided rebellion by reconciling idea with reality.[1]

On the face of it, the repetition of formulaic settings, characters, and moral or social dilemmas in literary texts calls into question the usefulness of plays as a source for historians. In practice, however, even for historians of society and politics, literature is able to highlight aspects of human experience that may be difficult to ascertain from state archival documents. Plays in particular are expressive of social relationships both because they are designed for public performance and because their structure depends on dialogue that mirrors discussion, conversation, and debate. When eighteenth-century fictional characters living in invented circumstances addressed questions of contemporary concern, they spotlighted historical specificity in otherwise predictable plots. The life situations of stock characters may have followed a familiar course defined by the formulas of tragedy, drama, comedy, and comic opera, yet the concrete attitudes and actions of these characters—not so much what they did but how they went about doing it—spilled over the boundaries of genre and literary movement into the realities of everyday life. Like the policy debates of high-level officials, which remained hidden from public view, and like the critical commentary of the unofficial periodical press, which barely existed in eighteenth-century Russia, literature and theater more specifically could articulate a range of opinions and perspectives on important social questions.

LITERARY FORMULAS

No matter what the source base chosen for study, historians must contend with the formulaic presentation of information. That is to say, any body of documentation is the product of concrete human purposes that impose formal or implicit rules of selection, analysis, categorization, and presentation. It is not, therefore, the formulaic progression or outcome of a play that interests historians; it is the definition of the problem or conflict to be resolved that conveys the social assumptions and attitudes contained within the body of literary sources. To the extent that historians distinguish formulaic expression from information unique to the historical situation being described, they read sources of any genre—including legislation, statistical compilations, judicial proceedings, and official reports—as literary texts. Thus when historians analyze literature in order to understand social consciousness, they do not ask how literary formulas are realized in a particular work but rather how historical conditions render meaningful the presence of particular formulas or how the formulas in turn represent historical conditions. Approached in this manner, the literary formulas unlock social meanings that are important for understanding what people thought and consequently how society functioned in a specific historical context.

Although the literary formulas of neoclassicism, sentimentalism, and pre-romanticism dominated the Russian stage during the eighteenth century, the formulas were neither rigid nor inviolable.[2] Even playwrights who tried to follow recognized rules of composition—for example, the neoclassical unities of place, time, and action—deviated from the rules in order to enhance literary expression.[3] In the introduction to *The Nun of Venice* (1758), M. M. Kheraskov explained his abandonment of the standard five-act structure with reference to "authenticity." To achieve greater realism, he wrote a three-act tragedy, introduced his play with an historical account of the seventeenth-century events that provided the basis for the plot, and admitted to taking poetic license with some established facts.[4] Decades later, in the introduction to the comic opera *Milozor and Prelesta* (1787), V. A. Levshin invoked naturalism to justify his departure from "the rules approved by many." "So what if this opera is not performed even once," Levshin continued, "it still represents my feelings."[5] Ignoring any strict boundary between tragedy and comedy, his play combined sadness with laughter, and in contrast to opera characters who sang continuously, his characters sang only at those moments when real people would want to sing. Would a person condemned to death be singing? "Is it possible to sing as one sobs?"[6] Catherine II likewise neglected formalistic composition in her imitations of Shakespeare's historical plays: the title pages accompanying *From the Life of Riurik* (1786) and *The Beginning of Oleg's Reign* (1787) openly acknowledge disregard for "the usual theatrical rules."[7] Like so many educated Russians of the time, the empress was eager to try her hand at literary self-expression and ready to take liberties with formal poetics.

From the 1750s onward, Russian playwrights experimented with a broad range of European theatrical models and most often identified their creations as tragedy, drama, comedy, or comic opera. The classical distinction between tragedy and comedy remained important, but as in other parts of Europe, the proliferation of blended labels—bourgeois tragedy, bourgeois comedy, heroic comedy, lyric comedy, comic opera, dramatic opera, drama, lyric drama, drama with music, drama with voices, bourgeois drama, tearful drama, among others—demonstrated a readiness to abandon accepted rules of composition that interfered with historical accuracy or authorial self-expression. For technically unschooled authors, the blending of dramatic forms permitted freer expression. For those endowed with literary talent, it extended the boundaries of appropriate content and diversified the arsenal of poetic techniques. Even among strict neoclassicists such as A. P. Sumarokov, the combination of tragedy and comedy was evident in the tendency to dispense with tragic endings. Long before the age of Enlightenment hopefulness, both ancient Greek and classical French tragedy had produced happy endings.[8] Their adoption in eighteenth-century Russia did not then represent a radical departure from European conventions. On the contrary, happy endings enriched the expressive possibilities of the tragic repertoire at a time when literary developments that had extended over several centuries in much of Europe burst onto the Russian scene in concentrated bundles.

It is tempting to attribute the eighteenth-century distaste for pure tragedy to Enlightenment utopianism or even arrogance. But if authors shied away from tragic endings, this was not because of undue optimism about human behavior. The avoidance of tragic endings generally accompanied reconciliation with rightful order, also a recognized characteristic of the classical system of tragedy. In tragedy, "the ethical order always has the last word, regardless of the hero's motivations."[9] Based on this principle, eighteenth-century Russian playwrights remained faithful to the rules of tragedy and even expressed a tragic view of social and political relationships. Too much realism and too many hopeless outcomes would have demoralized the audience and undermined the social utility of theater. Enlightenment belief in the possibility of earthly progress required that people possess moral choices and that at least some conflicts be resolved in favor of human happiness.

Thus, whether a Russian tragedy ended happily or sadly, there was a rightfulness to the outcome, for even death could represent freedom. Nor were happy outcomes achieved without struggle and suffering. What distinguished tragedy from the new serious drama—variously labeled drama, tearful drama, bourgeois tragedy, or bourgeois drama—was its focus on eminent personages. Tragedies invariably depicted courtiers, grandees, rulers, and mythological heroes, whereas drama (and later melodrama) also portrayed ordinary (nonheroic) characters. Russian *drama* (or *dramma*) derived from the French *drame bourgeois* advocated by Denis Diderot (1713–1784), and it incorporated features already familiar from tragicomedy, the mixed dramatic forms of the Renaissance, French classical tragedy and *comédie larmoyante* (the predecessor to *drame bourgeois*), and the sentimental neoclassical tragedies of Restoration England and eighteenth-century Russia.[10] Understood as a serious genre, as a combination of tragedy and comedy that depicted the everyday problems of ordinary (nonheroic) people who must face and overcome misfortune or danger, Russian *drama* was not bound by the rules of neoclassical composition, and like French *drame*, it aimed to teach a moral lesson by directly appealing to human emotions.[11]

In contrast to Britain, where scholars associate George Lillo's (1693–1739) sentimental bourgeois drama with the development of a distinct middle-class culture, in Russia the diversification of dramatic forms cannot be pegged to changes in social structure.[12] Even though the concept of the public or educated society implied social heterogeneity, Russia's educated classes were overwhelmingly noble, and theater based on literary texts belonged primarily to the realm of noble culture. In Russia, the blending of dramatic forms emerged from the newness of *all* the literary models, which had never been precisely defined in the first place, and from a broadening of the subject matter explored by playwrights. Writing in 1788, the translator Ivan Iakovlev praised Denis Diderot's "bourgeois tragedy" *Le Fils naturel* (1757) for showing that the fate of nonheroic yet good people also could make an impression and be worthy of public attention. Is it possible, Iakovlev asked, that "the unhappiness of only eminent persons, heroes, conquerors of empires, and destroyers of myriad peoples deserves general sympathy *(chuvstvitel'nost')?*"[13] At roughly the same time—a time when sentimentalism had become an established literary movement in Russia—V. A. Levshin defended drama, which he described as a "middle sort" of theater between the extremes of tragedy and comedy, on grounds of naturalism: on stage, the actions and feelings of characters should approach nature, and what could be more natural to human experience than the combination of amusement and sorrow?[14] It was not, then, the rise of a new social class but an expansion of ideological and artistic horizons that accounted for the appearance and appeal of serious drama in Russia.

The same blending of dramatic forms that encouraged disregard for neo-classical rules, the phenomenon of "happy" tragedy, and the spread of drama also affected comedy. Russian comic opera combined substantial spoken dialogue with musical numbers, and in the 1780s, both N. P. Nikolev and V. A. Levshin associated it with drama. "This drama with voices," Nikolev wrote of *Rozana and Liubim*, "or comedy with songs, or comic opera, or pastoral drama with music, or pastoral drama with whatever one wishes, I wrote in 1776."[15] Similarly, in the introduction to *Milozor and Prelesta* (1787), V. A. Levshin explained that he "called this drama a Comic Opera because [characters] sing in it, and because its beginning and end are not sad."[16] But comedy also could be difficult to distinguish from drama. Particularly among less gifted writers, sentimental emotions and philosophical digressions imparted to comedy a serious tone reminiscent of tragedy. Even in D. I. Fonvizin's (1744/5–1792) classic comedy satire *The Minor* (1783), deliberate philosophical explication played a visible role. When Starodum discovers Sof'ia reading François de Fénelon's *Education of Girls* (1687), he seizes the opportunity to elaborate his own moral instructions.[17] In D. V. Volkov's *Upbringing* (1774), the *raisonneur* Dobromysl likewise provides endless advice on good living and the proper upbringing of children.[18] Volkov understood that his comedy might not be suitable for performance precisely because actors would find the long monologues difficult to recite and because audiences hungry for "something new and extraordinary" would be bored by the didactic discussions. Still, the author insisted, "I will not become angry if somebody, without swearing, can show that my reasoning about love for the Fatherland is unjust." Volkov hoped to enlighten people about how to educate the young in a manner useful to the fatherland. Whether *Upbringing* possessed literary merits was of secondary concern: the comedy deserved to be published for its beneficial ideas and moral message.

The desire to reform behavior produced a range of comic characters whose exaggerated faults—greed, ignorance, credulity, vanity, frivolity, cruelty, and conceit—contrasted sharply with the goodness of serious characters. Through the mockery of vice and the unmasking of deceit, comedy restored rightful order by giving victory to the virtuous. Yet at the same time that the exposure of deceit brought rightful resolution, the victory of virtue frequently depended on deception. Classical playwrights such as Aristophanes and Plautus had deployed deception scenes and clever slaves to effect the reintegration of society, and Molière had relied on playacting for purposes of unmasking.[19] These techniques were pervasive in late eighteenth-century Russia. Comedy after comedy represented deception *(obman)* and the joke *(shutka)* as legitimate means to set things right in a world beset by disorder.[20] The joke performed multiple functions and could be used by both the strong and the vulnerable to assert social control.[21] Like the slaves of antiquity, some servants swindled superiors while others resorted to trickery to solve a master's problems.[22] Within the patriarchal household, parents and guardians tricked young lovers to test their faithfulness, and children staged deceptions, often with the assistance of servants, so that rightful love could triumph against the tyranny of their elders.[23] When authority thwarted true love, either the parental figure deserved to be deceived, or the imposter who manipulated well-intentioned people deserved to be exposed. In both situations, the joke became a weapon of the weak, and justice demanded the deception.[24] Reason almost always effectively unmasked imposters so that virtue could triumph, and only rarely did a villain's deception succeed in defeating honor.[25]

Of course, in everyday life imposters frequently had their way, a reality also duly represented in numerous tragedies, dramas, and comedies. That the joke could serve both the virtuous and the corrupt revealed the sense of power and powerlessness characteristic of social experience in late eighteenth-century Russia. The staged joke that restored rightful order or unmasked an imposter gave voice to the belief that human beings could manipulate and hence control their environment. The unmasking of vice likewise proclaimed that society could be improved by reforming individual behavior. Even though some characters were not reformable, others who committed evil deeds were essentially good. Once exposed, the individuals driven to corruption by poor education and social circumstances could be rehabilitated. Clearly, the spread of Newtonian science and Enlightenment ideas gave to educated Russians, as to their counterparts across Europe, an unprecedented confidence in the capacity of human beings to bring about earthly progress. Yet physical life remained fragile, and God-given order continued to define social and political relationships. The limits to human powers, manifested in the gap between idea and reality, could not be denied. Playacting, whether to disguise oneself or to unmask another, helped worthy people to survive the uncertainties of everyday life. That people needed deception to protect themselves resulted not only from the effects of tyranny and corruption but also from human inadequacy before divine truth, transcendent nature, and superordinate authority. On stage, a sudden reversal of fortune constituted literary formula, but the reversal made sense because people understood the fragility of happiness. When eighteenth-century playwrights employed the word "shchast'e," usually translated as "happiness" but also implying "good fortune," they had in mind both the happiness of personal desire rightfully realized and the good fortune only God and fate could bestow.

By the nineteenth century the aesthetic sensibility of eighteenth-century Russia seemed glaringly artificial and chimerical. Already by the 1790s, the satirist I. A. Krylov denounced as unnatural the popular technique of the joke and insisted that the moral instruction (nravouchenie) so often found in Russian comedies emerge from the action of the play rather than from the long monologues of "old men."[26] But literary formulas that a mind imbued with realism found unconvincing effectively conveyed moral truth to an eighteenth-century audience. Krylov was a great poet concerned with the rules of artistic composition, yet for most eighteenth-century Russian observers, believability on stage did not demand the naturalistic portrayal of human actions. The concept of verisimilitude required "playwrights to invent stories and motivations that will produce the effect and illusion of truth."[27] Artificial plots, simple character development, and formulaic speech—these artistic "failings" did not detract from the truthfulness of the human behavior being portrayed.[28] Even dramatic resolution that occurred at the expense of historical plausibility did not necessarily undermine the realness of a story. The sudden appearance of a benefactor, the unexpected return of a lover or parental figure, the fortuitous recovery of a lost identity—the deus ex machina of intervening circumstances made sense because a religious or providential view of the world prevailed. In the eighteenth century, when life and death formed an integrated whole, and chronic ailments reminded people of how precarious physical existence could be, the plausibility of plots and characters, whether tragic or comic, was secondary to the truth of the moral message being conveyed.[29] Verisimilitude did not require that the characters and situations on stage be understandable in terms of social reality, but rather in terms of human behavior.

All literatures, regardless of time and place, explore archetypal problems and dilemmas, yet social meaning is historically specific and determines which archetypal problems appear in a particular literary product. Social questions also can be so specific to time and place that they lose their resonance for subsequent generations. Few eighteenth-century Russian plays lived on in the nineteenth century, and only a handful became canonized as literary classics. The renowned prerevolutionary historian V. O. Kliuchevksii described one of these classics, Fonvizin's *The Minor,* as an educational play for gymnasium students, and while he recognized its artistic and historical significance, he dismissed the virtuous Sof'ia as a "freshly manufactured dolly of good behavior, from which the dampness of the pedagogical workshop still blows."[30] For Kliuchevskii, the character of Sof'ia existed not in nature but in the minds of late eighteenth-century educational reformers. This was precisely the point, as V. I. Lukin made clear in defending the heroine of his comedy *The Spendthrift Reformed by Love* (1765).[31] Although critics complained that few Kleopatras could be found in Russia, Lukin attributed this to bad education, which he blamed on parents. To provide a model of good behavior that might encourage people to change was, in fact, his goal.

Indeed, numerous late eighteenth-century plays replicated the model of virtuous girlhood represented by Fonvizin's Sof'ia. Despite subsequent literary oblivion, and regardless of whether such a person ever actually lived, at the time of its inception the model conveyed social meaning. Playwrights, policymakers, and enlightened commentators in general encouraged young

Russian women to acquire European education, display cultural refinement, use their reason to think independently, and live with feeling and sincerity—all while remaining virtuous wives and mothers respectful of patriarchal authority and bounded by Orthodox Christian morality. The model of Sof'ia corresponded quite closely to the social demands placed on elite educated noblewomen in late eighteenth-century Russia.[32] Clearly, the terms in which playwrights represented abstract virtues could carry historical specificity.[33] Characters did not need to appear real in order to possess believable moral traits. Nor did plot sequences need to be believable in order to address real social problems. Plays that failed to reproduce actual social relationships nonetheless commented truthfully on social experience. When Kliuchevskii dismissed Sof'ia as a lifeless artifact, he ignored the power of ideas to influence social behavior—not because in the eighteenth century ideas became reality but because educated people believed that over time human beings could use their enhanced understanding to make life better. On and off the stage, what people thought or believed about social reality conditioned behavior and guided action.

AUTHORIAL SELF-DEFINITION

So many translations, adaptations, and imitations, so many archetypal social themes—what can plays from the second half of the eighteenth century possibly reveal about contemporary Russian society? Russian authors were keenly aware of their debt to European literature, yet they participated in Enlightenment culture with enthusiasm and resolve. Did their comfort with imitation indicate a limited understanding of Enlightenment ideas, or did it represent an uninhibited willingness to learn from foreign models? The "reviewer" of the comedy *Unsuccessful Stubbornness* (1779) doubted that the play was a Russian original, but he could not be certain, because the title page did not indicate the comedy's origin.[34] His erroneous conclusion that the play was a translation—in fact it is a Russian work by A. A. Volkov—testified to the meaningfulness of cultural borrowing.[35] To borrow brought membership in the cosmopolitan world of European letters, in which the empress Catherine II and a few talented Russians—Lomonosov, Sumarokov, and Fonvizin—already had achieved glorious recognition.[36] To borrow meant also to follow the lead of Emperor Peter I and his daughter Empress Elizabeth, both of whom had done so much to place Russia on an equal military, political, and cultural footing with the great powers of Europe. Borrowing did not imply inferiority or ignorance; borrowing belonged to the "continuity" and "echo" that was high culture.[37] The Enlightenment culture of eighteenth-century Europe, at least as received in Russia, was an open-ended cosmopolitan affair.

Eighteenth-century playwrights, however, did more than borrow; they adapted foreign plays to Russian mores. They changed vocabulary, characters, and settings to impart Russian meaning to the European models. That the results seemed artificial, imitative, and unoriginal to subsequent generations of educated Russians does not negate the significance of the effort. In the productions of late eighteenth-century court, public, and domestic theaters, renowned literary figures mingled with amateur playwrights, and together they imagined the social relationships of everyday life. Among the most prominent of Russia's amateur playwrights was Empress Catherine II, who authored over two dozen dramatic works published in Russian, German, and French. Catherine's personal friend, the courtier Princess E. R. Dashkova, wrote two plays, whereas the memoirist, provincial landowner, and military officer A. I. Bolotov composed three. Because playwrights could be monarchs, courtiers, churchmen, state officials, military officers, serfowners, educators, and actors—precisely because so many playwrights were not recognized or even aspiring literary figures—their plays expressed ideas, attitudes, beliefs, and emotions that, taken as a whole, represented the thinking and moral universe of Russia's educated service classes. Although small in number within Russian society as a whole, and consisting predominantly but not exclusively of nobles, these educated classes dominated the important tasks of policymaking and government.[38]

When in letters, memoirs, and published introductions authors of the later eighteenth century described the circumstances inducing them to write, they also shed light on the social meaningfulness of theater. Historians have long recognized the educational, polemical, and political goals of Catherine II's literary activities. Her 1785–1786 trilogy, *The Deceiver, The Deceived,* and *The Siberian Shaman,* sought to expose Freemasonry as a dangerous occultist fraud.[39] But Catherine also appreciated the entertainment value of theater. In need of a Russian play for her Hermitage Theater, she pressed Princess Dashkova to attempt a theatrical composition. The empress, Dashkova relates, "knew from personal experience how much it amused and occupied the author," and so in 1786 the princess obliged her sovereign and spent several days writing the comedy *Mr. This-and-That.*[40] To please friends and patrons, to please oneself—these were sufficient reasons to pen a play. Even when authors did not write in response to a direct request, numerous dedications indicated a desire to honor benefactors with literary creations.[41]

Authors such as Bolotov and Catherine II also recognized the pedagogical, not to be confused with the political, value of theater by writing plays for their children and grandchildren.[42] Bolotov records that in December 1779 he spent two days writing the children's comedy *The Braggart,* which flowed "from my pen, like a river," and the following year he devoted three days to the composition of *Unfortunate Orphans.* Bolotov's children performed in both plays at the makeshift theater he organized in Bogoroditsk, where after retiring from military service he administered crown estates.[43] D. V. Volkov, a close advisor to Peter III, can hardly be called a lover of theater, yet he too acknowledged its value as a tool of moral instruction. Hoping to be useful to society and fatherland, Volkov employed the dramatic medium to put forth a social and political argument in favor of noble service.[44] Utility and principle likewise motivated another critic of theater, the Moscow mason I. V. Lopukhin, whose drama *Celebration of Justice and Virtue, or The Good Judge* (1794) could, in the view of his publisher, be read with profit even if its "sermons on virtue" made it unsuitable for performance.[45] Whether or not these eighteenth-century commentators approved of theater, they appreciated its power to influence behavior.

But not all authors sought to shape morals or teach a lesson; some simply reacted to works they had seen or read. Dashkova's second play, a continuation of August von Kotzebue's *Armuth und Edelsinn* (1795), aimed at highlighting the contrast between the noble spirit of Lieutenant von Cederström and the greed of Fabian Stöpsel. Reportedly completed in only two and a half hours in 1799, the play was performed at the serf theater of Dashkova's brother, A. R. Vorontsov.[46] Whether Dashkova actually wrote her play with the speed claimed, the story of its composition suggests that Kotzebue's original moved her spontaneously to compose a response. Friedrich von Schiller's *Don Carlos* (1787) had a similar effect on V. I. Kireevskii, who chose to emphasize the romantic rather than the more central political themes of the original. In introducing the "dramatic fragment" *Elizabeth* (1800), Kireevskii explained that at the conclusion of Schiller's play, Don Carlos is turned over to the Inquisition for judgment, and so "I wanted to represent his death and the death of Elizabeth [Don Carlos's stepmother and lover]—that is why I composed this play."[47] Audience became author when Dashkova and Kireevskii, neither of whom can be called an accomplished playwright, responded to the works of recognized literary figures by penning their own theatrical compositions. That they did so with such ease and speed indicated their familiarity with dramatic dialogue and the discussion it fostered.

Theater facilitated public discussion precisely because the composition and performance of plays were as much sociable as professional literary activities. Although permanent public theater started to take hold only in the late 1750s, when classes of professional writers and performers quickly began to form, troupes of enthusiasts continued to populate the cultural landscape.[48] In a published letter to B. E. El'chaninov, the translator and adapter V. I. Lukin described how one amateur performance actually changed his career. Curious about a play he had viewed at the public theater on Brumberg Square in St. Petersburg, Lukin queried the head of the troupe, a compositor at the Academy of Sciences publishing house. The compositor knew nothing about the play's origins—the script had been sent to him—but he allowed Lukin to read it. Subsequently, Lukin dreamed the play, and it became his comedy *The Trinket Vendor*, published in 1765 as an adaptation of the French comedy *La Boutique de Bijoutier*, based on an English original. The French play was Claude Pierre Patu's version of *The Toy Shop* by Robert Dodsley (1703–1764).[49] Written in 1735, Dodsley's *Toy Shop* underwent sev-

eral reincarnations before becoming fixed in Russian thirty years later as
Lukin's *Trinket Vendor*.[50] Never mind that Lukin had dreamed the play in response to a Russian adaptation of a French adaptation; he regarded his
composition as a contribution to the development of authentic Russian
comedy. The modern distinction between amateur and professional theater
did not fully apply, nor had the modern concepts of intellectual property
and national literature become firmly established.

However one defines professional literary activity, by the end of the
eighteenth century permanent public theater in Russia had yet to achieve
commercial viability or independence from court patronage. Impresarios
regularly staged plays, pantomimes, concerts, and dances, but these productions lacked the permanence of institutional theater dedicated to the performance of a literary repertoire. The status of author remained similarly amorphous, providing neither a secure social identity nor an adequate livelihood.
Few eighteenth-century playwrights expressed the pretensions or claimed
the authorial rights of an A. P. Sumarokov, "the father of Russian theater"
and arguably the empire's first professional writer.[51] But if Sumarokov pretended to professional status, he nevertheless relied on the monarchy to
guarantee an income and a forum for the staging of his plays. Sumarokov
was a court poet, able to devote himself to literature because he received a
lifelong pension after retiring as director of the imperial Russian Theater.
Courtier, serviceman, poet, and playwright—all could belong to the same
social milieu and be combined in the same person. No major Russian cultural figure of the late eighteenth century subsisted solely through artistic
endeavors, or even through private publishing and teaching.[52]

Like so many of his contemporaries, V. I. Lukin also depended on state
service and his connections to Catherine II in order to pursue a literary career. But in contrast to his literary opponent Sumarokov, he found it difficult to employ the concept of author.[53] When Lukin published his collected
works in 1765, he gave two reasons for the unusual action: he needed
money and he hoped to squelch rumors that I. P. Elagin was the actual author of his compositions.[54] Lukin dedicated his *Works* to Elagin, who publicly supported his protégé, and he countered anticipated accusations of
"pride and ignorance" by explaining that circumstances had forced him to
undertake publication. In the introduction to *The Spendthrift Reformed by
Love*, Lukin reiterated that in contrast to some writers, he did not seek glory
and honor, profit, or the means to malign opponents.[55] Encouraged by the
empress to write, he wanted to be useful to his countrymen by composing
comedies "in our mores that condemn our main vices."[56] Lukin called himself a "scribe" (*pisets*), a word he used interchangeably with "writer" (*pisatel'*), and admitted to a want of talent. But, he insisted, a play could be socially beneficial even if it lacked literary merit. Noting the absence of
gifted Russian writers, Lukin proclaimed the usefulness of his compositions and denied that in publishing his works he had been "infected with
authorial arrogance." Indeed, he rejected the notion that he ever would

be a "professional Author" *("remeslennyi Avtor").* Rather, he wrote come-dies when he felt so inclined during his free time.[57]

In disclaiming the status of "professional Author," Lukin downplayed his literary abilities and aspirations. His was a common refrain among eigh-teenth-century writers who felt compelled to apologize for their limited lit-erary talent. The reluctance to declare oneself an author stemmed from a variety of circumstances and should not be taken entirely at face value. Russian playwrights surely understood that they were imitators of foreign models. Private publishing, journalism, and consistent attention to the de-velopment of the Russian literary language were creations of the eigh-teenth century, and with few exceptions, the empire's educated classes were newcomers to the pan-European literary culture that had emerged with the help, crucially, of the printing revolution of the late fifteenth cen-tury.[58] The glorification of human endeavors that served only earthly needs also was a recent phenomenon. During the eighteenth century, as already seen, Russian theatrical performance expanded beyond religious and court ceremony, school drama, and fairground entertainment to in-clude the public display of political power and cultural refinement. But like Renaissance humanists, eighteenth-century Russian playwrights who took pride in their individual achievements also remained sensitive to the smallness of human life. Against the backdrop of their Orthodox religious sensibility, pride easily became arrogance.

Not surprisingly, the arrogance, ignorance, and mediocrity of authors re-ceived regular treatment on the late eighteenth-century Russian stage. Al-though historians generally connect this criticism to the impassioned liter-ary polemics of the time, the theme of bad authors echoed an Enlightenment rhetoric that distinguished the truly enlightened from those who followed the latest fashions and pandered to popular taste.[59] Given that the polemics often targeted specific authors, those who claimed imma-turity may have acted out of political expediency. If they could not blunt the inevitable criticism, perhaps they could save face or their political skin by publicly acknowledging their own deficiencies. But both in relation to other writers, who also functioned as critics, and in relation to patrons, whose protection was needed, deference begged recognition. Toward the end of the century, when feeling and spontaneity had become enshrined as aesthetic principles, sentimentalist writers sought to appear unschooled in order to claim greater authenticity for their work.[60] As in French autobio-graphical and epistolary novels of the eighteenth century, the assumption of amateur status sometimes represented literary convention.[61] Whether the pose of inexperience served a rhetorical purpose or expressed a genuine sense of inadequacy, it revealed a consciousness of writing as a public activ-ity. In striving to appear humble, playwrights inadvertently advertised their self-awareness as authors.

Ironically, playwrights who pretended to shun personal profit and celebrity eagerly claimed moral superiority. V. I. Lukin's approach to the question of originality illustrated the combination of humility and self-assertion. An advocate and practitioner of adapting foreign plays to Russian mores, Lukin admitted in the 1765 introduction to *Constancy Rewarded* that it is better to write original plays.[62] But he possessed neither the time nor the strength to do so, and he criticized Sumarokov's "original" comedies for depicting characters and situations nowhere to be found in Russia.[63] Leaving aside the literary disputes—Sumarokov's plays are rich in Russian content—Lukin provided moral justification for the practice of adaptation. True to the belief in comedy's pedagogical efficacy, Lukin's main concern was that a play depict Russian mores; otherwise it would fail to correct behavior. People would be unable to see themselves in such a play and would assume that not they, but foreigners, were being satirized. Better to imitate or adapt a foreign play than to write an original that had nothing to do with Russia. In response to critics who denounced adaptations as shameful, Lukin invoked the names of literary luminaries—Destouches, Voltaire, Molière, Regnard, and Boissy—who had adapted the comedies of others.[64] Adaptation brought no shame, but surely it was shameful to quarrel and to attribute another's work to oneself. Driving home the point, Lukin further distinguished between adaptation and imitation. To imitate *(podrazhat')* meant to borrow a character or an insignificant part of the story but otherwise to write an original play. To adapt or rework *(peredelyvat')* meant to add or remove content here and there but in the main to leave the original and adapt it "to our mores." Lukin was very careful to call *Constancy Rewarded* an adaptation.[65] In his view, to adapt one scene and then present the play as an imitation would have represented blatant conceit.

Not all authors bothered with such a fine distinction between adaptation and imitation. O. P. Kozodavlev stressed the difference between adaptation/imitation and translation, though clearly he also recognized the need to change foreign originals so that they became understandable in Russian terms.[66] In adapting *Der Diamant* (1773) by Johann Jakob Engel (1741–1802), Kozodavlev replaced the Jew who sold the ring in the German original with a Frenchman: "in Russia, Jews are unusual, and so I represented in his place a trading Frenchman—such Frenchmen are as numerous among us as Jews in Germany." For neither Lukin nor Kozodavlev did borrowing bring dishonor. As Lukin explained the matter, to borrow meant simply to recognize a teacher or a person more accomplished than oneself. But as Lukin also noted, his was a time when the most distinguished writers "steal better than others" by presenting "skillfully covered-up" work as their own.[67] The debate over originality blended into the very concrete problem of plagiarism.

Aware of the plagiarism problem, the anonymous author of *A Reasonable Choice* (1773), announced that the comedy was an adaptation of a one-act French play "dressed in Russian clothes" and reworked into three acts: "I sincerely declare to all readers that it [the play] is not entirely my creation, for it is not good to present the ideas of other people as one's own."[68] But what constituted a creation of one's own? When N. P. Nikolev published his comic opera *Rozana and Liubim* in 1781, he responded to critics who attacked him for "stealing" theatrical decorations and scenery from various French operas.[69] Is it possible, Nikolev asked, that an author's imagination will not be met with "in the poetic imagination, ideas, feelings, and expressions of innumerable ancient and new writers?" Is Racine less worthy than Euripides because he borrowed from the ancient master? Originality had become an issue the moment authors set out to define a Russian literary language, but originality did not yet require romantic self-creation.

Although contemporary commentators distinguished the problem of plagiarism from the artistic debate about adaptation, eighteenth-century authorship remained elusive and difficult to establish. The Russian publishing industry did not achieve commercial viability before the nineteenth century, and many literary works appeared anonymously or without proper attribution. Plagiarism was rampant, authors' wishes were ignored, and copyright laws were nonexistent. Even as prominent a writer as A. P. Sumarokov could be accused of stealing another's work and claiming it as his own.[70] In the 1793 edition of V. A. Levshin's *Works,* the author announced that the first version of his comic opera *Your Own Burden Doesn't Drag as Much* had been stolen; he appealed to theater directors who might receive a copy not to stage the opera or put it to music. "Otherwise, I shall claim insult *(obida)* from them without any reason; for my right *(pravo)* will have been taken, like that of a writer whose works are disposed of by others."[71] The former serf M. A. Matinskii did find his work disposed of by others: the 1791 version of *The St. Petersburg Bazaar* was published without his permission and with errors.[72] In the realm of copyright, authorial self-awareness developed ahead of both the law and social practice. However assertive authors had become by century's end, and however much recognition they received in fashionable society, authorial status continued to lack legal rights and protections.

Of course, to steal another's work and call it one's own implied identification, so that for purposes of understanding social ideas, correct authorial attribution is not necessary. Nor had later eighteenth-century writers imbibed romantic notions of originality, nationalism, and individual genius. Even so, by the 1790s a change in attitudes became discernible. Whereas in 1765 V. I. Lukin vigorously defended adaptations, in 1792 P. A. Plavil'shchikov, writing in the *Spectator,* just as vigorously condemned "blind imitation."[73] That Lukin felt compelled to defend the honor of adapting foreign plays to Russian mores indicated some early criticism of the practice; however, the more vehement nationalistic tone of the 1790s marked a qualitative shift. In contrast to the early 1770s, when N. I. Novikov's satirical journals had promoted Russian theater by satirizing the notion that French plays and actors were superior, the *Spectator* questioned the effectiveness of translations and adaptations to Russian mores on the grounds that Russian theater now possessed identifiable attributes *(svoistva)* different from those found on the French, English, or German stage.[74] The idea of a distinctively Russian national theater that expressed distinctively Russian national traits clearly was taking hold. In addition, by 1800 Russian playwrights began to associate talent with "the creative spirit." A romantic understanding of the arts based on individual and national uniqueness soon would transform the eighteenth-century concept of the author as a cultivated, socially useful participant in European Enlightenment culture.[75] Professional writers and artistic geniuses stood poised on the horizon.

Virtually all late eighteenth-century playwrights and many spectators belonged to the nobility, yet authors addressed themselves to the public *(publika)* or society *(obshchestvo)* rather than to a particular social group. The public was both an abstract concept and a social body consisting of patrons, fellow writers, critics, readers, and the parterre or general theater audience. Even servants, V. I. Lukin argued in *The Spendthrift Reformed by Love,* could imitate the good behavior represented in theater: by implication they too could belong to the public, for "all people can think," and all are born with ideas "except for idiots and frivolous people."[76] That the public extended beyond the theater-going audience, about which historians possess so little information, was also evident from the regular publication of plays deemed unsuitable for performance. Introductions addressed "to the reader" show that playwrights expected to be read, whether or not their works were staged.[77] Although any play that is staged also must be read, in late eighteenth-century Russia, drama was as much a form of literature, like poetry or the rising novel, as a distinctive performing art. Performance elicited praise, and plays might be written with particular actors in mind, but many works that were published and presumably read never made it to the public stage. The public, understood as a court of public opinion or judge, stood as a counterpoint to the author. B. E. El'chaninov regarded the 1767 staging of his comedy *The Giddypate Punished* as a success, yet in the published introduction, he addressed the reader as judge and called himself a novice: "I hope that my judges will be tolerant and not judge me too harshly, because this is the first test of my penchant for the literary sciences."[78] Both rhetorically and in the flesh, the public conferred authorial identity.

As self-conscious educators and carriers of enlightenment, playwrights expressed ambivalence toward the public that judged their work. Once again V. I. Lukin's extensive introductions pinpointed the problem. Lukin wrote at a time when the monarchy had committed itself to the development of Russian public theater and the writing of plays had become a fundamentally social activity. "Believe me, lovers of the literary sciences," Lukin declared in the dedication to his *Works* (1765), "I am publishing my works, borrowed from other Authors and composed by me, for your satisfaction."[79] Although Lukin attributed the success of *The Spendthrift Reformed by Love* to the abilities of the actors, he also adapted the play with an eye to the audience's diverse inclinations. Only a small part of the parterre "loves mournful [plays] filled with noble thoughts"; most people prefer "cheerful comedies." Thus Lukin included sad scenes and repentance to satisfy the taste of the minority and comic characters to amuse the rest. Indeed, through the very practice of adapting foreign plays to Russian mores, Lukin hoped to please the public. But tastes varied, he lamented, and spectators in search solely of entertainment preferred inferior translations. Ultimately, however, even though Lukin accommodated the need for entertainment, he rejected the idea of writing for people who wanted only to laugh. Lukin labored "for those who have true taste." To read his comedy *The Trinket Vendor*, Lukin equated with reading a book or satirical composition: he did not write for people who used books to decorate a room but for those who understood "that books adorn our souls and minds."[80]

Lukin's attitude toward the public echoed across Europe in the conflict between the didactic moralism of Enlightenment playwrights and the popular taste for entertainment. The idea that art should be moral and didactic encouraged censorship and subordinated theater to literature. In Leipzig, Johann Christoph Gottsched (1700–1766) had replaced harlequin comedies and improvisational theater with a set repertoire based on literary texts. In contrast to improvisations, literature could be subjected to censorship and hence more easily controlled. Thus after 1770, censorship and repression also hit the Viennese commercial stage, established in a permanent theater as early as 1710. The Austrian reformers, however, succeeded only in part: although literary theater became preeminent in central Vienna, the improvisational forms continued to flourish in plebeian suburbs. Historians have yet to identify parallel efforts in Enlightenment Russia, perhaps because there were no permanently housed improvisational troupes to banish.[81] Certainly, there is no evidence that the authorities regarded extemporaneous performance as a public problem. The official newspapers, the *St. Petersburg News* and the *Moscow News*, announced theatricals, staged by impresarios, that were not limited to the literary repertoire.[82] In Russia, permanent public theater spread at the behest of the government and court. The improvisational theatricals of foreign and Russian impresarios belonged to this effort, even though public taste also challenged the pedagogical goals of Enlightenment playwrights and officials.

The playwright and sometime official A. P. Sumarokov addressed the problem of audience reception by defining the public *(publika)* as people who possessed taste and knowledge, whether or not they were nobles. He distinguished people of taste from uncultivated social groups *(chern')*, usually equated with the common people, yet insisted that not all nobles belonged to the worthy public. Although the question of taste appeared bound up with social hierarchy, Sumarokov's concerns were overwhelmingly literary. Railing against noble pride, he refused to exclude from the public those non-nobles who possessed taste—all in response to the lack of literary taste exemplified, in his opinion, by the popularity of the "comedy" (actually a *drame larmoyant*) *Eugénie* (1767) by Pierre-Augustin Caron de Beaumarchais (1732–1799). Sumarokov was a critic of the "tearful comedies" that had begun to compete with neoclassical theater, and his attitude toward the public that embraced *Eugénie* reflected the literary debates of the day.[83]

N. P. Nikolev, a practitioner of the blended dramatic forms Sumarokov decried, likewise collapsed the public into literary polemics. In the published edition of *Rozana and Liubim*, Nikolev included a letter to the publisher, N. I. Novikov, complaining about the personal criticism leveled against authors.[84] The introduction to his "drama with voices" bemoaned the public's inability to distinguish good from bad plays yet invoked public taste to justify specific literary choices. Thus, Nikolev explained, his characters spoke a Moscow dialect, and in one case a mixture of Moscow and peasant speech, because spectators and readers of taste would be disgusted by "the low and base dialect of the Russian common people, such as for example the dialects of factory and steppe peasants." Nikolev acknowledged a literary role for the public but then distanced himself from the reality of public judgment. "Enlightened Moscow spectators," he wrote, "while tolerating a small number of creators, somehow still tolerate bad creations; and Russian orangutans, not understanding the reasons for such indulgence, applaud the performance of a bad show *(igrishche)* as much as a performance of *Sinav and Truvor,* and often even more zealously."[85] As portrayed in Ia. I. Blagodarov's *Funny Assemblage* (1787), ignorant townspeople, servants, clergy, musicians, and artists might pretend to be performers and playwrights, and equally ridiculous spectators from the merchants and townspeople might mistake real life for the ending to a tragedy.[86] Playwrights could not escape the need to please audiences, but neither did they accept the public as a reliable arbiter of taste. From their perspective, self-conscious authors, not the ignorant or fickle public, were the true representatives of Enlightenment culture.

In the small-scale world of Russia's eighteenth-century educated service classes, the judgment of the public could be intensely personal. Yet authorial awareness of the public also hinted at the presence of an impersonal, commercialized relationship. In the final scene of the comic opera *A Lucky Haul of Fish* (1786) by D. P. Gorchakov (1758–1824), the spirit Iezrad addresses the parterre: having shown that "true treasure" lies not in wealth but in the harmony between husband and wife, he also notes that for authors, "there is treasure where the writer is in harmony with the parterre."[87] Late eighteenth-century playwrights understood the commercial benefits of pleasing the parterre. Lukin admitted as much when he explained that financial circumstances had forced him to publish his *Works.* But to exploit the commercial side of theater did not indicate acceptance of the profit motive or audience judgment. Nor did playwrights necessarily need to think in commercial terms. Russian public theaters were overwhelmingly state sponsored, and while financing remained a chronic problem for directors and impresarios, authors did not write for a fully commercialized market. As late as 1800, A. I. Klushin, playwright and inspector of the Russian troupe of the Imperial Theater, declared that while he felt sincerely grateful to the public for its applause, he had written the comedy *It's Bad to Be Short-Sighted* to honor his patron A. L. Naryshkin, chief director of theatrical productions.[88] Uneasy with public success and unwilling to give his soul to the public—"my heart was disgusted by the praise"—Klushin paid tribute to Naryshkin for his ability to appreciate and cultivate talent.

Personal, professional, or political rather than commercial concerns informed Klushin's behavior. Yet when it suited his purposes—for example when he needed to justify his reworking and publication of I. A. Krylov's comic opera *The Americans* (1800)—Klushin readily subjected the author to the public's putative judgment.[89] A weak opera should be corrected, he argued, and in order to judge the quality of an opera, "it is necessary to love the national theater." Furthermore, "the success of a play depends on the Public. The good does not lose its value because of momentary opinion, just as the bad does not become good because writers and translators applaud themselves." Although Klushin professed to disdain applause, in rewriting Krylov's play, he assumed the mantel of the public and declared its judgment superior to authorial self-promotion. Krylov did likewise in an open letter to P. A. Soimonov, director of the St. Petersburg theaters from 1789 to 1791.[90] Embroiled in conflict with Soimonov and the playwright Ia. B. Kniazhnin, Krylov expressed frustration at the failure to stage his translations and plays: "I chose the theater to be my court of law, the public—to be my judge, and I dared to ask . . . only that my creation be displayed before the court."

Dissimulation, judgment, and counterjudgment notwithstanding, authorial self-definition hinged upon the abstract concept of the public. Authors had begun to distinguish personal attacks from impersonal public judgment. Given that the public was assigned the moral authority to judge, such judgment also can be seen as the precursor to modern public opinion. For the moment, however, public opinion remained a semantic point of reference exercising authority in the prepolitical literary public sphere.[91] Russia's educated classes did not yet invoke public opinion to effect political or social reform, nor did they conceive of a society in opposition to the state. Rather, society stood opposed to the individual, and the problem of the author's relationship to the public represented the problem of the individual's relationship to society. The literary polemics and institutional relationships of the late eighteenth century underscored the vulnerability of the individual writer.

Yet in relation to the general population, Russia's late eighteenth-century educated classes shared the tutelary assumptions of officialdom. Playwrights understood their enterprise as part of a broad social mission to bring enlightenment to Russia. To that end they acted in concert with the monarchy, and their identification with society emerged not in opposition to the state, but by its side, in loyal service. The role of the writer as moral arbiter also may seem to contradict the role of the public as judge, except that in the small world of late eighteenth-century Russian letters, author and audience frequently belonged to the same self-contained social milieu. Playwrights did not respond to an independent audience; their function was to bring enlightenment to people blighted by ignorance, including any person who failed to recognize the moral authority of "literary science." That literature represented a form of knowledge—a literary science—helps to explain the abstract quality of the late eighteenth-century Russian plays.[92] Free of the need to achieve commercial viability through interaction with a socially and culturally diffuse audience, even a terrible poet could write verses filled with "important and intelligent opinions."[93]

THE SOCIAL FUNCTIONS OF THEATER

In 1786, the Russian Academy of Sciences in St. Petersburg began to publish a multivolume anthology called *The Russian Theater,* which proudly proclaimed theater the mark of an "enlightened people" *("prosveshchennyi narod").*[94] Russia, like other countries, now possessed theatrical works capable of extirpating prejudice and vice. Purporting to be a "collection of all Russian tragedies, comedies, dramas, and operas," *The Russian Theater* aimed "to serve the greater glorification of our writers" as well as "the satisfaction of the public." The following year the *St. Petersburg News* used similarly glowing language to celebrate the establishment of a theater in Tambov: since antiquity "enlightened peoples" had esteemed "loyal theatrical performances that serve to correct morals."[95] The opening of the Tambov theater coincided with Catherine II's nameday, and the prologue that began the spectacle advertised the public schools her government had created—schools that "for the simple people can with justice be regarded as the first stage of enlightenment." If before Catherine's provincial reforms of the 1770s—specifically the establishment of the governor-generalships—Tambov had been little more than "a steppe village," now it boasted the ability to organize local talent and artistry in theatrical productions.

The compiler of *The Dramatic Dictionary,* published in Moscow in 1787, reiterated the perception that theater's influence had spread out from the capitals. "The entire enlightened world" benefited from useful and entertaining theatrical compositions, which did not overburden the human mind.[96] As a result of education, the Russian nobility had acquired "taste" and learned to appreciate "enlightenment." Thus in contrast to the crude and violent amusements of earlier times—fisticuffs, pigeon races, horse races *(konskie ryskaniia),* and the hunting of hares—nobles now enjoyed reading, music, and theater. Even in the provinces, the new cultural refinement represented by theater had taken hold: "commanders" and local nobles organized useful entertainment that included the writing and translation of dramatic compositions. Children of nobles and "people of various ranks" *(raznochintsy)* attended theatrical performances and entered into discussions about the plays. Indeed, the compiler had prepared *The Dramatic*

Dictionary for young people whose parents strove to give them a good education, even though they lived far from St. Petersburg and Moscow. Calling theater "a mirror in which each person can clearly see himself," the compiler assumed that the mere display and recognition of moral corruption would induce spectators to change. Among the correctable vices shown on stage, he identified miserliness, dissipation, the squandering of wealth, cruelty, hypocrisy, jealousy, insolent timidity, caprice leading to weakness, being in love to the point of idiocy, a predilection for passion, credulity, impudence, shyness caused by suspicion, disobedience, and "many other human defects." Thanks at least in part to the influence of the stage, he averred, enlightenment and polite sociability had begun to replace ignorance and cruelty everywhere in Russia. Thanks to playwrights such as Sumarokov, tastes had been reformed and the children of nobles knew how to reason.

Of course, commentators did not conceive of refined behavior or improved morals in a uniform manner. *The Dramatic Dictionary* condemned hunting, which, however, remained a favorite pastime of wealthy, cultivated nobles from the late eighteenth to the mid-nineteenth century.[97] Nor did the growing visibility of Russian public theater mean that its beneficial effects were universally recognized. Like Rousseau, some Russians began to see in the content and sociability of theater a source of moral corruption. Rousseau had penned his critique in defense of Geneva, a republic of citizens with a strict civic code that included a ban on theater; echoing Plato, he assumed that entertainment and instruction were incompatible. Theater, Rousseau contended, neither changed people nor instructed them morally: it either reflected or exacerbated existing mores. Relying on illusion and imagination, theater lacked authenticity and therefore could only entertain. In an already corrupted city such as Paris, theater might offer a useful diversion, but in a virtuous republic such as Geneva, it could only bring harm.[98] Writing in 1786–1787, Prince M. M. Shcherbatov, a harsh critic of the Russian court, also expressed misgivings about theater. He too associated theater with moral corruption, represented in his account by divorce, Catherine II's love of flattery, and the bad education acquired at the Smol'nyi Institute, where young ladies acted in comedies instead of improving "their hearts, morals, and reason."[99] Given the human proclivity for corruption, theater seemed just as likely to encourage vice as to improve morals.[100]

The effective power of theater also could be abused, as suggested by M. M. Kheraskov's comedy *The Hater* (1789), in which the evil Zmeiad (Snake-Venom) attempts to engineer his personal advancement by slandering competitors and creating dissension.[101] Although himself a critic of theater, Zmeiad stealthily uses it to attack opponents. On one level, Kheraskov defended theater by making its critic an evil character, but he also showed that corrupt people could manipulate theater for their own purposes. According to Zmeiad, comedy not only fails to rid people of passions, it teaches vices and confirms the prejudices of spectators who witness on stage the stupidity and foolhardiness of great people. Zmeiad further exploits the influence of theater by sending his cronies to ridicule a play so that it appears to flop. In this instance the vile Zmeiad ends up being cursed, but in V. I. Lukin's *Constancy Rewarded,* Evgraf confirms that raucous audience behavior can be planned in advance to spoil a play.[102] Indeed, historians of the eighteenth-century French parterre document the presence of "organized cabals," designed to promote or destroy productions regardless of merit. Sometimes these cabals existed only in the minds of rejected authors and actors, but whether real or imagined, they threatened the public's status as honorable judge and underscored theater's vulnerability to the machinations of evildoers.[103]

Suspicion of the public's ability to judge and of its taste for mere entertainment consistently challenged belief in the social utility of theater. But to challenge was not to deter, and throughout the eighteenth century, Russian commentators expected theater to provide moral instruction. By combining the pedagogy of religious drama with the pleasure of popular entertainment, the creators of Russian literary theater hoped to deliver an edifying cultural experience. As early as 1739, the *St. Petersburg News* compared theater to a school or philosophical assembly in which people learned virtue. If theater sometimes failed to restrain the passions, this was not the fault of the "science" *(nauka)* itself but of the particular artist's "maliciousness or foolishness." The practice of medicine provided an analogy: "When a certain physician is unable to treat human wounds, usually it is said that he does not know his science; nobody says that surgery is of no benefit."[104] Writing in *Useful Entertainment* in 1760, the student Ivan Sokolov (not to be confused with the court actor and playwright of the same name) also insisted that theater did more to correct than to corrupt morals.[105] The real reason for the corruption of morals was unrestrained human will *(volia)*. Countering critics who thought that comedy taught children and servants to deceive parents and masters, Sokolov argued that the display and mockery of vice led to its correction. Everyday life offered endless instruction in immorality, whereas comedy helped people to avoid vice by exposing its vile nature and sad consequences. If reasonable people gleaned a few rules of good behavior from comedy, it served a useful purpose. Moreover, given that "laws, punishments, and other cruel means" inadequately tamed vice, Sokolov concluded that theater helped to reform people precisely because it combined mockery "with a little pleasantness." Enlightenment and entertainment did not represent contradictory goals. On the contrary, useful instruction that also entertained effectively improved morals.[106]

If some eighteenth-century comedies sacrificed amusement to moral instruction, others realized Sokolov's injunction simultaneously to entertain and teach. Addressing readers of *The Windbag* (1765), V. I. Lukin expressed his intention to provide "innocent amusements, that while nourishing your mind and sincere feelings, [also] entertained your sight."[107] Even if the comedy brought no concrete benefit, it offered "pure pleasure" that could stave off harmful behavior during leisure time. The desire to instruct and amuse also was evident in the anonymous comedy *The Imitator* (1779), which after condemning merchant backwardness and forced marriage, ends with an appeal to the parterre: "We hope," a maid declares, "that today we entertained you without in any way putting too much sugar into it."[108] The comic opera *Baba Iaga* (1788) by D. P. Gorchakov likewise fulfilled the promise of didactic entertainment by representing the reward of virtue and the punishment of vice in a lighthearted comical fashion.[109] Assisted by the witch Baba Iaga, a malevolent figure of Slavic folklore who sometimes became a magical friend, a poor orphan recovers his inheritance and marries his beloved.[110] At the end of the play, Baba Iaga promises that evil and vice will be eliminated from the world: adultery, frivolity, uncontrollable passion, excessive luxury, bribery, godless usury, foppishness, hypocrisy, envy, and idle talk—all will disappear. But in the meantime, "We will try to drive away / The heavy burden of boredom, / And in innocent games / Spend our time." At the very least, theater provided people with a pleasant diversion, and perhaps eventually it also would help to bring about a reform of morals.

In order for theater to improve society, however, it needed to address real social problems and extend its appeal beyond the small world of the educated service classes. In *The Spendthrift Reformed by Love* (1765), an adaptation of Philippe Néricault Destouches's *Le Dissipateur* (1736), V. I. Lukin depicted a Russian problem of which he had personal experience.[111] Claiming to have witnessed the ruin of a hundred noble youths sent to the capitals without adequate supervision, Lukin selected the content of his comedy to warn young people about the dangers of card games and extravagance.[112] N. I. Novikov agreed that plays should present models of good behavior, but in the journal *The Purse* in 1774, he described the comedies of Destouches as useless for the general population. Thus Novikov urged playwrights to create models for the people *(narod)*—good servants, honest merchants, and industrious peasants—and by way of example published a popular play or comedy that portrayed a good servant.[113] The anonymous *Play about Christmastide*, published the same year, seemed also to be designed to entertain and instruct "the people."[114] The play associated traditional celebrations and forms of sociability with vulgarity and ignorance by representing an urban household in which holiday games led to violence. Finally, in an imitation of Molière's *Le Bourgeois Gentilhomme* (1670), V. P. Kolychev directed the instructional power of theater against upwardly mobile merchants who ruined themselves trying to live like nobles.[115] *Merchant Becoming a Noble* (1781) highlights the errors of a misguided merchant by staging a conversation about Molière's play. The social climber himself fails to appreciate the parallel, but other characters—including a wise merchant whose son is both a successful trader and a playwright—assume that Molière's satire will help the wayward merchant to understand his mistake.[116] "Theater," wrote V. A. Levshin, "is devised to mock vices, expose excessive passions, and depict the triumph of virtuous souls."[117]

For all their enthusiasm about theater's power to teach morals and bolster civilization, commentators in late eighteenth-century Russia understood only too well that human beings, not institutions, possessed virtue. Theater was no unassailable fortress from which virtue spread out into society and conquered moral corruption. As Christianity long had taught, and as Freemasonry secretly proclaimed, virtue belonged to the individual moral being. Recent studies of eighteenth-century European culture have drawn attention to the practices and lived experience of the Enlightenment as opposed to the Enlightenment of intellectual and political movements.[118] Scholarly attention has shifted from defined sets of ideas and principles to the self-conscious task of fostering enlightenment through education, sociability, and public discussion. But where was the judgment of moral virtue to be located in secular society? Did the church, the monarchy, the bureaucracy, the educated classes, or the people define enlightenment and virtue? In western Europe, this question fueled the "new politics" of open contestation that developed within the institutions of the old regime.[119] In Russia, the absence of constituted political bodies and the Orthodox Church's undisputed authority in matters of religious belief meant that instead of institution-based oppositions and movements, the "new politics" took the form of abstract literary debates. By implication, it was the educated classes who defined what was just and virtuous, and throughout the eighteenth century the educated classes consisted overwhelmingly of individuals who served the monarchy and owned, or aspired to own, serfs.

CONCLUSION: TO SEE AND BE SEEN

When in 1794 Joseph Haydn attended a performance at the Little Haymarket Theater in London, the phrase *spectas et tu spectabere* (see and be seen) appeared inscribed above the curtain.[120] The phrase also resonated in France, where one critic of the transparent windows popular in Parisian churches after 1650 complained that the earlier "taste for prayer" inspired by "a sombre light" had been "rashly replaced with a dangerous itch to see and be seen."[121] To light was to see, and theater lay at the center of Enlightenment sociability. In terms of both participants and content, late eighteenth-century Russian theater incorporated diverse social perspectives. Its public discourse was neither purely official (though censors could intervene at any time) nor purely noble (though nobles dominated as playwrights, patrons, and critics). Ultimately, however, Russian Enlightenment theater's vision of social and political integration represented the voice of a tiny elite who assumed abuses would be corrected, justice achieved, and conflicting interests reconciled. While less pervasive than modern myths of political equality, social and economic opportunity, or national culture, theatrical "myths" of integration and reconciliation reinforced a cognitive reality in which the educated service classes could justify their privileges, assert their authority to govern, and proclaim their belief in Enlightenment principles without having to question the legitimacy of serfdom, inherited social status, legal inequality, or absolute monarchy. Like children's play, eighteenth-century Russian theater allowed people to examine themselves and their society free of responsibility for the social dilemmas represented.

In eighteenth-century Russia, permanent public theater developed in conjunction with a new print culture that encouraged social criticism and individual self-expression on an unprecedented scale. Never before had educated Russians devoted so much effort to examining themselves, their society, and the secular world beyond. Like their counterparts across the European world, educated Russians sought to understand human society in order to make it better, yet they also feared the instability that knowledge could bring. The desire to see and the fear of being seen embodied the Enlightenment tension between philosophical principles and everyday experience. The desire to see encompassed the will to know and understand in order to transform. The fear of being seen represented the cognitive barriers and ideological assumptions that inevitably came to the fore when the principles of human equality and the dignity of the individual contradicted the harsh realities of social and political life. The theatricality of eighteenth-century public culture—the masquerade, the rules of etiquette, and the splendor of ceremony—was the product of a time when people accepted, and lived comfortably with, a vast dichotomy between idea and reality. The realm of the philosophical mind, like the realm of the religious spirit, was not equivalent to the realm of material life. Nor was a correspondence between the two expected. Instead a fragile psychological harmony allowed the educated public to believe that its own moral universe embodied the common good. Philosophers such as Immanuel Kant, monarchs such as Catherine II, and republicans such as Thomas Jefferson imagined that eventually all people could become enlightened, as they themselves had become—in Catherine's case through self-education—and only then could society and government be based on universal civic, or in the promises of the American and French Revolutions civil, rights.[122] In the eighteenth century, educated Russians followed the lead of great thinkers and powerful politicians at home and abroad; they explored social questions without giving up cognitive equilibrium. How did they do it? What did they see? And how did they want to be seen?

3

THE PATRIARCHAL HOUSEHOLD

• The reconciliation of social differences and the justification of social hierarchies—these were fundamental attributes of the good society envisioned by Russian Enlightenment theater. The basic unit of this society, and the place from which good order emanated, was the patriarchal household. In broad outline, the stage version of the patriarchal household embodied principles familiar from ancient literature, biblical teachings, and Muscovite law and practice.[1] The archetypal patriarch governed a household consisting of parents and children together with wards and dependent relatives, tutors, bailiffs, laborers, and servants. Whether the patriarch functioned as husband, father, guardian, or master, his was the immediate authority linking the household to the civic and spiritual communities beyond. All members of the household owed him unquestioning obedience, in return for which he assumed responsibility for their material and moral well-being. Like the biblical God, or the monarch sitting on high, the patriarch was at once merciful and awe-inspiring. It was his duty to educate dependents and punish their transgressions. If he failed in this obligation, or abused his authority, he answered to society, sovereign, and God.

Of course, in reality, household relationships were much less well ordered, for repeatedly the experiences of everyday life contradicted the patriarchal ideal. Love and genuine bonds of affection surely defined some family relationships; however, duty and belief in the sanctity of marriage also dictated that wives and children turn the other cheek when subjected to humiliation and abuse.[2] To determine with any empirical precision how patriarchy actually functioned is extremely difficult. Because memory and personal accounts can be so spotty and subjective, and because the vagaries of individual character and human psychology render intimate relationships so variable, contradictory depictions inevitably emerge from the sources. Not surprisingly perhaps, in present-day scholarship patriarchy has become as much an ideological as a sociological or historical category. Scholars who see in patriarchy the framework for household, community, and seignorial relationships tend to emphasize mechanisms of social control and the inequitable distribution of power. Feminist critics may recognize the functional benefits of patriarchy as a principle of social organization but reject the notion that it could also serve the moral and emotional needs of women. In their conception, patriarchy institutionalized female inferiority in the interest of male domination. Overwhelmingly, historians conclude, patriarchy mirrored absolute monarchy in sanctioning oppressive subjugation.

Yet historians are equally quick to point out that while patriarchy subjugated women and children, it could not deny them subjectivity and agency. Like "the people" of the new social and cultural histories, the women of gender studies emerge as autonomous historical actors as well as "victims." Male domination did not go unchallenged, for women successfully subverted subordination through acts of self-affirmation and conscious resistence. Eighteenth-century Russia provides especially rich material for exploring the interplay between female agency and patriarchal authority. From 1725 to 1796, four of Russia's rulers were women, and all told they reigned for approximately 66 years. In addition, the regent Sophia, half-sister of Tsar Peter I, ruled from 1682 until 1689, and the mother of Ivan VI served as regent from 1740 to 1741. Equally significant, historians of the nobility document the strength of women's property rights already in the seventeenth century, as well as the economic power they wielded.[3] But the political and economic visibility of Russian women could not change the fact that hierarchies of gender and age invariably assigned primacy to the male head of the household and, only at his death, to his widow or eldest adult son. It was no accident that once crowned, the female rulers of the eighteenth century remained unwed. Because eighteenth-century Russian elites expected a wife to be subordinate to her husband, to marry would have brought the empress into conflict with patriarchal authority. Female agency there may have been, and in the case of Elizabeth and Catherine II at least, it included the absolute power of reigning monarchs, but female agency was not necessarily opposed to patriarchy. In a variety of ways, though not necessarily those of nineteenth- and twentieth-century feminism, patriarchy incorporated female agency.

To assume an essential opposition between female agency and patriarchal authority yields limited results when applied to a society in which the abuses of husbands, fathers, and masters were regularly acknowledged, but without reference to the feminist critique of patriarchy or the principle of equal rights for all citizens. As an analytical category, patriarchy is most effective when it encompasses hierarchies of gender *and* age *and* social station. As a moral ideal of benevolent hierarchical authority without which there could be no good society, the patriarchy of Russian Enlightenment theater looked beyond the question of gender relations to the greater problem of the individual's relationship to God-given social order. If the biblical Abraham, guiding his household and followers toward the realization of a special relationship with God, provided a sacred model for patriarchal authority, eighteenth-century Russian playwrights superimposed onto providential history the struggles of human beings in search of personal happiness. In the stage version of this quest, it became possible, within the boundaries of the patriarchal household, to reconcile individual aspirations with social order.

But could this proposed reconciliation have any basis in reality? Was it sincere, misguided, cynically manipulative, or simply disingenuous? From today's perspective it seems obvious that any dramatic resolution in favor of an idealized patriarchy must have resulted from the overwhelming dominance of male voices among eighteenth-century playwrights. Yet if historians are serious about the vitality of female agency, they also must explain why women accepted (and continue to accept) patriarchal authority. What was the meaning of their apparent silence? What did the absence of a Russian feminist critique of patriarchy prior to the mid-nineteenth century reveal about social attitudes in the empire? One possible explanation for the lack of any overt challenge is that in eighteenth-century Russia patriarchy represented much more than the principle of male authority. By adopting a broad definition that incorporates hierarchies of gender, age, and social station, it becomes clear that patriarchy functioned not only as an instrument of male domination but, more importantly, as a mechanism for controlling human passions in the interest of stability and good order. Herein lay the chief obstacle to the satisfaction not only of female aspirations but of all individual aspirations. How could personal happiness be achieved without unleashing destructive human passions?

REASON AND PASSION

Long before the eighteenth century, classical and biblical literature had portrayed love as divinely sanctioned yet also threatening to morality and social order. Eighteenth-century Russian playwrights elaborated upon these themes both by extolling romantic love and by confronting the tension between affective relationships and patriarchal order. In the process, they neither condemned passion in favor of reason nor justified male power with reference to female seductiveness. Playwrights did indeed give center stage to the victory of reason, because passion so often led to unhappiness, tyranny, and civic strife, but they also showed that passion could motivate people to defend justice, honor, and right. When equated with romantic love, passion became a source of virtue, and in play after play it provided a powerful metaphor for personal happiness and freedom. In their stories of romantic love, and particularly of its challenges to patriarchal authority, playwrights explored the problem of how to reconcile passion with social order. If good order required at once that human emotions be contained and individual aspirations be satisfied, how could the passions be civilized so as to allow for personal happiness?

The Natural Right of Love

Classical and biblical archetypes suggest, and historians of early modern Europe confirm, that affection became the preferred basis for family relationships long before the rise of nineteenth-century "bourgeois" domesticity.[4] Less certain, however, is the extent to which individuals in premodern societies were able to realize romantic love. Perhaps the spread of education and capitalist market relations, by increasing the choices available to individuals and their families, also made it easier for such sentiments to prevail over economic, social, and political interests. At the very least, it became easier to imagine the possibility of romantic fulfillment, as European literature from the late Middle Ages onward plainly attests. Thus, however daunting the obstacles encountered in real life, on the eighteenth-century Russian stage, all enlightened and virtuous people assumed that romantic love should be the basis for marriage. Repeated paeans to passion proposed that while people did not always know how to find love, and sometimes feared the emotions it aroused, there could be no happiness without romantic union.[5]

Unequivocal expression of this attitude appears in the 1779 drama with music by V. I. Maikov (1730–1778), *Pygmalion, or The Power of Love*, where the gods Venus and Cupid intervene to help the ruler of Amathus find the love he needs not only to attain happiness, but also to secure the legitimacy of his throne.[6] After Pygmalion falls in love with a female statue he has sculpted, Venus brings the statue to life, so that she can become his wife. Pygmalion's romantic ideal is transformed into empirical reality.[7] The celebration of love continues in the anonymous dramatic opera *The Good Wizard* (1787), in which magic cures a prince of intemperateness and a passion for sailing so that he can marry the daughter of the Turkoman tsar.[8] With marriage comes the promise of children, who, in the words of the joyous tsar, represent love and the laws of nature. That nature not only sanctions but indeed requires love is again the message in the opera *Love Magic* (1799) by Prince I. M. Dolgorukov (1764–1823).[9] Gippolit is a prosperous noble admired by his peasants, but unable to find personal happiness because he associates love with dependence, captivity, and extravagance. In his quest for happiness, Gippolit receives assistance from Cupid, who allows him to witness a blissful peasant girl engaged to be married. Cupid's love magic soon takes effect, and Gippolit falls in love with a poor noble orphan. To love, he discovers, is a divinely ordained natural obligation.

Indeed, love was a natural right *(pravo)* that extended to all social groups—from kings and nobles to peasants and lowly serfs. For this reason, church, state, and Enlightenment thought were united in publicly condemning forced marriages.[10] In the comic opera, *The Parting, or The Departure from Kuskovo of the Chase with Hounds* (1785), the aunt and guardian of a peasant girl has designs on her niece's lover.[11] Herself the unhappy victim of a forced marriage, the aunt is thwarted by the master of hounds, the estate manager, and ultimately the landlord, who orders that the true lovers be allowed to marry. At every level of seignorial administration, the principle of marriage based on love receives affirmation. Even the love-starved aunt eventually concedes that the young couple should not have to share her own unfortunate fate. By recognizing the right of love, she at once maintains her position as head of the household and upholds social order. The aunt's own "patriarchal" authority prevails through acceptance of romantic love.

But while *The Parting* ended in reconciliation, it also showed that passion could impel children to ignore the hierarchy of age and resist parental authority. Indeed, playwrights readily acknowledged that the very principle of love carried within it the seeds of rebellion against patriarchy. *Olin'ka, or Original Love* (1796), by A. M. Belosel'skii-Belozerskii (1752–1809), confronts the problematic nature of love head-on.[12] Olin'ka's girlfriends seem innocent enough when they become jealous of her feelings for Tsarevich Khlor. But then amidst kisses and expressions of love, they insist that the happiness of women requires separation from men. The play appears to challenge social order by depicting romantic love between women. The challenge evaporates after the threat of punishment from the priest of the goddess Lada (Beloved) causes the girls to repent and promise to love men; a second challenge soon arises, however, from the rightful lovers themselves. Olin'ka is secluded in the *terem* (the female living quarters of noble and royal households in Muscovy), and Khlor's father insists that the tsarevich is too young to marry. First Khlor must learn that law *(zakon)* governs feeling *(chuvstvo)*; he must be patient and moderate his passion with reason. But neither Khlor nor Olin'ka can contain the passion that consumes them. After communicating innocently through the *terem* window, Khlor takes the drastic step of breaking into his beloved's quarters. This leads to confessions and pleas before the tsar, who becomes convinced of Khlor's faithfulness and blesses the marriage. "Live," he tells the lovers, "according to your feelings, live!" In *Olin'ka*, affective relationships and defiance of parental authority, both the product of passion, threaten to undermine social order. But happy resolution occurs through the affirmation of that very same romantic love. Love emerges as both the cause of dangerous disorder and the guarantor of good order.

Tragic Love

At once natural and problematic, love engendered a host of contradictory human emotions. Happiness appeared inconceivable without romantic satisfaction, but not before love also produced misery and peril. As one might expect, based on the history of eighteenth-century royal marriages, the genre of tragedy showed that interests of state frequently took precedence over the personal happiness of monarchs and grandees.[13] In the tragedy *Sophonisba* (1787) by Ia. B. Kniazhnin (1740–1791), the lovers Sophonisba and Masinissa choose suicide over submission to Rome.[14] V. I. Maikov's *Femist and Ieronima* (1775) likewise portrays two lovers who prefer death to political subjugation.[15] In both stories, military defeat prevents the realization of love, prompting the rightful lovers to seek freedom and romantic union in death. But foreign conquest was not the only form of political necessity capable of crushing legitimate love. In an early tragedy by A. P. Sumarokov (1717–1777), *Sinav and Truvor* (1751), the fulfillment of duty leads to the lovers' demise.[16] The Russian prince Sinav has asked for the hand of the boyar's daughter Il'mena, but she loves the prince's brother, Truvor. Even so, Il'mena obeys her father and meets her obligation to society by marrying Sinav. Duty appears victorious until a messenger brings news of Truvor's suicide—news that immediately prompts Il'mena to end her own life. Appropriately, the powerful Sinav also is unable to escape the tragic consequences of love: overcome with guilt, he bemoans the fate that has made him a tyrant while awaiting punishment from heaven.

Rightful lovers who became the tragic victims of conquest and politics occupied morally certain ground, even when they defied necessity and sought freedom in death. Less heroic and far more ambiguous emotionally were those who succumbed to a cruel fate that stood apart from important political events. In the tragedy *Marteziia and Falestra* (1767) by M. M. Kheraskov (1733–1807), the Amazon queen Marteziia longs to marry the Locrian tsar Ajax, who landed on her shores following a shipwreck.[17] But after agreeing to the marriage, Ajax has fallen in love with the queen's sister, Falestra, and is unable to keep his earlier promise. Falestra, by contrast, overcomes her passion, adheres to duty, and refuses to run away with her lover. Reason seems to prevail as Ajax says goodbye to his beloved and prepares to set sail, but then Marteziia becomes suspicious of her sister's intentions. Military confrontation ensues, Falestra again declines to leave her country, and both lovers end up committing suicide. At once the cause of love and the obstacle to its realization, impersonal fate wreaked havoc on human happiness.

The role of tragic circumstances in destroying individual happiness highlighted the mighty powers aligned against love. But in a Christian Enlightenment culture concerned with earthly well-being, the vicissitudes of impersonal fate or unknowable providence could not provide an entirely satisfactory explanation for human happiness and suffering. On the Russian stage of the late eighteenth century, both fate and providence represented omniscient forces that transcended human powers and molded human experience. At the same time, however, both Christianity and the Enlightenment viewed the individual human being as a moral subject who actively participated in the God-given natural order. In this scenario, neither classical fate nor Christian providence could be absolutely determinative of outcome. On the contrary, the Christian and the Enlightenment morality of individual responsibility called for an understanding of order in which rightfulness and personal happiness to some extent depended on the choices and actions of self-conscious human beings.

The idea that individual choices determined whether a love turned tragic appeared with disturbing force in revenge stories in which uncontrolled passion caused acute psychological suffering. In the bourgeois tragedy *Calamity Caused by Passion, or Sal'vinii and Adel'son* (1781) by V. P. Kolychev (1736–1794), Sal'vinii's love for Nelliia, the bride of his benefactor, Adel'son, opens the door to manipulation by evildoers.[18] Sal'vinii knows that his passion is wrong, yet he allows Adel'son's enemies to convince him that Adel'son is at fault for allowing him access to Nelliia. Once Adel'son and Nelliia receive permission to marry, Sal'vinii loses all self-control and shoots Nelliia. He quickly repents, however, and exposes a plot against Adel'son. Nelliia survives, and the lovers forgive the criminal. In this moment of profound crisis and pain, reconciliation remains possible. But as things turn out, Sal'vinii is unable to live with his crime; he stabs the evildoer who had encouraged his passion and then kills himself in despair. In place of the rightful resolution promised by repentance and forgiveness, passion has unleashed ever greater destruction.

The gruesome consequences of excessive passion erupt with special vengeance in another bourgeois tragedy *Garstlei and Florinichi* (1787) by V. A. Levshin (1746–1826).[19] Based on the novellas of the popular French writer François-Thomas-Marie de Baculard d'Arnaud (1718–1805), *Garstlei and Florinichi* depicts an Italian lover whose passion for his benefactor's bride also leads to bloody murder and suicide. Rosaliia's uncle, seeking revenge against the family of Garstlei, persuades the rejected Florinichi that Garstlei is to blame for allowing contact with Rosaliia. When Florinichi fails to execute a plot to abduct Rosaliia, his passion intensifies, and violence quickly follows. As Rosaliia prepares to leave for her wedding, Florinichi kills her with a dagger. Later in prison, he repents and commits suicide, which prompts Garstlei to kill Rosaliia's uncle and then take his own life as well. A story of deep emotional suffering, *Garstlei and Florinichi* portrays passion as a problem beyond the ability of human beings to control—a problem that only death can resolve.

Whether tragic love resulted from political necessity, merciless fate, or dangerous human emotions, its painful consequences precluded any simple understanding of even the most rightful love. Eighteenth-century Russian playwrights repeatedly associated the natural right of love with freedom, and its hindrance with tyranny, but the association conveyed an ambiguous moral message. Thus, for the heroine in M. M. Kheraskov's 1765 tragedy *Plamena*, freedom is neither political nor individualistic; it is the freedom to fulfill one's duty as required by conscience, nature, and God.[20] Plamena's tragic dilemma results from her love for the Kievan prince

Pozvezd (Pozvizd), son of Vladimir, the semi-legendary tenth-century Christianizer of Russia. Plamena's father, the captive prince Prevzyd, opposes this love and refuses to accept Christianity, declaring that while he may be a prisoner in body, he is not a prisoner in spirit. By the time the tragedy opens, Plamena has loved Pozvezd for three years and has come to believe that while religious laws may vary, there is one God, one Creator. Still, she remains bound by the principle of filial obedience, which her attraction to Christianity has only strengthened. Plamena's dilemma reaches a crisis point when in accordance with Vladimir's decree she must convert and marry Pozvezd or go into exile with her father.

Tragically, both Plamena and her father represent freedom of conscience. Prevzyd chooses the course of open rebellion and organizes a military force to march against the Christians. Plamena, by contrast, decides to convert and appeals to her father to make peace. Prevzyd rejects his daughter, which leaves her irreconcilably torn between love and obedience; she begins to see herself as an evildoer and blames Pozvezd for denying freedom to her father. Resolution comes only after lover and father face off in battle. Prevzyd kills Pozvezd and later, while awaiting punishment, commits suicide. Freedom of conscience has yielded conflicting results. Even though Plamena's decision to follow love seems rightful because it leads to Christianization, forced conversion remains problematic. Caught between authority and freedom of conscience, Plamena seeks refuge in a convent where she can devote herself to God. Hers is an individual moral solution to tragic love.

Given that eighteenth-century Russian playwrights embraced romantic love as a source of virtue and happiness, why did they also so often stress the suffering it caused? Why did the ambivalent attitude toward love characteristic of tragedy resonate in eighteenth-century Russia? Certainly, the educated servicemen who wrote plays intended to warn against the dangers of excessive passion—to show the ways in which passion led people astray. But they also saw in love a symbol of something much greater than personal desire. The moral and emotional dilemmas of tragic love drew attention not only to the individual human being in search of happiness, but also to his or her destiny in relation to family, society, and polity. On the eighteenth-century Russian stage, tragic love represented nothing less than the universal conflict between reason and passion in human affairs. Lacking the language of romanticism or modern social science, playwrights described human psychology in terms of moral struggle—a struggle at once highly personal and greater than any single human being. Through the clash of reason and passion in the consciousness of tragic heroes and heroines, playwrights gave philosophical expression to complicated emotional states.

The Realization of Romantic Love

On the eighteenth-century Russian stage, the struggle between reason and passion also appeared in mundane settings where duty (equated with authority) again threatened rightful love (equated with freedom). But whereas tragedy, even when it ended happily, tended to require the death of a protagonist, comedy and drama taught that the obstacles to romantic love could be overcome without resorting to suicide or murder. The obstacles might seem insurmountable, but they resulted from immediate circumstances that in many cases could be remedied by a change of attitude or social position. Instead of political necessity and amoral fate, which stood outside the individual human being, nonheroic lovers confronted economic interests, considerations of social status, and parental abuse. Dramatic conflict arose when accepted moral principles clashed, or rightful relationships were violated. Kings, nobles, merchants, peasants, and servants all sought to enjoy romantic love, and all struggled to find happiness without violating etiquette or duty. Although these more commonplace barriers to happiness echoed the elevated dilemmas of tragic heroes and heroines, they also established a closer correspondence between the realization of love and the reward of virtue. By transposing conflicts familiar from tragedy into stories of everyday life, writers of comedy and drama showed that rightful love and good order could indeed be reconciled. Individual freedom did not inevitably challenge patriarchal authority.

Although duty frequently required the mastery of personal desire, the realization of love remained paramount. For together, the combination of love and duty symbolized the harmony of nature and civilization. In the verse drama *Celebration of Friendship* (1773) by P. S. Potemkin (1743–1796), Milon (Nice) has fallen in love with Zaida, the Turkish prisoner and fiancée of his friend Modest.[21] Duty and honor require that Milon forget his love, which, in any event, he regards as less important than service to society, fatherland, and monarch. For Milon duty is foremost, but for Zaida love cannot be a sin. In her state of natural reason *(razum)*, Zaida is unable to understand how law *(zakon)* can forbid love. Unencumbered by the rules of civilized living, unaware of the need to repress natural feelings—Zaida appeals directly to Modest, who does not want to be a tyrant and concedes to Milon. But Milon refuses to accept the favor in the belief that his love for Zaida is a betrayal of friendship. Thus before happy resolution can be achieved, both men struggle with the conflict between duty and desire. In Rousseauian fashion, civilization seems to thwart rightful nature. Honor requires each man to concede to the other, for neither wants to cause the unhappiness of either Zaida or his friend. Eventually, Milon accepts Modest's concession, and the natural right of love emerges victorious without, however, violating duty. Modest also finds natural happiness by marrying Milon's sister, who has loved him all along.

Late eighteenth-century Russian playwrights made very clear that rightful love rested on feelings of mutual inclination *(sklonnost')*, shared mores *(nravy)*, and appropriate etiquette. The anonymous comedy *A Reasonable Choice* (1773), billed as an adapted French play "dressed in Russian clothes," stresses the point by abandoning the usual preference for lovers of similar age.[22] A young military officer arrogantly assumes that Varvara loves him, and her guardian, Nikanor, a retired serviceman around age 60, readily agrees to the match provided his charge is willing. The problem is that Varvara loves Nikanor, but being a virtuous girl, she is too modest and shy to tell him. Nor is Nikanor sufficiently vain or presumptuous to understand the repeated hints Varvara struggles to express. At last Varvara gets her point across by having her guardian write a letter to the man she loves, that is to himself. Yet even then Nikanor does not believe he is worthy of Varvara, and herein lies the proof of his superiority over the proud officer. Although marriage to an older man can bring concrete advantages, Varvara loves her guardian for his moral qualities, particularly his constancy and forbearance. Despite Nikanor's advanced age and parental relationship to Varvara, their union is rightful based on mutual inclination.

In an age of enlightenment, playwrights preferred to judge the rightfulness of marriage partners on the basis of individual merit rather than economic or social gain, yet they also recognized that attention to interest repeatedly blocked romantic satisfaction. In Ia. B. Kniazhnin's comic opera *The Miser*, the greedy Skriagin (Miser), uncle and guardian of Liubima (Beloved), ignores his niece's happiness and education in order to control her property.[23] Nor, as the anonymous comedy *The Letter, or The Rich Bride* (1788) shows, is the pursuit of interest confined to avaricious guardians and suitors.[24] Identified as the work of a female author, *The Letter* depicts the wealthy Liumilova, who is determined to marry the sweet-talking Den'gov (Money). Liumilova's deliberate manipulations accord well with Den'gov's "modern" view of courtship. Women, he argues, are free to socialize with potential grooms, so it is incumbent upon men to flatter them by expressing affection. Intent on mastering foolhardy passion in order to preserve his own freedom *(vol'nost')*, Den'gov courts girls but avoids romantic feelings. A marriage based on interest, he concludes, can indeed be happy. Liumilova agrees and sets out to secure a match by writing to Den'gov about her wealth. She also seems genuinely attracted to the man, though she knows little of his character and does not care if he marries her out of greed. Liumilova's overriding concern is to get what she wants, or at least what she thinks she wants. Men and women, young and old—anybody can seek benefit *(pol'za)* in matters of love.[25]

The cynicism of "modern" courtship notwithstanding, playwrights hoped that interest and love could be harmonized. They also made clear, however, that economic necessity easily threatened the realization of love. Nobles were neither agriculturalists nor tradesmen capable of subsisting from their own labor. They were landowners and servicemen who relied on serfs and salaries to keep their families afloat. While one should not bemoan the economic plight of nobles in a society organized around serfdom, it nonetheless is important to recognize the pressures they faced. On the consumption-oriented estates of the eighteenth century, crop failures, natural disasters, shortages of cash, and geographical isolation could bring ruin, or at the very least make it difficult to maintain a lifestyle appropriate to noble status. Nor in a preindustrial and only barely commercialized economy could people simply go out and earn a wage; economic and personal ties could be difficult to distinguish. Survival thus required that marriage be viewed as an economic partnership, and that noble families use marriage to acquire land and income. Even if romantic love remained the primary goal of marriage, prospective partners also needed to consider the physical survival of person, family, and estate. The economic realities of the eighteenth century limited the means by which families could achieve economic stability. Material constraints muted personal aspirations, including the satisfaction of love, despite the hope that happiness and practical necessity could be reconciled.

In the late eighteenth-century, Russian playwrights did indeed foster this hope by assuming in their plays that mutual love derived from the personal merits of marriage partners. But if virtue took precedence over lineage and wealth, it cannot be said that dramatic resolution ever endorsed a love match grounded in poverty. In the anonymous comedy *Guess and I Will Not Say* (1772), the retired dragoon major Gadalo (Guess) is dissatisfied with the suitors who seek the hand of his daughter Nadezhda (Hope).[26] One suitor, he is certain, will squander Nadezhda's estate, the second lacks all honor, and the third is an evil tax collector. Gadalo claims to value honor over wealth, yet he has neglected to consider Artemii, a poor noble in his charge, as a possible groom. The good Artemii is convinced, moreover, that his poverty precludes any union with Nadezhda. In formulaic fashion, circumstances change once Artemii and Nadezhda declare their love: a rich uncle who had wronged Artemii's father decides to make amends by adopting his nephew. The apparent conflict between economic security and honor is joyously resolved.[27]

But just how serious the economic obstacles to rightful love could be is evident from *Fomushka—Grandmother's Boy* (1790) by P. A. Kropotov (1736/7–1790).[28] The noble Dobrovidov (Looks-Good) must choose between two suitors who seek the hand of his daughter Malan'ia. The first is an ignorant, socially awkward sergeant in the guards named Foma, who has never served but whose grandmother has brought him to town in hopes of securing his promotion to major. Though morally unworthy, Foma is a wealthy serfowner, and he has offered to deed a village of five hundred souls to Malan'ia.[29] Because Malan'ia is generous to the poor but not rich, Dobrovidov is justifiably concerned about her future and therefore receptive to Foma's marriage proposal.[30] Malan'ia, by contrast, despite the threat of economic hardship, is not at all interested in Foma; she loves the worthy Ostromyslov (Sharp-Thinker), a decorated lieutenant raised by her father. Ostromyslov is a man of many virtues but also a poor man: he owns only five souls and about ten hectares of land. Nor is his salary sufficient to rent quarters and support a wife. Rightful love and material security seem irreconcilable until Count Chistoserdov (Sincere) comes to the rescue of the desperate couple. A general who rails against the ignorance of judges and insists that service appointments and rewards be based on merit, the count is moved by the lovers' plight to provide a village of three hundred souls.[31] With this gift Malan'ia and Ostromyslov acquire the essential resources needed to marry. Once again rightful love can be realized after the economic question is resolved.

Economic gain was not the only advantage or necessity compelling parents to ignore the happiness of their children. Social status, exemplified by lineage, also played a role. Count Chistoserdov rejected family connections as the basis for advancement in service, advocating instead personal virtues such as enlightenment and zealousness. By contrast, in V. A. Levshin's lyric comedy *Let Bygones Be Bygones* (1791), Starolesov (Old-Woods), after promising his daughter Liza to Cheston (Honorable), has become concerned about corrupting the blood of his ancestors. Now he wants Liza to marry old Partazanov (Partisan), age 50, whose noble lineage goes back twelve generations to the time of Dmitrii Donskoi's victory over Mamai.[32] Oblivious to the notion that individual merit is preferable to lineage, Starolesov demands blind obedience from his daughter. He assumes that passion and compatibility are irrelevant in marriage: a wife, he believes, must adapt to the ways of her husband. But Liza cannot abide her father's callousness; she insists that her heart belongs to Cheston and that while parental authority can ruin her, it is beyond her will to love another. Still, despite Liza's strong plea for freedom of the heart, she remains obedient and refuses to elope with Cheston. This prompts action from the lovers' servants, one of whom notes the impossibility of living without deception.[33] Liza and Cheston are able to sneak away and be married, Liza's uncle makes Cheston his heir, and the patriarchs Partazanov and Starolesov are forced to reconcile with the newlyweds. Bygones can be bygones as rightful love once again triumphs.

For eighteenth-century Russian playwrights, adherence to the merit principle in the selection of marriage partners provided clear evidence of enlightenment or the lack thereof. In the anonymous comedy *The Satisfied Groom*, Plenira (Captivating) loves Cheston (Honorable), who is honorable and intelligent, but her parents want her to marry Fadei, who is rich and stupid.[34] Old-fashioned and uncultured, the parents of Plenira abuse their servants and deride refined sociability. Fadei's lack of enlightenment is equally striking, represented by his interest in gypsy entertainment. Certainly, the vices of the unenlightened justify the use of deception to bring about the marriage of Plenira and Cheston. The same message echoes in *The Betrothal of Kuteikin* (1799) by P. A. Plavil'shchikov (1760–1812)—a comedy filled with characters from Fonvizin's *The Minor*.[35] The merchant Preslep wants his daughter Paraskov'ia to marry Kuteikin, because the former seminarian is a Christian who has studied God's truth and is free of heresy. Paraskov'ia, by contrast, received her education in St. Petersburg, where she acquired literacy, learned French, and in the words of Preslep, became an infidel. Much to her father's dismay, she has learned to think and love, and as a result she wants to marry the like-minded officer Pimen. Although Preslep previously had promised Paraskov'ia to Pimen, he lacks the sense of honor that would compel an enlightened man to keep his word. Rightful love prevails only after Pimen and Paraskov'ia defy parental authority, prompting Kuteikin to flee and forcing Preslep reluctantly to concede.[36] While it cannot be said that virtue has triumphed—much ignorance and abuse remain—manipulation of the unenlightened does allow the worthy lovers to marry.

Russian playwrights of the late eighteenth century agreed that irrespective of wealth and lineage, mutual inclination and compatible moral qualities provided the basis for happy marriage. Attention focused on the individuals involved, for without happy unions, there could be no good order in society. To be sure, economic security represented an important consideration, one that even the most enlightened stage characters could not ignore, yet it was hoped that financial obstacles could somehow be overcome. Perhaps this was less likely to be achieved in real life than on stage, though certainly playwrights intended to present any sacrifice of romantic love to economic or social gain as a great misfortune. The realization of personal happiness may not have been the be all or end all that it would become in later times, but the satisfaction of individual desire still was highly valued. Within the constraints imposed by economic and family survival—the two were understood to be one and the same in the eighteenth century—playwrights assumed that personal happiness was possible and that it was most likely to be found in romantic love. Indeed, playwrights even went so far as to sanction resistance to authority figures who stood in the way of rightful love. In proposing such resistance, they in no way questioned the legitimacy of patriarchal authority but rather sought to ensure that it functioned properly.

DUTY AND THE BONDS OF AFFECTION

To forestall potential conflicts between the rights of romantic love and the maintenance of social order, Russian playwrights looked to the principle of duty. It can be argued that in the patriarchal household, duty invariably corresponded to the will of the paterfamilias. But duty was more than a euphemism for raw patriarchal power, although sometimes it may well have functioned in this manner. Duty also implied reciprocal obligations and genuine bonds of affection. Personal obligations that today seem arbitrary and oppressive were imposed and accepted in the eighteenth century to ensure the economic and social survival of the family. Because marriage represented an ethical institution in which the interests of the family superseded those of the individual, personal satisfaction resulted from carrying out one's duties, which did not represent limitations on the real self.

On the contrary, the real self could be realized only through the fulfillment of duty, grounded as it was in the emotional altruism of family relationships. To live up to one's institutionally and morally imposed duties thus constituted not only virtue but also happiness. When individual desire corresponded to the requirements of duty, it brought the freedom and calm of rightful order; when desire and duty clashed, the lack of freedom and the suffering of moral breakdown ensued.

On the eighteenth-century Russian stage, the patriarchal household provided the social framework for the fulfillment of duty and the good order it promised. For this reason, wayward women effectively symbolized the dangerous "unfreedom" that could result from weak patriarchal power. In Fonvizin's well-known comedy *The Minor,* a major reason for the disarray in the Prostakovs' (Simpletons) household, as well as for the ignorance and moral incapacity of their son Mitrofan, is the failure of Mr. Prostakov to assert proper authority over his wife.[37] Mrs. Prostakova rules the roost, and the result is moral degeneration. The "unfreedom" of freedom is equally characteristic of the widow Pul'kheriia (Beautiful), portrayed by B. E. El'chaninov (1744–1770) in *The Giddypate Punished* (1767).[38] Pul'kheriia is a frivolous coquette admired by multiple lovers, and once she has obtained freedom in widowhood, she regards marriage as boring and unnecessary. Like other coquettes and fops, Pul'kheriia is ignorant of the Russian language and disdainful of Russian culture. Her speech is interspersed with French phrases and Russified French words; her friends, convinced that Russians cannot be "great people," ridicule Mikhail Lomonosov and Feofan Prokopovich. Although eventually exposed and abandoned by her admirers, Pul'kheria remains indifferent to her reputation. Self-absorbed and unreformed, she is last seen going off to attend a masquerade.[39]

Wives and widows who possessed too much power or freedom surely caused social chaos, yet it did not invariably follow that the good order of patriarchy hinged upon male dominance. Eighteenth-century Russian playwrights echoed classical and biblical archetypes, and foreshadowed modern feminists, in also recognizing women as legitimate bearers of independent authority. This is the image conveyed in the comedy *Mr. This-and-That* (1786) by Princess E. R. Dashkova (1743/4–1810).[40] Widowed herself at the age of 20, Dashkova was a woman of the world—forever in search of favorable appointments for relatives and protégés, forever in need of money to pay off the debts of her husband and children. In *Mr. This-and-That* she depicts a man of weak character—a type "unfortunately so common in our society"—who is saved from economic ruin by a domineering aunt, the widow Reshimova (Decisive).[41] Strong women like Reshimova (and her creator) upheld and themselves embodied patriarchal or, in this case, matriarchal authority. Patriarchy may have institutionalized the subordination of women to men, but within its boundaries, hierarchies of age and moral virtue repeatedly overshadowed or even reversed gender relations.

Husband and Wife

Indeed, with respect to marriage, eighteenth-century Russian playwrights did not represent the requirements of good order in terms of gender relations or the subordination of women to men, but in terms of the proper relationship between husband and wife. The principle of love-based marriage assumed that a bride and groom entered into holy union not only voluntarily but also individually. As autonomous moral beings united by mutual inclination and respect, they faced the duties of marriage with serenity and determination. Among the many obligations assumed by spouses, none was more important than loyalty—understood as both sexual fidelity and the ability to withstand extreme adversity. Playwrights admonished husbands and wives to be true by carrying out their obligations to each other, to their children, and to the larger family. Although the concept of duty assumed that marital responsibility would be shared, it also was the case that wives performed the most extraordinary feats of faithfulness. Such displays of female fidelity not only reinforced the double standard imposed by patriarchy in matters of carnal love, but also recognized how difficult it could be for wives to adhere to duty given the trials and tribulations of their lives.

To this day the archetype of the loyal wife remains Euripides' Alcestis, brought to Russia in 1759 by A. P. Sumarokov.[42] In both the Greek original and Sumarokov's opera, Alcestis, wife of Admetus, king of Pherae in Thessaly, symbolizes the true love of the ideal wife. When Admetus married, he neglected to make the obligatory sacrifice to Artemis and consequently faced a sentence of death. Through the intercession of Apollo, however, Admetus obtained a concession from the Fates allowing another to die in his place. Alcestis turns out to be the only person willing to die for him, and both plays open at the time appointed for her death. Scenes of grief, dying, and mourning ensue until Alcestis unexpectedly returns after being wrested from death by Heracles. Husband and wife are rightfully reunited, though the troubling question of why Admetus allowed Alcestis to die remains. Significantly, neither play answers the question in terms of the *mutual* obligations between husband and wife. The Greek chorus attributes Admetus' decision to the rule of Necessity, and Sumarokov agrees that humans cannot oppose the gods. Sumarokov also adds a political twist: the king is needed for the happiness of the people. Nobody is more important than the monarch, and because the monarch is the source of happiness—an official theme of Empress Elizabeth's reign—somebody must die instead of Admetus. That Alcestis agrees to do so epitomizes the loyal wife who is rewarded by being returned to life.

However lopsided the sacrifice of Alcestis, it made sense not only as the fulfillment of duty, but also as the fruit of a happy marriage. That of Fedima, in the tragedy *The False Smerdis* (1769) by A. A. Rzhevskii (1737–1804), is explicable solely in terms of duty.[43] Although Fedima married the Persian tsar Smerdis (Vile) only after he threatened to kill her father and beloved Darius, she is no less bound by duty than Alcestis. Indeed, her husband's evil character deepens her sense of obligation. A typical tyrant of the eighteenth-century Russian stage, Smerdis assumes that tsars are gods rather than human beings devoted to the people's tranquility.[44] He insists that the people exist to please him, that his power is unlimited, and that the only way to secure the throne is by destroying every enemy. Nor does Smerdis's passionate love for Fedima bring him happiness. Tormented by jealousy and unable to subjugate Fedima's heart, he expects to find inner peace through revenge. Fortunately, before Smerdis can act against Darius, rebellion among the grandees reveals that he is a pretender. The confrontation also leads to Smerdis's death, after which Darius is crowned by popular acclamation. Fedima plays no role in these events and even tries to protect her husband. When Darius declares his desire to marry her, she is unable to respond: instead of embracing her beloved, she expresses despair over the spilled blood of her spouse. However much tyranny justified the killing of the imposter tsar, no human deed could break the sacred bond of marriage.

Fedima was not alone in believing that the sanctity of the marriage vow extended into death. In the comedy *Constancy Tested* (1776) by N. P. Nikolev (1758–1815), Prospekh returns home after seven years of captivity plagued with doubts about the loyalty of his wife.[45] But in reality, ever since Nizmena received the erroneous news of her husband's death, she has honored his memory with continual mourning and tears. For years she has neither gone out nor received visitors, yet Prospekh still wants to test her fidelity. To that end, he enlists Dobromysl (Good-Thinking) to play the role of a renowned prince and field-marshal who has fallen in love with a portrait of Nizmena. Dobromysl arrives with a large suite, claims to have spent a year searching for Nizmena, declares his love, and asks her to marry him. Despite the urging of her servant, who thinks enlightenment has eliminated the need for lifelong mourning, Nizmena is unmoved. She insists that love does not change even in death and that it is impossible for her ever to love another. Heaven does not grant a virtuous husband twice in life. Although Nizmena's steadfastness appears miraculous, it nonetheless fails to satisfy Prospekh. Happy reunion occurs only after Dobromysl threatens to use force, and Nizmena responds by attempting suicide. In contrast to the dark suspicions of her husband, Nizmena's virtues shine.

Not all the good wives of the Russian stage performed such amazing feats of fidelity, and depending on circumstances, some could be forgiven their transgressions. In the comedy *Word for Word*, "written in Simbirsk in 1774," M. I. Verevkin (1732–1795) describes the aftermath of the destructive Pugachev rebellion (1773–1774), including the rape and murder of local notables.[46] Two women, one unmarried and the other married, have been violated by the rebels, and their social positions are now in doubt. Pul'kheriia (Beautiful), daughter of the governor *(voevoda)*, has lost all self-respect as a result of her captivity and wants to enter a convent, but her lover, the young military commander Miloi (Nice), disregarding her sense of shame, seeks and obtains her father's permission for the couple to marry. The plight of the already married woman is equally complicated; she was forced to marry the Cossack ataman who took her captive, but her husband is less forgiving than Miloi. Although the woman is eager to return and bear the name of her first spouse, he is reluctant to take her back because she has learned to change husbands. As judge and representative of state authority, the governor agrees that the wife is innocent and urges her husband to reconcile. In both cases, men in positions of authority uphold the rape victim's honor by restoring rightful love and sacred marriage.[47]

The Pugachev rebellion created a highly unusual set of circumstances, yet it is noteworthy that Verevkin's play did not hold sexually violated women responsible for any moral transgression. To the contrary, the dramatic action focused on providing assistance to victims of the uprising, including women deprived of legitimate social position. Of course, the playwright's need to address the question of female honor in conditions of rape and forced marriage suggests that society held men and women to very different standards of sexual behavior. But the problem is less an illustration of female subjugation than an affirmation of how important women were to family honor and social order.[48] If the play's resolution appears insensitive in assuming that a victim's suffering will end once men accept her as an honorable daughter and wife, perhaps this is because emotional conflict was understood in moral rather than modern psychological terms. Pulkheriia assumed she had become unworthy of Miloi even though she was innocent of wrongdoing; her married counterpart, by contrast, believed that precisely because of her innocence she remained worthy of her husband. For both women the experience of rape raised moral questions about the sacrament of marriage—questions that patriarchal authority decided in favor of the victim.

Patriarchal authority was less generous in cases of intentional infidelity, but even here reconciliation remained a possibility. A 1772 adaptation of Nicolas-Thomas Barthe's (1734–1785) *Les Fausses infidélités* (1768)—itself a loose adaptation of William Shakespeare's *The Merry Wives of Windsor*—depicts two couples who feign infidelity out of jealousy, insecurity, and boredom.[49] While all ends well when the couples decide to marry, the comedy reveals just how readily lovers manipulate and deceive. Similarly, in *Exchange of Hats, or An Attempt [At Infidelity] Destroyed by Prudence* (1782)—a free translation from the German by A. M. Krutitskii (1754–1803)—a sensible wife breaks off a love affair after her husband becomes suspicious.[50] Better always to see her spouse's gloomy face and listen to his orders than to deserve his reproaches, the wife concludes. All is forgiven once husband and wife agree to live happily: he will avoid jealousy and she empty-headedness. Common sense and forgiveness again occupy center stage in the comedy *Love Joke* (1800) by N. M. Kugushev (1777–1825).[51] The unfaithfulness of both husband and wife is uncovered when the lover of Mrs. Milovidova

(Nice-Looking) visits, disguised as a woman, and her husband tries to seduce the guest. Each spouse has doubted the other's love, and both are prepared to reconcile and forget the past on the assumption that all people are sinful. The rightful order of the patriarchal household, without which there could be no good society, depends on the ability of individuals to repent and reform.

When Peter I brought elite women out of the seclusion of the *terem*, required courtiers to attend French-style assemblies, and forbade forced marriages, he encouraged a new public sociability that allowed more open communication between the sexes.[52] The many coquettes and fops who peopled the eighteenth-century stage were among the negative products of the new freedom, which when accompanied by an absence of virtue, led to corruption and disorder. In the pseudonymous comedy *Revenge for Infidelity* (1781), young Blezor courts two women simultaneously—one for her beauty, and the second, a widow of 50, for her money.[53] Even though the younger woman has known all along that Blezor is deceiving the widow, both women desert him when the betrayal is discovered. The unfaithful wife in the anonymous comedy *Female Infidelity* (1788) is similarly abandoned after her lover flees from exposure and her husband sends her back to her father in Moscow.[54] Finally, the behavior of the adulteress Amarilla in Ivan Mikhailov's comedy *One Is Like the Other* (1788) appears equally reprehensible, though her fate is left to the reader's imagination.[55] She wants to marry her lover, whereas the lover wants her wealth. Presumably these goals are not incompatible: the play concludes as the deceived husband learns that the lovers have run away with his wife's possessions. Light-hearted in tone and entertaining in effect, romantic comedies did not punish every carouser or adulterer. They did, however, invariably associate unfaithfulness with frivolity and immorality.[56]

Themes of adultery and sexual impropriety were not new to Russian literary culture in the eighteenth century, though clearly playwrights expressed concern about loose social mores that, in their view, had penetrated Russia along with fashionable European sociability.[57] At the same time, however, they also consistently associated enlightenment and the rightful realization of romantic love with "modern" social practices—that is, with the forms of sociability imported from abroad.[58] In the comedy *Virtue Crowned with Faithfulness* (1774), M. I. Prokudin-Gorskii (1744–1813) contrasts the marriage of the widow Sueverova (Superstitious) with that of her niece Beznadezhdova (Without-Hope).[59] Sueverova is an uneducated representative of the old thinking, and although she was married against her will, for 40 years she took her husband's beatings as evidence of love and friendship. Now, after consulting the district fortune-tellers, Sueverova insists that Beznadezhdova marry the rich Uedinennov (Solitary), who is empty-headed and boastful, mistreats his servants, and does not care that his bride objects to the marriage. Beznadezhdova avoids unhappiness precisely because state law encourages the freer forms of social intercourse. Friends and servants, citing the legal prohibitions on forced marriage, defend Beznadezhdova, so that when her beloved Postoianov (Constant) returns from war, the lovers are able to announce their engagement. In defiance of Sueverova's patriarchal authority, Beznadezhdova and Postoianov can legitimize their action with reference to the official support accorded love-based marriage.

Alongside the near universal association of happy marriage with enlightenment, eighteenth-century playwrights also showed the extent to which a lack of enlightenment affected family relationships. A. P. Sumarokov's comedy *Empty Quarrel* (1781) depicts a miserable husband and wife who cannot agree on the choice of a groom for their daughter.[60] Salmina is a typical domineering wife of the eighteenth-century Russian stage, particularly vulgar in the belief that she possesses all the social graces. For her, nobility *(blagorodie)* inheres in the ability to pay compliments. Never mind that she beats her husband, regards him as an idiot, and feels neither love nor respect toward him. After decades of marriage, she is satisfied because he remains subservient. Consistent with Salmina's false refinement, her chosen groom is a Frenchified fop who does not like to be called Russian, yet knows French poorly. Her husband's choice is a meek man like himself who also enjoys "old" forms of entertainment—the popular game *svaika,* for example—and assumes that wife-beating is necessary in marriage. Lack of enlightenment and indifference to enlightenment—these are the attributes of the rude and barbarous couple. It comes as no surprise, then, that their daughter does not believe a noblewoman needs to love her husband. But neither does she want a husband. The daughter resolves her parents' dispute by refusing to marry either proposed groom.

However much eighteenth-century Russian playwrights tried to associate virtue with enlightened reason, they also understood that in marriage reasonableness frequently proved elusive. In Ia. B. Kniazhnin's comedy *The Unsuccessful Peace-Maker, or Without Dinner I Am Going Home* (1787), Mr. and Mrs. Kuter'ma (Commotion) cannot speak to each other without arguing.[61] Their friend Mirotvor (Peace-Maker), who believes that education can enlighten natural reason and be used to make people happy, sets out to effect a reconciliation. The futility of the effort is foreshadowed by Mirotvor's own failure to distinguish false enlightenment from genuine learning: he mistakes the drunkard Sinekhdokhos (Synecdoche) for a well-educated person capable of using logic to end marital strife. If an ignorant fraud can present himself as an erudite scholar, what does it mean to possess enlightenment? Is enlightenment, moreover, an effective instrument of reformation? Mr. and Mrs. Kuter'ma cannot live without each other precisely because they love to argue. Perhaps if they were truly enlightened, logic could be brought to bear in their relationship. But with or without enlightenment, the playwright seems to suggest, logic is not necessarily an essential component of marriage.

By juxtaposing enlightenment to ignorance and by associating ignorance or lack of enlightenment with adultery and marital strife, late eighteenth-century playwrights employed abstract principles to describe the gap between the idea and reality of marriage. Although Enlightenment thinkers often are accused of ignoring human passion in order to preserve a blind faith in reason, they actually were quite realistic about the extent to which individual virtue could be realized and hence society reformed. As noted in *Revenge for Infidelity*, "the action [that is, deception and betrayal] is here and everywhere." Unlike modern purveyors of utopia, eighteenth-century playwrights recognized the limits to human power and understanding. They walked a middle ground amid the extremes of moral purity and violent self-destruction, and in the process effectively explored the everyday give and take of love and marriage. Their literary depictions, however lacking in naturalism and nuance, conveyed a common-sense sensitivity to the dynamics of gender relations in a patriarchal society.

Duty inspired by mutual love and respect—this was the basis for the happy marriages that guaranteed good order in society. Although fathers and husbands dominated the patriarchal household, male authority was not unlimited. It was bounded by genuine bonds of affection and by the expectation of a correspondence between the requirements of duty and the desires of the individual. Real life—characterized as it might be by personal unhappiness, loveless marriage, physical abuse, and adultery—challenged the patriarchal ideal without weakening its power to define duty. In the name of duty, eighteenth-century Russian playwrights reconciled individual aspirations with familial needs, and in the process envisioned a household that embodied the natural harmony of God's universe. Since the days of Abraham, providential history had unfolded within the framework of patriarchy, so that to deny its rightfulness would have represented nothing less than defiance of God. No matter how often everyday experiences might contradict moral principles, social order could not be separated from patriarchy.

Parent and Child

After God and monarch, no authority exceeded that of the parent, for as stage parents repeatedly reminded their children, it was parents who gave the gift of life. On this basis, filial obedience represented a sacred duty that superseded personal happiness and precluded any conflict between parent and child. The sacred tragedy *Jephthah* (1778) by Apollos [A. D. Baibakov (1737–1801)] illustrates with painful finality the embedding of filial obedience in duty to God.[62] In an effort to show that biblical stories also could provide compelling subject matter for the theater, Apollos dramatized a story from Judges (11–12:7) in which judge of Israel Jephthah makes a fateful vow to the Lord: if victorious against the Ammonites, Jephthah will give to the Lord as a burnt offering whatsoever comes first out of his house to meet him. The "whatsoever" turns out to be Jephthah's maiden daughter and only child, called Tselomudra (Chaste) by Apollos. Previously, Tselomudra had accepted her father's choice of groom; now she accepts death, so that Jephthah can fulfill his promise to God. After mourning her virginity in the mountains, Tselomudra is sacrificed, much to the despair of her grief-stricken father. Her warrior groom, wishing to be reunited with his beloved, simply falls unconscious and dies. A more tragic and complete act of filial obedience would be difficult to imagine.

A second example of absolute filial loyalty is Plamira in P. A. Plavil'shchikov's tragedy *Riurik* (early 1790s).[63] Plamira is the daughter of the Slavic prince Vadim, who rebels against Riurik following the establishment of Varangian rule in Novgorod. Consistent with other dramatic renditions of the Vadim legend, Plavil'shchikov's Riurik is a good ruler who has restored peace among the Slavs and strives to make his subjects happy.[64] His Vadim, by contrast, is a cruel tyrant plotting to murder Riurik and eager to kill Plamira because she refuses to help. Even worse, Vadim urges the execution of his daughter when she is accused of attempting to assassinate Riurik. The evil machinations of Vadim are boundless, yet Plamira remains steadfastly silent, seeing no solution to her dilemma other than death. Out of loyalty to her father, Plamira cannot reveal that he is the would-be assassin, and at no point in the tragedy does she speak out against him. Eventually, it is Vadim who experiences remorse and confesses, opening the door to rightful resolution. Riurik is forever eager to forgive the transgressions of his subjects and offers Vadim the throne. Vadim responds in kind by conceding to Riurik. Plamira, who had every reason to disobey her father, avoids the sin of disloyalty and as a result, facilitates the happy reconciliation of all.

In the best of all possible worlds, which surely the stage sought to represent, the principle of filial obedience assumed that the child's inclination naturally coincided with the parent's will. Upbringing was key to achieving the desired harmony, because virtuous children grew up to be virtuous parents. Yet while playwrights made clear that good education taught virtue, the path to good education remained uncertain. Good parents could corrupt their children by giving them a bad education, and corrupted children could be reformed by receiving timely instruction. Alternatively, corrupt parents could raise good children, for even though education instilled virtue, goodness also existed in nature. Playwrights in late eighteenth-century Russia made no attempt to decide the age-old question of whether human beings were innately good or evil. As practitioners of the Enlightenment, they tended toward a Rousseauian image of children as naturally good, which meant that even a fully grown child, old enough to serve and be married, could be reformed. But playwrights also embraced the Lockean assumption that the goal of education was to teach the child, whether boy or girl, "to get a mastery over his inclinations and submit his appetites to reason."[65] Without civilization natural goodness could not be realized.

To submit the appetites of children to reason required that parents reward goodness and punish transgression. But when parental authority proved unequal to the task, divine authority took its place. In M. M. Kheraskov's heroic comedy *The Godless One* (1761), Rufin, the favored son of Leon, commits a series of evil acts.[66] When at last confronted by his father, Rufin blames him for ruining his soul with overindulgence. While there is truth to the accusation, Kheraskov nonetheless holds Rufin responsible for his own misdeeds. The wicked son attacks his father with a sword, and divine retribution ensues. Thunder erupts, an abyss opens up, and Rufin perishes. The godless, the chorus notes, are punished by the Creator. In less extreme cases, however, earthly punishment proved sufficient. In the anonymous opera *Three Lazy Ones* (1791), a retired corporal, invoking military discipline, employs the lash to reform his nephews, whose parents have failed to educate them properly.[67] Going even further in the direction of leniency, the children's drama *A Doll for Lizan'ka, or Diligence Rewarded* (1799), by G. N. Gorodchaninov (1772–1852), suggests that the carrot can effectively replace the stick.[68] Interested in pleasing her parents, Lizan'ka learns her lessons, while her sisters spend their time catching butterflies in the garden. As reward for her diligence, Lizan'ka receives dolls and other gifts from her parents. She then generously shares the gifts with her sisters, who presumably learn from her example the importance of not postponing their studies.

That the goal of education was to cultivate virtue, and that parents were responsible for educating their children, was a sine qua non of eighteenth-century Russian theater. When in 1779 A. T. Bolotov (1738–1833) wrote the children's comedy *The Braggart*, he intended on the one hand to ridicule "liars and boasters, ignoramuses and young philanderers" and on the other to present "as a model well-behaved and diligent children and virtuous acts."[69] Performed in the children's theater organized by Bolotov in Bogoroditsk, *The Braggart* spotlights nine-year-old Kleon, son of Blagonrav (Well-Behaved). Thanks to the upbringing provided by his father, Kleon is a paragon of virtue. In Lockean manner, he self-consciously has learned to control his natural propensity to lie, so that he will be praised rather than scolded by adults. He obeys his father and avoids doing anything that will anger him. Kleon also gives generously to the poor, for whom he feels genuine sympathy, and he avoids all forms of mockery. At every turn his goodness is evident, standing in stark opposition to the ignorance of the adolescent Chestokhvalov (Braggart). Chestokhvalov insults the people around him, abuses the poor, chases servant girls, and wants to marry the daughter of Blagonrav, with the aim of possessing her villages. Intent on having a good time at the expense of others, Chestokhvalov eventually is punished. He himself becomes an object of ridicule, whereas Kleon receives the reward of being named the heir of a childless neighbor.

Just as Kleon's father deserved credit for raising a virtuous son, the parents of Frenchified fops deserved condemnation for corrupting their children. In the comedy *Unsuccessful Betrothal, or Betrothed but Not Married* (1794), A. A. Maikov (1761–1838) blames parents for the bad education of their offspring.[70] Liza and Milon wish to marry, but Liza's mother, seduced by wealth and status, wants her to marry Count Razvratin (Depraved). Razvratin is recently returned from a six-year stay in Paris, and in three months he has spent his entire annual income, half of it on clothes. His goal is to marry, divorce, and quickly remarry, in pursuit of which he has made promises to multiple brides. The true lovers are rescued from unhappiness by the exposure of Razvratin, whose uncle, Postoianov (Constant), has been contending with the effects of Razvratin's bad education. Postoianov decries the view that children are better enlightened in foreign lands—such thinking defames the fatherland—and blames Razvratin's parents for having sent him abroad before his reason *(razsudok)* was adequately developed. Postoianov's program for reforming his nephew is twofold: first, he refuses to give Razvratin additional money, and second, he plans to take him on a trip around Russia. Not only will Razvratin be properly educated, he will become a Russian. Success appears likely, because Razvratin, who previously had declared that he did not want to be Russian, repents and promises to obey his uncle. Even the children of ignorant, corrupt or, as in Razvratin's case, misguided parents can with the appropriate supervision overcome their upbringing.

Precisely because the effects of bad upbringing could be corrected, it was important to acknowledge the social dangers faced by children. In addition to bad education, late eighteenth-century Russian playwrights identified a second threat to the assumed correspondence between the child's inclination and the parent's will: abuse of patriarchal authority. The threat posed by greedy guardians was strikingly evident in depictions of forced marriage, a topic addressed in another play for children by A. T. Bolotov. A year or two before Denis Fonvizin's Prostakovs appeared on the Russian stage, Bolotov portrayed a cruel and malicious Mitrofan in the drama *Unfortunate Orphans* (1781).[71] Bolotov's Mitrofan intends not only to marry the virtuous orphan Serafima, but also to poison her younger brother in order to take control of her villages. Locked up and threatened by her guardian, Mitrofan's father, Serafima escapes forced marriage thanks to the intervention of a kind passerby. The passerby learns of the orphans' plight from a loyal servant and quickly seeks help from soldiers he meets on the road. He also is able to provide medicine that saves the life of Serafima's brother. And if that were not enough, the passerby is so taken by Serafima's innocence and natural reason—at their first encounter she is reading a book called *A Christian in Solitude*—that he follows up his good deeds with a proposal of marriage. The virtue of the orphans is thus rewarded, whereas the wickedness of Mitrofan and his father is sure to be punished. The soldiers arrive to escort the evildoers to town where they will be judged according to the law.

Repeatedly in the patriarchal household of the late eighteenth-century Russian stage, the abuse of children and wards revolved around the problem of forced marriage. Ia. B. Kniazhnin's comic operas *The Sbiten Seller* (1787) and *The Sham Madwoman* (1787) depict cruel guardians who keep their female wards under strict guard in order to prevent them from developing romantic relationships. In *The Sbiten Seller* (sbiten is a hot drink made with honey and spices), the merchant Valdyrev, age 50, wants to

marry the bashful Pasha, daughter of his deceased partner, in order to re-
tain control over her inheritance.[72] But innocent Pasha has fallen in love
with a young military officer and cannot hide her natural feelings. Aware
that a relationship has formed, Valdyrev decides to hire a woman to
watch Pasha, and with the help of the sbiten seller, the officer, disguised
as an old lady, obtains the post. The deception then produces rightful resolution by allowing the true lovers to slip away and be married. Similarly,
in *The Sham Madwoman,* set in Italy and based on *Les Folies amoureuses*
(1704) by Jean-François Regnard (1655–1709), the jealous Albert loves his
ward Liza and keeps her locked up like a prisoner.[73] Ultimately, the effort
fails to thwart rightful love because the heart is a site of freedom, and
Liza's heart belongs to Erast. The lovers devise a plan to escape Albert's
watchful eye and successfully elope to Venice, affirming once again the
right of love.

In contrast to the avaricious Valdyrev, Albert sincerely loved his ward,
suggesting that even the most well-intentioned guardians, and parents,
could do wrong by their dependents. How to achieve the necessary balance
between parental authority and the freedom of young people to choose
their partners was a difficult problem—one that echoed, as will be seen, in
treatments of the monarch's authority over his or her subjects. As long as
the object of a person's love was virtuous, eighteenth-century Russian playwrights endorsed the natural right of love. Understood to exist in nature,
love frequently took precedence over parental authority. At the same time,
however, because playwrights were committed to happy outcomes, they
also sought to reconcile the aspirations of love-stricken children and errant
parents. In stories of rightful love realized, true lovers found a way to marry
because corrupt characters were exposed, circumstances changed, or parents saw the light. Parents who did not see the light—who tried to force
marriage on their children or concocted schemes to ensnare unwilling
brides—represented ridiculous or despicable characters. Frequently, therefore, when young people were faced with the prospect of unwanted marriage, the filial duty to obey fell by the wayside, and evasion, if not outright
rebellion, became justified. Obedience did not require that personal happiness be sacrificed to the whims of parents and guardians.

Yet, however much late eighteenth-century Russian playwrights endorsed the notion that children should be free to choose their lovers, they
also assumed that parental knowledge and consent would be sought. In the
anonymous comedy *The Victory of Innocence, or Love Is More Cunning than
Caution* (1788), Milon (Nice) and Milana (Nice) have met on the riverbank
and kept their relationship a secret.[74] Their love comes to light because Milana's spinster aunt, assuming that marriage should be based on friendship
rather than passion, wants her to marry Milon's uncle. Milana's mother, a
selfish coquette for whom marriage to an old man brought freedom to
commit adultery, also threatens her daughter's happiness; she wants a rich
groom who likes to entertain. The voice of reason is Milon's uncle: an hon-

orable man who believes happy marriage depends on love, he agrees to marry Milana only if she is so inclined. Men, he insists, are born to labor, and women reward men for their labor by giving them their hearts. Soon he learns that Milana has given her heart to Milon, and although the lovers were wrong to hide their relationship, he blesses the marriage, paving the way for general reconciliation.

Indeed, although the brides and grooms of the Russian stage frequently met in secret, they nonetheless recognized that a love blessed by parents was more likely to bring happiness. The drama *The Hermit* (1800), by V. S. Viazemskii (d. 1823), relates the story of Alfons and Dalenda who meet at the Fountain of Love, but then must wait three years before obtaining the necessary parental permission to declare their feelings.[75] In the comedy *The Usurer* (1768), by A. P. Sumarokov, the lovers Isabella and Dorant also get what they secretly have come to want, and what rightfully is their due, without directly defying the authority of Kashchei (Miser), Isabella's uncle and guardian.[76] Although Kashchei deserves to be challenged—he is a soulless usurer and cruel master who wants Isabella to remain unwed—she hesitates to marry Dorant without his permission. If absolutely necessary, Isabella is prepared to elope, but clearly she prefers to avoid dishonorable conduct. Money talks to Kashchei, and eventually he agrees to the marriage in return for interest payments and other illicit profits. The means to happiness may be questionable, but the message is unambiguous: even when a corrupt parent or guardian does try to usurp the right of love, it is better to evade than openly to defy parental authority.

Time and again, manipulation and trickery held out the hope that rightful lovers could challenge patriarchal authority without overturning the presumably God-given edifice. In Johann von Berg's comedy *Unexpected Marriage, or The Old Man Deceived* (1766), the miser Lizimor wants his daughter Melanta to marry a friend, aged 70, who has no heirs and demands no dowry.[77] Although Lizimor claims to oppose forced marriage, he assumes that Melanta will recognize the advantages of the match and obey his wishes. But Melanta loves Doriman and employs deception in order to marry her beloved. Ultimately, father and daughter reconcile, and Melanta apologizes for the ruse, but she also insists that her love for Doriman is beyond her power to control. Rightful love cannot be thwarted by parental opposition. The lovers in M. I. Verevkin's *Nameday Celebrants* (1774) would agree, for they too manage to find happiness despite the machinations of a jealous stepmother and lustful father.[78] Although on her deathbed, Glafira's mother had given her daughter to Dostoinov (Worthy), the girl's father, swayed by his second wife, has decided that she should marry Dostoinov's uncle. Required by God and nature to obey her father, Glafira seems destined for unhappiness, especially when she is threatened with confinement in a convent. But such an outcome is more than the good Dostoinov can bear: he reminds Glafira's father that parental authority is not unlimited, for it has become possible to seek justice from the laws. Fortunately, the legal challenge proves unnecessary, and happy resolution is achieved, thanks once again to the use of deception.

The role of deception in protecting the right of love made clear that parents who abused patriarchal power should be resisted. The anonymous comedy *Dobronrav* (1789) portrays another greedy parent, this time a merchant, who ignores his daughter's happiness and insists that she marry a wealthy man of 80 who seeks no dowry and has no heirs.[79] To escape this predicament, the daughter and her lover stage a consultation with a magician (played by the bride) who declares that the old groom will live three days after he marries. Happily for the lovers, he runs from death. The young couples in the anonymous comic opera *The Veiled Bride* (1790) respond in like manner after a tyrannical merchant commands his daughter and niece to marry each others' lovers.[80] When open appeals fail to change his mind, the grooms agree to exchange brides, something they can do because the women go to the altar wearing veils. Presented with a fait accompli, the chastened merchant concedes. The women ask forgiveness for the deception, but also remind the merchant that he cannot force them to marry. In marrying for love, they fulfill divine, tsarist, and human law.

Prohibitions on forced marriage had existed in pre-Petrine Russia, so that when playwrights associated the abuse of patriarchal authority with boorish old-fashioned characters, they were not accurately portraying the mores of earlier times. Their goal was to distinguish enlightenment and virtue from stupidity and moral corruption. This is evident in the verse comedy *A Frivolous Person Mocked* (1796) by N. I. Seliavin (1770s–1833), where Glupilova (Stupid), herself a victim of unwanted marriage, does not care that she is imposing the same fate on her daughter.[81] Glupilova has chosen a groom who exemplifies the corruption of fashionable society *(svet)* in which external splendors are more valued than spiritual qualities. The groom is obsessed with lineage, disdains the Russian language, and arrogantly assumes that Roza adores him. But Roza loves another, and while she is outwardly obedient and ashamed to reveal her true feelings, she also agrees to run away with Postoianov (Constant)—a man who believes that birth is meaningless without virtue. Unable to challenge her mother openly, Roza takes leave to dress, and a servant returns in her place. While Glupilova's guests celebrate the anticipated wedding, Roza and Postoianov return married from the church. Immediately they ask forgiveness, and Glupilova recognizes her stupidity.

In the eyes of late eighteenth-century Russian playwrights, filial disobedience and abuse of parental authority represented equally serious violations of social order. For this reason, a less than virtuous suitor could be morally superior to a cruel parent. In the comedy *The Invisible Father, or Courted the Mother, Married the Daughter* (1799) by Prince A. I. Golitsyn (1765–1807), Ugar, the object of Henrietta's love, needs the girl's dowry to pay his debts.[82] Despite his moral shortcomings, Ugar is on the side of right and appears less despicable than Henrietta's mother, who not only tyrannizes her family and servants, but also insists that her daughter marry Ugar's father. Henrietta remains silent in the face of her mother's severity, though secretly she plots to marry Ugar. The deception succeeds, and although Ugar's motives in seeking the hand of Henrietta cannot be called pure, the effort of Henrietta's mother to impose an unwanted marriage is far more egregious an act. Social order did indeed require submission to patriarchal authority, but it also required that parents not abuse their power by thwarting rightful love. To do so threatened the very existence of the good society and appeared analogous to the tyranny of evil rulers.[83] Both forms of tyranny justified disobedience, which by default became the instrument of social order.

Master and Servant

That the right to resist tyranny did not appear to threaten social order is evident from the role of servants in late eighteenth-century Russian plays. In contrast to peasants, whose lives increasingly took center stage, servants functioned as facilitators in plots revolving around nobles.[84] Even so, their presence represented more than a mere mechanism for moving forward the dramatic action. Servants also were individuals with their own virtues, vices, and desires. Repeatedly, it was their voices and actions that conveyed the moral message of the play. Still, to present servants as moral beings did not translate into a realistic understanding of their everyday existence. The educated servicemen who wrote plays could not effectively reproduce the thoughts of servants, though they did shed light on how masters imagined the attitudes and behavior of their human property. In dramatic depictions, the master-servant relationship, like the husband-wife and parent-child relationship, combined adherence to patriarchal authority with genuine bonds of affection. Within the household, relationships based on principles of deference and natural hierarchy did not preclude deep emotional ties. Precisely because social hierarchy was God-given, it need not imply disdain for the person of inferior status. To the contrary, good order in the household, and by extension in society as a whole, hinged upon personal relationships grounded in virtue and respect. Ideally, servants functioned as members of the family unit.

As is well known from Russian history and literature, however, familiarity and intimacy also produced vile and unsavory behavior. On the late eighteenth-century Russian stage, masters and servants came in good and bad types. More often than not, the behavior of the servant mirrored the character of the master—a pattern that denied servants individuality but also emphasized the moral responsibility of the master. As the representative of God-given authority, the master or mistress, like the monarch, was obligated to ensure the good behavior of all dependents through education, punishment, and personal example. Good masters respected the humanity of their servants, treated them with care, and on occasion educated them alongside their own children. Cruel masters, by contrast, demanded sexual favors, inflicted physical and verbal abuse, punished the innocent, and neglected servants' spiritual and material needs. Given that the master acted with the moral authority of a father, his servants, like children, responded to the "education" they received. Those who suffered abuse or lived in disorderly surroundings were more likely to steal, deceive, and drink. In the anonymous comedy *Domestic Disagreements* (1786), the servants Potap and Mavra enhance their own position in the household by telling lies that encourage conflict between the master and mistress.[85] And they feel no moral obligation toward their social betters. But is it Potap and Mavra who are to blame? Family disputes over property and marriage allow them to manipulate their masters, who, as Potap describes matters, spend a great deal of time thinking up ways to torment servants. Not surprisingly, when he and Mavra are discovered, they promptly run away—a unique occurrence in eighteenth-century theater but not an unheard-of phenomenon in legal-administrative sources.

The servants on the late eighteenth-century Russian stage represented both the human aspirations of serfs and the potential abuses of serfdom. Servants fell in love and married, served loyally and deceitfully, rescued orphans and accepted bribes. Disaffected servants complained of hunger, lack of rest, ill treatment, and the incessant demands of masters. However playwrights described the social condition of servants, the main effect was to situate them within the intimate relationships of the patriarchal household. The sincere affection that good masters and their good servants expressed for one another resembled that between family members and friends. Their mutual trust could run so deep that servants felt free to correct masters while masters confided their true thoughts, feelings, and fears to servants. Servants facilitated illicit love affairs and in cases of rightful love acted to bring about the happy resolution of family disputes. Wise servants also functioned as the moral teachers and protectors of foolish or vulnerable masters. In Bolotov's drama *Unfortunate Orphans,* the good servant of the deceased master repeatedly risks his life to protect Serafima and her brother from their evil guardian. In contrast to social hierarchy, which allowed only for the subordination of servants, the hierarchy of moral virtue frequently placed them above social superiors.

Yet no matter how wise or virtuous the individual, masters and servants performed different functions in society and polity. That a servant or peasant could rise above his master in terms of goodness and enlightenment did not entitle him to occupy a higher social status or exercise legal-administrative authority. Enlightenment assumptions about the dignity of the individual and Christian belief in the sameness of all human beings before God did not automatically bring acceptance of social equality or universal civic rights. In material terms, human equality conformed more closely to the subsistence-oriented principles of Christian moral economy than to the consumer and utilitarian principles of modern political economy.[86] All members of the household were entitled to shelter, clothing, and subsistence, though not necessarily to the same shelter, clothing, or subsistence. Because human equality belonged to the transcendent spheres of God and monarch, it could not serve as the basis for large-scale social organization. Human equality did not mean earthly equality, but suggested instead the potential for realizing moral equality, a concept familiar from religious teachings. While the principle of moral equality may seem to have carried little weight beyond mere semantics, to imagine servants as individual moral beings created cognitive dissonance in a society within which these same servants were also the master's property. When juxtaposed to corrupt and frivolous nobles, images of morally and intellectually superior servants possessed the potential to turn social hierarchy on its head. The conclusion drawn by eighteenth-century Russian playwrights was not, however, that social hierarchy was flawed, but that flawed individuals, who did not deserve the status and authority they possessed, needed to be reformed.

The same can be said of patriarchal authority in general. Abuses, late eighteenth-century Russian playwrights assumed, were individual and particular; they did not represent a reason to restructure patriarchy, but rather indicated that good order had been violated and needed to be restored. Indeed, everyday life taught that happiness and physical survival hinged upon the fulfillment of duty within the framework of patriarchal relationships. While it may appear to a more modern sensibility that hierarchies of gender and age lay at the center of these relationships, to an eighteenth-century mind, patriarchy promised solutions to the problem of human passion. Through adherence to duty, as defined by patriarchy, it might be possible to resolve the great conflict between reason and passion—not simply by subordinating passion to reason but by recognizing the rightfulness of both. But the effort could be only partially successful. When passion corresponded to the natural right of love, it represented happiness and freedom; yet all too often passion contradicted duty and in the guise of freedom challenged legitimate authority. Authority also could be dangerous and illegitimate, as when it tried to thwart romantic love, the natural product of passion. Although most eighteenth-century plays effectively distinguished rightful from wrongful passion and in so doing held out the hope of good order, the right of love still offered an unstable basis for the reconciliation of freedom and authority. However much playwrights might wish to calm the stormy waters of human emotion, they could not find an unambiguous solution to the problem of passion.

M. M. Kheraskov, a writer who repeatedly avoided coming down on the side of either reason or passion, highlighted the problem in his 1758 tragedy *The Nun of Venice*.[87] Reported to be based on actual events resulting from a Venetian law that imposed capital punishment on citizens who associated with foreigners, *The Nun of Venice* is a moving story of unrealized love. The nun of Venice, Zaneta, believing her lover is dead, has entered a convent out of obedience to her deceased parents. But Korans, to whom she had pledged her love, returns and demands that she abandon her life of devotion to God. For Zaneta, duty is paramount, and although she loves Korans, she decides to abide by her parents' wish that she spend her life in prayer. Her answer to the suffering of Korans is that he trust in God. Korans, by contrast, cannot forget Zaneta and gets caught passing through a foreign embassy when he tries to visit her. Accused of treason, he refuses to defend himself: by dying a traitor he can at once preserve Zaneta's honor and punish her betrayal. The innocence of Korans eventually becomes public, and he affirms his love for Zaneta, but she stands firm in her decision to live for God. Soon Zaneta dies—it is not clear how—and once Korans learns of her death, he commits suicide.

Neither the suicide of Korans nor Zaneta's adherence to duty brings rightful resolution. Throughout the tragedy Zaneta represents the ability to master passion, though her suffering is in no way ameliorated by devotion to duty. The behavior of Korans also is problematic. Zaneta had attributed his insistence that she leave the monastery to weakness of spirit, and his father seems to concur when he declares Korans's suicide the fruit of excessive passion. For even if, as Korans had argued, duty does not deprive us of freedom, and love also possesses legal rights, it does not inevitably follow that love leads to happiness. On the contrary, the conflict between reason and passion represents an infinite source of suffering that cannot be resolved in favor of one or the other principle. Patriarchy is needed, eighteenth-century Russian playwrights assumed, not to control women and children but to control the passions of all human beings.

4

CIVIC SOCIETY

• Although an Enlightenment print culture, sites of public sociability, and participation in civic institutions attained a visible presence in late eighteenth-century Russia, it would be misleading to speak of a politically organized civil society independent of state authority. A realm of free market relations (called civil society by Hegel) did exist, though often illicitly and without legal protections, as did a prepolitical literary public sphere grounded in print culture, learned and philanthropic societies, social clubs, commercial associations, and masonic lodges.[1] Russia also possessed strong family units, autonomous local communities, and a variety of legally defined social categories, which had been created as tools of administration by the government and only partially corresponded to actual social and economic relationships. Scholarly understanding of these aspects of Russian society is well researched and analytically sound, though insufficient to explain social consciousness.[2] The preceding chapter focused on the patriarchal household in order to explore how members of the educated service classes defined the primary social roles and relationships that were constitutive of their moral universe. This chapter examines social consciousness in terms of a broader "society," or social way of life, beyond the immediate spheres of kinship and locality. Eighteenth-century theater represented one of the earliest forums in which Russians self-consciously imagined themselves as members of a social collective.[3] Without such awareness of a collective social body, administrative state building, the sustained mobilization of material and human resources, and nineteenth-century notions of nationhood and citizenship would have been unthinkable.

The dictionary of the Russian Academy defined "society" *("obshchestvo")* as "a people *(narod)* living together under the same laws *(zakony)*, under known regulations *(ustavy)*, [and] rules *(pravila)"*; while a "people" *("narod")* designated "the inhabitants of a state, [or] some country, living under the same laws, and speaking the same native language."[4] In a polity that recognized equality before the law, the principle of a people living under common statutes would have described a universalistic society encompassing all citizens. But such a meaning could not apply to late eighteenth-century Russia, where each individual belonged to a juridically defined social category distinguished by specific tax and service obligations, and to a lesser extent by rights and privileges. Thus a second meaning of society referred to a specific assembly *(soslovie* or *sobranie)* of people identified by a shared activity—for example, the society of educated people *(obshchestvo uchenykh muzhei)* or the society of merchants *(obshchestvo kupecheskoe)*. In literature and journalism the term "society" also could indicate *"le grand monde,"* "the civil society of the educated," or "educated Russians who are neither agents of the government *(pravitel'stvo)* nor, in the traditional sense, its subjects *(narod)."*[5] The independence from government implied by a "civil society of the educated"—what Marc Raeff has called a yearning for autonomy and privacy—clearly was evident in late eighteenth-century social thinking, but it was not necessarily associated with the concept of society.[6] True to their Enlightenment principles, eighteenth-century Russian playwrights expressed deep ambivalence about society, which they depicted as both a source of corruption and a site for the realization of moral virtue. The tension between these images is strikingly evident in depictions of social hierarchy and in calls for civic engagement. Their reconciliation, within the terms of eighteenth-century plays, highlights a new consciousness of society as an abstract translocal entity.

EQUALITY AND SOCIAL HIERARCHY

Identification with a social way of life inevitably raised questions about the human relationships contained within the larger social collective. In late eighteenth-century Russia, playwrights portrayed these relationships through the prism of Enlightenment ideas and natural rights theory that posited the underlying equality or moral worth of all human beings, the efficacy of properly cultivated human reason, and the ability of educated people self-consciously to improve themselves and their society. While eighteenth-century observers saw no reason why equality of human worth should lead to equality of social status, from today's perspective, it may be necessary to explain what moral equality meant in a society based on serfdom and hierarchies of birth, age, and gender. Already in the first decades of the nineteenth century, social critics denounced as callous and hypocritical the Enlightenment notion that serfdom could be rendered humane or that the social inequality embodied in serfdom somehow could be consistent with belief in the dignity of the individual human being.

Modern scholars have been similarly dismissive of the eighteenth-century Russian Enlightenment, which produced no articulate philosophers or representative political institutions. In the words of Viktor Zhivov, "the Russian Enlightenment was a Petersburg mirage."[7] Yet even if one rejects the notion of "the Russian Enlightenment" as a coherent philosophy capable of generating progressive reform, there is no denying the presence of Enlightenment thinking in the laws, policies, and literary culture of eighteenth-century Russia. To explain how members of the educated service classes understood the relationship between human equality and social hierarchy, it is important to set aside the modern definition of equality as "the possibility of an equal route" or "equality of rights."[8] The corporate, "constitutional" order granted by Catherine II's charters of 1785 to the nobility and towns, and further represented by her unpromulgated project for a charter to the state peasants, defined equal obligations and privileges *within* but not between social categories.[9] In philosophical terms, equality was understood as the potential for morally transcending social hierarchy through individual virtue. It lacked political connotations, not having been joined to the Rousseauian general will, and it underscored the correctness of Daniel Roche's judgment that "the Enlightenment was forever hesitating on the road to progress."[10]

Serfdom

The Enlightenment focus on moral virtue may have allowed equality and social hierarchy to coexist, but it could not change the painful reality of human bondage. In theatrical depictions, as in actual life, limited legal-administrative controls and extensive reliance on landlord authority made it difficult to counter abuses. For most Russian representatives of Enlightenment thinking, it was not serfdom as an institution but the abuses of individual masters that appeared problematic; consequently, late eighteenth-century playwrights repeatedly attempted to show how belief in the dignity of the human being could be reconciled with, and could properly temper, seignorialism. Their understanding of a well-ordered serfdom was simple and straightforward. In *Village Holiday, or Virtue Crowned*, a pastoral drama with music by V. I. Maikov (1730–1778), a good master describes the mutual obligations of lord and serf.[11] Upright estate management requires that peasants not be ruined. Otherwise they cannot fulfill their duty, which is to obey the master and pay quitrent. The master's duty, in turn, is to protect his peasants from abuse, and "when serving Sovereign or fatherland, to fight for them in war and die for their tranquility." Only if his peasants are rich and free—free from abuse and insecurity—can the good master find pleasure and comfort. At the time *Village Holiday* was published and staged in 1777, noble serfowners no longer performed mandatory state service; yet the assumption of useful activity and the message of reciprocity and mutual obligation remained, as did the tradition, if not the necessity, of temporary state service.

However reassuring the message, when playwrights attempted to condemn abuses and describe a humane serfdom, they implicitly challenged the imagined ideal. Abuses might arise from the very organization of the serf estate where the bailiff or steward, who exercised authority on behalf of the landlord, could act unjustly. In *The Bailiff* (1781) by N. P. Nikolev (1758–1815), the commune of "all the peasants" has complained to the master against a dishonest bailiff who is intent on marrying an unwilling local girl.[12] The master deals with the immediate problem by dispatching his manager to remove the bailiff and banish him from the estate. But the potential for social unrest remains, and so the master also must instruct his peasants to live peacefully, remain obedient, and remember the fate of the bailiff. Peasants again seek the removal of an abusive bailiff in the comic opera *Milozor and Prelesta* (1787) by V. A. Levshin (1746–1826).[13] To prevent delivery of a communal petition, the bailiff places a respected peasant under guard and prepares to sell his daughter into marriage. The girl hides, the master arrives, and the bailiff is punished. Right again is restored once the landlord learns of the bailiff's crimes.[14]

Bailiffs were not the only estate officials who could abuse their power. In *The Clerk Who Was Unsuccessful in Love* (1795) by I. V. Nekhachin (1771–1811), a good bailiff rescues two lovers whose happiness is threatened by the machinations of a village clerk and guard.[15] The clerk tries to force Stepanida to marry him by accusing her father of various crimes and offenses: failure to pay quitrent, theft of communal monies during his tenure as elder, and negligence in protecting the master's property. The clerk then has the poor man taken into custody and threatens to send Stepanida to the master's factory. Finally, in an effort to break the girl's resolute resistance, the clerk falsely informs her that her father has admitted his guilt and agreed to the marriage in return for judicial representation before the master. Stepanida is not deceived, believing throughout that the bailiff and master will protect her. Once the bailiff arrives, justice is indeed restored: the peasants complain against the clerk and guard, both of whom are dispatched to the master in town. Having refused the bribes offered by the offenders, the bailiff declares his satisfaction with the salary he receives and urges the peasants to be happy with what is theirs. In the words of the chorus: "Whoever is not created to possess something should not seek to have it." Even while writing happy conclusions to their plays, playwrights expressed unease about the possibility that peasants might become dissatisfied with their social station.

Dramatic resolution that brought corrupt bailiffs and peasant officials to justice generally resulted from the intervention of masters or superior officials. In historical practice, the petitioning of higher authorities for redress of grievances also was integral to estate management and to the functioning of state law and administration.[16] But what happened if the master himself was abusive or the responsible official corrupt? In the comic opera *Aniuta* (1772), written by M. I. Popov (1742–1790) and best known for its effort to reproduce peasant speech, the peasant Miron (Peaceable) describes nobles as people who drink, eat, carouse, and sleep—whose only labor is to collect money.[17] In order to provide for himself, Miron wants his adopted daughter Aniuta to marry his landless laborer Filat, but Aniuta is in love with the noble master. The stage is set for a clash between the peasant father and noble master until it comes to light that Aniuta is in fact a noblewoman. The enemies of her real father have perished, he has returned to his estate, and her social position can be acknowledged. The apparent inappropriateness of a noble-peasant marriage, complicated by the master's threat to ignore the peasant father's will, conveniently evaporates. Even so, before this happy resolution is achieved Filat's behavior toward the master becomes dangerously belligerent. Of course a master can do as he pleases, and the peasants must obey, though as it turns out, Filat is the one not created to possess Aniuta. The preservation of social hierarchy thus corresponds to the restoration of rightful order.

Another noble-peasant love triangle drives the plot of Nikolev's drama with voices, *Rozana and Liubim*.[18] The rich noble Shchedrov (Generous) covets Rozana (Rose), who consistently repulses his advances. "The lord's happiness is our unhappiness," the chorus of serf huntsmen declares, and so it seems when Shchedrov imprisons Liubim (Beloved) and abducts Rozana. This compels Rozana's father, the retired soldier Izlet (To-Pour-Out), to go down on his knees and beg Shchedrov to spare Rozana. Filled with outrage, he also threatens to petition the tsarina: "She will defend me," Izlet proclaims, for "in her justice all subjects are equal." This outpouring of righteous indignation touches the conscience of Shchedrov, who overcome with shame, asks and receives forgiveness from his peasant victims. The master's remorse then prompts Izlet to seek forgiveness for his impertinent words. Rightful order again is restored because the noble recognizes his crime, having learned from social inferiors "that virtue does not know inequality," and because the retired soldier returns to an attitude of public deference.

In *Rozana and Liubim* awareness of imperial justice brings a corrupt noble to his senses. In *The Minor* by Fonvizin, one of the few eighteenth-century plays to remain part of the classic Russian repertoire, no such happy rehabilitation occurs.[19] The tyrannical noblewoman Prostakova (Simpleton) unjustly curses and punishes her servants while excessively indulging her ignorant son. Although Fonvizin does not detail Prostakova's treatment of her peasants, clearly she is an abusive landowner. The prerevolutionary historian V. O. Kliuchevskii described her as one of those Russian landowners who had interpreted the 1762 emancipation from mandatory service as emancipation from estate *(soslovie)* obligations with the preservation of estate rights.[20] To counter such attitudes, the landowner Pravdin (Righteous) has been appointed by the governor-general to take action against abusive masters. Pravdin has reported the Prostakovs, and toward the end of the play, receives instructions to place their house and villages in trusteeship at the first outburst that might bring harm to their serfs. The moment comes when Prostakova is unable to force the ward Sof'ia to marry her son. Prostakova blames her servants and threatens to beat them to death for failing to carry out her orders. In her view, the ukase on the freedom of nobles gives them the freedom to beat their serfs. Pravdin objects that "nobody is free to tyrannize" and quickly deprives the Prostakovs of seignorial authority.

The Minor holds out the possibility that the Prostakovs can be reformed but leaves unanswered troubling questions about serfdom as an institution. That Prostakova is an abusive mistress whose actions exceed her legal authority is unquestionable; the expectations and demands she places on servants surpass any reasonable measure of their natural obligations. But Prostakova is unaware of the legal and moral limits to her authority; she assumes that all her orders should be obeyed and that she is free to punish at will. Only outside intervention by powerful provincial officials can bring her to account. *The Minor* contains no instance of a serf taking action to protect himself. Nor is it certain that by placing the Prostakov estate in trusteeship, the government will induce the mistress to mend her ways. Prostakova expresses shame and seems to repent at the end of the play, but the future of her serfs remains uncertain. Moreover, unlike her son, who is to be sent off to service, the means for reforming Prostakova are not identified. The threat of punishment sends the only resounding message: Prostakova's "depravity cannot be tolerated in a well-established state." A solution to the abuses of serfdom is found not in institutional change, but in individual moral transformation backed by the force of legal-administrative authority.

The notion that abuse of power reflected the moral failings of individuals was widespread in imperial Russian law and administration. To question the rightness of institutions was to question God-given monarchical authority, which by nature was just and immutable. Not surprisingly, eighteenth-century Russian playwrights did not challenge the institutional basis of master-serf relations, and there was no "peasant question" in the sense of an emancipation debate. Such debates had begun in educated and official circles during the reign of Catherine II, but playwrights did not engage the issue directly.[21] They did suggest, however, that seignorial abuses might represent more than the corruption of individuals. In the anonymous comic opera *Evening Gatherings, or Tell Fortunes, Tell Fortunes, Pretty Girl, Tell Fortunes* (1788), the marriage of Nenila and Panfil is threatened when their master demands the payment in silver of three years' quitrent and the delivery of ten peasants to be sold as substitutes for drafted peasants, five unmarried men to serve as lackeys, and five girls to become housemaids.[22] Among the girls, he specifically wants Nenila. Nenila's father appeals to the bailiff for mercy: his daughter is betrothed, and the master would not take a married woman. But the bailiff is unmoved; he cannot deceive the master, and besides, Panfil is to be sold as a soldier. The matter is resolved, and the lovers spared, when Nenila's upright father promises to bring valuable gifts to the bailiff. Perhaps, as one character claims, the threat to send Panfil to the army was simply a joke designed to elicit gifts. Joke or not, there were no formal limits to the demands a master could impose on his peasants, no legal contracts or inventories. Of course, there were informal expectations, and peasants did resist increased or unreasonable obligations, sometimes even by initiating lawsuits.[23] But there was no precise legal definition of serf obligations, and sequestration depended on vague notions of excessive cruelty. Thus *Evening Gatherings* implies that the abuses of serfdom stemmed from the very nature of the peasant-lord relationship, which allowed the master to determine the occupations and concrete obligations of his serfs. That serfs could negotiate with their lord and challenge his demands did not change the underlying juridical principle. There could be no peasant will in a legal-administrative or philosophical sense, only seignorial will as an extension of monarchical authority.

The Common Soldier

While depictions of rural life complete with serfdom provided the most obvious setting in which to explore abuses of hierarchy and authority, theatrical treatments of the common soldier also confronted the problem. In contrast to nobles, who after 1762 chose whether or not to serve, ordinary soldiers were forcefully conscripted from social categories subject to the capitation ever since the reign of Peter I. Upon induction, these former serfs, state peasants, and lesser townspeople became exempt from the capitation and legally free from the authority of the landlord or local community.[24] As a social group, soldiers, their wives, and any children born to them while in active service were upwardly mobile. For the soldier in uniform, however, his newly acquired freedom was not implemented until retirement. Given the lengthy term of service—initially for life, but reduced to 25 years in 1793 and to 20 in 1834—conscripts could hardly view conscription as a path to liberation. Although laboring people accepted the obligation to serve with relatively little resistance, and Russian soldiers were renowned throughout Europe for their endurance and steadfastness in battle, conscription created a moral dilemma for at least some enlightened observers.[25] The effective performance of brave men could not eliminate the uncomfortable realization that popular attitudes challenged the idea of service as a glorious calling, or that the social condition of the common soldier contradicted the imagined honor of military rank.

Without ever denying the monarchy's right to demand manpower or its desire to ensure an equitable distribution of the service burden, playwrights consistently questioned the moral authority of the landlords and local officials who were responsible for implementing conscription on the ground.

In the well-known comic opera *Misfortune from a Carriage* (1779) by Ia. B. Kniazhnin (1740–1791), abuses occur at the hands of the bailiff, who represents seignorial authority.[26] Aptly interpreted by scholars as an exposé of serfdom and superficial Europeanization, *Misfortune from a Carriage* is the story of two peasant lovers, Aniuta and Luk'ian, who are threatened with separation. Their owners have decided to sell a conscript in order to purchase a French carriage, and the bailiff, who wants Aniuta for himself, selects Luk'ian. When the frivolous masters discover that Aniuta and Luk'ian can speak a few words of French, they spare the couple, but only because they have other serfs who can be sold to buy the carriage. That similar abuses also occurred outside serf estates is suggested in *Coachmen at the Relay Station* (1788), a comic opera by N. A. L'vov (1751–1803).[27] An elderly coachman already has two sons in the army when the local community issues an order to conscript *out of turn* his third and only remaining son. The son accepts the unjust decision and has no intention of running away, even though the escort sent by the community to haul him off turns out to be a coachman who previously had avoided conscription by becoming indentured to the local police official. Eventually, the hapless recruit is rescued by a passing officer, symbol of state and military authority. As soon as the officer learns who is who (not an easy task in eighteenth-century Russia) and what has transpired, he rescinds the order of the local community, promises to inform the marshal of the nobility about the family's situation, and dispatches the errant coachman to the army.

Justice is served in *Coachmen at the Relay Station*, but not because the parties involved adhere to a regularized process of conscription. Justice is served because an outsider who represents state authority intervenes to set things right. Justice requires that the autonomy of the local community and police official be subverted because they have wrongfully exercised their authority. Whether the aggrieved coachmen are unwilling or simply afraid to challenge the arbitrary selection process, they accept that their interests might conflict with those of neighbors and the unseen community. Their fatalistic resignation does not, however, indicate a positive identification with the military calling. Given that the community's agent is a scoundrel, and that his punishment for evading conscription as well as stealing a hat from his master is to become a soldier, where are the virtue and honor in military service? How can a willingness to serve remain indicative of moral worth when the status of soldier also can be seen as a punishment? One answer offered by state policy, and reiterated by late eighteenth-century playwrights, was fairness in distributing the burden of conscription. Only then could soldiers be expected to embrace the dreaded obligation to serve. Fairness remained elusive, however, and the conscript's attitude toward service problematic. From 1762 until the restoration of a universal service obligation in 1874, equality of treatment in conscription could be imagined only in terms of particular communities or categories of laboring people who also were liable for the capitation.

From the moment a conscript assumed the status of soldier by taking the oath of allegiance to the monarch, the consequences of military service for family life and by extension for the social order became apparent. In contrast to soldiers whose complete emancipation could not be realized until retirement, that of soldiers' wives had immediate repercussions. Freed from the authority of landlords and local communities, soldiers' wives also could be driven from their homes and forced to fend for themselves in conditions of social and economic distress.[28] Probably the best known literary portrayal of a soldier's wife is the nineteen-year-old sergeant's widow, Martona, in M. D. Chulkov's *The Comely Cook* (1770). Although Martona holds the title of sergeant's wife, her husband had been neither a noble nor a landowner; lacking a source of subsistence, she survives by attaching herself to a series of lovers. In explaining her anomalous social circumstances, Martona notes, "My misfortune seemed to me unbearable, for I knew nothing of human relationships and could not find for myself a place *[mesto]*, and so I became free *[vol'noiu]* because they did not assign us to any position *[dolzhnost']*."[29]

Martona's description is not entirely accurate; as a widow she could remarry and hence regain a position in society. But for the soldier's wife who had no proof of her husband's death, the conditions of life could become even more dreadful and uncertain. In the comic opera *Happiness by Lot* (1780) by A. O. Ablesimov (1742–1783), a soldier's wife who has been driven from her home takes up with the nephew of a peasant widow.[30] Believing that the soldier's wife also is a widow, the nephew has brought her to his aunt's home and expects to marry her. Meanwhile, the soldier husband returns to claim his lawful wife, whom he defends as blameless. Having been ostracized at home, the soldier's wife is fortunate to avoid Martona's debauchery. Yet in order to survive, she deliberately conceals her legal identity and comes close to violating the sanctity of marriage. For her, conscription has caused a painful loss of social moorings. In the larger arena of society and polity, a household has been destroyed, a marriage threatened, and structures of authority undermined.

Even when formal marriage was not at stake, conscription severed bonds of affection and prevented personal happiness by separating friends and lovers. The anonymous comic opera *Sailors' Jokes* (1780) portrays the sailor Provor (Swift), who has returned home after a seven-year absence, hoping to be reunited with his beloved Krasana (Beauty).[31] But before Krasana learns of Provor's return, she must resist pressure from her mother and the village bailiff to marry another.[32] Defiant and intrepid, Krasana declares that she will marry only Provor, even though she has not received a single letter in seven years. A similar plight threatens the peasant lovers Stepanida and Aleksei in the comic opera *A New Family* (1781) by S. K. Viazmitinov (1749 [or 1744]–1819).[33] Aleksei has been conscripted, and Stepanida's aunt has promised her to the village farrier. Although Stepanida refuses to marry the farrier, her unhappy fate seems sealed until Aleksei's brother offers to serve instead, and also gives the couple his earnings from trade to start their household. The noble masters are so moved by his generosity that they provide money to purchase a substitute and assign land allotments to both brothers. Stepanida and Aleksei escape the suffering caused by conscription, but it means another potential Luk'ian will have to be purchased, and perhaps another family or love affair destroyed, in order to deliver a conscript to the army. Justice again prevails, but only within the confines of a particular estate, and only because kindly masters arbitrarily intervene to set things right.

Neither historical nor theatrical reality offered satisfactory solutions to the social disruptions caused by military service. Throughout the second half of the eighteenth century, Russian comedies, comic operas, and dramas employed formulaic plots to rescue stock characters from unhappiness, but they could not resolve the larger social questions that formed the backdrop for the dramatic action. Precisely because playwrights viewed the common soldier through the moral lenses of the educated service classes, they inadvertently highlighted the contradiction between his inferior social status and the idea of service as a glorious calling. Equally significant, in their ambiguous portrayals of relationships between noble officers and common soldiers, the association of service with virtue implicitly challenged hierarchy and authority.

M. M. Kheraskov (1733–1807) explores the conflict between the moral worth of the common soldier and his base social origins in the comic opera *Good Soldiers* (1779), a love story about the soldier Prolet (Flighty) and Plenira (Captivating), the daughter of a wealthy townsman.[34] Plenira had become separated from Prolet when his regiment left winter quarters, and she now has come looking for her beloved. Problems arise, however, because Prolet's commanding officer, Zamir (For-Peace), also is in love with Plenira. Although Plenira boldly refuses to marry Zamir, Prolet assumes that his superior will prevail and begs to be shot dead. Zamir quickly recognizes the depth of the lovers' feelings, resolves to control his own desire for Plenira, and concedes to Prolet. To celebrate the atmosphere of collective goodwill and reconciliation, he proclaims a regimental holiday so that his subordinates can rejoice in love and friendship. Good and brave soldiers, an honorable and judicious commander, mutual respect and goodwill—the glorious principles of military life seem unassailable.

But there remains a hint of ambiguity. Toward the end of the play, a camp follower identifies Prolet as the orphaned son of an impoverished yet good noble. The worthy soldier Prolet already has won his beloved and received his due in service. His fellow soldiers honor him, his commander recognizes his merit and promotes him to sergeant, and his lover is ready to die if she cannot be his. As it happens, however, the possibility emerges that Zamir has not given up Plenira to a common soldier but to a fellow noble. To the faithful Plenira it is unimportant whether Prolet is a simple soldier or a noble, and Zamir acknowledges that noble status does not augment Prolet's merits, though it "does increase our general attention to him." The play never conclusively resolves the question of Prolet's true identity; the social question is left unanswered. The natural human equality between honorable soldiers, regardless of rank, exemplified by the noble officer conceding to the common soldier, suddenly becomes redefined as potential social equality in the formal sense. The need to suggest that the soldier hero might in fact be a noble hero, or that Prolet must be noble in order to be truly virtuous, reveals the friction between the ordinary soldier's inferior social status and the imagined honor of military service.

Because Zamir is a virtuous commander, the unresolved ambiguity in his relationship with Prolet does not undermine the harmonious and joyful images of military life. By contrast, theatrical depictions that juxtaposed worthy soldiers to unworthy officers evoked potentially more disturbing challenges to hierarchy and authority. In A. O. Ablesimov's comic opera *March from Stationary Quarters* (1782), Captain Ratobortsov (Fighter) appears to be an experienced military man, eager to please the common soldier.[35] In reality, he leaves the training and preparations for the march to subordinates, while he entertains himself chasing women. He generously provides money to buy liquor for his men but then runs short of state funds to pay for repairs and faces distraint of his personal estate for monies borrowed from the regiment. Worse still, he has seduced one widow with a promise of marriage, and having abandoned her, he tries to persuade the wife of a rich farrier to take her husband's money and run off with him.

If Captain Ratobortsov at least possesses an ability to get along with ordinary soldiers, Lieutenant Nezhniakov (Delicate) represents an egregious example of misplaced rank and authority. The lieutenant, who is new to the regiment, lived at home in the countryside, tended by nurses and nannies, until he reached officer rank. He lacks all military experience, declines to participate in training exercises, and thinks that on campaign he is entitled to travel in comfort. Equipped with a note from his parents promising to cover expenses, Nezhniakov sends the sergeant to purchase goods for the march: black and green tea, coffee, a cow to make cream, smoking tobacco, and all the customary table provisions. Oblivious to the need for transport and fuel, he also arrogantly assumes that the sergeant can obtain goods on credit. Undermining the paternalistic ideal of the father-officer who cares for his subordinates, the childlike Nezhniakov is completely lost without the sergeant. A seasoned serviceman, the sergeant stands to attention whenever the lieutenant appears, but then ridicules his ignorance and softness behind his back. The moral and professional superiority of the sergeant eloquently challenges the formal superiority of officer rank.

Undeserved rank receives further satirical treatment in *Campaign against Sweden* (1790), a comedy with choruses and ballet by I. A. Kokoshkin (1765–1835).[36] A foolish, doting mother has brought her son Falalei to the capital to secure a military rank, and after obtaining his appointment as a guards corporal, she expects to receive passports for the trip home.[37] Instead a soldier arrives with orders that Falalei join his regiment on campaign. Because the mother sees no connection between rank, described as "the tsar's favor," and service, she is distressed by the news, attempts to bribe the soldier to leave her son behind, and when this fails, goes off to petition for a leave. Falalei's potential usefulness to his regiment is highly questionable. He is a pampered child, still bathed by a nurse, and has no understanding of military organization or equipment. When told that he must join his regiment, he cries at the thought of not being able to skate and play games. The clever soldier reassures his noble charge with stories of the merry lives and endless amusements that servicemen enjoy. (In an aside, he also explains that while this is not the entire truth, military life is indeed joyful, and once a man becomes accustomed to it, he does not want to be anywhere else.) Falalei seems persuaded and leaves for war in cheerful ignorance, though clearly his formal rank indicates neither moral virtue nor professional competence.

Of all the social transformations wrought by military service, retirement—the one transformation that promised tranquility and prosperity—could also sow disorder.[38] This was the experience of the retired soldier Pafnut'ich, portrayed in V. M. Fedorov's *Russian Soldier, or It's Good to Be a Kind Master* (1803), who has returned to his native village after twenty years of service.[39] Lacking a family, Pafnut'ich is an honored outsider but not a member of the peasant community. When the play opens, the good soldier has despaired of finding a wife and is ready to leave for a town, where if he sells some jewels in his possession, he can live quietly. Unfortunately, the very jewels that would allow him to start a new life are also a source of deep mental anguish. Pafnut'ich took the jewels during the storming of a fortified town in the Turkish war, and now that he has left the service, he regards his action as robbery.[40] Instead of enjoying a tranquil retirement, Pafnut'ich suffers from a troubled conscience and fears of eternal torment. His only hope is that through a good deed, he can redeem himself in the eyes of God.

Pafnut'ich's quest for personal redemption coincides with the misfortune of his former landlord, Dobrov (Good), who has become the victim of a crime committed long ago by his own father. The senior Dobrov had allowed a family of runaway serfs to settle in his village, their original owner brought suit, and a court has decided that the younger Dobrov must pay compensation. Unable to come up with the money, Dobrov is going to lose his village. This drastic outcome is avoided, thanks to the sin of Pafnut'ich, who begs Dobrov to use the jewels to pay the claim of the aggrieved landlord. With a single act of charity, Pafnut'ich redeems his soul and becomes the benefactor of his former lord. By choosing personal redemption over the promise of social mobility, Pafnut'ich also restores the authority of his fallen master and wins the love of the village girl he has longed to marry. Dobrov resumes his rightful place as father-master to his peasants, and Pafnut'ich resumes his rightful place as member of a village family. The social order, which the sins of the noble father and common soldier had turned upside down, returns to its natural configuration. Individual characters find happiness in their respective social stations, and the implications of a former serf displacing a master in the role of patron remain unexplored.

By emphasizing administrative arbitrariness, ruptured personal relationships, and unworthy officers, late eighteenth-century Russian playwrights portrayed military service as a source of social disorder. Precisely because, as members of the educated service classes, they understood the common soldier in terms of their own moral universe, they inevitably became aware of the contradiction between the idea of service and its social consequences. In social terms the common soldier was naturally and rightfully inferior, but as a zealous serviceman he acquired noble virtue and deserved to be rewarded with a prosperous and tranquil retirement. To imagine the soldier as anything other than a zealous serviceman would have been unthinkable; consequently, popular dread of the obligation to serve became associated with inequities in the process of conscription. Vivid theatrical representations exposed social tension but also imposed happy endings: husbands, wives, and lovers were reunited; timely intervention by persons in authority corrected administrative abuses; and social hierarchy returned to its natural configuration. Given that comedy and comic opera required joyful resolution, while drama required that misfortune be overcome, the attention to historically identifiable points of conflict acquires added significance. Rightful social order invariably was restored, but only because potentially disruptive questions about hierarchy and authority remained unanswered.

Social Mobility

The common soldier's liberation from serfdom symbolized the possibility of social mobility, though in situations somewhat removed from the everyday life of the educated service classes. By contrast, depictions of love and marriage across social boundaries placed the question in more immediate emotional settings. In V. A. Levshin's *Celebration of Love* (1787), the drama version of the comic opera *Milozor and Prelesta,* the innocent love between a peasant girl and a young nobleman comes to fruition.[41] Unaware of his true social station *(sostoianie),* Milozor has been raised as an orphan by Prelesta's father, Chistoserd (Sincere). Following the death of Milozor's mother, and the departure and reported death of his father, an evil aunt had plotted to poison the young boy in order to seize his property. To save him, Chistoserd took Milozor to a village where his identity has been kept secret. As the drama unfolds, Milozor's father, the master Dobronrav (Good-Morals), returns to discover that his son is alive and well. All is as it should be, except that Milozor and Prelesta have fallen passionately in love. Their feelings torment Chistoserd, who is absolutely certain of where duty lies: a master cannot love his slave, and if Dobronrav learns of the relationship between Milozor and Prelesta, he will accuse Chistoserd of trying to rise above his natural social station. Fearing that Chistoserd could lose the master's favor and be punished, the virtuous lovers accept their fate. They agree to separate, yet pledge to love each other for eternity. Fortunately, the painful parting becomes unnecessary once Milozor confesses his love. Touched by the virtue of all concerned, Dobronrav blesses the marriage. Love, it seems, can triumph over social hierarchy.

As seen earlier (in chapter 3), marriage based on romantic love was the ideal of eighteenth-century Russian playwrights, but they also understood that love could not always be decisive. Duty, property, and legal status represented equally compelling concerns. It was one thing for nobles of unequal status to be united in holy matrimony, but quite another for commoners to marry their social superiors. The happy union of Milozor and Prelesta definitely appeared exceptional. No matter how often love triumphed over social difference, playwrights rarely extended this principle to marriage between nobles and non-nobles. In M. M. Kheraskov's tearful drama *Friend of the Unfortunate* (1774), love and virtue clash openly with social hierarchy.[42] When the drama opens, the virtuous Milana (Nice) and her young brothers have not eaten for two days; Milana also has been threatened with forced labor to repay a debt. Still, she refuses to obtain money by shameful means. When her father returns home with stolen money and bread, she insists that the money be returned and refuses to eat the bread. The family's situation seems utterly hopeless until a benefactor appears in the person of the judge robbed by Milana's father. Sensitive to how the rich rob the poor, the judge forgives the crime and soon falls in love with Milana. He learns that she was brought to the deceased wife of her father by a noble who has not been seen for ten years. The judge would like to marry Milana—his feelings tell him that "poor people are equal to me"—but her unknown social status poses a problem. In the end, Milana's real father, who had been unjustly disgraced, returns; her noble identity is established, and the social barrier to marriage is removed. The social question is not resolved, however, precisely because of the judge's concern for the virtuous poor. Whether the declared equality of the poor can extend to marriage remains untested. The judge appears to object to the unknown, not the unequal, social origins of Milana, yet as it turns out, she is not unequal at all.

K. F. Damskii describes a similar dilemma resulting from unknown social origins in the comic opera *Vinetta, or Taras in the Beehive* (1799).[43] Hoping to marry the orphan Vinetta, who lives in the country as a peasant's daughter, the noble Milon (Nice) has run away from his parents and supports himself as a shepherd. The lovers plan to marry in a nearby village and then appeal to Milon's parents for forgiveness. When Milon's father arrives in search of his son, he becomes enamored with the virtues of rural life and immediately recognizes Vinetta as a woman born to live in society. Yet because of Vinetta's unknown ancestry, he cannot allow the marriage. Rightful resolution occurs when Vinetta's noble identity is revealed. Heiress to a great estate, Vinetta had run away from a guardian who tried to control her property by forcing her to marry. But perhaps because of his own orphan status, Damskii answers the social question unequivocally: Vinetta does not become a suitable bride until her noble origins are established.

Nor, in the eyes of late eighteenth-century Russian playwrights, was socially appropriate marriage strictly a noble problem. In A. O. Ablesimov's popular comic opera, *The Miller—Sorcerer, Deceiver, Matchmaker* (1779), a peasant and his wife cannot agree on a groom for their daughter.[44] Born a noble, the girl's mother does not want her daughter to marry a peasant; her peasant husband, by contrast, wants his son-in-law to be a farmer. Exploiting both parents' belief in sorcery, the miller presents the girl's lover as both noble and peasant. He is in fact a single householder (*odnodvorets*), which makes him landlord and peasant, slave and noble, farmer and collector of quitrent.[45] Despite the suggestion that social status should not determine the selection of a spouse, marriage across social boundaries consistently appears problematic.

In treatments of noble-merchant matches, playwrights sent an especially strong message to those who would aspire to rise socially through marriage. Osip Cherniavskoi's comedy *In the Company of Merchants* (1780) describes a merchant girl whose parents have chosen a noble groom so that their daughter can become well-born.[46] Social pretensions have led them astray, however, for the groom is a complete scoundrel, a carouser and gambler, who uses his post in the city magistracy to enrich himself at the expense of others. The girl is saved from the unhappy match when a relative returns from a business trip financially ruined. The relative had gone to purchase grain from a landowner who persuaded him to sign a letter of credit that subsequently was used to deprive him of 30,000 roubles.[47] The parents likewise have jeopardized their property in questionable dealings with nobles. They acquired a serf woman as payment for a debt, but because it is illegal for non-nobles to possess serfs, they can lose their human property and hence also the payment on the debt.[48] As a friend explains, merchants who think they can own villages in the name of a son-in-law risk losing everything. Fortunately, Cherniavskoi's merchant parents recognize the parallel between their relative's ruin and their own potential ruin at the hands of the noble groom. They postpone the wedding for a year, the groom understands the hint, and catastrophe is avoided. The chastened father remembers that "God provides for us," and reminds his family "that a noble person is not one who possesses a noble rank, but one who has a noble spirit and lives virtuously." Compelled to abandon their hope of upward social mobility, the merchants find solace in the hierarchy of moral virtue.

Because formal social status was inherited from the father or transmitted from husband to wife, only women could legally achieve upward mobility through marriage. A man in search of social eminence could either rise in service or cultivate prestigious personal relationships. On the late eighteenth-century stage, the merchants who chose the latter route tended to associate with dishonorable nobles, thereby revealing their inability to understand the noble way of life. In *The Wedding of Mr. Voldyrev* (1793), a comic opera by V. A. Levshin, extravagant living has brought a noble widow and her lover to the brink of ruin.[49] The widow's creditor, the merchant Mr. Voldyrev, is threatening to have her house placed under distraint. Her solution is to marry him on the assumption that this will allow her to live freely in the French manner. The deception is successful, and Voldyrev falls for the noblewoman. Not only does he destroy her promissory notes, he also gives her property. Blinded by the noblewoman's rank, Voldyrev's social pretensions are no match for her moral corruption. The ease with which she robs him provides a clear warning. *The Wedding of Mr. Voldyrev* assumes that in noble-merchant marriages, merchants seek to rise above their natural social station and nobles seek unsavory economic gain. Neither motive corresponds to virtue, and the possibility of romantic love does not even enter the picture.

A second approach to the question of male mobility appeared in plays about wealthy merchants who ruined themselves trying to live like nobles. In *Merchant Becoming a Noble* (1781) by V. P. Kolychev (1736–1794), an imitation of Molière's *Le Bourgeois Gentilhomme*, the young merchant Razmotaev (Squanderer) is falling into ruin.[50] His creditors are hounding him, his credibility is being undermined, and his business deals are failing. Instead of tending to trade, Razmotaev sleeps late, maintains an elaborate toilet replete with servants, entertains nobles, and attends theater, assemblies, and masquerades. He utterly disdains the merchant way of life yet foolishly plays cards with dishonorable nobles. To escape merchant baseness, Razmotaev hopes to sell his factories and shops, enter service, obtain a rank, purchase an estate, and visit Paris. Filled with illusions of grandeur, he cannot see that while his noble friends pretend to teach him refined behavior, their real goal is to fleece him at cards.

Can Razmotaev become a real noble? In a stage discussion of Molière's comedy, Kolychev suggests not, and Razmotaev himself appears to accept his merchant destiny as he is being escorted to the magistracy to face his creditors. The young spendthrift's financial recovery is assured thanks to a sensible family friend, who also has the last word on merchants becoming nobles. In the friend's view, all social groups can be happy if they live according to their status *(sostoianie)* and do not try to leave it. Nobles and merchants are "equal citizens and equally useful" to the state. Nobles defend the fatherland with their lives and administer affairs of state; for this labor they receive ranks and villages. Merchants possess the right to trade, which is useful to the state and protected by the government. Merchants and nobles have different privileges, "but all the parts of the people are so connected that one [part] cannot manage without another. Not everybody can be a noble, a merchant, or a farmer, but all are equally useful and important." This vision of society was fully consistent with the Catherinean "constitutional" structure, which sought not to prevent social mobility but to ensure that it served the common good and preserved rightful order.[51]

Praise for useful merchants and warnings about the dangers of social pretension did not condemn mobility as a matter of principle. In *Merchant Becoming a Noble*, Razmotaev's aspirations are laid to rest; in the anonymous comedy *Change of Morals* (1789), however, a similar plot line produces a more ambiguous result.[52] *Change of Morals* is the story of Bogatov (Rich-Man), the son of a wealthy merchant, who has become an officer and is preparing to petition for ennoblement. Bogatov disdains his merchant origins, ignores the advice of his enlightened uncle, and leads a frivolous Frenchified life in the company of nobles interested only in his money. Although Bogatov has squandered his property and fallen into debt, he gambles, attends parties into the early morning hours, thinks about how to order fashionable buttons from Paris, and sees no reason to obtain a service appointment. Eventually, when Bogatov is rejected by his self-serving friends and faces incarceration for debt, he experiences feelings of shame, recognizes his errors, and repents.[53] His uncle, Dobronrav (Good-Morals), who all along has blamed "faulty education and pernicious acquaintances" for his nephew's behavior, eagerly reconciles and accepts Bogatov as his own child. Generosity and obedience abound: Dobronrav's daughter and future son-in-law agree to share their inheritance so that Bogatov's debts can be paid, while Bogatov decides to obey his uncle's injunction that he enter the Sovereign's service.

Throughout the play, the moral corruption of *le grand monde*, represented by the willful depravity of Bogatov, is contrasted to rightful social order, represented by the "healthy reason" of Dobronrav. Dobronrav's thinking defines society as it should be organized, whereas the behavior of Bogatov symbolizes the ongoing threat to good order found in society. Through Bogatov's moral transformation this threat is removed, and a vision of social harmony emerges. In keeping with the Catherinean "constitution," Dobronrav leads an ordered life: he rises early, tends to business, and provides for his family. In contrast to Bogatov, who has used his inheritance to join the army and obtain a rank only so that he can quickly retire and live undisturbed, Dobronrav regards nobility as a title *(dostoinstvo)* granted by the Sovereign for important services to the fatherland. Dobronrav recognizes that commerce also is useful to society, yet he does not aspire to become a noble or take up the military calling. His nephew's desire to obtain nobility without ever really serving is nothing short of unforgivable, laughable, and foolhardy. Thus while Bogatov pursues happiness in eminence and wealth, Dobronrav finds it in the love and respect of honorable people, in virtue and justness, and in a calm spirit. Bogatov also is wrong, in Dobronrav's opinion, to regard merchants and peasants as base. Nobles do indeed enjoy privileges before these groups, but the latter are equally necessary for the fatherland. The only real scoundrels are the people who are useless to society.

When Dobronrav rejects the idea that his commercial contribution to society merits social elevation, he also assumes the absence of a correspondence between the hierarchy of social status and the hierarchy of moral

worth. Dobronrav's understanding of propriety is no disingenuous justification of social hierarchy. Setting aside social distinctions, Dobronrav believes
that one should behave humbly before those exalted by spiritual worth,
courteously with one's equals, and tolerantly toward the unfortunate. To
the poor, one should offer assistance. The character of Dobronrav belongs
to a sizeable group of enlightened patriarchs assigned by eighteenth-
century playwrights to be the voice of moral virtue. Dobronrav is unusual,
however, in being a merchant rather than a noble. By assigning the role of
enlightened *raisonneur* to a merchant, the anonymous author not only re-
inforces social hierarchy—Dobronrav is happy with his merchant status—
but also shows that the voice of enlightenment and moral authority actually transcends it. Bogatov's moral regeneration does not require that he
abandon his noble aspirations, only that he become useful to society.

In late eighteenth-century Russia playwrights did not condemn upward
mobility outright; they simply suggested that the desire to rise above one's
original social status, to obtain that which one was not created to possess,
could lead to moral disaster. This was not because social hierarchy reflected
moral virtue, but because in the arena of civic society, beyond the patriarchal household, individuals easily lost their moral bearings. The good society of Russian Enlightenment theater was a society of moral rather than social relationships, and the source of those relationships was God-given
natural order. When Bogatov repents, Dobronrav acknowledges that his
sudden change of heart may seem strange. But the change is not so strange,
he explains, if one attributes it to "Divine providence." The deus ex machina
of providential intervention, a dramaturgical technique traceable to Greek
tragedy, equated Bogatov's change of morals with the restoration of rightful
order. The social question remained, however, because rightful order implied
virtue, and no matter how rightful the return of a good noble to appropriate
social status, it also happened that good serfs suffered abuse and good soldiers remained socially inferior. How could virtue and merit be rewarded
without disturbing social hierarchy? And how could authority be justified
when its representatives ignored virtue and abused power? An answer appeared in the separation of legitimate authority from the requirement of individual moral virtue and in the separation of individual moral virtue from
the reward of social mobility. Frequently at odds, the hierarchy of moral
virtue and the hierarchy of social status occupied two separate realms.

A SOCIAL WAY OF LIFE

The disjunction between virtue and social hierarchy suggests that the
philosophical and moral principles accepted by eighteenth-century Russian
playwrights could have led to transformation of the social order. But
throughout the eighteenth century such an outcome remained inconceivable to the vast majority of educated Russians, for whom "society" cohered

not so much as a legally defined social structure but as sets of moral relationships rooted in natural order. Belief in God permeated Enlightenment theater, which by focusing on the improvement of earthly life also encouraged the application of a religious standard to civic relationships. Thus abuses of hierarchy and authority appeared to be the result of individual moral failings, and the question of how best to cultivate moral virtue became central to the understanding of society. The preceding chapter showed that although in Russian theater of the late eighteenth century the patriarchal household sometimes represented a site of tyranny and abuse, more often than not it exemplified the realization of moral virtue. The image of virtue within personal family relationships stood in stark contrast to the image of corrupt sociability beyond the household. On the eighteenth-century Russian stage, personal morality and civic society seemed to conflict.

Fashionable Sociability and Evil Usury

Historians of eighteenth-century France situate Enlightenment sociability in a "republic of letters" that treated educated individuals of diverse social origins as equal citizens.[54] By contrast, Russian playwrights, like Enlightenment figures such as Rousseau, saw in fashionable sociability not only intimate relationships of sincerity and equality, but also civic relationships of deception and hierarchy. Within the patriarchal household, hospitality encouraged persons of equivalent social station to communicate without regard for the service ranks that distinguished them in civic life.[55] An explicit statement of this attitude appears in the anonymous play *Neighborly Celebration* (1790), set on the estate of the young nobleman Dorast.[56] Recently returned to his patrimony, Dorast has invited his noble neighbors to visit. Among these, Valeriian is particularly deferential and mindful of Dorast's superior education. But Dorast wants to converse "without ranks" and urges Valeriian to forget the compliments: "The only difference between us," he declares, "is that you are sitting on one side, and I on the other, of the table that separates us; in all else we are equal." Dorast displays the same familiarity toward other noble neighbors, but his understanding of equality in society *(obshchestvo)* excludes social inferiors. When a merchant arrives to do business with Valeriian, Dorast insists that the honored assembly not be disturbed. The equality between Dorast and his noble neighbors does not extend to the service and commercial relations of civic society.

In *Reward of Virtue* (1780), a drama written by I. A. de Teil's (1744–1815) for the wards of the St. Alexander School, equality also is achieved in intimate relationships.[57] The noble Postoianov (Steadfast), who as a young man squandered his inheritance on fashionable entertainment, now earns a living as a shoemaker. Although Postoianov blames his youthful frivolity on faulty education, he is repentant and generally satisfied with his lot, except that he wants his children to acquire formal learning in order to be useful to the fatherland. The children find a benefactor in the noble Miloserdov (Charitable), whose sole satisfaction comes from using his wealth to assist the poor, especially when he can "mold young hearts for the good of the fatherland." A paragon of virtue, Miloserdov's charity extends to a house full of poor, orphaned, and aged people. He invites Postoianov to join them for the sake of his children. Having lost his moral bearings in society, Postoianov has redeemed himself in family life and now brings honor to his social status. As a reward, his children will enjoy the benefits of personal charity; in intimate household relationships they find protection from the dangerous consequences of fashionable sociability.

In the eyes of late eighteenth-century Russian playwrights, happiness existed in quiet and peace of mind rather than in frivolous entertainment and material possessions.[58] *Experience of Friendship* (1799), an anonymous drama performed at the Voronezh noble theater of 1798, contrasts virtuous love and friendship to corrupt society.[59] In formulaic fashion, Aniuta loves the impoverished Prince Cheston (Honorable) but her mother wants her to marry the wealthy Count Velikodushin (Magnanimous). A simple and sincere country girl, Aniuta finds the count too courtly in his behavior, too adroit and unrestrained in social intercourse. The count, though quite taken with the quiet and solitude of rural life, also is a friend of Cheston, who has lost his estate because a guardian falsified claims against his late father. The count rightly attributes Cheston's misfortune to the corruption of society *(svet)*, which is filled with traitors: "at every step traps are set for you; in the guise of the most noble virtues in the world, terrible craftiness and malice hide their sharp stings." Cheston's happiness is restored when the count makes it possible for him to marry Aniuta. The count has discovered a deed *(krepost')* by which his aunt, the first wife of Cheston's father, left her husband an estate. If the deed does not correct Cheston's financial situation, never mind, the count will share his own property. That Cheston suffered at the hands of a legal guardian, and that the count's happiness depends on the well-being of his friend, suggest the superiority of personal over juridical relationships.

But in civic society, personal relationships also could be deceiving. Eighteenth-century Russian playwrights associated corruption in society with two places: 1) the world of high society or *le grand monde,* including the court and town, where French fashion, frivolous sociability, ostentatious display, and careerist ambition overshadowed sincerity and virtue; and 2) the world of commercial relations where greed, consumerism, and extravagant living led thoughtless individuals to economic and moral ruin. Among persons teetering on the brink of disaster, the most endearing was the reformable young spendthrift whose taste for fashionable sociability led him to live beyond his means. In the comedy *The Spendthrift Reformed by Love,* V. I. Lukin (1737–1794) explicitly addresses what he perceives as a pressing social problem.[60] The prodigal Dobroserdov (Good-Hearted) is deeply in debt and under the influence of the deceptive Zloradov (Malicious), who delights in the misfortune of others. Dobroserdov's uncle has threatened to disinherit him, and his merchant creditors intend to call him before the magistracy. Dobroserdov has one virtuous creditor, however, Pravdoliubov (Lover-of-Truth), who does not want to ruin young nobles or receive payment from the sale of their villages. Instead, he extends credit to distinguished nobles for a ten-year period and relies on Dobroserdov's conscience to ensure repayment of the debt. Dobroserdov's love for Kleopatra already has led him to repent, but because Pravdoliubov is his only honorable creditor, he prepares to flee and hopes to reconcile with his uncle. He also wants Kleopatra to run away with him, so he pretends to love her aunt, the princess, in order to obtain money for the journey. Virtuous Kleopatra refuses to elope, and Zloradov, scheming to get his hands on the princess's wealth, exposes Dobroserdov's deception. But all ends happily: Dobroserdov inherits property from his magnanimous uncle, Kleopatra and the princess reconcile, and Zloradov is excluded from the company of the potentially virtuous.

Another reformable spendthrift appears in *Profligacy Corrected by Right-Thinking* (1781), a comedy by V. P. Kolychev.[61] Like Dobroserdov, Viktor is deeply in debt and wants to flee his creditors with his beloved Khristina. The lovers receive assistance from Viktor's maternal uncle, Kalist, who guides his nephew along the path of truth. Viktor admits that it is difficult for him to live in the world *(svet)* because the distinction and status of his family force him to dress fashionably and participate in society *(obshchestvo)*. At assemblies he feels impelled to play cards so as not to appear idle and superfluous. Kalist, by contrast, refuses to accept that card games, a metaphor for debt and corruption, are a necessity in society. To play cards for profit, as a trade, leads people to ruin and uselessness; to accumulate wealth from card games is nothing less than robbery. Although Kalist rescues Viktor from his creditors and persuades his tyrannical father to allow the marriage to Khristina, there is a second threat to the family's well-being. Viktor's sister, Kleopatra, wants to marry Count Parmen, who denies the need for decorum in society and assumes that debt is inevitable. According to Parmen, social custom requires that honorable people entertain sumptuously in magnificent houses, wear rich clothing, and maintain servants and horses. Kalist emerges as the voice of virtue: he accepts that fashion and foppishness are characteristic of youth, but insists that they be contained and that people who dress in old styles not be ridiculed. While it is important for the court and grandees to project state splendor, other people should not accumulate debts in order to shine. Kalist cannot change the harmful sociability embraced by Parmen, but he is able to expose the count as a fraud and save Kleopatra from an unhappy marriage.

Both Lukin and Kolychev described young spendthrifts whose upbringing left them vulnerable to incorrigible swindlers, frauds, and usurers. Society was a dangerous, seductive place that encouraged profligacy and threatened virtue. In contrast to the patriarchal household, where love, duty, and obedience defined goodness, in society appearances were deceiving, and vice easily assumed the guise of virtue. In Ia. B. Kniazhnin's verse comedy *The Braggart* (1786), a wealthy provincial noblewoman has been lured by the pretense of rank and status to promise her daughter to a false count, in reality an indebted petty noble who pretends to have wealth, access to court, and the power to grant ranks, service appointments, and pensions.[62] By the time the play concludes the count has been exposed, the daughter has received permission to marry her true lover, and a police official has intervened to settle claims. Without effective policing, Kniazhnin seems to suggest, the social problem represented by the false count cannot be solved. When personal virtues fail, state authority is needed to ensure the good order of society, a place where charlatans and cheats easily feign love and friendship in order to swindle the unsuspecting.

An important function of Enlightenment theater, and of print culture more broadly, was to expose vice in order to correct morals and reform society.[63] For this reason, portrayals of spendthrifts and swindlers consistently associated corruption with the pleasures of fashionable sociability. In *The New Eccentrics, or The Projector* (1800) by Prince A. I. Golitsyn (1765–1807), a dishonest judge, usurer, and gambler, who sees gaming as a way to acquire an estate, live in luxury, and buy ranks, is last seen going off to play cards. In another comedy by Golitsyn, *Worldly Intercourse, or The Morals of Our Time* (1800)—an adaptation of *Bon Ton, or High Life above Stairs* (1775) by David Garrick (1717–1779)—the central characters continually cheat, lie, and betray.[64] The sole voice of virtue is the old-fashioned Pravdin (Righteous), who hopes to save his already depraved niece and sister from moral ruin. In the process, he condemns the city as a den of iniquity and the times as a reflection of foreign mores. Adultery, coquettes and Jezebels, drunkenness, crime, disorderly and lazy servants, masquerades, card games, fashion, luxury, debt, and dueling—all are denounced as urban vice. Echoing Rousseau, Pravdin explicitly equates worldly social intercourse with the corruption of morals. Rightful resolution comes when Pravdin's niece and sister repent and agree to return with him to the country, where presumably they can recover their moral virtue. Thus Pravdin is able to wrench "from the jaws of the monster, known as worldly intercourse, his unfortunate victims." Pravdin also assumes that every thinking Russian will applaud his worthy enterprise and begs the pardon of the spectators who sit in judgment of his actions.

On the late eighteenth-century Russian stage, fashionable sociability clearly threatened virtue. Good people could be seduced by frivolous pleasures or manipulated by the many swindlers and imposters who inhabited *le grand monde*. The young, the thoughtless, and the vain, led astray by the truly corrupt, could return to a life of virtue. But what of the vile characters and anti-heroes who most fully embodied the vices of society? What drove these individuals to abandon virtue and conscience? Eighteenth-century playwrights were not morally or socially naive. The rightful outcomes required for dramatic resolution and the underlying Enlightenment belief in the possibility of human progress left troubling social questions unresolved. Even though law and duty embodied virtue, corrupt individuals effectively corrupted society.[65] The achievement of earthly right depended on the actions of individuals whose moral virtue could not be guaranteed.

Among the enduring vices that threatened human progress, cynicism, ambition, and greed loomed large. In M. M. Kheraskov's verse comedy *The Hater* (1779), the cynical Zmeiad (Snake-Venom) successfully manipulates a foolish country noble in order to marry his daughter Priiata (Pleasant) and take possession of her dowry.[66] Blinded by Zmeiad's sham status, Priiata's father believes that the marriage will bring his family wealth and honor. The sad truth is that Zmeiad does not believe it possible to live by "the laws of honor." In his view, honor brings no benefit because there is no escaping envy and malicious anger. Indeed, Zmeiad epitomizes these vices: he shamelessly promotes his personal interests by spreading slander, creating dissension, insisting that friends and servants curse others on his behalf, and quickly abandoning people who no longer serve his needs. Nobody other than he, Zmeiad claims, is worthy of appointment to the Senate. Fortunately for Priiata, both her true lover and her uncle understand the need to counter deception with deception. They expose Zmeiad, and while Priiata's father remains inclined to reconcile, eventually he too sees the reality. After Zmeiad is deprived of rank and sentenced to exile—having been judged a person harmful to society—Priiata's father gives her permission to marry her beloved. The innocent girl is saved from the evil Zmeiad, who loves nobody, quarrels with everybody, and acts solely out of cynical ambition.

The successful courtier whose social adeptness produced undeserved reward exemplified the problem of ambition, defined as the pursuit of advantage and rank. A classic statement occurs in a story recounted by Starodum (Old-Thinking) in Fonvizin's *The Minor*. In old age, Starodum regrets that he did not serve the fatherland longer, having recognized what he failed to understand in youth: that a man of honor aspires to deeds not ranks, that ranks often are solicited whereas true esteem is earned, and that it is better to be overlooked without blame than to be rewarded without merit. Starodum left service as a young man after enduring combat wounds that failed to bring promotion. Unlike a boyhood friend who obtained higher rank without going to war, Starodum was not well versed in the ways of *le grand monde*. He lacked social skills, having been taught to value heart and soul over intellect (*um*) and learning (*znanie*). Even so, Starodum decided to seek his fortune at court but again found no straight path to success. Court life, he discovered, is filled with danger, and attention to rank only undermines sincerity. Next Starodum journeyed to Siberia, where at last he prospered through honest labor.[67] Starodum's virtue received its reward, but not before he left the world of service and fashionable society.

A more light-hearted portrayal of the courtier who embodied corruption in society appears in the verse comedy *Laughter and Sorrow* (1793) by A. I.

Klushin (1763–1804).[68] Born at court, Vetron (Empty-Headed) lacks education and disdains duty. A Frenchified fop and manipulative courtier, he
seeks rank and reward yet avoids going to war. Courage, Vetron proclaims,
is dangerous for the body. Instead, he finds honor in fashionable dress and
dismisses intellect as "empty day-dreaming." Ever mindful of the need to
wear a mask in society, Vetron is a man in search of advantage. Although
Vetron's association with the court could be construed as criticism of the
monarchy, it is in fashionable society as a whole that honor and duty are
forgotten. Indeed, the rich widow Vzdorova (Nonsense) wants Vetron to
wed her niece, which forces the latter to feign obedience and resort to deception. During a masquerade, a servant dressed as the niece dances with
Vetron while the true lovers slip away to be married. As in so many Russian
plays of the late eighteenth century, deception is needed to set things right,
an indication that virtue and vice can be difficult to distinguish.

Alongside the quest for advantage, symbolized by the courtier, greed
stood as another potent source of corruption in society. In eighteenth-
century England, sociability was understood as an aspect of commerce, and
commercialization provided the basis for an autonomous civic culture
clearly distinguished from the court.[69] In Russian Enlightenment theater,
by contrast, the connection between credit-worthiness and life in *le grand
monde* invariably appeared in a negative light. Fashionable sociability encouraged consumerism, which because of evil usury created ruinous debt.
In Russia, the charging of interest on monetary loans became legal only in
1754, so it is no surprise that playwrights tended to identify merchants as
cruel usurers.[70] The virtuous merchants who did appear on stage either for-
gave debts or managed to prosper without charging interest on credit. Vile
moneylenders from the nobility also played a role, suggesting that it was
not solely merchants whose commercial activities deserved condemnation.
The problem of usury did not inhere in social identities, but in moral corruption and economic inequality. The circulation of goods that accompanied fashionable sociability created material needs that could be satisfied
only through money lending and the expansion of credit.[71] The dangerous
new consumerism thus encouraged borrowing which in turn bolstered the
long-standing hostility toward moneylenders.

All too often money lending led to usury, which educated Russians
could not condone. An unequivocal denunciation of usury appears in I. V.
Nekhachin's *Flight from Debt, or The Repentant Spendthrift* (1792), the story
of Count Dobroserd (Good-Hearted), who has fled St. Petersburg hoping to
create a new identity in Moscow.[72] Although a weakness for fashion encouraged Dobroserd to squander his estate, he now feels remorse, shame,
and guilt. All ends well when his beloved Kleopatra arrives and pays his
debt to the merchant Plutiagin (Swindler), epitome of the evil usurer. Plutiagin disdains the poor, bribes officials to ensure that his debtors are punished, and values riches above conscience and honor. What good is honor,
he asks, if a man dies of hunger? By contrast, a second creditor, Dobroserd's

friend Councilor Pravdoliub (Lover-of-Truth), demands no timely repayment, believing instead that he should wait for the debtor to turn over a new leaf. Poverty, Pravdoliub insists, is not a vice, and society benefits when the poor recover. Corrupt officials who assist usurers eventually will be punished, for "now the poor have access to the throne of justice; the laws are established equally for all." Finally, Pravdoliub concludes, the duty of honor requires moneylenders to protect the young from ruin. A virtuous creditor does not lend to spendthrifts and does not lend at all unless there is a real need. In Pravdoliub's conception, the correct practice of money lending can serve the cause of enlightenment.

The distinction between good and evil money lending recurs in *As You Live, So You Are Judged* (1792) by the serf M. A. Matinskii (1750–ca. 1820).[73] Skvalygin (Miser) is a heartless creditor who believes that merchants should enrich themselves at the expense of others. The essence of commerce is profit, he argues, and a merchant who puts virtue before profit inevitably remains poor. Not surprisingly, Skvalygin cheats debtors and creditors by falsifying documents and overcharging for loans, goods, and rents. Nobles, merchants, men, women, widows, and orphans—all fall victim to the greed of a man who rejoices in the ruin of others. Skvalygin's own downfall begins when a military officer comes to collect money before leaving on campaign and notices an altered promissory note. The officer reports the matter, local authorities investigate, and Skvalygin is arrested. Not only is vice punished, virtue shines forth. Juxtaposed to Skvalygin is his nephew Khvalimov (Praiseworthy), who is willing to accept partial payments from debtors. Khvalimov believes that his uncle's lack of conscience and compassion gives the position *(dolzhnost')* of merchant a dishonorable name. Honor, he believes, is the merchant's primary duty and sweetest blessing; commerce can and should be conducted honorably. Khvalimov sounds more like a serviceman than an entrepreneur, and his indignation falls on deaf ears. Only through the intervention of state officials can Skvalygin be stopped and his wickedness punished.

As You Live sees the solution to avaricious usury in vigilant administration, an approach that was consistent with cameralist concepts of government.[74] Stories of reformable spendthrifts suggested a second solution—the cultivation of individual moral virtue—that was more in tune with the distinction between the virtuous household and corrupt society. In contrast to playwrights who portrayed young prodigals as victims of swindlers and greedy merchants, D. V. Efim'ev (1768–1804) blamed uncontrollable passion. In the comedy *Criminal from Gaming, or The Sister Sold by Her Brother* (1790), Bezrazsudov (Reckless) has squandered his inheritance and his sister's dowry in an effort to enrich himself at card games.[75] When Bezrazsudov's merchant creditor refuses to postpone payment on a debt, and his friend Cheston (Honorable) refuses to give him money, he sells his sister to Cheston, claiming that she is a serf educated by his mother. Bezrazsudov then runs away, only to be saved by Cheston, who stages his friend's arrest and pretends to be enjoying the pleasures provided by the "serf girl." That Bezrazsudov remains honorable and hence reformable is evident from the outrage he feels upon hearing the news of his sister's supposed violation. When Bezrazsudov next meets Cheston, he immediately draws his sword. His sister, by then engaged to Cheston, intervenes, and a happy denouement follows. Bezrazsudov realizes that his passion for gambling has deprived him of all reason and resolves to seek self-mastery and financial solvency in military service.

It is telling that Efim'ev dedicated *Criminal from Gaming* to Catherine II. In emphasizing reason as the solution to harmful gambling, Efim'ev echoed the empress's own dramatic treatments of vice. But while Efim'ev focused on the need to control human passion, Catherine advocated the need for enlightenment to eradicate ignorance and superstition. Her renowned antimasonic trilogy—*The Deceiver* (1785), *The Deceived* (1786), and *The Siberian Shaman* (1786)—also can be read as an exposé of human vulnerability to deception, a vice comparable to the ruinous passion for fashionable sociability.[76] In *Oh, These Times!* (1772), an adaptation of *Die Betschwester* (1745) by Christian Fürchtegott Gellert (1715–1769), Mrs. Khanzhakhina (Sanctimonious) exemplifies ignorance and superstition.[77] Instead of educating her granddaughter and fulfilling her obligations to creditors and servants, she seeks virtue in lengthy prayer and strict fasting. But her outward religiosity masks a malicious gossip and miserly usurer who cheats poor widows and beats innocent servants. Thanks to a clever servant girl and a persistent suitor, Khanzhakhina's granddaughter has the opportunity to escape ignorance by marrying a serviceman who can cultivate her natural reason. As the servant explains in the closing scene, the times are such that people condemn, judge, mock, and speak spitefully of others but fail to see that they themselves deserve laughter and condemnation: "When our prejudices take the place of healthy reason, then our own vices are hidden from us, and only the errors of others are visible."

Oh, These Times! attributes the corruption of society more to ignorance than to the dangers of fashionable sociability, for it is ignorance that makes people vulnerable to vice.[78] The parade of ignorant characters continues in *The Nameday of Mrs. Vorchalkina* (1774), the tale of another miser whose two daughters are besieged with suitors.[79] As the prospective grooms and their associates play out their roles, Catherine targets a range of undesirable social behaviors: the corporal punishment of serfs, the Frenchified fop who plays cards but does not pay creditors, the bankrupt merchant who spends his time writing useless reform projects, noble concern with lineage, indifference toward the dignity of noble status, false notions of honor, tyrannical parental authority, distrust of medical treatment, excessive petitioning, idleness, miserliness, gossip, superstition, and the plain unwillingness of people to recognize their own vices and idiocy. As the comedy concludes, the virtuous lovers receive permission to marry, the idiots with their vices are driven away, and one rejected but repentant suitor answers his father's

call to live in the country. There in solitude, he expects to correct the inde-
cision and empty-headedness caused by living in *le grand monde (svet)* and
to make himself into a suitable member of society *(obshchestvo)*.[80]

Repeatedly, late eighteenth-century Russian playwrights associated fashionable sociability and evil usury with the corruption of morals in society,
yet they did not condemn sociability and commerce outright. Enlightened
merchants contributed to good order, and refined sociability was superior
to the alleged superstition and violence of old.[81] Playwrights ridiculed boorish characters—often Frenchified fops and poorly educated provincial nobles—who thought they were cultivated but obviously lacked enlightenment. Their critique of civic society amounted to a secular exposé of
everyday vice—frivolity, cynicism, ambition, greed—caused more by ignorance than sinful human nature. It was a moral dissection of human folly,
not a proto-Slavophile rejection of cosmopolitan European culture. The
concern of eighteenth-century playwrights was to expose the gap between
false refinement and genuine enlightenment. On the assumption that outward behavior was a sign of inner worth, corrupt characters became visible
in word and deed, though not before they took advantage of the powerless
and the foolish, who then had to be rescued by the truly enlightened. Just
as playwrights understood equality to mean the potential for equality based
on individual moral virtue, so too their answer to corruption in society lay
in the reform and enlightenment of its individual members.

Retreat from Society

If individual virtue represented the solution to moral corruption in society, how could it be effectively realized and preserved? Flight from life
beckoned as the surest path and one that accorded well with traditional
Orthodox religious belief. In *The Hermit* (1769), a drama by A. P.
Sumarokov, Evmenii has left the corruption of the secular world to devote
himself to God.[82] In order to overcome the power of passion, he also has
abandoned and deeply hurt his parents, brother, and wife. While Evmenii
claims that in rejecting the vices and vanities of the world, he is following
the path of reason, his loved ones accuse him of opposing heart, intellect,
nature, and God's commandment to love thy neighbor and parents. Reasonable or not, their endless entreaties fall on deaf ears. Evmenii believes
that he already has served society, lived for his parents, and loved his
wife; now he wants to serve God in quiet and peace. This resoluteness
leads directly to the play's dramatic resolution: Evmenii's wife attempts
suicide with a dagger before finally deciding to enter a convent. Through
her decision to leave secular society and through the acceptance of
Evmenii's monasticism by his parents and brother, devotion to God is reconciled with family duty and romantic passion. Not surprisingly, reconciliation subordinates personal obligations to the unquestionable supremacy
of the divine order.

On the eighteenth-century Russian stage, escape from worldly corruption also could be achieved by flight into the wilderness. M. M. Kheraskov's tearful drama *The Persecuted* (1775) takes place on a deserted island where Don Gaston has sought refuge from the persecutions of Don Renod.[83] By the time Gaston's whereabouts are discovered, he has learned to bear his misfortune with indifference and has found happiness "in the interior of his heart." Gaston's concrete circumstances also change when the Spanish monarch declares him innocent and grants him the authority to decide Renod's punishment. Renod would like to redeem himself in exile; however, Gaston insists that they go to the city to reconcile before the ruler. Unexpectedly restored to fortune by the hand of God, Gaston is overjoyed to witness the love of human fellowship and the reward of virtue. The return of his title and estate signifies the reconciliation of virtue with civic society. Even so, society remains suspect. Together Gaston and Renod decide to leave the city and return to the island wilderness, which they hope to turn into "a quiet, pleasant, and serene dwelling."

Life in either a monastery or the wilderness symbolized the possibility of complete retreat from civic society. A less drastic solution was to live in the country, where happiness and moral virtue could flourish, away from urban sadness and corruption. The superiority of the country is vividly displayed in the opera *Serdtseplena* (1793) by L. M. Ivanov (d. before 1793).[84] The wise and virtuous Filosofan (Philosopher) has fled passion and worldly vanity for rural quiet and beauty. Determined to calm his soul, he has abandoned his beloved Serdtseplena (Captive-of-the-Heart) along with the pursuit of rank and status. Filosofan's peace and freedom evaporate, however, when Serdtseplena comes looking for him. She has been attacked by a robber and clearly needs protection; having risked her life to find Filosofan, she stubbornly demands that he admit his love. Feeling wins out over wisdom when Filosofan concedes that human well-being requires the reasonable use, rather than the complete suppression, of passion. The lovers reconcile and return to the city. There Filosofan finds favor with the sovereign and all too easily becomes convinced that with love and friendship he can live quietly. His happiness proves fleeting as the falsity of *le grand monde* reasserts itself. In a realm *(derzhavstvo)* where the ruler can be swayed by malevolent advisors, the innocent sometimes are condemned. Filosofan's downfall comes at the hands of a false friend, who defames him before the sovereign and then seduces Serdtseplena (who has not forgotten the suffering Filosofan previously inflicted on her). After reconciling with love and civic society, Filosofan learns that things are not as they appear, and virtue is not necessarily rewarded. Again he makes peace with society, this time by leaving it for good.

For the educated servicemen who dominated the late eighteenth-century Russian stage, however, flight from life did not represent a satisfactory course for the realization of moral virtue. D. I. Fonvizin directly confronts the question in the comedy *Korion* (1764), an adaptation of *Sidney* (1745) by Jean Baptiste Louis Gresset (1709–1777).[85] Korion lives in seclusion on his estate, unable to come to terms with his betrayal of Zenoviia. Fearing she is dead, he prepares to commit suicide. In his emotional despair, Korion has come to despise rank, town, court, and "all the secular world"; he seeks quiet and freedom from vanity. Countering Korion's decision to escape life is his friend Menandr, who regards suicide as sinful and selfish. Invoking duty, obligation, friendship, and love, Menandr appeals to Korion to take control of his heart and overcome his feelings. Korion, he argues, can be whatever he wants to be, if only he will subordinate feeling to reason. An honorable and reasonable man, Menandr continues, is obligated to dedicate his life to the fatherland: nature requires that he live in society *(obshchestvo)* for the benefit of the people. Only by directing all his efforts toward the common good and the glory of the fatherland can he hope to attain gaiety and spiritual calm. Menandr recognizes that in society morals have become corrupted, but this is no reason to abandon one's duty to live among people. Whether Korion heeds the call for civic engagement remains unclear. It turns out that Zenoviia also has been living in seclusion, overwhelmed by sadness and longing. Although the lovers reconcile and Korion's suicide attempt backfires, Fonvizin leaves unanswered the question of whether the lovers' will return to society.

A clearer judgment on the virtuous individual's relationship to society appears in *The Converted Misanthrope, or The Lebedian Fair* (1794), a comedy by A. D. Kop'ev (1767–1846).[86] Drawing upon characters and themes developed in Fonvizin's *The Minor*, Kop'ev addresses the problem of enlightenment by satirizing provincial nobles. The misanthrope is Marshal of the Nobility Pravdin (Righteous), who has retired to the country after serving in the College of Foreign Affairs. Having left service because of poor health, Pravdin values his secluded life, removed from the immorality, insincerity, and flattery of people in society *(svet)*. As a serviceman and visitor to foreign lands, Pravdin "saw society from all sides and found it full of pretense, deception, lies, and limitless self-love, which tramples all affection, friendship, and merit." Appropriately, Pravdin is in love with an innocent, poorly educated country girl whose Russian language has been corrupted by French but whose feelings and social behavior remain in a virtuous state of nature. In Rousseauian manner, *The Converted Misanthrope* juxtaposes the goodness of nature to the corruption of civilization, and the dichotomy is filled with ambiguity.

Although Pravdin disdains society and extols his lover's natural goodness, he also recognizes the inadequacy of innocence and the importance of education. The virtues of his lover—sensitivity, sincerity, and a noble soul—are precisely the qualities that prevent her from understanding the stupidity of her parents, who do not want her to marry Pravdin. Pravdin's praise for the educational and administrative reforms of Catherine II highlights the gap between ignorant and enlightened nobles. Pravdin works hard to persuade provincial nobles to send their children to the new state schools, but some simply refuse because they have no experience of the capitals or of ordered societies *(poriadochnye obshchestva)*. These nobles also ignore the new judicial institutions, especially the conscience courts, which offer an alternative to the corruption of the old governor *(voevoda)*. Pravdin recognizes that not all provincial nobles are ignorant and unscrupulous, but what sort of societies can they have when five or six homes are dispersed over 500 versts—a distance that allows people to meet only for hunting or every three years for elections?[87] The problem, Pravdin implies, is not the corruption of society but an absence of society: there are too few nobles in the district who can constitute society. Contradicting his earlier critique of *le grand monde*, Pravdin emerges as an advocate for well-ordered civic society.

Pravdin's thinking seems to suggest that while society is needed to make the Catherinean reforms work, the reforms are needed to stamp out ignorance and corruption in society. Significantly, his understanding of society extends beyond fashionable sociability, which he, like so many other contemporary observers, finds wanting. Although Pravdin's lover appears to represent unspoiled natural innocence, his own flight from town and court is not a Rousseauian affirmation of virtuous nature over corrupt civilization. Pravdin's struggle arises from the Kantian (and Catherinean) distinction between genuine and superficial enlightenment. Thus he notes that the freedom to enjoy entertainments away from the court and service is pleasant for people who know how to live correctly, but harmful for those who do not. Pravdin embraces the true enlightenment represented by well-ordered society which must be distinguished from the false enlightenment represented by poor education and injustice. Once Pravdin obtains what he has been denied—the hand of his beloved—he sees the world in a new light and can return to service, society, and material comfort. He can regard with indifference rather than excessive sensitivity the arrogance of exalted personages and the barbarity of rural ignoramuses. Ironically, it is through romantic satisfaction that Pravdin reconciles sensitivity with civic society. The suggestion that his previous abhorrence for society resulted from personal unhappiness seems justified. Precisely because individual moral virtue cannot purge society of corruption, personal happiness makes it possible for the virtuous individual to remain publicly engaged.

Another ambiguous Rousseauian treatment of enlightenment appears in the comic opera *The Americans* (1800) by I. A. Krylov (1769–1844), reworked by A. I. Klushin (1763–1804).[88] The efforts of two Spanish soldiers to persuade their American lovers to return with them to Spain set the stage for debate about the relative merits of primitive societies and enlightened civilizations. Seeking to show the superiority of Spanish wealth and grandeur, the Spaniards reveal their own lack of heart and admit that the wisdom gained from Philosophy can be used to advantage by swindlers. As one Spaniard puts it, he is unable to win the respect of the Americans because they are an "unenlightened people" who appreciate only genuine intelligence and bravery. The ironic treatment of civilization suggests that to be enlightened is to know how to deceive, with the result that Europe is filled with conflict and corruption. Criticism of the Europeans also emanates from the American leader, brother of the Spaniards' lovers and himself in love with the captive sister of the Spanish commander. The American is torn between the desire to befriend the brother of his beloved and anger toward the Spanish who not only steal the natives' gold but also want to deprive them of innocence and virtue. As one of the American women explains, she sees much wisdom but little goodness among the Spanish. Enlightenment and virtue are at odds.

Open confrontation erupts when the Americans capture the two Spaniards and prepare to burn them. The alternative to corrupt civilization seems to be primitive barbarity, but then natural virtue reemerges. The American leader decides to spare the prisoners out of love for the captive Spanish woman; in exchange he wants her to remain with him. This proposition prompts the Spaniards to urge the American to come to Europe. Again the heart, virtue, and quiet of America are contrasted with the false brilliance of Spain where learning is a source of darkness that blinds natural reason. In their unenlightened state the Americans are happy, and primitive society appears morally victorious over civilization. The pendulum swings once more, however, after Spanish soldiers defeat the Americans and place their leader in chains. At the moment that European force and cruelty seem to crush American innocence and justice, the Spanish commander frees the native leader. Responding to the Spaniard's love of his fellow man, the American's heart is softened, his enmity toward Europe disappears, and he agrees that all three couples should go to Spain. Despite the falsity and deception of European enlightenment, *The Americans* unequivocally proclaims the superiority of civilization. The crucial choice is not between nature and civilization, but between true and false enlightenment.

As teachers of morals, late eighteenth-century Russian playwrights grappled with the problem of how to spread enlightenment throughout civic society. Whether understood simply as a social way of life or an assemblage of moral and immoral beings, society embodied relationships that consistently threatened goodness. This negative perception did not represent emergent political opposition or rejection of the monarchy and court. It resulted from the tension between two competing images of the individual's relationship to society, both of which were needed to arrive at a vision of good order. On the one hand, corruption in society—exemplified by fashionable sociability and evil usury—reflected the vice and inadequate enlightenment of its individual members. A solution thus appeared in the cultivation of individual moral virtue, independent of society's harmful influences. On the other hand, individual moral virtue became manifest in usefulness to society, which meant there could be no realization of moral virtue apart from society. The virtuous individual effectively detached himself or herself from the vices of society while remaining thoroughly engaged in civic life. The inclination to cultivate virtue in private seclusion directly challenged the government's goal of productive mobilization. Consequently, as the voice of Russia's educated service classes, eighteenth-century plays countered the tendency to escape into a localized social life based on intimate relationships. Although acknowledging the corruption found in society, playwrights sought to reconcile civic engagement with individual moral virtue.

5

THE COMMON GOOD

• Historians of imperial Russia have long suggested that, prior to the creation of the Duma in 1906, the absence of constituted political bodies and universal civil rights precluded any meaningful separation between the state and organized civic society. At the same time, however, generations of scholars have also drawn attention to the administrative weakness of "absolute" monarchies across the European continent. Ironically, because the Russian version of absolute monarchy did not need to compete with territorially constituted law codes and corporate bodies, it appeared to be all-powerful when in fact its effective administrative reach remained exceedingly shallow.[1] Instead of implementing reform and negotiating political power through the structures of local and translocal corporate bodies, the Russian monarchy struggled at once to create a regularized administrative apparatus and to project political power through ad hoc consultation, personal patronage, and monarchical intervention. Instead of coming to terms with constituted institutions, sanctified by centuries of political struggle and juristic reasoning, the Russian monarchy created new institutions that individuals and communities then were called upon to fill. Small wonder, given the reliance on personal relationships to implement policy and exercise legal-administrative authority, that educated Russians found it difficult to conceive a separate society representing the interests of imperial subjects in relation to the state. Although household patriarchy and community self-administration stood out as enclaves of social autonomy, such legally constituted civic institutions with translocal linkages as existed appeared inseparable from government. Not before the mid-nineteenth century did Russia's landowning and service elites begin to view these civic institutions—for example, the district and provincial noble assemblies established in the reign of Catherine II—as potential instruments of political contestation.[2] For much of the imperial period, Russian subjects were more likely to eschew than to seek participation in state-engineered public institutions.[3]

In the depictions of civic society discussed in chapter 4, eighteenth-century playwrights suggested that the reluctance of individuals to participate in public institutions resulted not from the weight of an autocratic state but from the conflict between moral virtue and social vice. Being for the most part themselves also active servicemen, playwrights attempted to counter such tepid civic engagement by propagating the concept of "the common good" ("obshchee blago," "obshchaia pol'za," "pol'za obshchestva," "pol'za naroda," "obshchee dobro," "obshchaia vygoda")—a concept invoked by state officials to justify unprecedented mobilizations of human and material resources. Frequently interpreted by historians as a tool of absolutist state building and a euphemism for the primacy of the state interest (raison d'état), the concept of the common good did indeed serve the goal of constructing and maintaining instrumentalities of rule and imperial defense. But in a broader sense, it referred to the general well-being of the fatherland (otechestvo), which encompassed the institutions of the monarchy and state (gosudarstvo) in addition to the population and territorial expanse of the empire. The common good also was inseparable from social organization at the local level and civic society in the sense of shared interests, functions, and relationships outside the household and immediate community. Precisely because constituted bodies did not link communities to one another or to the monarchy, integration of the imperial polity depended on an understanding of the common good as civic authority exercised for the benefit of all. By associating the common good with authority that was both legitimately constituted and rightfully exercised, eighteenth-century playwrights addressed the question of how to preserve individual moral virtue amid the corruption and injustice so often found in civic relationships.

THE NOBLE OBLIGATION TO SERVE

If inequity and moral corruption threatened to alienate the virtuous individual from civic institutions, the concept of the common good showed how such an individual could be integrated into society and polity. The most immediate source of integration was the broad-based obligation to serve, which lay at the core of social and political organization in eighteenth-century Russia.[4] Across society, service bound individuals and communities to the person of the monarch and to the administrative structures of the state.[5] On the Russian stage, a commitment to serve represented the highest of moral virtues. Yet while the honor of service and the promise of social advancement through service promoted identification with the imperial polity, harsh reality exposed the gap between moral principles and concrete rewards. Even though the obligation to serve encouraged a larger vision of society, one that transcended the injustices of everyday life, in actual experience the injustices not only persisted but also seemed more egregious because of the human suffering caused by service, especially military service. With humor and empathy, eighteenth-century playwrights articulated the tension between service as a source of positive identification and service as a challenge to hierarchy and authority. Their depictions of service raised difficult moral and practical questions to which they could offer no fully satisfactory answers.

Noble Identity and the Debate over Service

When in 1694, at the death of his mother, Tsar Peter I became effective ruler of Russia, he inherited a complex hierarchy of service ranks associated with multiple privileges and functions. Through various mechanisms, Muscovite law and practice had linked the attainment of noble ranks to heredity and service. As the proprietors of estates held in hereditary and/or service tenure, Russia's landed serf-owning ranks derived their status from service to the tsar. Theoretically, their land holdings and serfs constituted grants from the ruler for services that they or their ancestors had performed. Of course, individual families also successfully augmented their estates through marriage, commercial purchases, and private gifts. But when Peter's government began to define an agglomerated noble category (shliakhetstvo, or later dvorianstvo), the ownership of populated estates did not automatically confer noble status. The Heraldry Office recognized nobility when a landowner could document that he or his ancestors had acquired their property specifically for noble service.[6] Nor did the ownership of populated villages and individual serfs become an exclusive noble right before the second half of the eighteenth century.[7] In contrast to the Muscovite rank ordering of aristocratic families (mestnichestvo), which stressed the connection between social status, service, and heredity, Petrine legislation made clear that henceforth service would take precedence over heredity in legal definitions of nobility. Through the Table of Ranks, which with minor alterations functioned from 1722 until 1917, the principle of meritorious service became formally institutionalized as the primary basis for promotion and the sole basis for ennoblement. Service to the tsar, not the mere acquisition of noble lands or serfs, constituted the only legitimate source of noble status.

Early in his reign, Peter I had also emphasized the disciplinary aspect of the obligation to serve when he subjected male nobles to a harsh regimen of forced education and lifelong service that could begin in the lowest ranks alongside commoners. From the start, however, educational opportunity and childhood enrollments in elite guards regiments lightened the burden of service by allowing nobles to rise through the ranks in ways unimaginable for ordinary soldiers. After Peter's death, service duties continued to ease, beginning with a temporary military demobilization in 1727. Preferential treatment for nobles was further formalized in 1731 with the founding of the Noble Cadet Corps, graduates of which entered service with officer rank. Then in 1736 the noble term of service was reduced to 25 years, followed in 1762 by complete emancipation from compulsory service. Although historians generally regard the emancipation as a popular measure, it probably weakened the moral authority and political power of its putative beneficiaries. Nor did emancipation end the close relationship between noble identity and service. For the monarchy, emancipation had become desirable precisely because sufficient numbers of qualified individuals were eager to serve. Policymakers assumed that most nobles would continue to serve, which in fact they did long after business and professional careers became plentiful in the nineteenth century.

Ironically, however, by making the legal rights of hereditary nobles unconditional, the emancipation from compulsory service raised troubling questions about the meaning of nobility. If nobles no longer served sovereign and fatherland, on what grounds could their privileges be justified? Perhaps more disturbing for nobles—especially those with limited economic resources—if they no longer were entitled to appointments in service, how they could reap the rewards of service and preserve a noble way of life?[8] In posing these questions, late eighteenth-century playwrights moved beyond the legal sphere of noble privilege into the moral sphere of noble identity. They reiterated the Petrine principle that noble privilege derived from service, but also recognized that the disjoining of noble status from service required a new conception of nobility. The need to reconcile the emancipation from compulsory service with the preservation of noble privileges produced a moral definition of nobility.

Representing the official ideal, enlightened patriarchs or *raisonneurs* insisted that nobles should serve, whether or not they were required to do so. A classic statement appears in *Upbringing* (1774), a comedy by D. V. Volkov (1727–1785), one of the framers of the 1762 emancipation.[9] The wealthy Moscow noble Dobromysl (Good-Thinking) has lost two sons in combat, and as a result, expects his daughter Sof'ia (Wisdom) to assume responsibility for the family's debts to sovereign and fatherland. Sof'ia believes that the deaths of her brothers are sufficient repayment, but as her father explains, "it is important to me that you replace your brothers and restore our dying family."[10] Equating female service with reproduction, Dobromysl reveals his wish to see Sof'ia married, so that his family will have descendants who can serve: "I owe to Sovereign and Fatherland a most sacred debt. The degree *(stepen')* to which our family has been elevated and the wealth in which our house abounds derive from Monarchical munificence for the services of my father and grandfather; consequently, I am obligated to serve Sovereign and Fatherland eternally, and to be as like my father and grandfather as possible." When Sof'ia invokes an archaic distinction, abolished by Peter I, between lands held in hereditary tenure and those granted on condition of service, Dobromysl is indifferent to the status of the family's property. He describes his patrimonial lands as grants from the monarch for the loyal services of his father and grandfather. "I do not know," Dobromysl declares, "whether they [the lands] are called patrimonial: but I do know that a family possessing such tokens of Monarchical favor is incomparably more obligated to serve to the uttermost." For Dobromysl, it is absolutely essential that he and his descendants provide continual evidence of the ancestral service and merits that elevated the family to its present degree and wealth.

The notion of a family debt that each successive generation must repay through state service leads Dobromysl to a broader discussion of noble identity. He insists that nobles are set apart by their ability to devote themselves to good deeds beyond the patriarchal household. Unlike the most well-behaved, kind, and honorable peasant agriculturalist or poor townsman, who is burdened by labor and a large family and whose virtue rarely can function outside his own household, an educated noble possesses the means and ability to perform good deeds. As a military commander, he can be useful to sovereign and fatherland; to his subordinates, he can be a father and protector. As a state official, he can eradicate slander and ensure justice in his administrative domain. If he returns to his villages (presumably after service), all his peasants—male and female, old and young—can rejoice in the presence of their father, guardian, and protector, who presumably will work to reduce ignorance and superstition, heal sickness, teach improved methods of cultivation and handicrafts, eliminate idleness and drunkenness, and transform quarrels into friendship and harmony. In Dobromysl's conception, service can be broadly defined, but nobility cannot be disjoined from service.

That the 1762 emancipation had indeed disjoined noble status from compulsory state service also explains Dobromysl's concept of rank. Peter I's Table of Ranks had established an order of fourteen grades that corresponded to specific ranks or offices in military, civil, and court service. Because promotion in service followed the Table of Ranks, the attainment of a higher grade signified social advancement. Although nobles usually rose more quickly than commoners, and over time entered service at ever higher grades, noble status did not in and of itself guarantee the possession of rank.[11] Rather the granting of rank resulted from education, patronage, seniority and merit in service, and recognition by superiors. Nor, after 1762, were nobles entitled to receive the service appointments that promised to bring the rewards of rank. Dobromysl's understanding of rank incorporates into the Petrine definitions the changed circumstances following the nobles' emancipation. His notion of the honor of rank distinguishes genuine nobility, which represents a moral quality, from mere noble status in the legal sense. Dobromysl insists that a noble cannot be a true son of the fatherland simply on the basis of legacy and the possession of estates, which in fact belong to the fatherland. In his view, nobles are not entitled to rank, which is separate from honor. Ranks are for the court to present; therefore,

nobles should seek appointment to service, and if they prove able to perform their duties, they then may hope for recognition of their zeal and tal-
ents. If the monarch decides to award rank to an infant, the honor derived
from that rank belongs to the parent whose services the monarch has favored; consequently, the child recipient is forever obligated to emulate his
father in service. Because all nobles theoretically attained their status in
recognition of their own or their forebears' service, nobility and the honor
of rank are meaningless in the absence of an earnest devotion to service. In
the post-emancipation context in which nobles were free to choose
whether to serve, Dobromysl's understanding of nobility and honor implied a moral debt to monarch and country.

Stage characters of Dobromysl's generation consistently shared his commitment to service, and it is tempting to attribute their zealousness to the
ideals of an earlier age when every noble was required to serve. Certainly in
the plays depicting service, all the patriarchal figures—even those devoid of
moral authority—believed that their sons should serve. The sons exhibited
more varied attitudes, though the virtuous among them also embraced the
service ethic of the fathers.[12] Sof'ia's future husband, Colonel Dobromysl,
who is in Moscow recuperating from wounds suffered in the Russo-Turkish
War, seems ready to sacrifice all for sovereign and fatherland. He is, if anything, even more zealous than the older Dobromysl. By the time the
colonel arrives on the scene he has served in the Seven Years' War, in
Poland, and in the Danubian campaign under General [P. A.] Rumiantsev.
News of this long service record prompts the older Dobromysl to suggest
that perhaps the colonel needs to take care of his estate. Duty does not demand that nobles neglect their property, for a person who tends to his estate is better equipped "to perform State service."

But Colonel Dobromysl counters that his house and villages are not suffering. Moreover, even if they fell into ruin, "when the Fatherland demands
service, one should think only of this." The colonel does not consider the
requirements of estate management a legitimate reason to leave service, especially in wartime when the only good reason to retire is poor health.[13] If
nobles leave service to manage their estates, and many do this, it follows
that the more generously a family is endowed with properties, the greater
right they have not to serve and not to be useful. This would mean "that
Monarchical favor brings harm to Sovereigns, and rulers would find themselves contradicting the principle of generosity, because the longer their
true servitors served, the less they would reward them."[14] Echoing the older
Dobromysl, the colonel notes that the purpose of wealth is to possess the
means to serve the fatherland. He also is uncomfortable with the practice
of granting promotions at retirement: because his ancestors could not have
obtained his present rank so quickly, he insists on achieving higher rank
through active service. The character of Colonel Dobromysl personifies the
close relationship between virtue and the desire to serve that is so central to
the older Dobromysl's thinking.

In the character of Colonel Zasluzhenov (Meritorious), the comedy *Mitrofanushka in Retirement* (1800) by G. N. Gorodchaninov (1772–1852) introduces another zealous officer and virtuous suitor.[15] Zasluzhenov sincerely believes that a man who devotes his youth to "useful labors" will be rewarded with a quiet and prosperous old age. Love for the fatherland, honor, and his own family obligate a noble to serve. In fact, Zasluzhenov declares, "we all are servants." Domosedova (Stay-at-Home), the mother of a competing yet clearly unworthy suitor, objects that a noble cannot be a servant; servants are household serfs, and a person who is wellborn is born a master. While Domosedova equates nobility with noble birth, Colonel Zasluzhenov draws a clear distinction between mere nobles, who are born, and noble souls who do good irrespective of personal interests. By way of example, he does not want recognition for assistance rendered to Domosedova's son, Mitrofanushka. Because, in Zasluzhenov's words, "all [people] are obligated to serve each other," the help he has given represents nothing more than the fulfillment of a human duty. Zasluzhenov's idea of service as a human duty takes him beyond the question of whether a particular individual deserves noble status. Instead, he arrives at the universalistic concept of noble souls, concluding that the soul of a servant can be more noble than the soul of a master: "in the eyes of a right-thinking person, a kind servant is incomparably preferable to a dishonorable Lord."

Alongside the zealous servicemen and enlightened patriarchs who internalized the Petrine service ethic, late eighteenth-century Russian playwrights portrayed another type of young noble who also possessed education and rank yet openly disdained service. Although harshly condemned for their immorality, these nobles articulated an understanding of noble privilege that did not depend on service. In *Upbringing*, the ignorant Francophile Makhalov (Runner-After), who arrogantly expects to marry Sof'ia, articulates a view of nobility and honor that separates these concepts from the notion of a moral debt to monarch and country. Believing that he is entitled to recognition, Makhalov is willing to serve only if the court grants him a rank that a person of his "nature and education can accept with decorum." In his view, nobles should serve out of honor and not for reward, which is to say that nobles possess honor by definition, as opposed to honor being the just reward for service. Furthermore, Makhalov insists, he already has served and brought honor to the fatherland by cutting such a fine figure in France. It would be laughable, in his eyes, if he served under a commander who had never seen Paris. For young Makhalov, genuine nobility is not a matter of service, because honor and social merit derive from nature (that is, birth) and education (that is, seeing Paris). While not a clear statement of noble autonomy based on inviolable rights, Makhalov's position defines merit as an innate quality rather than an attribute derived from service.[16]

Mitrofanushka in Retirement depicts an equally unworthy suitor who retires from service the moment war is declared. Mitrofanushka stands in stark contrast to Colonel Zasluzhenov, who earnestly believes that a noble is obligated to serve in a useful manner. Zasluzhenov recognizes that while Mitrofanushka is both a noble and a captain, he also is "an unheard of ass, a boor, who has no respect for his parents, without education, without understanding of honor and decency; a scoundrel, who is completely ignorant of noble feelings; dissolute, self-righteous, capable of the most vile deeds; a parasite who does not want to serve the fatherland." With this characterization in mind, Zasluzhenov is forced to question whether a noble with the personal qualities of Mitrofanushka can be at all useful to the fatherland. That Mitrofanushka has attained the rank of captain, Zasluzhenov decries as "a blow for a person with merit" and "a stain for noble souls." The obvious contradiction between the idea of nobility and the everyday behavior of Mitrofanushka threatens to undermine the moral basis of noble identity. If the important "title of noble" is a reward for service, and service is an obligation of nobility, what becomes of the noble whose individual vices render him incapable of useful service?

A further challenge to Zasluzhenov's concept of the relationship between nobility and service arises in the person of retired Ensign Khrabrilkin (Courageous), a landless noble living on the Domosedov estate. Burdened by poverty and the loss of a leg in battle, Khrabrilkin behaves in a soldierly manner out of nostalgia for military life. Determined to maintain the honor of officer rank, and proud of his military past, which understandably he prefers to his present life, Khrabrilkin condemns Mitrofanushka's decision to leave service. Yet even as he defends the dignity of servicemen, Khrabrilkin embodies the gap between idea and reality.[17] He combines noble status with devotion to service, but he is physically disabled and bereft of material security. Ordered to eat with the servants when esteemed guests visit the Domosedovs, his retirement is a far cry from Zasluzhenov's image of the quiet prosperity that awaits the noble who spends his youth performing "useful labors." In contrast to Mitrofanushka, who refuses to accept service as a moral obligation, Khrabrilkin embraces the obligation to serve, yet his only reward is to suffer neglect and humiliation. His life experience clearly contradicts the moral principle of service.

The final challenge to Zasluzhenov's service ideal appears in the relationship between the enlightened patriarch Brigadier Zdravomyslov (Sensible) and a noble raised by Zdravomyslov's father. As young men, they lived like brothers and began military service together in the same regiment. But the friend turned out to be a good politician and a poor officer. He left the military, obtained a position at court, and from this exalted post, received Zdravomyslov with preference. Expecting to benefit from the patronage of his friend, Zdravomyslov spent many years waiting for promised appointments. Promises they remained, until eventually Zdravomyslov announced his dissatisfaction and departed, thankful that he had not completely squandered his estate. Disappointed in friendship and unrewarded in service, Zdravomyslov concluded that any effort "to construct prosperity at

Court" is like trying "to build a palace on ice." Well-being does indeed require a tranquil spirit, but "tranquility flees from courtiers."

Although disillusioned by the realities of service, Zdravomyslov nonetheless continues to believe that all young nobles are obligated to serve. At the same time, by questioning the moral worth of courtiers, he also questions the imagined relationship between service and virtue. Like Zasluzhenov, he is compelled to recognize that while Mitrofanushka's decision to retire is disgraceful, the young noble would be of little use in service. Nor, he regrets, is it any longer fashionable to disdain an officer who does not want to sacrifice his life for the fatherland. In fact, the services that bring institutional rewards are not necessarily equivalent to true merit. Resourceful seekers are ready to sacrifice tranquility, health, life, and honor in order to please a grandee, who also may lack merit. As a result, they obtain rewards that a man with true merit dares not hope to receive.[18] In Zdravomyslov, the combination of disappointment in service and belief in the noble obligation to serve places the obligation on a higher moral plane. Service is a duty, even though the benefits are uncertain and the unworthy frequently rise.

• On the Russian stage of the late eighteenth century, the obligation to serve represented a fundamental yet inherently ambiguous source of noble identity. Plays written after 1762, when nobles were emancipated from compulsory service, depicted service as a moral obligation indicative of nobility, enlightenment, and virtue.[19] Given that nobles such as young Makhalov and Mitrofanushka were indifferent or even hostile toward service, playwrights distinguished true nobility or nobleness from mere noble status in the legal or hereditary sense. Once virtue, enlightenment, and the desire to serve became crucial markers of nobility, the role of birth receded, and lowly servants could potentially possess the attributes of nobility. Once an association existed between noble identity and the moral obligation to serve—an obligation that a commoner could embrace and a noble could disdain—the social reality of noble status and the moral reality of nobility no longer necessarily coincided. As the worthy Colonel Zasluzhenov described it, all people, including nobles, are servants.

Ironically, the greater precision in legal definitions of nobility represented by the 1762 emancipation and Catherine's II's 1785 Charter to the Nobility encouraged this orientation toward moral criteria, which in turn clouded the social foundations of noble identity. Not only on the stage but also in historical reality, regularized ennoblement through service blurred distinctions between nobles and commoners at the same time that the emancipation removed the primary justification for noble privilege by making hereditary noble rights unconditional. In this context, playwrights invoked service to articulate a predominantly moral definition of nobility that transcended concrete legal requirements. The utilitarian language of the Petrine common good remained, but instead of legitimizing coercive legislative measures, usefulness became a moral obligation for all virtuous, enlightened, and properly educated nobles. By transforming the social obligation to serve into a personal moral obligation, the internalization of service values also encouraged an awareness of individuality. Increasingly, playwrights suggested, nobility inhered in the individual moral being and became manifest in personal behavior.[20]

The emphasis on morality in definitions of nobility also had important political implications that may help to explain the longevity of Russia's old regime. Following the 1762 emancipation, the language of noble virtue diverged from the legal attributes of noble status. Given that noble virtue was realized in service, and simultaneously, service reflected virtue, the moral legitimacy of noble rights also derived from service, clearly an official domain. The need to find a moral basis for nobility then made it difficult, or perhaps unnecessary, to develop a political language of noble rights that functioned independently of state definitions. Precisely because state definitions assigned legal rights to social groups rather than to individuals, individuality became associated with predominantly moral qualities.[21] The personal authority of a serf master, state official, military commander, or sovereign ruler could then be accepted or rejected on moral grounds, without directly challenging the legitimacy of social and political institutions. Although a political language of noble rights might be discernible in young Makhalov's belief that as an educated noble he is entitled to rank, his character is morally reprehensible, and his idea of rights is limited to the privileges accorded a particular social group. His demand for the *privilege* of rank contains no concept of potentially universal natural rights.[22] Nor did Russian nobles, in contrast to their counterparts further west, possess legal rights that were proprietary or historically constituted in the local laws, offices, and institutions of an identifiable territory. The monarch alone granted rights or privileges to nobles and until 1906 remained legally empowered to change them at will.

Combat

Whatever the basis, legal, moral, or both, for the maintenance of noble privileges, eighteenth-century warfare created numerous opportunities for nobles to prove their moral worth in heroic and honorable deeds. Peter I not only imposed lifelong service on nobles and commoners, he, like his predecessors and contemporaries all over Europe, also led troops in continual warfare. The Great Northern War against Sweden dragged on for more than 20 years (1700–1721), stretched from the Baltic to Ukraine, and spilled over into Moldavia, where Russia and Turkey fought a war in the years 1710–1713. Military actions in Persia began toward the end of Peter's reign and persisted for a decade (1722–1732), and during the 1730s, Russian troops fought in the War of Polish Succession (1733–1735), the Turkish War (1736–1739), and four related Crimean campaigns (1735–1738). Although lifelong service for nobles ended in the 1730s, intensive warfare did not. Following the Swedish War of 1741–1743, the Russian army enjoyed a brief respite, until the Seven Years' War (1757–1762)[23] sent imperial troops deep into Prussia. The reign of Catherine II brought aggressive diplomacy and unprecedented military fortune: the First Polish War (1768–1772); the First Turkish War (1768–1774), which began the military subjugation of the Caucasus; the annexation of Crimea (1783); the Second Turkish War (1787–1791); the Swedish War (1788–1790); and the Second Polish (Insurrectionary) War (1794–1795). Finally, in 1799 the wars against revolutionary France led to Russian campaigns in Holland, Italy, and Switzerland—campaigns that marked the beginning of one of the most dramatic periods in the history of European warfare.[24] During the more than 150 years of ongoing imperial expansion and military engagement that culminated in the Crimean War (1853–1856) and the era of the Great Reforms, broad sectors of the educated service classes experienced warfare firsthand.

Repeatedly, this combat experience provided the inspiration for original literary creations that, while justifiably excluded from the corpus of Russian literary classics, nonetheless suggested deep identification with military service. Playwrights assumed that although conscription and mobilization caused acute suffering and dislocation, servicemen not only adapted to military life but also embraced its principles of courage, heroism, and glory.[25] Two dramas by the officer-playwright P. S. Potemkin (1743–1796) expressed a decidedly heroic view of military service, yet also communicated the bloody horror of combat—its thunderous sounds, blinding sights, and unnatural destruction. *Russians in the Archipelago* (1772) recounts the historic defeat and destruction by the Russian navy of the Turkish fleet at Chesme in 1770.[26] Although lavishly celebrated at the time of Catherine II's First Turkish War, Russian victories in the archipelago under A. G. Orlov proved less significant than those achieved on land under P. A. Rumiantsev and V. M. Dolgorukov. Anticipated uprisings of Greeks and Balkan Slavs failed to materialize, and the Treaty of Kuchuk Kainardzhi (1774) returned the islands of the archipelago to Turkish rule.[27] *Russians in the Archipelago* is both a dramatization of these historic events and a political panegyric celebrating imperial military successes, the heroism and sacrifices of the Russian troops, the wisdom of the empress, and the zeal of the Orlov brothers.[28]

Throughout the drama, Potemkin glorifies Russian civilization by juxtaposing two images: 1) the moral and military superiority of Russians over Turks, Greeks, and other foreigners; and 2) the heroism of Russian fighters who despite their generosity and deep-felt horror of bloodshed always are ready to die for the good of the fatherland and society. In Potemkin's rendition of military glory, Russians emerge as the greatest heroes. Just before the decisive battle, Rear Admiral Elphinstone concludes that victory is impossible given the Turks' numerical superiority. Aleksei Orlov counters that numbers are irrelevant; Russian bravery will ensure success. As the Orlovs, Prince Iurii Dolgorukov, and Admiral Spiridov declare their willingness to spill blood and die for the glory of society, the Scot Elphinstone and the Englishman Rear Admiral Greig marvel at the honor and zeal of the Russians.[29] Unlike the barbaric Turks, the disorderly Greeks, and the cautious Scot, Russian warriors are dedicated to the pursuit of glory. Even as Aleksei Orlov grieves over the mistaken news that his brother has perished, he preserves the belief that love of the fatherland demands sacrifice. Even while lamenting his own limited military accomplishments, he maintains that victory brings glory to the monarch, the fatherland, society, and every Russian. The heroic warfare of *Russians in the Archipelago* assumes identification with transcendent historical arenas beyond the immediate concerns of family and personal advancement. Instead of a profitable marriage, a secure social position, or a recognized service rank, the Russians in the archipelago strive for glory, a quality that accrues less to the individual than to Russia.

An even more broadly conceived idea of glory informs Potemkin's lyric drama in verse about the Second Turkish War, *Zel'mira and Smelon, or The Capture of Izmail* (1795).[30] One of the legendary events of Russian military history, the storming of Izmail, took place on 11 December 1790 under the command of A. V. Suvorov.[31] Potemkin himself served with distinction at Izmail, and he recounts the experience through the eyes of two lovers being torn apart by the war. Zel'mira is the daughter of Mukhafiz Osman, the commander of the Turkish forces; her beloved Smelon (Bold), though a mere colonel by rank, commands the Russian troops set to attack unless the Divan (Turkish Council of State) agrees to surrender Izmail.[32] At a time in the recent past, when Smelon was a wounded prisoner in the home of Osman, he and Zel'mira had fallen in love. Now duty and honor force the lovers to sacrifice their personal feelings for the higher good of the fatherland. Zel'mira is prepared to leave country, parent, and home in order to follow her lover, yet when Smelon urges her to persuade Osman to relinquish the city, she vehemently refuses. To use her father's love to betray duty, respect, and blood would be an evil act. Smelon possesses an equally strong sense of duty. During his imprisonment Osman had treated him like a son, and although the Turkish unwillingness to capitulate now impels him to view Osman as an enemy, he cannot be unfaithful to his benefactor by carrying off his daughter. Smelon's personal duty to Osman supersedes his love for Zel'mira. Osman is likewise pained by the inevitability of battle. As he explains to Smelon, "We cannot be personal enemies, but for the fatherland we must forget the bond of friendship. From the hour that we were born into this world we became subjects of the Tsars and sons of society."[33] Personal honor and the common good demand the subordination of friendship to this transcendent identity.

Faced with the possibility of destruction, Zel'mira, Smelon, and Osman all display an unequivocal understanding of where duty lies. In word and deed, they sacrifice personal happiness for the good of the fatherland. By contrast, the lovers portrayed in the comedy *A Soldier's Happiness* (1779), an adaptation to Russian mores of Gotthold Ephraim Lessing's *Minna von Barn-*

helm, oder Das Soldatenglück (1767), draw attention to the unheroic consequences of war, particularly its wounded bodies and broken spirits.[34]
Evgeniia's betrothed, Major Dobroserd (Good-Hearted), has returned from
war against the Turks a dispirited, dishonored, and mutilated man. He has
lost the use of his right arm, faces charges of corruption, refuses financial
assistance from trusted friends, and regards himself as unworthy of the
wealthy and stylish Evgeniia. Dobroserd's troubles began when he conducted a levy of conscripts in Iaroslav province and, out of concern for the
poverty of local nobles, lent out 10,000 rubles from the regimental treasury.
When at the conclusion of the war the regiment's accounts were reviewed,
the authorities suspected that Dobroserd had accepted bribes during the
levy and pocketed the missing money. Toward the end of the comedy, an
imperial decree clears Dobroserd of all suspicion and invites him to return
to service, but his response to the monarch's appeal for "officers with your
merits" is suggestively ambiguous. Although with his honor restored, Dobroserd initially declares his intention to marry and serve, soon he expresses a desire to live with Evgeniia in a remote corner of the country. He
even is prepared to tear up the imperial decree after Evgeniia, pretending to
have been disinherited for refusing to marry the groom chosen by her uncle, insists that she is dishonored and thus cannot live with him in civic society. More important than a soldier's glory and his sovereign's personal
plea is Dobroserd's wish to serve Evgeniia.

Dobroserd's understanding of honor also seems detached from military
service. Before Dobroserd is cleared of the charges against him, Sergeant
Major Tverdov (Steadfast) repeatedly tries to help his former commander.
Dobroserd just as stubbornly refuses to accept financial assistance. His
pridefulness offends Tverdov, who during the Danubian campaign shared
precious water with Dobroserd and twice saved his life in combat. When
the weather was hot and water scarce, Dobroserd did not hesitate to ask
Tverdov for a drink. Now, in another time of urgent need, he refuses to take
money, which is no more precious than the water he drank on campaign.
The equality of men in arms—an equality that forms so easily on the field
of battle—evaporates in civic society. Outside the combat environment,
Dobroserd is ashamed to accept charity from a social inferior. His alienation
from military life becomes even clearer when Tverdov announces plans to
return to service. Dobroserd questions Tverdov's motivations, declaring
that if his decision to serve reflects a penchant for the bestial, wandering
life—a desire to shed blood, make other people unhappy, and then search
for profit in their ruined shacks—he is a brigand, not a warrior. The only
worthy reason to serve is to defend the fatherland. Dobroserd's ambivalence is a far cry from Potemkin's heroism. Although Evgeniia and Dobroserd keep the decree inviting Dobroserd to serve—suggesting that they
remain committed to the idea of service—they also seem poised to subordinate this higher duty to the immediate satisfactions of love.

Clearly, service produced conflicting responses in the hearts and minds of educated Russians. *Campaign against Sweden* (1790), a comedy with chorus and ballet by I. A. Kokoshkin (1765–1835), reproduces both honorable and dishonorable reactions to the call to arms.[35] When the play opens, both the count and his servant Provor (Adroit) are frantic over how to break the news of war to their lovers. While Provor has no choice but to accompany his master, he nevertheless declares that his beloved means more to him than duty and honor: "Better to live a lifetime in leanness than die once in glory." The officer Skorodum (Fast-Thinking) does not question the concept of glory but is distraught over his inability to carry out his wedding plans: instead of acquiring two thousand souls (male serfs) through marriage, he must go on campaign.[36] A quite different response comes from an adulterous wife who is only too eager to send her husband off to war. Her amorous schemes are rightfully thwarted when her husband, convinced she is dying of grief, gives up his regimental place to the officer Modest, who is keen to fight but has been unable to obtain an assignment. Worse still, the wife's lover receives orders to replace Mr. Trusov (Coward), who has bribed a doctor to certify that he is too sick to serve. Yet another reluctant serviceman who cannot avoid the obligation to serve feigns concern about his father's health, when in reality he is sorry to leave the social and cultural amenities of the capital.

Russia has a fair share of shirkers, *Campaign against Sweden* suggests; however, alongside the unworthy characters who put personal interest before duty, the play also depicts virtuous characters who embrace the opportunity for sacrifice: a wife who insists on accompanying her husband while he defends the fatherland, two officers who are overjoyed at the prospect of testing the Russian sword and proving the worthiness of Russian fighters, and the young Modest, who is encouraged by his father to prove himself in battle and proudly prepares to join his comrades. In *Campaign against Sweden* an atmosphere of uncertainty and conflict surrounds the call to arms. For despite the unequivocal association of virtue with the desire to serve, the individual responses to war do not necessarily bring glory to the military calling.

• Eighteenth-century Russian playwrights bore personal witness to the social cost of military service, and their stories of combat evoked the bitter sorrow and suffering of that experience. At the same time, however, military life also gave rise to countervailing stories of fellowship and cooperation—stories filled with gaiety, fearlessness, and spirited anticipation. Juxtaposed to a sense of loss was a sense of belonging. Adding to the emotional ambiguity was the moral judgment that not every noble who questioned the obligation to serve or articulated an unheroic view of war necessarily deserved condemnation. A. P. Sumarokov's tragic hero Khorev speaks openly against the barbarism of war, in which murder and robbery are called heroism, and V. K. Trediakovskii's King Lycomedes condemns war's evil, inhumanity, and violence.[37] In Ia. I. Blagodarov's comedy *Maternal*

Love (1786), a mother who idealizes military glory and welcomes war as an opportunity for her son to distinguish himself breaks down once the son actually goes off to battle.[38] Unable to see the glory, a broad range of sympathetic characters answer the call to arms with distress and ambivalence.

By allowing laudable nobles to display an aversion to war and by spotlighting principles of courage, heroism, and glory that were not socially specific, playwrights implicitly challenged hierarchies of status and authority. Portraits of combat emphasized the natural human equality of all servicemen, regardless of rank, who devoted themselves to the fulfillment of duty. In addition, ignorant young nobles who possessed undeserved rank and officers who abused their power showed that social superiors could be morally inferior. Yet whether command authority was deserved—based on moral virtue and professional merit—in military service, discipline remained crucial to victory and survival. As Modest's father explains to his son, "Before you can be victorious over the enemy, you must learn to master yourself." Precisely because war required extraordinary self-mastery, command authority, even though it tended to mirror social hierarchy, might not depend on social hierarchy for its effectiveness. At moments of grave danger social differences could be transcended without weakening military discipline. Formal command structures receded, and hierarchies of strength, steadfastness, and courage emerged. In combat, playwrights suggested, all men became equally capable of heroism and equally vulnerable to death, even if they could not be equally capable of command. Heroism and glory were not jingoistic concepts designed to gloss over the chauvinism and injustices of war. On the contrary, the belief in heroism and the pursuit of glory produced a state of mind that made it psychologically possible for soldiers to confront war and its atrocities by moving beyond immediate relationships and actions to identification with a higher social purpose. Through this externalized identification, eighteenth-century Russian playwrights showed how servicemen might overcome emotional ambivalence and commit themselves to the common good.

THE PROMISE OF JUSTICE

Indeed, on the late eighteenth-century stage, the Russian serviceman realized his commitment to the common good by embracing the moral principle of service whether or not he received recognition and reward. Similarly, the concept of the common good also assumed that servicemen, and imperial subjects in general, accepted monarchical justice whether or not they could be assured of concrete satisfaction. Broad-based identification with the common good, without which there could be no effective social or political integration, required that Russian subjects associate the collective and their own personal good with the monarchy and government. For this reason justice permeated the language of civic authority, and judicial practice presented the monarch as the guarantor of earthly right. Concrete display of the monarchy's commitment to justice appeared in the righting of specific wrongs and the granting of mercy. Thus both on stage and in historical reality, subjects from all social groups enjoyed the right to petition officials, initiate lawsuits, and appeal the decisions of courts. Based on formal laws, every imperial subject, no matter how humble, could hope to obtain justice at the hands of higher officials or even at the foot of the throne.[39]

Reliability was an entirely different matter, however, for despite sincere intentions, the realization of justice remained unpredictable, both on stage and in real life. The number of individuals who actually sought or received judicial satisfaction in official courts is not now known. Minor crimes and private relationships often lay beyond the reach of official justice, belonging instead to the customary realms of lordship and community. Especially in the countryside, serious crimes and civil disputes covered by legislation could remain hidden from official eyes, decided instead by seignorial dictate or village practice. The Orthodox Church also played a visible judicial role through the imposition of penance for confessed sins and the mediation of marriage and other family conflicts. Nor can one assume that large numbers of imperial subjects possessed the stamina or resources needed to negotiate the complicated judicial structures leading to St. Petersburg. The road to ultimate monarchical authority was long and arduous. Yet along the way from the village or estate to the town and on to the capital, the high- and low-born effectively used laws to protect or promote their interests. In order to do so, however, they had to overcome widespread arbitrariness and corruption.[40]

On the eighteenth-century Russian stage, justice represented a concrete response to particular grievances or abuses. It could take the form of payment for goods and services, repayment of or release from a loan, compensation for dishonor or injury, recognition of true legal identity, the reestablishment of individual honor, or the return of property. Justice also required protection of the downtrodden and the independence of judges. Swayed by neither money nor power, honest judges decided cases based on law (zakon) and right (pravo). Finally, justice depended on the identification of injustice, several sources of which made vivid stage appearances: 1) the corruption not only of dishonest judges but also of individuals who used the judicial process for personal gain; 2) the incompetence and indifference of judges, which produced erroneous decisions and allowed abuses to go unpunished; 3) distance from the central government and monarch, which made it difficult to control corrupt or negligent subordinates; 4) the assumption by honest people that corruption was inevitable; and 5) the vulnerability of the poor, the naive, and the profligate, who could be manipulated by greedy officials and usurers. Even though playwrights invariably condemned injustice and pinpointed its causes with considerable historical accuracy, the path to reliable justice remained uncertain.

Playwrights confronted the uncertainty by identifying various forms of judicial corruption and also suggesting possible remedies. One comically prosaic but still powerful source of abuse was simple incompetence. Better known for satirizing Frenchified foppishness and the literary pedantry of V. K. Trediakovskii (1703–1769), the comedy *Monsters* (1781) by A. P. Sumarokov also portrays a husband and wife, Gidima and Barmas, who literally come to blows over the question of their daughter's marriage.[41] After Gidima slaps her husband in the face, he retaliates by hauling her into court, demanding that she pay compensation for dishonor and injury. An administrative clerk *(pod'iachii)* who serves as protocolist and secretary for the court testifies against Gidima, even though he did not witness the incident being investigated. In addition, he appoints Barmas's servant to be court guard and messenger. Thus a false witness (the clerk/protocolist/secretary) judges the woman against whom he has testified, and Barmas's servant exercises authority over his master's fate. The court's presiding judges, while not portrayed as corrupt, are grossly ignorant of the law and judicial procedure. One is a retired soldier with no experience of administrative affairs, and the other, who has spent his entire career in chancery work, lacks all legal knowledge. As the latter explains, judges decide cases, whereas secretaries know the relevant laws. After questioning the witnesses, the members of the court, including the clerk and servant, agree that Gidima should be fined, but they fail to reach a final decision because their deliberations degenerate into an argument over the order of rank in voting. In the end, the court appears irrelevant and its members ridiculous; Barmas and Gidima are reconciled because their daughter's true lover (neither parent's initial choice for her future husband) has saved their estate from creditors. Informal reconciliation effectively substitutes for esteemed, technically proficient judges bound by strict legal procedures.

For the predominantly noble elite represented in late eighteenth-century Russian plays, official justice could either threaten or secure such fundamental attributes of social status as property rights, service rank, and legal identity. Sumarokov's *The Guardian* (1765) describes just how uncertain legally defined social status could be.[42] The money-worshiping scoundrel Chuzhekhvat, who as his name indicates, snatches what does not belong to him, has amassed a fortune by assuming guardianship over orphaned nobles. Fortunately for his victims, Chuzhekhvat's greatest swindle also becomes his undoing. Some twenty years earlier, when Chuzhekhvat had become the guardian of twin boys, he entrusted one to Palemon, a sincere friend of the boys' father, and left the other with a wet nurse. Claiming that the second boy had died at age two, Chuzhekhvat stole his inheritance. But because the twins wear matching crosses engraved with their names and date of birth, Chuzhekhvat's servant, Paskvin, is discovered to be the allegedly dead Valeriian. Insecurity of property and social status was a fact of Russian life, and *The Guardian* also shows how such egregious abuses could transpire. Long ago the honest Palemon had reported the situation to a Count Otkupshchikov (Concessionaire), who after receiving

10,000 rubles from Chuzhekhvat, promptly instructed Palemon to ignore the matter or else lose any chance of obtaining a service appointment, even in remote Kamchatka. Spotlighting the extent to which noble fortunes depended on service and the protection of powerful patrons, Palemon complied, but once the count died, and justice returned, he again took action. Now at last, by order of the College of Justice, the Senate, and the monarch, Paskvin/Valeriian receives his rightful title and inheritance, while Chuzhekhvat faces distraint of his estate, arrest, and trial. Suggestively, although local officials had thwarted the law for many years, justice became possible the moment evidence of abuses reached the central government.[43]

The comedy As It Should Be (1773) by M. I. Verevkin (1732–1795) depicts another case of lost social identity that also results from local administrative corruption.[44] The action occurs in an extremely remote town to which the landowner and former military officer Doblestin (Valiant) has returned after being held captive by the Turks for twenty years. When Doblestin petitions the town governor (voevoda) to certify his noble status, he is promptly imprisoned as a vagrant, left to live out his remaining days in chains. Doblestin's noble status, property, and honor are restored only after a virtuous nephew discovers his identity and confronts the indifferent local officials. Not only does young Doblestin demand recognition of his uncle's status, he also insists that the governor and administrative clerk formally apologize before an assembly of noble servicemen. Convinced that conditions have changed in the present reign and the innocent now have access to the throne, he nevertheless accepts the reality of corruption and gives the clerk a purse of money so that his uncle's chains can be removed. Nor does his threat to seek justice in St. Petersburg have any effect on the local officials; repeatedly, they have neglected to send reports to superiors, even though the head of the provincial government (guberniia) is investigating numerous complaints against them.[45] Young Doblestin's belief in the promise of monarchical intervention notwithstanding, As It Should Be gives no indication that well-ordered administration has reached distant areas of the empire. In fact, it seems that even after the Catherinean legislation of 1775–1785 had extended the monarchy's reach to substantially larger numbers of people and remoter parts of the empire, the irregularities described by Verevkin remained.[46]

In the eyes of late eighteenth-century Russian playwrights, neglect of duty and the overt corruption of judges largely explained the persistent abuses. One particularly despicable figure appears in The Judge's Nameday (1781), a comedy by court actor I. Ia. Sokolov (b. 1739).[47] The occasion is the nameday celebration of the judge Khamkin (Lout), whose many crimes come to light in a parade of gift-bearing visitors. The case of Bedniakov (Poor-Man), who is barely able to feed his family, has dragged on for fifteen years, and while Khamkin recognizes the justness of Bedniakov's suit, he continues to collect small gifts from the plaintiff (and even larger gifts from his rich opponent). Only after the judge concludes that Bedniakov has nothing more to give does he agree to decide the suit in return for a share of the settlement.[48] When the trading woman Iadova (Venomous) visits, she and Khamkin plot to swindle a noble spendthrift by providing generous loans that can be called once the man inherits the estate of his rich father. (Indeed, Khamkin already has stolen the estate of another innocent noble debtor.) The final well-wisher is the merchant Korystoliub (Profit-Seeker), who provides substantial handouts in return for instructions about how to fix the upcoming auction for a state contract. On all counts—including the cruel mockery of a servant who fervently believes that honor derives from virtue and intellect rather than from money—Khamkin is a caricature of brazen dishonesty completely devoid of conscience.[49]

In a society dependent on local self-sufficiency and intermittent justice from above, mutual obligation provided a measure of social and economic security that also easily masked corruption and abuse. It is no accident that petitioners and associates bring gifts to Khamkin's home on the occasion of his nameday celebration. Aware that the authorities have received a denunciation accusing him of bribery and violation of the law, Khamkin expects to resolve the matter by entertaining the councilor and secretary in charge of the investigation. When they arrive, however, it is not to celebrate the judge's nameday but to charge him with crimes and seize his estate. Khamkin again tries to employ bribery, but the investigating officials stand firm in defense of justice. The exposed judge realizes that no court will exonerate him and begins to talk of suicide. In *The Judge's Nameday,* a social environment of hospitality and gift giving blurs the boundary between bribery and the exchange of personal favors. Only administrative intervention from above can correct the situation.

The role of bribery and personal favors in Russian judicial process appeared with special force in stories of debt and property disputes. Probably the best known dramatic treatment of eighteenth-century property litigation is the verse comedy *Chicanery* (1798) by V. V. Kapnist (1758–1823).[50] The publication and performance history of the comedy also suggests broad recognition of its historical veracity. After four St. Petersburg performances in August and September of 1798, an imperial decree banned *Chicanery* from the stage. In addition, authorities confiscated the published copies of the play, which had appeared with censorial deletions the same year. Sale of the published copies resumed in 1804, and the comedy returned to the stage in 1805. In revival, *Chicanery* again aroused controversy, as critics and audiences debated the reality of the legal practices represented. In 1814, as Kapnist prepared the text for a new staging, he responded to critics who claimed that *Chicanery* undermined respect for judicial authority. His preface, not published until 1886 and then only in French translation, explains that "already long ago" changes instituted by "the supreme authority" (Alexander I's judicial reform of 1801) eliminated the shortcomings described. The irregular procedures and corrupt officials of *Chicanery* belonged to an earlier era, when all the members of the civil chambers were appointed and judges carried out sentences without Senate review.[51] By depicting "the dishonorable actions of a few judges," which nonetheless hinted at the reality of such behavior, Kapnist "wanted to arouse in the audience a still greater aversion to chicanery." Under cover of comedy, Kapnist's preface removes *Chicanery* from any immediate Russian context while defending the verisimilitude of its content.

Chicanery portrays a possible murderer, the incorrigible Pravolov (Law-Trapper), who bribes officials, falsifies documents, and generally manipulates judicial process in order to deprive innocent landowners of their property. His current fraud targets the principled Priamikov (Straight), a military officer recently returned from service, who resolutely refuses to defend himself with bribery. Taking advantage of a discrepancy in the genealogical record, Pravolov claims that Priamikov is not his father's son but an imposter who acquired his estate illegally.[52] Despite the gravity of the accusation, Priamikov knows his case is just and expects vindication based on the law. Twenty witnesses already have testified on his behalf, and both the district and upper land courts have rejected Pravolov's suit. Now, however, the case has reached the civil chamber, which except for one lowly clerk does not contain a single honest official. In the home of Chairman Krivosudov (Crooked-Judge), where the chamber meets, eating, drinking, gambling, and the celebration of holidays openly intermingle with judicial procedure. Worse still, the judges accept bribes and ignore legitimate cases for years on end.[53] Although a well-wisher urges Priamikov to employ bribery because "nothing is effective against chicanery," the comedy ends with a potential victory for justice. Pravolov is arrested by order of the Senate, and the judges fearfully assume that they too will face criminal charges.

Cases of lost identity and property, such as those catalogued in *Chicanery*, appear repeatedly in archival sources.[54] Kapnist himself had personal experience of extended litigation over a disputed estate. More interesting than the historical parallels, however, is the playwright's understanding of how judicial process worked and why abuses seemed to flourish. At first glance the situation on the ground appears hopeless. Although two lower courts have supported Priamikov, the corrupt civil chamber has the authority to overturn their decisions.[55] Fearing the intervention of higher authorities, Krivosudov and his associates effectively mask their crimes behind legality, evidence, and procedure. If the chamber rules against him, Priamikov will appeal to the governor-general, a man of conscience whose associates believe it is shameful to lie. Indeed, Krivosudov describes another official—the governor—as "a guardian of humanity," and constantly worries that evidence of judicial irregularities will reach the Senate. For this reason, the court secretary must identify laws that can be used to pardon the guilty and then incorporate the misrepresented legal provisions into senseless judicial summaries.

When Priamikov attempts to speak directly with Krivosudov and to reconcile publicly with Pravolov, he is rudely rebuked. The civil chamber does not allow personal petitions or adversarial explanations, and reconciliation belongs to the jurisdiction of the conscience court. No matter that Pravolov privately visits every member of the chamber or that he receives a warm reception at Krivosudov's nameday feast. Priamikov's case, Krivosudov shamelessly claims, will be decided based on the law and written evidence. No matter either that the judges can interpret poorly worded legislation to benefit Pravolov, or that documents can be falsified with ease. The intent of the law may be to foster good, but in the hands of corrupt officials, it is powerless to transform human souls. *Chicanery* ends with the fall of Pravolov and the salvation of Priamikov, but it is not at all clear that the judges will be punished or reformed. Priamikov himself is in love with Krivosudov's daughter and eagerly offers to assist his future father-in-law in any way possible. This incomplete moral resolution reveals a narrow, particularistic definition of justice: the punishment of a single individual and the preservation of what rightfully belongs to another. Pravolov becomes criminally responsible only through the intervention of higher authorities, and once Priamikov's concrete grievance is remedied, his commitment to legality as a broad principle seems to disappear.

On the late eighteenth-century Russian stage, to uphold consistently the principle of legality required the herculean fortitude of uncommonly virtuous individuals. In the verse comedy *Unheard-of Wonder, or The Honest Secretary* (1802), N. R. Sudovshchikov (1770/1–1812) portrays a young civil servant, Secretary Pravdin (Righteous), who repeatedly challenges his corrupt superior.[56] Krivosudov (Crooked-Judge), recently appointed chairman of the court, is determined to use his office for economic gain. He receives only petitioners who offer a payment, and he fleeces the local contractor, who must supply the chairman's household before being paid for goods already delivered to the government. When Pravdin questions the justness of a decision that has put 500 rubles into Krivosudov's pocket, he is told that "for a judge conscience is a completely unnecessary feeling." The proposed marriage of Krivosudov's daughter, Milena (Nice), provides the occasion for the great swindle that the chairman hopes will allow him to retire with a small estate. A landowner intent on stealing the property of another has initiated a sham suit and offered Krivosudov 10,000 rubles to decide in his favor. Because Pravdin and Milena are passionately in love, Krivosudov expects to persuade the secretary to accept the deception by promising him his daughter's hand.[57] But Pravdin refuses in uncompromising terms: he will not deprive an innocent man of his estate, nor will he buy Milena or violate his duty. Better to remain poor and unhappy than to commit such vile deeds. Just when happy resolution seems impossible, Milena's uncle, Priamikov (Straight), arrives for a visit. His intervention, including the gift of a dowry, persuades Krivosudov to allow the young lovers to marry.

In contrast to the marriage question, *Unheard-of Wonder* leaves the judicial question unresolved. Krivosudov's corruption is neither discovered nor addressed; presumably he will continue in his old ways. Pravdin's position is equally ambiguous. He remains subordinate to Krivosudov, who hopes that marriage will render him more pliable, but he also receives praise and encouragement from his deliverer, Priamikov. The instructions of Priamikov—a decorated military officer, wounded veteran of the Turkish wars, and serviceman of thirty years—represent the possibility of moral resolution. Priamikov reminds Pravdin that he is "the monarch's nursling"; therefore, he must follow the straight path, treating the service as his father and mother. While obligated to obey the authorities, he should not bow low to superiors, but devote himself to truth and honor. Silent on issues of institutional reform and criminal prosecution, Priamikov's answer to the problem of judicial authority focuses on the character of the monarch's servitors. His advice to Pravdin implies that every serviceman of any rank enjoys a personal relationship to the ruler, whom he serves as an individual moral being. Such autonomous moral beings, as opposed to political or legal citizens, were the offspring of classical and Enlightenment universalism in Russia. Short of the monarch, it was these moral beings, these "unheard-of wonders," who guaranteed justice.

Another "unheard-of wonder" from the late eighteenth-century Russian stage struggled not against the corruption of judicial officials but against the corruption of the human heart. *Celebration of Justice and Virtue, or The Good Judge* (1794), a drama by the Moscow mason and judicial offical I. V. Lopukhin (1756–1816), portrays the righteous judge Pravdoliubov (Lover-of-Truth), who must sacrifice the happiness of his own son for the sake of truth.[58] In a melodramatic tale with parallels to the binding of Isaac, Pravdoliubov's commitment to justice impels him to reach a decision that threatens the life of his beloved son, Chestnodum (Honest-Thinking). Samoliubov (Self-Love), the father of Chestnodum's beloved Nezhna (Delicate), possesses hereditary lands that are not rightfully his. Pravdoliubov must deprive him of the property, and as a result, Samoliubov refuses to allow Chestnodum and Nezhna to marry. Although Samoliubov admits the justice of the case against him, he also firmly believes that wealth is the only basis for a happy marriage. Chestnodum is poor, and if Samoliubov loses his estate, Nezhna will have no dowry. Chestnodum accepts his fate on the grounds that virtue is dearer than life, yet he is overcome with grief and begins to consider suicide. Nezhna responds similarly; when her father forbids her to see Chestnodum, she falls unconscious and for a time remains close to death. Moved by the plight of his daughter, Samoliubov begins to feel truth and love in his heart. He experiences a moral conversion, embraces a new life of virtue, and decides to bless the marriage.

While lofty paeans to truth and virtue echoed the masonic beliefs of Lopukhin, *Celebration of Justice* also explored the mundane activities of an unusual theatrical phenomenon, an honest court. Honesty, however, was not sufficient to ensure justice. Chief Judge Pravdoliubov is assisted by a secretary who sincerely strives to carry out his superior's instructions, but two other associates prefer frivolous sociability to the fulfillment of duty. In the course of everyday proceedings, it becomes clear that Pravdoliubov constantly must struggle against the indifference of colleagues who regard him as "a fanatic." Moreover, although Pravdoliubov is known to be a man of principle committed to the sanctity of the court, litigants repeatedly attempt to influence judicial process in their own favor. Invariably, he rebuffs their petitions—a prudent judge relies on the law instead of personal appeals—but he is hounded by a steady stream of self-seekers. Pravdoliubov also is deeply troubled by the conflict between his official duties and personal feelings. Even if a criminal clearly is guilty and deserves to be punished, the judge sheds tears before ordering an arrest or harsh sentence.[59]

Pravdoliubov believes the court can follow a "just course" yet fears that erroneous decisions cause the innocent to suffer. Nor will he detain a suspect before judicial investigation establishes evidence of possible guilt. Acts of severity can induce an innocent person to confess, which generates disrespect for the law and further violations. Better to pardon several guilty people than to punish a single innocent suspect, he declares. For all his attention to just process and the careful weighing of evidence, Pravdoliubov still assumes that before a judge can make a decision based on "the laws," he first must "penetrate the essence of the case." Pravdoliubov recognizes that judicial reasoning does not necessarily lead to discovery of the truth. Like honesty, reason is inadequate; a judge also needs to search his conscience. Comparing himself to a warrior who goes to battle for the fatherland, Pravdoliubov notes that "a judge fights for truth, and for the tranquility of society, which vices constantly try to disturb." Justice is more than a technical legal function, more than the law and jurisprudence; justice is a high moral calling. In light of the limited investigative capacity of eighteenth-century Russian government, which made reliable information difficult to obtain, Pravdoliubov's emphasis on abstract justice seems eminently sensible.

• Against the backdrop of transcendent justice guaranteed by a monarch who answered to God and conscience, right implicitly reigned supreme. In practice, however, while concrete grievances could be remedied, judicial procedures remained inefficient and riddled with irregularities. Indeed, judicial corruption so threatened the principle of the common good that illegality could be imagined as justice. In the comedy *Unsuccessful Stubbornness* (1774) by A. A. Volkov (1736–1788), a servant deploys not only deception but also bribery so that two lovers can marry.[60] Corruption serves right when the notary called to compose a marriage contract substitutes the name of the true lover for that of the groom chosen by the tyrannical father. No matter that the notary will receive 300 rubles for the mistake; his duty is "to force people to do justice." Deception was a common literary formula in late eighteenth-century Russian theater, yet it also is clear from archival research that justice represented a malleable concept. Although generations of reformers strove to create a government of laws and procedures, judicial practice consistently distinguished justice from strict adherence to legal prescriptions. To uphold and implement the law, the primary goal of judicial process, did not mean that the law was ultimately sovereign. Whenever existing legal prescriptions failed to ensure justice, the monarch could change or ignore the law at will. Even local officials and military commanders, who lacked legislative authority, could receive pardons for administrative abuses that facilitated the fulfillment of duty.[61] To ensure that justice was done appeared more important than to preserve the rule of law, especially when corruption threatened the common good.[62]

In this context, late eighteenth-century Russian playwrights suggested that in order to compensate for unreliable legal institutions, technically inadequate notions of legality, and the absence of jurisprudence, judicial authority should be grounded in moral virtue and personal responsibility.[63] In the playwrights' eyes, morality superseded law and substituted for its effective implementation. Thus the judge's obligation to uphold justice, like the noble's obligation to serve, became an individual moral obligation consistent with personalized political authority. Although in practice the Russian monarchy consciously employed law to transform society, and imperial subjects from all social statuses turned to courts for protection, eighteenth-century playwrights did not present legality as the cornerstone of judicial authority. Uncertain of what to expect from local judicial institutions, aggrieved parties on the Russian stage looked to the intervention of higher powers to achieve justice, defined as the righting of specific wrongs. Petitioners and litigants based their claims on legal prescriptions, but justice and legality were not equivalent. Justice corresponded to the natural order created by God and preserved on earth by the monarch, whose authority transcended both legality and judicial process. Precisely because the purpose of judicial process was not to transform but to restore a social order that had been violated by corrupt individuals, justice represented an unchanging moral principle to be embraced despite chronic abuses. Justice could not then be equated with civic authority, for only through the actions of virtuous individuals, including the monarch, could the transcendent principle of justice and the unstable reality of judicial practice be reconciled.

LOVE OF THE FATHERLAND

Eighteenth-century Russian playwrights consistently looked to virtuous individuals to uproot the inequity, corruption, and injustice that prevented realization of the common good. Indeed, given the unreliability of legal-administrative institutions, neither state service, which primarily rewarded nobles, nor justice, which theoretically benefited all subjects, provided an adequate basis for broad-based identification with the imperial polity. A source of virtue beyond individual responsibility also was needed, and playwrights found this source in "Russianness," understood as a moral quality

or set of cultural mores rooted in love of the fatherland.[64] Russianness provided an especially effective form of identification with the common good
because, like virtue, it was not socially specific. Nor was Russianness equivalent to the ethnic or political nation: the Russian polity was a vast multi-
ethnic, multiconfessional empire governed by elites from diverse territories
and peoples. Although educated Russians sought to distinguish themselves
as a cultural nation—from the 1750s onward, monarchs, officials, playwrights, and journalists publicly devoted themselves to the development of
original national theater—their concept of Russianness embodied the virtue
of patriotism more than the possession of ethnicity.[65]

Because love of the fatherland was understood as a personal virtue, its
absence indicated moral corruption. Memorable among the caricatures created by late eighteenth-century Russian playwrights were the Frenchified
fop and coquette who spoke a mixture of Russian and French, devoted significant amounts of time and money to dressing in the French fashion, and
behaved with a superficial refinement that revealed disdain for Russian
mores. Preferring Paris to the fatherland, these Russians were objects of explicit criticism that scholars generally interpret as evidence of an emergent
national consciousness.[66] D. I. Fonvizin's Ivanushka, son of the brigadier, is
a prime example. Completed in 1769 and first performed in St. Petersburg
in 1772, *The Brigadier* is a story of ignorance, deception, and romantic intrigue.[67] Ivanushka and the councilor's wife, mother of his intended bride,
are carrying on an illicit love affair; the councilor is pursuing Ivanushka's
mother; and Ivanushka's father hopes to seduce the councilor's wife.
Ivanushka himself is a thoroughly corrupt fop, educated by a French coachman at a private boarding school. He has visited Paris and speaks a mixture
of French, Russian, and russified French that his parents find difficult to understand.[68] Ivanushka regards himself as worldly, enlightened, and intelligent, yet he despises his parents, reads nothing but novels, and does not
love his nation *(natsiia)*. Although born in Russia, he openly proclaims that
his "spirit *(dukh)* belongs to the French crown." Worse still, Ivanushka
plans to run off to Paris with the councilor's wife, another Francophile,
who also reads novels and sees herself as too cultivated for Russian life.
Based on his experience of *le grand monde,* and despite the absence of any
service record, Ivanushka believes he deserves respect. As the comedy ends,
and the romantic entanglements are exposed, Ivanushka learns how little
respect he actually inspires: the young fop is sent home with his boorish father, who all along has been threatening to give him a thrashing.

In the characters of Ivanushka and the councilor's wife, Fonvizin clearly
associates Frenchness with moral corruption and disdain for Russia. Even
so, Russianness is no guarantee of virtue. Characters such as the brigadier
and his wife are unaffected by the fashionable sociability of *le grand monde,*
yet they appear no less ignorant or ridiculous. The brigadier's wife possesses
some knowledge of estate management but is miserly and does not want
her son to serve; her husband is a retired serviceman, though also a wife

beater. The councilor is similarly corrupt: he left service because of intensified prosecutions against bribery and seeks to marry his daughter to Ivanushka in order to gain entrée to the brigadier's wife. When coupled with Fonvizin's *The Minor,* in which Mitrofan's French teacher is an ignorant German coachman and his reading teacher a greedy seminarian, and when viewed in association with the broad theatrical critique of frivolous sociability, the condemnation of Ivanushka's Frenchness seems less an expression of national sentiment than a plea for good education and an exposé of false enlightenment. Frenchness is primarily a symptom of moral failings caused by poor upbringing, which is the fault of ignorant Russian parents.

Russianness could not then ensure virtue, but neither could virtue exist apart from love of the fatherland. Proper education taught loyalty to the fatherland, which like the commitment to serve, consistently appeared as a marker of virtue. In Volkov's *Upbringing* (1774), the enlightened Dobromysl explicitly attributes young Makhalov's Francophilia and refusal to serve as evidence of poor education, which however can be corrected. Young Makhalov speaks excellent French but his Russian is poor; he can describe Paris but is ignorant of Moscow. By contrast, Dobromysl regards knowledge and love of the fatherland as the highest science, the source of Rome's greatness, and the necessary basis for every young Russian's education. In his view, Russia's children should not live in confinement with foreign tutors and then be sent to Paris. To be useful to the state, they must learn about the fatherland by visiting the outlying regions of the empire. Better to be familiar with the mores of Russia's wild Asiatic neighbors and non-Orthodox peoples, Dobromysl insists, than with the latest Parisian fashions. Only after serving and learning about one's own fatherland is it beneficial to visit foreign states; only then is it possible to distinguish the good from the bad. If a young man's first taste of independence from parents, teachers, and study comes from travel abroad, how can he not prefer foreign lands? In Dobromysl's pedagogical prescriptions, the solution to the corruption fostered by French culture is proper education, which teaches love of the fatherland.

Less reassuring in its outcome is *The Russian Parisian* (1787), a verse comedy by D. I. Khvostov (1757–1835).[69] Like young Makhalov, Frankoliub (Francophile) has not benefited from travel to Paris where he passed the time among purveyors of fashion. Instead of improving himself through exposure to foreign mores and laws, the real purpose of travel abroad, he learned to detest the fatherland. In the eyes of his enlightened uncle, Frankoliub can no longer be counted a human being; he has become separated from the fatherland by his "soul." Frankoliub does indeed manifest a lack of humanity: he steals from his father, betrays his Russian fiancée, and hopes to become an expatriate by purchasing a rank and regiment in Paris. He peppers his speech with French words, refuses to smoke Russian tobacco, and agrees to sell stolen goods for a price below market value simply because the purchaser has been to Strasbourg. In the end Frankoliub is exposed but remains unreformed: his French bride, who expected to marry a marquis, leaves him, while he and his similarly corrupted servant decide to sell their wardrobe and go to Paris. In the case of Frankoliub, Khvostov holds out no possibility of rehabilitation through education; his Francophile is a permanently lost son of the fatherland.

Although late eighteenth-century Russian playwrights subjected French mores to relentless criticism, love of the Russian fatherland remained fully consistent with a cosmopolitan European identity based on Christianity and Enlightenment culture. One historian has noted, interestingly, that by the 1730s educated Russians had secured their own identity as westernized and European by imagining Siberia as a foreign Asiatic colony, a "non-European geographical Other."[70] A similar self-definition characterized imagined relations with Muslims and Turks. Claiming to have written a play for the amusement and benefit of "honored society" that, within the bounds of decency, depicts actual Turkish customs and "malicious speech," M. O. Parpura (1763–1828) contrasts Christian/European/Russian civilization to Muslim/Turkish barbarism. *Misfortune from Ochakov, or Celebrating Perfidy in Constantinople* (1789) highlights the despotism of the Porte in sketches of political conflict, intrigue, and corruption among Turkish officials.[71] The sole virtuous individual among the entire cast of Turkish characters meets his death by execution in the last scene of the play. Parpura's harsh judgment is unequivocal: at the Ottoman court there is no place for goodness.

Given Parpura's Enlightenment language, one also might interpret his condemnation of Turkish slavery and despotism as a veiled attack directed against Russian serfdom and autocracy. Such a reading would correspond to the findings of European historians who argue that eighteenth-century images of Turkish despotism contributed significantly to the production of a political analysis indicting the French monarchy.[72] A similar conclusion also might be drawn from the 1785 comedy by P. A. Kropotov (1736/7–1790), *Fomushka—Grandmother's Boy,* in which the worthy Ostromyslov, who has visited the monarchies and republics of England, Holland, Venice, and Portugal, condemns Turkish despotism—defined as a state in which the sovereign can change the laws at any time without first seeking general counsel *(obshchii sovet).*[73] It is important to remember, however, that criticism of serfdom and denunciations of tyranny appeared frequently on the late eighteenth-century Russian stage.[74] If from the perspective of the twenty-first century it appears that Russian monarchs, like Turkish despots, could indeed change the laws without asking general counsel, eighteenth-century Russians nevertheless drew a clear distinction between the tyranny of emperors Peter III or Paul, on the one hand, and the exercise of legitimate monarchy, or absolute power, by Catherine II, on the other. Catherine did consult with her subjects in the Legislative Commission of 1767–1768, and she fostered a pluralistic public culture by actively engaging in literary debates. Only late in her reign, after the French Revolution had led to regicide, did she begin to perceive condemnations of tyranny as potential attacks on her own government. When the Moscow governor-general, Ia. A. Brius, recommended that performances of N. P. Nikolev's tragedy *Sorena and Zamir* be halted, Catherine reportedly replied that the verses critical of monarchy have "nothing to do with your Empress. The author challenges the despotism of tyrants, whereas you call Catherine a mother."[75]

Not only did Russians, in contrast to Turks, embody European civilization, they also possessed good morals and acted out of love for their fellow human beings. The anonymous drama *Good Deeds Win Hearts* (1770) takes place following the defeat of the Muslims in Catherine II's First Turkish War.[76] The Turk Rustan (In-the-Russian-Camp) had been saved by a Turkish-speaking Russian commander, who not only prevented him from committing suicide but also set him free with generous gifts. Out of gratitude, Rustan vowed to redeem a Christian slave every year and never to fight against the Russians. Rustan's father also had been rewarded at the Russian court, but after being sent home by the empress, he praised the Russian enemy, and the Turkish authorities sentenced him to death. Thus, given the gap between Russian goodness and Turkish depravity, Rustan has decided to reject his "bleak fatherland." Russian ships are approaching, and he wants to take his beloved Selima—Rustan also has learned from the Russians to love only one woman—to live in Russia. There he hopes to devote himself to prolonging the Russian empress's reign "for the felicity of the human family." Before embarking on this course, Rustan fulfills his pledge to free Christian slaves, which leads to the unexpected rescue of the officer who previously had helped him. Again one can read the description of the Turkish slave market as an allusion to Russian serfdom. But the drama ends by glorifying Russian goodness: how magnificent Russia's good deeds must be, if at a time of bloody war "they win the hearts of our enemies." Russianness emerges as a moral quality that non-Russians can embrace.

A similar paean to Russian and Catherinean goodness appears in Potemkin's *Zel'mira and Smelon, or the Capture of Izmail* (1795), which also presents Turks in a more positive light. As the characters of Zel'mira and Osman show, non-Russians too can live by lofty principles. Like Smelon, the Turks behave with uncommon courage and virtue, sacrifice personal happiness to duty, and treat the enemy with love. Still, it is Russian goodness that proves decisive. After the Turks are defeated, Zel'mira and Osman are taken prisoner, and Smelon's orders become law. Much to the prisoners' amazement, they receive food, clothing, and medical treatment from their Russian conquerors. (In reality, the capture of Izmail was followed by three days of unbridled pillaging, Suvorov's customary reward to his men in moments of victory.[77]) Smelon attributes this munificence to the sensitivity and heroism of Russian nobles "whose ambition is to defend the Tsarist Throne, love the fatherland, honor, elevate glory." The lovers also are reunited when Smelon asks Zel'mira's father for her hand in marriage. Osman readily agrees, and the Turks declare their desire to live in Russia, where reportedly, "eunuchs are forbidden to lock wives in the seraglio." Heralded by the chorus as a victory comparable to the 1709 defeat of the Swedes at Poltava, the capture of Izmail ends with Russians and Turks dancing in unison to songs of the monarch's glory. Russian superiority appears unassailable yet it remains possible for barbarians to enter the orbit of Russian virtue.

In contrast to nineteenth-century nationalism, eighteenth-century love of the Russian fatherland did not derive from innate ethnic characteristics. In the eighteenth century, the myriad peoples of the empire, including the Russians, were distinguished by name, territory, customs, traditions, language, and religion.[78] Because the absence or possession of specific traits and virtues did not inhere in a particular nation, both the Frenchified fop and the barbaric Turk could assume the mantle of Russianness through education and enlightenment. Theatrical criticism of foreign ways had more to do with moral corruption and superficial Europeanization than with national identity per se. In Gorodchaninov's *Mitrofanushka in Retirement*, Domosedova tries to appear cultivated in the French manner, and in Fonvizin's *The Minor*, Prostakova listens to the advice of the German tutor/coachman but ignores her son's Russian teachers. Both women think of themselves as refined, though in reality they are ignorant and devoid of genuine enlightenment. The problem they represent is not the corruption of Russian goodness by foreign influence but a particularly superficial form of Europeanization—an aping of foreign/French manners, an identification with foreignness that leads to denigration of things Russian, and most importantly, an outwardly refined behavior that masks a lack of inner virtue. Russian plays derived from foreign models, and truly enlightened characters read foreign books and quoted foreign authors. Moreover, even when Russian soldiers and commanders appeared more heroic or generous than their foreign counterparts, playwrights attributed this to moral virtue rather than national essences. In the thinking of late eighteenth-century Russian playwrights, who were themselves members of the educated service classes, patriotism and cosmopolitanism seemed fully compatible. Frenchness did not signify French ethnicity but French high culture, fashions, and manners, which elites across Europe had adopted and which increasingly, especially after 1789, became objects of domestic criticism.[79]

Even before the French Revolution cast a shadow over Enlightenment culture, educated Russians expressed ambivalence and uncertainty about the empire's European identity. Official histories, designed to glorify the state and nation, presented civilized Russia as foreign in origin. Prior to the arrival of the Scandinavian prince Riurik in the mid-ninth century, historians claimed, the "Russians" did not possess "politics, history, religion, and Enlightenment."[80] But late eighteenth-century playwrights also suggested that while Russia was not yet fully European or fully civilized, neither was European enlightenment necessarily indicative of virtue. In the drama *The Slavs* (1786), I. F. Bogdanovich (1743–1803) moves beyond the familiar association of fashionable sociability and foreign culture with moral corruption.[81] Instead, Bogdanovich foreshadows nineteenth-century arguments about the advantages of backwardness and the unique goodness of the Russian people by explicitly connecting Slavic virtue to the absence of philosophy and enlightenment. When the drama opens, the victorious Greek "tsar" and military commander Alexander fears that he will be remembered as a robber. Troubled by his warriors' treatment of the Slavs, and unable to restrain their violent behavior, he speaks openly against war, which is justified only by absolute necessity. More importantly, Alexander censures Greek culture, which he contrasts to the good taste and mores of the Slavs. Wisdom has brought the Greeks unhappiness, filling them with self-love and ruining their morals. According to Alexander, Aristotle's teachings would be more useful among the simple Slavs, who are happy, judicious, and loyal. As the failure of Greek learning shows, philosophy is an unreliable guide to virtue, and Slavic natural reason *(razum)* is superior to enlightenment.

At first glance, *The Slavs* seems to espouse a Rousseauian critique of civilization; however, the dialogue leads to a quite different conclusion. When Alexander asks the Slavic emissary how it is that his people successfully control their military impulses, he is told that Slavic upbringing distinguishes moral education from philosophical wisdom and that the Slavs have few books to teach them about virtue. Rather than write about virtue, they preserve it in human actions. Nor are writers a special group in Slavic society: all Slavs are writers, and they write for the sole purpose of nurturing the goodness of hearts and minds. But when pressed to explain how such good rules became established among the Slavs, the emissary looks to civilization, specifically the sacrifices and glorious achievements of Catherine II. The drama's earlier association of happiness with simplicity and of superior reason with lack of enlightenment leads to praise for the empress, whose policies instill good morals. Thus neither natural reason nor sophisticated learning is sufficient to guarantee virtue, and although backwardness, in the sense of a limited literary heritage, carries advantages, it is the role of monarchy to establish good rules that can provide the basis for moral education. Under Catherinean government the Slavs find happiness and virtue. By implication, civilization does not stand condemned. Just as the Frenchified fop symbolizes the distinction between true and false enlightenment, Catherinean government represents the distinction between good and bad civilization.

That the monarchy embodied the fatherland and guaranteed the people's happiness is again evident from M. M. Kheraskov's tragedy *Moscow Liberated* (1798).[82] Based on the events of the Time of Troubles (1598–1613), when the end of the first Russian dynasty unleashed a period of social rebellion, civil war, and foreign occupation, *Moscow Liberated* describes the Russian military campaign of 1612, which expelled the Polish ruler from Moscow and led to the election of Mikhail Romanov as tsar.[83] Whether or not the historical Muscovites viewed their situation in terms of national liberation, in Kheraskov's rendition they exemplify loyalty to the fatherland, understood as the totality of the people *(narod)*, supreme power *(derzhava)*, tsardom *(tsarstvo)*, state, throne, crown, faith, land, and Moscow. Faced with social crisis and foreign occupation, every good Russian is prepared to sacrifice life, property, and personal glory to defend the fatherland. All Russians, including boyars, churchmen, merchants, and the people, act to promote the common good, defined not as peace but as liberation from foreign rule and the return of the tsar to his throne in Moscow.

In *Moscow Liberated,* the Russian leaders of 1612 recognize that the fatherland and much-needed authority have been lost because of dissension among the boyars. Lacking a tsar, the people are without a head, and a people without a head is "a body without a soul." Whatever their past differences, as well as present suspicions about individual motives, the boyars agree that supreme power cannot exist without a tsar, and that all the people must be under the authority of the Russian crown. Revealingly, however, in the absence of a tsar, the fatherland remains, or as Pozharskii explains, the tsar is in his heart even if there is no tsar who rules. Tsar and fatherland are distinct yet inseparable. At a time when memories of palace coups and popular rebellion remained vivid, and when French armies were beginning to spread revolution across Europe, *Moscow Liberated* conveyed a message about the relationship between tsar, fatherland, and people that spoke to contemporary historical conditions: internal strife threatened the existence of the fatherland, and the Russian people needed a monarch to rule over them. By unifying to save the fatherland, the boyars defined the common good as the collective existence of the Russian people. Through the concept of the common good, the Russian political nation could be glimpsed. More importantly, to equate the common good with the people suggested, in the eighteenth-century context, a broad-based social identification, for the time being free of egalitarian implications, that did not depend on the unstable realities of state service and imperial justice.

*I*n the cosmopolitan intellectual environment of late eighteenth-century Russian theater, patriotic cultural identification produced an elusive concept of Russianness best defined as love of the fatherland. Russianness represented moral virtue in contrast to foreignness, which exemplified lack of enlightenment or rejection of a Russian way of life. The corruption of the Frenchified fop and coquette resulted from neither Frenchness nor Russianness but from inadequate education that failed to instill the virtue of patriotism. Nor was the barbarism of the Turk or Muslim ethnically determined. Barbarians who embraced the superior Russian civilization assumed the mantle of Christian and European enlightenment. For the corrupt fop, the return to Russianness brought moral regeneration, and for the infidel, the acquisition of Russianness brought enlightened civilization. Adding to the ambiguity of Russian identity was the distinction between true and false enlightenment, which meant that civilization in and of itself could not guarantee goodness. Thus the Greek "tsar" distinguished the morally inferior philosophy of his people from the superior natural reason of the seemingly backward Slavs. Just as Rousseau understood human imagination to be both a source of corruption and a tool of moral transformation, the virtuous Slavs lacked philosophical sophistication but possessed good rules of behavior given to them by a wise empress.[84] Moral virtue assumed diverse forms, and it was the possession of this *acquired* quality that lay at the core of Russian identity. Russianness was amorphous, fluid, and accessible to non-Russians. Its multiple meanings provided an unstable foundation for ethnicity but an effective principle for integration of the imperial polity. At no time in its long history did the Russian monarchy fully embrace nationalism as the basis for social and political integration. Instead, it subordinated all forms of nationalism to the categories of dynasty and empire.[85] When understood as the virtue of patriotism or love of the fatherland, as on the late eighteenth-century stage, Russianness became an inclusive concept that by encompassing the monarch and all the people, allowed the individual to be reconciled with civic society and integrated into the common good.

6

MORAL MONARCHY

• After the suppression of three military rebellions, the confinement of the regent Sophia to a convent, and the death of
co-ruler Ivan V, the Russian throne was at last fully secured by
Peter I in 1698. Following his death, in the years 1725 to
1796, seven different individuals, including four women, wore
the Russian crown. The great Catherine II, herself a usurper,
died of natural causes in 1796, but her son Paul, like his father
before him, fell victim to a murderous overthrow in 1801.
Throughout the eighteenth century, the vulnerability of the
supreme sovereign power was visible to all. Yet Russian nobles
remained unable, or perhaps unwilling, to assert proprietary
claims to authority beyond the family estate—claims that
could be historically and politically constituted in the local
laws, offices, and institutions of an identifiable territory.[1]
Lacking a politics grounded in constituted bodies, Russian
elites viewed civic authority in terms of personal relationships. Although frequently condemned by historians as a
source of arbitrariness and abuse, the reliance on personal authority to bring order to government imparted ideological
continuity to Russian monarchy in an era of chronic politcial
uncertainty. Personal authority allowed the sanctity of the office of sovereign to survive the demise of the living sovereign,
so that the authority of monarchy could be preserved even
when confronted with the misdeeds of individual monarchs
and officials.

As the sovereign, the Russian monarch was thought to exercise God-given and hence inviolable authority, but as a human
being, he or she behaved rightly or wrongly and was judged ac-
cordingly. The language employed by Princess E. R. Dashkova to
justify the assassinations of two legitimate monarchs illustrates

the extent to which Russia's educated classes understood monarchy in personal moral terms. In her political memoirs, Dashkova noted that Peter III (ruled 1761–1762) "smoothed out for us the difficulties in the way of his own overthrow," for although he was not evil, "his incompetence and lack of education, as well as inclination and natural bent, all combined to make of him a good Prussian corporal and not the Sovereign of a great Empire." If Peter III's "total incapacity to govern" justified removal, the elimination of his son Paul (ruled 1796–1801) had more sinister origins. "Exile and detention left few families without a victim." "Bewilderment and fear gave rise to apathy and stupor, fatal to the most important of all virtues—love of one's country." Banished to a family estate in 1796, Dashkova could count herself a victim of Paul's "despotic tyranny." In recording his demise, she wrote that "Providence allowed the Emperor's existence to be brought to a close, and with it all the public and private disasters."[2] Notwithstanding the acknowledgment of a role for divine providence, Dashkova judged monarchs on the basis of strictly secular criteria: the performance and moral character of the individual.

Like Dashkova, the vast majority of educated Russians believed (or abided by the belief) that monarchy, embodied in the reigning monarch, represented God's will on earth and that the natural (sociopolitical) order expressed divine rationality. Many also continued to revere the sovereign as divinely anointed. At the same time, however, beginning in the reign of Peter I, a fully secular language appeared to justify political power. Throughout the eighteenth century, classical imagery dominated court ceremonial, and the very creation of the Russian Empire, including the adoption of the title "emperor," aimed to invoke Russia's great-power status in Europe through association with imperial Rome.[3] Without abandoning the idea of divinely sanctioned monarchical authority, Russian monarchy became secularized or, more accurately, resanctified in a secular classical idiom.[4] In this context, Peter I's abolition of hereditary succession at once enhanced the sanctity of the reigning monarch and established fitness to rule as the primary basis for earthly power. Monarchical authority remained in principle infallible and absolute, so that the monarch, as the guardian of monarchical authority, represented the sole source of law and the final guarantor of earthly justice. But the monarch also became an individual moral being, who like the gods and goddesses of classical antiquity combined power, glory, and wisdom with everyday human foibles.

THE TYRANNY OF DESIRE

To reconcile the assumption of divinely sanctioned authority with the reality of human behavior, playwrights articulated a moral conception of rulership capable of bridging the gap between the transcendent principle of monarchy and the everyday actions of reigning monarchs. The good monarch of the late eighteenth-century Russian stage displayed not only the uncommon virtue and courage needed to justify heroic stature but also the personal shortcomings and emotions characteristic of any human being. Whether playwrights employed the lofty poetics of neoclassical tragedy, the satirical techniques of comedy, or the sentimentalist formulas of drama, they portrayed the monarch in terms that encouraged identification with his or her human vulnerabilities. Chief among these vulnerabilities was individual desire. When monarchs neglected duty and succumbed to desire, they also undermined authority by giving just cause for rebellion. Among the monarch's subjects, individual desire could be so strong that it produced challenges to rightful authority. In either scenario, playwrights posited a painful opposition between duty and desire that at once exemplified the humanity of rulers and paralleled the individual subject's relationship to the patriarchal household, civic society, and the common good. By condemning uncontrollable desire and assigning primacy to duty, playwrights posited a moral conception of monarchy based on reciprocal obligations. Precisely because individual desire so easily led to tyranny, which in turn violated reciprocity, heroes and heroines were expected not only to control desire but also to resist tyranny.

Throughout the eighteenth century, monarchs and grandees on the Russian stage struggled to preserve authority by subordinating personal happiness to duty. In A. P. Sumarokov's tragedy *Khorev*, first published in 1747 and performed at the St. Petersburg court in 1750, the lovers Khorev and Osnel'da are destroyed by the enmity between their peoples.[5] Osnel'da is a prisoner of the Russian prince who drove her father from Kiev, and she has fallen in love with the prince's brother and heir, Khorev. When her father returns to reclaim the throne, she seeks permission to marry, but he forbids her love for Khorev. Mindful of filial duty and of the wrongs inflicted on the Kievans, Osnel'da submits to parental authority and prepares to leave. Khorev is similarly loyal to his brother and steadfast in his commitment to honor; he fights heroically against Osnel'da's father, leading the Russians to victory. In the meantime, however, the Russian prince becomes convinced that Osnel'da is plotting to seize the throne and orders her to drink poison. The heroine welcomes the opportunity to escape unhappiness, as does Khorev, who commits suicide once he learns of her death. The virtuous lovers, both of whom obeyed the call of duty, die because of forbidden desire. Freedom appears in death, and desire leads to destruction. Yet Sumarokov also hints at the possibility of earthly happiness: the tragedy ends with reconciliation between Osnel'da's father and the Russians. Although the reconciliation comes too late to save the lovers, symbolically their love prevails.

Sumarokov's hesitant endorsement of personal happiness in *Khorev* turns to unequivocal affirmation in a most unlikely place: his reworking of the tragedy *Hamlet* (1748), in which Claudius, unreformed by education, plans to murder Gertrude and Hamlet and then force Ophelia into marriage.[6] For the virtuous Ophelia, who prefers death to unhappy marriage and separation from her beloved Hamlet, the struggle between authority and individual desire takes the form of disobedience to an evil father. Polonius not only bears responsibility for the former king's murder, he also is implicated in the plot against Gertrude and Hamlet. Hamlet's dilemma likewise results from the parent-child relationship: duty requires him to avenge his father's death—to forget love and act heroically—yet he is unable to overcome his desire for Ophelia. Resolution occurs when Polonius's hirelings attempt to carry out the murder plot, and Hamlet kills Claudius in the tumult. Polonius, after being spared by Hamlet at the behest of Ophelia, then commits suicide, and the repentant Gertrude prepares to become a nun. Having fulfilled the commandment to love and honor her father, Ophelia is freed by his death. God's punishment of Claudius and Polonius allows the lovers to unite without abandoning filial duty. Through providential intervention and adherence to moral obligation, personal happiness is brought into harmony with rightful order.

Respect for authority and the satisfaction of individual desire again clash in Sumarokov's 1768 tragedies *Semira* and *Vysheslav*.[7] Semira, the sister of Oskol'd (Askold) and Dir, has fallen in love with Rostislav, whose father, Oleg, had removed her father from the Kievan throne. Committed to die or be free, Oskol'd prepares to take military action against the usurpers, and Semira decides to leave her lover out of duty to the fatherland. Rightful resolution is achieved after the failure of the rebellion prompts Oskol'd to stab himself, reconcile with Oleg—fate has decided between us, he declares— and bless the marriage of Semira to Rostislav. Despite much struggle and pain, Semira's willingness to sacrifice personal happiness to duty allows happiness to prevail. Semira is not unique among the heroes and heroines of the late eighteenth-century Russian stage. Grand Prince Vysheslav of Novgorod also is prepared to give up personal happiness for duty and honor. Vysheslav has fallen in love with Zenida, princess of Iskorest, after promising her to the Iskorest prince Liubochest (Lover-Of-Honor), who had saved his life in battle.[8] Tormented by his passion, Vysheslav aspires to be a law-giver and father to his people, while Zenida, even after Liubochest leads an attack against Vysheslav, believes she must keep her pledge of marriage. Rightful resolution occurs after Vysheslav concedes and prepares to end his life, impelling Liubochest to give up his right to Zenida. Throughout the tragedy, Vysheslav and Zenida place duty above desire, yet their love also receives validation. In the "divinely rational utopia" of Sumarokov's neoclassical tragedies, authority and individual desire can be harmonized.[9]

Eighteenth-century Russian playwrights assigned a high value to personal happiness, but only within the bounds set by duty. In the tragedy *Deidamia* (1775) by V. K. Trediakovskii (1703–1769), the heroine is called upon to perform the supreme duty of giving her life to the fatherland.[10] Trediakovskii's play centers on a threat to Scyros arising from the anger of

the goddess Diana.[11] Because Lycomedes has dedicated his daughter Deidamia to the goddess, Deidama is required to remain a virgin. But Deidamia
has fallen in love with Achilles and as a result has unwittingly violated her
father's oath. In the tradition of classical tragedy, the goddess demands that
Deidamia be sacrificed, even though at the time of the transgression she was
ignorant of her obligation. Lycomedes accepts the necessity of submitting to
the fates, Achilles blames the priests and priestesses for the unhappy situation (a reference to Trediakovskii's clerical origins), and Deidamia pleads for
mercy but then courageously embraces death to save the fatherland. Dramatic resolution occurs, when Diana, like the god of Abraham, is appeased
by Lycomedes's zeal and spares Deidamia. Once again adherence to duty restores rightful order, which then makes possible human happiness.

Deidamia's willingness to die ensured not only her own happiness but
also that of her country. In the dramatic fragment *Codrus* (1799) by V. I.
Kireevskii (1773–1812), the king of Athens likewise places duty to his people above all other human relationships.[12] According to legend, the Dorians
who invaded Attica in the eleventh century B.C. learned from the Delphic
oracle that victory would be theirs if Codrus lived. Informed of the
prophecy, Codrus went out dressed as a woodcutter and started a quarrel
with the Dorian warriors; his resultant death gave victory to the
Athenians.[13] Kireevskii follows the Greek storyline in portraying a Codrus
eager to give his life for the fatherland: to invite death by challenging the
Dorian warriors is an opportunity he has long awaited. Codrus's wife is similarly committed to duty. She never wavers in support of her husband's decision, and although at one point she contemplates suicide, hers is a voice
of moral authority. After Codrus saves Athens, she explains the lesson of
his death to their children: "Learn from father to sacrifice life for the fatherland—and from mother, how to endure life for the children." For Codrus
there is no heart-wrenching struggle between duty and the natural feelings
of a husband and father. To die for the fatherland is the highest duty and
greatest happiness.

Precisely because rulers and grandees carried responsibility for entire
peoples and countries, their struggle to control desire touched on questions
far greater than personal happiness. In A. P. Sumarokov's tragedy *Artistona*
(1751), romantic feelings not only threaten the fulfillment of duty but also
become a source of tyranny and outright evil.[14] Darius has established himself on the Persian throne by promising to marry Fedima, daughter of Otan,
though in reality he intends to marry Artistona, who loves Fedima's brother,
Orkant. Virtue and duty compel Artistona to obey Darius, whereas jealousy
and revenge motivate Fedima and Otan. Orkant's posture is also problematic: he does not seek revenge but is prepared to challenge the tsar militarily.
Moral resolution becomes possible because Darius realizes that his love for
Artistona is making him a tyrant. Subsequently, upon returning victorious
from civil war, Darius forgives the rebels and gives Artistona to her beloved.
His ability to overcome individual desire transforms him into a father-tsar

loved by his subjects. Darius joins the ranks of those who achieve greatness not simply by ruling over peoples, but by being worthy to rule.

V. I. Maikov's queen Agriopa also deserves to rule, though she must employ practical cunning to preserve her power.[15] Both Agriopa's betrothed, the Greek prince Telephus, and the grandee Azor are plotting to seize the Mysian throne. Telephus has conquered Agriopa's people, and a marriage has been arranged, but he plans to ascend the throne and marry Azor's daughter. (The vile Azor is no less deceptive and has arranged to have Telephus called away to war so that he himself can take power.) Telephus acknowledges that he has violated duty, love, and honor; in conversation with a friend, he even seems repentant, noting that passion has defeated reason and expressing the fear that he has become a tyrant. But passion continues to drive Telephus, and when he tries to seize power, Agriopa's warriors meet the challenge. Long aware of the plots against her, Agriopa has feigned ignorance while secretly taking measures to defend her throne. Still, even after defeating Telephus, she remains tormented by unrequited love and must overcome suicidal impulses in order to devote herself to the welfare of her subjects. Unlike her enemies, who ended their shameful lives in the pursuit of base desire, Agriopa masters desire and endures life for the sake of others.

The experience of Agriopa suggests, and that of other heroines confirms, that men and women alike shared a common human vulnerability to desire. In V. A. Levshin's tragedy *Trajan and Lida* (1780), desire mercilessly destroys all whom it touches.[16] The Roman emperor Pertinax is in love with Lida, who has pledged herself to the deceitful Trajan. Lida's father wants to honor the tsar's marriage proposal, but she threatens to commit suicide if forced to marry against her will. Both Lida and Pertinax are tormented by love. Although Lida is under constant pressure from her father, who sincerely believes that subjects find happiness by fulfilling the tsar's wishes, she is unable to control her passion and constantly wavers between obedience, defiance, and suicide. Pertinax likewise contemplates suicide because he cannot live without Lida, whose rejection also threatens his authority. The love of Pertinax is genuine, and he tries to resist the impulse to use force or to punish unjustly, but in the end reason fails, and he orders the murder of Trajan. Lida kills herself after learning of Trajan's death, and Pertinax follows suit after admitting his guilt and entrusting his dominion to Lida's father. Lida's father alone retains a firm understanding of duty, whereas Lida and Pertinax both become victims of their own uncontrollable desire.[17]

Desire again leads to female defiance of parental and political authority in N. P. Nikolev's tragedy *Pal'mira* (1786), in which alternative endings also highlight the ambiguous meaning of duty.[18] Prince Omar, heir to the throne of Sidon, lives in disguise at the court of Tyre in order to be near his beloved Pal'mira. At the same time, Pal'mira's father, Tsar Iroksers, has been trying unsuccessfully to wed his son to the daughter of Sidon's ruler. Because Omar believes that forced marriage violates reason, he regards neither his love for Pal'mira nor the rejected marriage proposal as insults to Tyre. Tragically, Pal'mira's father thinks otherwise, and she agrees that duty is foremost. If Iroksers forbids her love, she must either forget Omar or die. Pal'mira's obedience holds firm until her brother's death in a killing rampage leads Iroksers to condemn Omar to burn at the stake. Torn between nature and love—nature representing the natural bond between parent and child—Pal'mira helps her beloved to escape, even though she knows he will oppose her father. Iroksers's reaction is swift and merciless, for his daughter has violated duty and honor. Guilty before him, the gods, and the people, she must die by fire. Pal'mira is set to go the way of other classical heroines and perish because of her own fateful action.

Pal'mira's story continues, however, and provokes discussion about whether wrongful actions caused by romantic desire can be forgiven. Iroksers's emissary urges forgiveness because all people suffer from the conflict between feeling and thinking. Love, the emissary argues, is humanity's only sweetness. Without love, people would be "dead in the world," and "the gods would not be gods but tyrants." Iroksers's refusal to forgive Pal'mira is a form of tyranny, and as a result, her disobedience, like that of Lida, lays bare the complicated problem of how to reconcile individual aspirations with constituted authority. Nikolev's equivocal response appears in alternative endings to the tragedy. In the first and more traditionally tragic ending, Omar attacks the city, and at the moment he returns victorious, Iroksers kills Pal'mira and then commits suicide. Iroksers dies because of his tyranny, Pal'mira because of her desire and disobedience. In the second and more typically eighteenth-century ending, Iroksers stabs himself, and Omar's warriors arrive in time to save Pal'mira from the fire. But Pal'mira, believing she is responsible for the destruction of her father and fatherland, rejects Omar. Rightful resolution is achieved only because the dying Iroksers assumes moral responsibility for the tragic events. Blaming his behavior on prideful revenge, he calls himself a tyrant, and names Pal'mira his heir. Iroksers then reconciles with Omar and declares as his last wish that Omar and Pal'mira marry. Ironically, although Pal'mira is freed from the guilt of disobedience caused by desire, the problem of desire remains. Unlike tragic heroes and heroines who submit to necessity by accepting unhappiness or death, Pal'mira satisfies desire by defying authority. But she by no means feels secure in her happiness. As the tragedy closes, Pal'mira exclaims in despair, "Oh calamitous love!"

Against the causal backdrop of rightful order, either pagan or Christian, but in any event divinely ordained, Russian playwrights addressed the difficult question of how to reconcile individual desire with the inevitable subjugation to constituted authority. In the story of Pal'mira, desire produces an unfortunate yet unavoidable challenge to legitimate authority. In A. P. Sumarokov's historical tragedies—*Iaropolk and Dimiza* (1768), *Dmitrii the Pretender* (1771), and *Mstislav* (1774)—desire gives rise to tyranny and abuse of power that not only violate moral monarchy but also call forth harmful rebellion. In *Iaropolk and Dimiza*, the Russian prince Vladisan believes his son must marry a princess in order to strengthen the throne, but Iaropolk is in love with the boyar's daughter Dimiza.[19] Unable to weaken the love between Iaropolk and Dimiza, Vladisan becomes a tyrant. Not only does he threaten the lives of the lovers, he also unjustly imprisons a favorite who reminds him that the people want mercy. His intransigence—Vladisan insists that a ruler who cannot control his passion is a prisoner—and cruelty toward Dimiza—he tries to force her to marry another—induce Iaropolk to rebel. The tragedy ends in armed confrontation followed by reconciliation between father and son. Vladisan realizes that he, not Iaropolk, is the prisoner of passion. "Although I am tsar," he proclaims, "I am also human."

Resistance to tyranny is again a central theme in Sumarokov's popular tragedy *Dmitrii the Pretender*.[20] Anticipated by the false Smerdis of A. A. Rzhevskii (1737–1804), the false Dmitrii is among the most despicable of late eighteenth-century stage tyrants.[21] Like the Persian tsar Smerdis, who is overthrown and then assassinated in a popular uprising, Dmitrii is a man driven solely by corrupt passion. Spiritually tormented, he punishes the innocent, wants Poles and Catholics to rule Moscow, and accepts no limits on the satisfaction of his base desires. As a tyrant, Dmitrii, like Smerdis, believes the people live for him, not he for the people. In reality, however, his subjects refuse to regard him as a divine being and feign loyalty only in order to survive. When a tsar is evil, Shuiskii explains, his subjects cannot be honest.[22] Even though Russia needs a single tsar, tsarist power should not be a burden to the people. Nor can rulers take away the freedom granted to human beings by God. Indeed, nature acts equally in all people, which explains why the clergy, nobility, and people eventually rebel against Dmitrii. Precisely because the false tsar has set himself up in opposition to the people, his demise through rebellion and suicide is consistent with rightful order. His tyranny, and the tyranny broadly condemned in Russian Enlightenment theater, is not the systemic despotism depicted by Montesquieu or the political libel of pre-revolutionary France. The tyranny depicted in *Dmitrii the Pretender* emanates from the whims of a single individual and thus can be overcome without structural change.[23]

In late eighteenth-century Russia, especially after the assassination of Peter III in 1762, bloody rebellion against tyranny appeared both historically sanctioned and immediately present. Perhaps it was the all too visible gap between historical reality and divine rationality that encouraged Sumarokov also to imagine, as he did in the tragedy *Mstislav*, a nonviolent solution to tyranny.[24] After the historical Mstislav of Tmutorokan (d. 1036) defeated Iaroslav of Kiev (d. 1054) in the Battle of Listven (1024), the brothers, both sons of Vladimir, made peace by dividing the territories along the Dnieper.[25] Sumarokov's Mstislav and Iaroslav likewise reach agreement, but only after desire has degenerated into tyranny. Mstislav and his first boyar both love Olga, who, in accordance with Vladimir's orders, has been chosen to marry Iaroslav. The malicious boyar urges Mstislav not only to claim

Olga but also to unite the lands apportioned among Vladimir's sons.[26] Persuaded by the boyar's evil tongue, Mstislav imprisons Iaroslav, who has come to claim his bride. Mstislav's conscience is troubled, however, for he associates heroism with magnanimity and understands that honor requires submission to fate. Honor, he declares, is the only source of glory. When Olga threatens suicide if she cannot marry Iaroslav, Mstislav initially concedes, believing that the country's happiness depends on harmony. But then desire again gets the better of him; he wavers and condemns Iaroslav to death for fomenting rebellion. Eventually it comes to light that the boyar instigated the unrest, and the stage is set for fraternal reconciliation. Throughout the tragedy Mstislav professes his intention to uphold justice, yet his underlying goodness does not prevent the lapse into tyranny. Although he repents before causing irreparable harm, his behavior reveals how fallible even a good tsar can be. Rulers cannot see their own vices, Mstislav complains, for they are surrounded by flatterers and too easily swayed by evildoers.

That good tsars, possessed by desire, could so easily become tyrants underscored the instability of rightful authority. Equally unreliable in the struggle against tyranny was the call of duty. If desire caused tyranny, duty helped maintain it, which raised questions about the assumed inferiority of desire. In the tragedy *Borislav* (1774), M. M. Kheraskov draws attention to the truth of feeling and turns on its head the expected opposition between duty and desire.[27] Duty becomes the weapon of the evil tyrant, desire that of the virtuous hero and heroine. The Bohemian princess Flaviia and the Varangian prince Premest, supported by the boyars, wish to marry, but the tormented Tsar Borislav, father of Flaviia, despises any human bond that does not promote his power. Invoking the language of duty to mask tyranny and destroy Premest, he insists that the lovers forget their feelings and devote themselves to the people. His demands go beyond the reasonable fulfillment of duty and thus lead Flaviia to question the subordination of desire to authority. Why, she asks, did nature give us feelings if we have no freedom to follow them? Borislav is a true tyrant who knows no virtue and persecutes his people; consequently, Flaviia's challenge is not an unequivocal elevation of feeling over duty. Like Sumarokov, Kheraskov strives to reconcile duty and desire rather than subordinate one to the other. The tragedy appears at an end when armed confrontation leads to the anointment of Premest by the priests and people. But then Premest forgives Borislav, saving him from the boyars, and Borislav forgives the rebels, declaring Premest tsar. Violence is superseded by a peaceful circular action as Borislav leaves the throne and Premest ascends it. The scepter, a repentant Borislav explains, goes to him who is like the gods. Alongside rebellion, the expected method for removing a tyrant, Kheraskov imagines the possibility of peaceful abdication in favor of a superior individual.

A repentant tyrant is again the vehicle for rightful resolution in the tragedy *Iaropolk and Oleg* (1798) by V. A. Ozerov (1769–1816).[28] Iaropolk wants to marry his brother Oleg's bride, the Bulgarian princess Predslava (historical Rogneda), and the servitor Svenal'd (historical Sveneld) is eager to manipulate the monarch's passion for purposes of revenge. Svenal'd had sent his son to serve Oleg, the son committed a crime deemed harmful to the people, and instead of recognizing the father's services, Oleg strictly followed the law and put the son to death. To Oleg's mind, the monarch must forget friendship and family relations when dispensing justice. Consequently, when Oleg arrives in Kiev to claim his bride, he has no inkling of the betrayal that awaits him. The vengeful Svenal'd convinces Iaropolk that Oleg is an enemy intent on taking his throne. Iaropolk's reason succumbs to passion, and he gives Svenal'd permission to murder Oleg. Then in a troubled sleep, he realizes his mistake and repents. By that time the people have gathered to defend Oleg, whose escape from death also has led to the suicide of Svenal'd. Iaropolk learns that Svenal'd has failed to kill Oleg and thanks the gods for preventing the evil act; however, his weakness and susceptibility to false friends have already revealed the fragility of goodness.

The fragility of goodness and the power of desire—such were the forces arrayed against rightful authority. Indeed, if it can be said that eighteenth-century Russian playwrights attributed human calamity to a single source of evil, that source was desire—the desire of love, the desire for power, the desire for revenge, and the desire caused by envy. Time and again, in the stories of tragic heroes and heroines, the good order supposedly ensured by monarchy appeared to crumble. Desire defeated justice and created tyranny, it led children and subjects to rebel, and it caused unbearable suffering. But desire also could represent virtue and honorable feelings. If sometimes, as in the case of Codrus, sacred duty clearly lay outside personal happiness, more often than not happiness, even when doomed by political necessity, also received legitimation. In the hearts of virtuous heroes and heroines, the natural right of love became a cry for individual freedom in the face of tyranny and oppression. Throughout the eighteenth century, Russian playwrights stubbornly insisted that individual desire could be reconciled with constituted authority, but they could not resolve the tragic opposition unequivocally. In order to ensure rightful order, monarchs and grandees needed to maintain the highest possible standards of behavior, for without their adherence to duty the wrongs of society could not be righted. Monarchs and grandees were not, however, uniformly worthy; some were patently unworthy, and even the worthy could succumb in tragic fashion to their own individual desire.

THE BURDEN OF RULE

The good monarchs of the eighteenth-century Russian stage were thought to possess extraordinary personal qualities that justified in turn the authority they wielded over "the people." But the heroism and moral worth of individual rulers could not provide a stable foundation upon which to build legitimate monarchical authority. If precisely because of their human qualities even good monarchs lapsed into tyranny, then monarchs in general certainly could not be counted upon to behave with exceptional virtue. By portraying the unheroic behavior of humanly flawed monarchs, playwrights challenged the assumption that monarchical authority derived from superior personal qualities. Given that the humanity of the monarch, symbolized by individual desire, contradicted the heroism required to preserve honor and duty, and given that the monarch's human weaknesses revealed a lack of moral superiority, how could constituted authority be justified? While upholding the ideal of the virtuous monarch, playwrights also acknowledged that bad rulers gained power and good rulers committed injustices. Evil tyrants surely deserved to be overthrown, but good rulers who faltered deserved the understanding and loyalty of their subjects. Their errors, playwrights suggested, did not result from tyrannical impulses but from the extraordinary burden of rule. Even the most well-intentioned monarch did not have "God's eyes" and could not be aware of all the wrongs carried out in his name. The human failings of monarchs not only created situations in which rebellion could be justified but also encouraged sympathy so that tyrannical behavior could be forgiven.

Eighteenth-century stage heroes and heroines adapted from Russian history encouraged sympathy for monarchs by concretizing their humanity and the burden they carried. Labeled a tragedy and described as an imitation of Voltaire's *Mérope* (1743), *Velesana* (1778) by F. Ia. Kozel'skii (1734–after 1799) is less concerned with lofty principle than historical reality.[29] The historical Velesana was Princess Olga, wife of Igor (d. 945) and mother of Sviatoslav. After Igor died suppressing a Derevlian rebellion, Olga ruled in Kiev, brought the Derevlians under control, and in the mid-950s received baptism from the emperor in Constantinople. According to the *Primary Chronicle*, during Sviatoslav's minority the Derevlian prince proposed marriage to Olga, who played along in order to avenge Igor's death. The deception succeeded, and prior to the promised marriage, Olga's warriors destroyed the Derevlians at a funeral feast held in memory of Igor.[30] In Kozel'skii's dramatization of the chronicle account, Velesana likewise agrees to marry the Derevlian prince, called Izrad, in order to avenge Igor's death and preserve the throne for Sviatoslav. Knowing that Izrad intends to eliminate both her and Sviatoslav once he obtains the crown, she secretly plans to attack the Derevlians at the funeral feast and even feigns loyalty when Izrad sentences a defiant Sviatoslav to death. Resolution occurs not because the unsuspecting Derevlians are slaughtered, but because Velesana's betrayal is discovered. Armed conflict erupts, and the Russians emerge victorious. Blaming passion for his weakness—he does in fact love Velesana—Izrad acknowledges that the gods punish earthly tsars for their evil and commits suicide.

Velesana illustrates very clearly that the men and women of Russian neoclassical tragedy could be equal in terms of heroic stature. Gender assigned to them different social functions—Velesana cannot defend the Russian throne by personally engaging in combat—yet they faced the same moral dilemmas and were equally effective as guardians of legitimate authority. Velesana inspires the Russians with her courageous use of love and wine to defeat the enemy, and although she regrets the need for bloodshed, she accepts it as the only means to save the fatherland. She is less a model of uncommon virtue and individual suffering than of the practical cunning needed to overcome harsh reality. With calculation and resilience, Velesana finds a means to avert the danger that she, her son, and by extension the entire people will be overrun by the barbaric Derevlians. Her worthiness to rule results not from the realization of abstract justice—which also is on her side—but from concrete action grounded in historical experience. Velesana possesses heroic stature because she bears the burden of rule with extraordinary foresight and fortitude.

The capacity to withstand the burden of rule vindicated many a monarch whose moral character could be questioned. On stage, the emotional complexity of the medieval prince Vladimir exemplified the ambiguity. In the tragedy *Vladimir the Great* (1779) by F. P. Kliucharev (1751–1822), the monarch is a troubled man surrounded by disaffection and danger.[31] A victorious military leader and a father to his people, who regard him as a god, Vladimir nevertheless fears that his wife Rogneda has tried to kill him. Indeed, Vladimir is the cause of her unhappiness: when Rogneda refused to marry him, he took her by force, devastating Polotsk and killing her family in the process. Now Rogneda hopes to die by admitting to the attempted murder, and the people, believing that Vladimir is dead, have rebelled. Vladimir finds momentary relief from the surrounding turmoil when his appearance calms the people and his love for Rogneda leads him to conquer his anger and forgive her. Soon, however, he is reminded that rulers enjoy no tranquility, freedom, or amusement. After surviving a second attempt on his life, Vladimir assigns judicial authority to his first boyar, who claims that Rogneda and the local governor are plotting to seize the throne. Convinced that he must master his passion in order to save the fatherland, Vladimir signs their death sentences. In reality, Vladimir's passion and the needs of the fatherland are one and the same. In response to Iziaslav, who insists on dying with his mother, Vladimir again succumbs to nature and tears up the sentences. The truth of feeling at last is confirmed when he discovers that Rogneda and the governor are innocent. The boyar, acting on orders from Iaropolk, is to blame. How unfortunate rulers are, Vladimir proclaims, when they entrust themselves to traitors.

The Vladimir portrayed in M. M. Kheraskov's tragedy *The Idolaters, or Gorislava* (1782) is, like Kliucharev's character, besieged by enemies and troubles.[32] Kheraskov picks up the narrative after the murder of Iaropolk, when Vladimir already has converted and is on the verge of forcing his subjects to accept Christianity. Sviatopolk, believing he is the son of Iaropolk, plots with the pagan priests against Vladimir. Gorislava (Sorrow), historical

Rogneda, is tormented by her love for Vladimir, who not only killed her parents but also rejects her affections. Vladimir accepts responsibility for Gorislava's unhappiness yet ignores her warnings about enemies. After all, Vladimir has given his subjects useful laws, extended the boundaries of the tsardom, built new cities and villages, and eliminated robbery and deception (all references to the reforms of Catherine II). Believing that Russia is his family, Vladimir is blind to the betrayal around him. First Sviatopolk leads a rebellion and suffers defeat, though instead of punishing him, Vladimir wants to be his father. (A letter from Sviatopolk's mother confirms the relationship, setting the stage for reconciliation).[33] Next the priests rebel because of Vladimir's conversion and implicate Gorislava by telling her that the gods have ordered her to kill her husband. Gorislava seems destined for execution until Iziaslav's desire to die with his mother moves Vladimir to forgiveness. Husband and wife reconcile, and Vladimir sends Gorislava and Iziaslav to Polotsk, where they will rule as his friends. Happy outcomes notwithstanding, Vladimir's good policies and efforts to Christianize his people have caused him countless hardships. Rightful order there may be, but how heavy is the burden of rule.

Playwrights who emphasized the burden of rule encouraged a humanistic understanding of the monarch that could be expressed either in neoclassical tragedy or in less lofty theatrical forms. Catherine II called *From the Life of Riurik* (1786) an "imitation of Shakespeare, an historical play without preservation of the usual theatrical rules."[34] Catherine was no poet, and her use of unconventional literary forms resulted in part from limited artistic talent. But her nonheroic portrayal of Riurik also made possible an examination of the monarch in mundane human terms. Outside the formulas of neoclassical tragedy, the struggle to preserve honor and duty took place in familiar historical settings. Instead of defining the good monarch in abstract heroic language, drama and comedy highlighted his or her personal relationship to the people. Alongside the transcendent monarch, guarantor of God-given justice and rightful order, stood the parent or friend who protected and rewarded deserving subjects.

The sentimental *Virtue Acquired at School* (1775) illustrates concretely the monarch's concern for needy subjects.[35] Written for performance at the Naval Noble Cadet Corps, the anonymous play depicts a virtuous cadet and orphan, Dobronravov (Well-Behaved), who provides shelter, food, and clothing to a weary old man. The man had suffered wounds and imprisonment in the Turkish War and has returned from Constantinople to find that his wife is dead, his home is gone, and his children have disappeared. Dobronravov also is a victim of misfortune, though at the cadet corps he has been receiving an education and all that he needs from commanders and benefactors who substitute for his missing parents.[36] Even so, like the old man, Dobronravov faces an uncertain future and worries that poverty will prevent him from finding a patron in the service. But as things turn out, Dobronravov is not so poor. The old man is in fact his father, and although the family lost its estate years ago, the money from the sale has been earning interest in a trusteeship. Nor, a friend insists, will the old man's services, wounds, and misfortune go unrewarded. The empress is a friend and protector of the unfortunate, the proof of which is that the old man's son has learned virtue and "enlightened reason" at the school.

The monarch's personal concern for his subjects is again spotlighted in Filiter Matveev's drama *The Virtuous Criminal, or Criminal from Love* (1792), in which a good marquis believes that his love for Sofiia not only deprives him of reason but also prevents him from meeting his obligations to sovereign and fatherland.[37] The marquis understands that love turns good people into evildoers and even forgives a competing suitor who tries to kill him, but still he fears for the safety of Sofiia. Convinced that he has caused her death simply by loving her, the marquis declares himself unworthy of the monarch's friendship and attempts suicide. The monarch is completely distraught over the suffering of his friend and valiantly struggles to calm him. Mercifully for all present, including the reader, the emotional tumult eventually dies down. Sofiia returns safely, the jealous suitor's repentance brings him forgiveness and rank, and the marriage of Sofiia to the marquis receives the blessing of her father. Clearly, the monarch is pleased to have such sensitive and virtuous subjects, yet a feeling of disquiet immediately overtakes him. Although he has sacrificed personal tranquility for the welfare of the people, they are dissatisfied, ungrateful, and unfeeling. The monarch also is disgusted by titles that mask tyranny and vileness: distinction and greatness, he believes, lie in virtue. Sofiia's father experiences a similar unease: he recognizes that the family happiness he now enjoys is possible only because he has retired from service and no longer bears witness to the misfortunes of the persecuted. Although the good monarch harbors no malice, he is unable to see and hear all. If he could, moreover, his sense of calm would evaporate forever.

To accept that the monarch could not see everything made it possible to challenge injustice while continuing to believe in the efficacy of monarchical authority. In the drama *Timely Assistance* (1794) by T. V. Konstantinov (1765–after 1798), Dobroserd (Good-Hearted) is a retired captain who at the outbreak of war volunteered to be a soldier.[38] Placing the needs of the fatherland above personal happiness, he left behind a wife and daughter, spent 25 years in service, participated in many battles, and survived multiple wounds. But like so many stage soldiers, Dobroserd returned home to find his wife dead, his daughter gone, and his estate plundered. Now at age 70, he is dying of cold and starvation, helped only by a poor laborer barely able to feed his own family. How can the misfortune of such a virtuous combat veteran be explained? First, the insensitivity of the rich leads them to ignore the suffering of the poor. Second, when Dobroserd left the army, he did not request a reward from the monarch. Because service is a duty, Dobroserd accepted the promotions he already had received as sufficient reward for his zeal. To seek money and villages at the time of retirement would have been shameful. Finally, after Dobroserd returned home to his ruined estate, the authorities refused to help him. Although he believes that conditions have changed since the creation of the governor-general-ship, when he retired, officials were neither enlightened nor prudent, and they did not understand the meaning of the laws. Judges were selected based on favoritism rather than ability, and the society of the nobility played no role in examining their qualifications. By contrast, the new jus-tice protects the property of orphans and widows, and the poor can attend tuition-free schools to enlighten their minds and souls. By way of illustra-tion, the old man's nephew, who arrives to provide "timely assistance," is the shining product of a gymnasium for the poor, where he had been sent to learn virtue after an evildoer stole his own father's estate.

Dobroserd's praise, which refers directly to the Catherinean reforms, is less a reflection of historical reality than of the years that T. V. Konstanti-nov spent in the loyal service of governors-general. All ends well once Do-broserd is reunited with his nephew and daughter, but the playwright's sug-gestion that good institutions have corrected what the monarch previously could not see appears exaggerated. Dobroserd's rescue results from the per-sonal intervention of his virtuous nephew, not from any official action based on the reformed judicial order. Granted, the nephew learned virtue in one of the new Catherinean schools, but the assistance he provides is an act of personal charity rather than the outcome of administrative proce-dures. Thus while good institutions might help to create virtuous subjects and officials, they could not provide impartial or reliable mechanisms for the realization of justice. As the depictions of judicial practice discussed in the preceding chapter also showed, without good people, beneficial laws and institutions fail to ensure rightful order.

Russian playwrights of the late eighteenth century consistently praised the Catherinean reforms. Yet however sincere stage monarchs appeared, their ability to implement policy remained problematic. Kniazhnin's Titus is deeply pained by his inability to distinguish falsehood from truth.[39] If only the emperor could look into the human heart, he would be able to el-evate the worthy, avoid shame, and correct the depraved. Instead, Titus must rely on the senators to be his eyes and on mercy to defeat enemies who pose as friends. In the anonymous drama *The Heroism of Love* (1794), Clovis, king of Austrasia (the eastern Frankish kingdom), is similarly dis-turbed by his failure to ensure justice and reward services.[40] "We are human beings *(cheloveki)*," he complains to his first minister, "and cannot contem-plate with accuracy all the distant parts of our state." Maybe there are peo-ple "oppressed by injustice" and others unrewarded for their services. Maybe "a large proportion of the people of the lower sort are not satisfied with the government *(pravlenie)* and are persecuted by commanders." Clo-vis worries that the information he receives concerning the established or-der is inaccurate because it comes from the evildoers themselves (that is, from the officials who neglect to implement his policies). True, Clovis's doors are open to petitioners, but do they really have access to him? In the words of the popular proverb, "God is on high and the Tsar far away." Although Clovis strives to appoint good administrators, he and his ministers make mistakes because "we do not have God's eyes." Clovis's first minister assures the king that he has indeed created a just order. Officials see and carry out the monarch's policies, the minister insists, because they are motivated to seek his favor. Oblivious to the Petrine distinction between the bureaucratic and charismatic principles of government, the minister imagines a complete blending of the two. Once again individual moral virtue emerges as the chief guarantor of good government.

If good government hinged upon good officials seeking the approval of a good monarch, it also happened that good monarchs made mistakes and acted arbitrarily. The tragedies discussed above reveal just how easily well-meaning rulers lapsed into tyranny. Less rarified treatments not only acknowledged the monarch's human failings but also assumed the inevitability of imperfect government. In contrast to tyranny, which emanated from evil individuals who deserved to be resisted, everyday government emanated from imperfect monarchs *and* subjects. Thus, Catherine II's comedy, *The Ante-Room of the Eminent Boyar* (1786), satirizes patronage and unrealistic popular demands by depicting petitioners in search of favors.[41] The boyar himself is never seen, having been called away to the palace, but his servant must contend with an endless stream of petitioners who arrive at sunrise and stay all day in hopes of encountering his eminence. Devoid of conscience, the petitioners rarely come on legitimate business, yet they offer a variety of excuses for why one or another should be first in line to see the boyar: exalted lineage, deference to women and age, an appointed meeting with a mistress, possession of urgent information obtained in a tavern, and initiation of a third appeal in a legal case.

In reality, the petitioners all seek material or social favors. One man hopes that his mistress can obtain permission to divorce her husband. A widow who owns a village of one hundred souls has heard that the boyar is giving away money to the poor and thinks that she deserves charity because liquor and sugar have become expensive. Indifferent to the proposition that handouts are for the truly needy, the widow also wants to be enrolled in an almshouse where she can collect assistance while continuing to live in her village. A second widow, granted a sum of money after her husband died, has squandered it and now expects a second endowment. The boyar already has helped a third woman to obtain a dowry, but her so-called groom is a dead man. She too has spent or pawned the dowry and asks permission to enter a convent. Several male petitioners want money, land, serfs, and/or rank: a Turkish noble, a Frenchman who thinks Russians need to be taught to walk upright (a reference to Paul Pierre Le Mercier de la Rivière), a German baron with a project, and a self-appointed Russian informant who eavesdrops on conversations in order to report on what people think of the boyar.[42] As Catherine II understood from decades of personal experience, the exercise of power requires constant vigilance against shameless self-seekers.

Catherine also was keenly aware of the need to cultivate good monarchs capable of opposing the foibles of their subjects. Her husband's "lack of education" and "incapacity to govern" supposedly had brought about his tragic downfall. At age fourteen she herself had arrived in Russia ill-prepared for court life, and certainly with no expectation that someday she would govern a great empire. As part of the effort better to educate her grandsons, Alexander (the future Alexander I) and Constantine, the empress wrote a series of plays devoted to comic heroes in need of instruction. In the allegorical play *Tsarevich Khlor, or The Rose without Thorns, Which Does Not Travel About* (1788), Catherine describes a young ruler who comes of age by learning to follow the path of truth and honor.[43] The people send Tsarevich Khlor to find the rose without thorns, a symbol of paradise and future happiness. Felitsa (Catherine) warns Khlor that in order to obtain the rose, he will have to forgo all amusements and overcome many obstacles. People will try to distract him with dishonorable pastimes, and smooth talkers will seek to deflect him from the true path. But if Khlor can remain straightforward, firm, well-intentioned, and diligent, he will succeed in his endeavor. Guided along the straight path by Reason, Khlor learns that the rose is not attached to any particular social group—that all people possess an equal capacity to achieve happiness through labor and patience. Although tempted by worldly amusements, with the help of Truth and Honesty, Khlor obtains the rose and discovers happiness in virtue.

Catherine further explores the question of preparation to rule in the comic operas, *Fevei* (1786) and *Woeful Hero Kosometovich* (1789), whose central characters are restless young men eager to prove themselves, but not yet ready to assume adult responsibilities.[44] In *Fevei* the empress insists that to come of age, a tsarevich must obey his parents, resist pressure to extend favors, and discover happiness in marriage. Fevei is both sincere and respectful, but he does not always succeed in following his father's orders; sometimes he fails to understand the meaning of obedience. Even so, his overall effort to obey indicates that with time he will acquire the qualities needed to govern effectively. This is surely not the case with the antihero Kosometovich (Throws-Askew), who leaves home to see the world and prove his worthiness. Kosometovich fancies himself an heroic warrior, when in reality he is cowardly, superstitious, and unsuited for adventure. Although interpreted by contemporaries and scholars as a caricature of the Swedish king Gustav III (ruled 1771–1792), Kosometovich also represents people who make a lot of noise but do nothing important—people who, like Catherine's other young heroes and tsareviches, have yet to prove they deserve to command.[45]

The need to provide evidence of a capacity to rule raises questions about whether Catherine II and educated Russians more generally truly believed in the sacredness of the monarch's sovereign will, or whether they simply understood that monarchy could not function without the presumption of God-given authority. Of course, the good policies and behavior that justified monarchical authority on secular grounds also could be seen as marks of divine favor. In any event, Catherine, like the great Peter, measured worthiness in terms of concrete achievements without assuming that appropriate behavior was God-given. Strong, upright character had to be learned, which is why Catherine's pedagogical plays highlighted the shortcomings of young heroes destined to rule. Her admonitions to tsareviches embraced a principle of moral equality that assigned to people from all social statuses an equal capacity for virtue and happiness. Precisely because the realization of moral virtue depended on individual actions, rulers and grandees were no more naturally inclined to goodness than ordinary people. On the contrary, the temptations of power were many, and persons born to elevated status were especially susceptible to manipulation and love of luxury. Demands to extend favors, and the ease with which monarchs could satisfy personal desires, encouraged extravagance and the perpetration of injustice. Not unlike the young spendthrift who lost his moral bearings by succumbing to fashionable sociability, the young tsarevich could be seduced by the endless efforts to curry his favor. To follow the straight path required uncommon self-control and represented one of the great burdens of rule.

Catherine II repeatedly suggested that in order to ignore flattery, labor diligently, and observe moderation in all matters, monarchs needed to recognize the potential moral equality shared by all human beings. V. A. Levshin also probes the question of moral equality in the comic opera *The King on a Hunt* (1793), the story of a count who steals peasant brides.[46] More a portrait of the good monarch than an exposé of serfdom, *The King on a Hunt* ends with banishment for the lustful count and happy union for the virtuous peasant couples. Like Catherine, Levshin's king believes that "noble feelings exist in any social status," and like the empress, he possesses an acute sense of the burden of rule: "Rulers are unhappy with their majesty / We are deceived, deluded. / We lack the power to see the hearts of all, / For this we are cruelly accused." Thus the king does not see the vileness of the count until he happens upon the family of the peasant Maksim. There, because his identity is unknown, he at last feels like a human being able "to see nature in her innocence." The king is moved to tears by Maksim's love for "our father" who is "such a kind, good Sovereign." If all his subjects loved him so, the burden of rule would be bearable.

The king also learns from Maksim's son, Ivan, that the peasants' love for him is more than abstract principle. Ivan recounts the many concrete benefits—a litany of Catherine's reforms—that the king has brought to his people: he has established subsistence for the poor, homes for the sick and wounded, and tuition-free schools in the towns. (Ivan himself attended a city school for three years.) The king is a friend to unfortunate infants (a reference to Catherine II's foundling homes); he has defended the state from enemies and extended its borders without bloodshed (a reference to successful imperial expansion); and finally, he has issued wise and salutary laws. The king loves his subjects as children, rewards their services, gently extirpates vice, and punishes malefactors with forgiveness. Most gloriously of all, anybody can write to him, as to a friend, about his or her needs. While Ivan's metaphorical account of Catherine II's actual achievements certainly is overdrawn, it accurately conveys what the empress would have liked her reforms to accomplish. Equally significant, his glorification of the king suggests that conscious support for monarchical authority is based on specific policies.

To provide concrete evidence of worthiness to rule at once humanized and sanctified the monarch because the human equality that a tsar shared with his subjects need not imply equivalent social or political authority. It was precisely the monarch's extraordinary power that enabled him or her to bring benefits to the people. The principle of worthiness to rule thus produced a form of humanization that made it possible to criticize individual monarchs without challenging political authority. There was a fine line, however, between legitimate criticism and unacceptable ridicule—a line that I. A. Krylov's farcical tragedy *Podshchipa* clearly crossed.[47] Written in 1800 for the home theater of Prince S. F. Golitsyn, *Podshchipa* was rejected by the St. Petersburg censorship committee in 1807 and not published in Russia until 1871. On one level, the farce delivered a devastating critique of eighteenth-century neoclassical tragedy that exemplified the well-established practice of employing fiction to conduct literary polemics.[48] Ironically, although the social and political message of *Podshchipa* simply carried to logical conclusion a theme that tragedy already had done much to promote—the idea of the monarch as a human being susceptible to the desires and struggles of everyday life—the monarchs in *Podshchipa* embodied a far too primitive form of humanity to be tolerated by censors charged with upholding God-given authority. It was one thing to condemn tyrants in the exalted manner of neoclassical tragedy and quite another to question the very dignity of monarchy by ridiculing monarchs as unheroic, uncivilized, and dishonorable.

In a familiar storyline, Podshchipa (Plucked-From-Below) can save her country and her father's throne if she marries the German prince Trumf (Trump). But she loves Sliuniai (Dribbler) and prefers death to unhappy marriage. The tone of the dialogue in *Podshchipa* effectively mimics the lofty poetics of tragedy, but the concrete language and details that carry forth the dramatic action are utterly mundane. Vulgar eating habits, uncouth pastimes, and base concerns render heroes into churls. Thus, the tsar and his boyars pay a gypsy fortuneteller to provide good predictions. The tsar also is extremely distraught when he breaks his favorite childhood toy, a calamity he describes as worse than war, conspiracy, or crop failure. Podshchipa's beloved Sliuniai turns out to be similarly unheroic, more the coward than honorable lover. Podshchipa would like to drown herself in a pond along with Sliuniai, but he rejects the idea, and when

Trumf threatens him with sword and pistols, he becomes afraid and agrees to give up Podshchipa. Nor does Podshchipa care if her beloved dies; she insists on publicly proclaiming her love even if he hangs for it. Finally, it is not the heroes but the gypsies who end the troubles by disarming the Germans. This brings the fortuneteller an appointment as maid of honor to Podshchipa, who at last marries Sliuniai. Throughout *Podshchipa* the ingenious combination of elevated tone and crass content produces a Rabelaisian satirical effect.[49] If in most late eighteenth-century Russian plays the humanization and secularization of monarchical authority encouraged sympathy for the struggles of good and even bad monarchs, in the hands of Krylov the result was a complete desacralization and loss of dignity that could not be tolerated.

Herein, it could be said, lay the problem of monarchical authority in eighteenth-century Russia. To elicit sympathy for the monarch, playwrights called upon subjects to identify with the monarch as a human person—as parent, patron, or master. On one level, this identification encouraged acceptance of constituted authority. For regardless of whether a monarch governed through consensual or absolutist forms of power, his or her personal authority allowed patriots, monarchists, and loyal subjects to criticize specific policies and even support regicide without seeking to change social and political arrangements. But on another level, the readiness of reigning sovereigns and court factions to ignore patrilineal succession created an atmosphere in which mere subjects—from elite servicemen to lowly peasants—might presume to judge the actions of earthly monarchs. The implications could be combustible, for such judgments not only appeared to contradict the principle of God-given monarchical authority but also opened the door to outright rebellion. Playwrights avoided explicit discussion of the succession question, but they too upheld the Petrine principle that a monarch must be worthy to rule. On the late eighteenth-century Russian stage, the good monarch embodied God-given authority, but human beings invariably sat in judgment of his or her goodness.

TO SIT IN JUDGMENT

When juxtaposed to the human behavior of earth-bound monarchs, the principle of God-given authority could seem meaningless. Yet when late eighteenth-century Russian playwrights highlighted the human flaws of monarchs, and even endorsed rebellion against tyranny, they did so in abstract terms that did not on the face of it resemble any actual situation. Most stage tyrants appeared so utterly evil and their opponents so remarkably virtuous that the rightness of resistance required little explanation. Other tyrants were simply misguided individuals who temporarily lapsed into tyranny and eventually saw the error of their ways. In both situations, the act of resistance was naturally contained and led to the restoration of rightful order. Indeed, the idea that tyranny represented an individual or momentary transgression rather than a systemic problem explains how, in an absolute monarchy, public theater could so openly display and condemn harmful monarchs without appearing to challenge political authority. But the problem of authority remained. In eighteenth-century Russia, the reality of palace coups and assassinations meant that any justification of rebellion carried potentially concrete implications. No matter how egregious and incontestable the evil of an individual tyrant, when playwrights assigned to subjects the ability to judge a monarch's actions, they inevitably introduced shades of moral gray. For how was tyranny to be defined, and when was rebellion truly justified?

In 1793, to the surprise of contemporaries, Catherine II banned Ia. B. Kniazhnin's tragedy *Vadim the Novgorodian* and berated Princess E. R. Dashkova for allowing its publication.[50] The incident suggested that the problem of rebellion against tyranny could quite easily move from the lofty abstractions of neoclassical tragedy to the concrete reality of history and politics. In the historical play *From the Life of Riurik* (1786), Catherine confronts the problem by recounting the rebellion of the legendary Slavic prince Vadim of Novgorod against the Varangian ruler Riurik.[51] According to the *Primary Chronicle*, the Varangians were invited to rule in Novgorod because of disorders among the local peoples. In Catherine's version of these events, based on contemporary histories, the Slavic prince Gostomysl, grandfather of Vadim and Riurik, extends the invitation.[52] Thus Vadim rebels not only against a cousin who is senior to him—Riurik is the son of Gostomysl's middle daughter and the Finnish/Varangian king—but also against his grandfather, the worthy ruler of Novgorod. Vadim's claim to rule rests on his Slavic blood and more importantly on his knowledge of Novgorodian customs. In contrast to Riurik, Vadim was born and raised in Novgorod. But Riurik's non-Slavic blood, like Catherine's, is no obstacle to legitimacy.[53] Gostomysl has selected Riurik to be his heir (an action consistent with the Petrine law of succession), and his will must be obeyed without debate. According to the loyal Novgorodian Dobrynin, a person such as Vadim, who cannot be obedient, is himself incapable of giving orders. Thus although Vadim musters enough support to cause unrest, once Riurik and the Varangians arrive, the Slavs submit or flee.

A usurper with no legal right to the Russian throne, Catherine II epitomized the principle of authority based on moral worth. If her worthiness was not perceived by the Cossacks, minority peoples, and peasants who joined the mass Pugachev rebellion or by the millions of serfs vulnerable to seignorial abuses, it nonetheless seemed obvious to the courtiers and high-level servicemen who placed her on the throne, acceded to her lengthy reign, and then overthrew her son several years after his ascension. Consequently, *From the Life of Riurik* does more than defend monarchical authority; it also explains why Riurik is a good ruler and by implication why Catherine deserves to rule. First, it is Gostomysl's will, based on sound judgment, that Riurik rule. Second, like Catherine, Gostomysl faces the problem of how to keep order among diverse peoples. Referring metaphorically to the vast Russian empire, one obedient Novgorodian explains that a judicious sovereign is needed to unite the many peoples of the land. Where laws, presumably granted by the monarch, correspond to the general and private good, disobedience disappears. Thus Riurik also deserves to rule because he exercises authority in accordance with his subjects' mores. Riurik intends to send out Varangian princes to rule in the cities, but first he will consult Dobrynin regarding local customs. Nor does Riurik wish to tie the hands of trusted personages who govern in his name. Just as Catherine entrusted G. A. Potemkin with the administration of the Greek project and the new territories in southern Ukraine, Riurik sends Oskol'd (Askold) to secure Kiev with permission to continue his campaign to Constantinople.[54] The final proof of Riurik's worthiness is his willingness to hear the unpleasant truth. When he and his advisors discuss whether Vadim should be punished according to the letter of the law, or whether the failure of his enterprise and condemnation by the people constitute sufficient loss, Riurik's wife speaks on behalf of the rebel. Vadim is young, people are born with passions, and not everyone can control his desires. Riurik's wife apologizes for her frankness, which along with Vadim's bold spirit, moves the ruler to grant clemency. Riurik realizes that Vadim's courage can be useful to the state and sends him with Oskol'd to Kiev. The hitherto belligerent Vadim responds with expressions of eternal loyalty, proclaiming that Riurik will defeat his enemies with mercy.

Ia. B. Kniazhnin's tragedy *Vadim the Novgorodian* depicts not an impetuous youth but a seasoned political and military leader who returns from war to find Riurik firmly in control of Novgorod and the grandees deprived of their freedom.[55] As in Catherine's account, Riurik was invited to Novgorod by Gostomysl to end civil disorder, his reign is based on virtue, and he is accepted by the people. Yet Vadim's supporters equate Riurik's sovereignty *(samoderzhavie)* with tyranny and their own loss of freedom with slavery. Rebellion ensues, the Varangians are victorious, and Riurik (as in the Catherinean version) seeks reconciliation. Reconciliation is exactly what Kniazhnin's Vadim rejects. Instead of rebelling and repenting as in the trajectory of the Catherinean Vadim, Kniazhnin's character remains defiant in the name of freedom.[56] Moreover, in contrast to the Catherinean Riurik, whose authority is upheld by loyal grandees, Kniazhnin's Riurik returns his crown to the people, who go down on their knees and ask him to rule. Monarchy is preserved because the people embrace it, yet Vadim finds the people's submissiveness to Riurik shameful and calling himself a man without a fatherland, commits suicide. His refusal to acquiesce follows the model of classical tragedy—it can be seen as the recovery of freedom through sacrifice to a higher moral principle—though for Riurik, it means that his own virtue has not been recognized.[57]

Both Catherine's *From the Life of Riurik* and Kniazhnin's *Vadim the Nov-*

gorodian vindicated the good monarch Riurik, even if, as was the case with the empress, Riurik's genealogical claim to the throne could be questioned. Perhaps this is why contemporaries claimed to be surprised by Catherine's belief that Kniazhnin's tragedy posed a threat to her person and authority. Kniazhnin's *Vadim* affirmed monarchy, Dashkova argued, and was "less dangerous than many a French tragedy acted in the Hermitage" and in public theaters.[58] In *The Mercy of Titus*, a tragedy published in 1787 and performed as early as 1785, Kniazhnin already had depicted a repentant conspirator forgiven by the Roman emperor and fully reconciled to his authority.[59] Be that as it may, to draw attention to the parallels between Catherine's *Riurik* (published 1786) and Kniazhnin's *Vadim* (written 1788–1789 and published 1793) misses the point. Catherine's banning of *Vadim* followed the intensification of censorship and repression evident in the exile of A. N. Radishchev (1790) and the imprisonment of N. I. Novikov (1792). The January 1793 beheading of Louis XVI also helps to explain Catherine's behavior. If Kniazhnin did indeed pen his tragedy in response to Catherine's play, clearly the empress was not interested in conducting a discussion. As Dobrynin reminds Vadim, there is no need for debate when one is supposed to carry out the ruler's will. An active reformer, Catherine was well aware of the practical limits to monarchical power, yet she regarded her will as unquestionably sovereign. Her attention to why Riurik was a good monarch revealed not how she *should* govern, given the conditions of Russian life, but how she *might wish* to govern, if circumstances allowed. More than a symbolic treatment of rebellion, Catherine's play emphasized the need to preserve calm and eliminate harmful disorder. The obvious problem with Kniazhnin's Vadim was that he chose death over acceptance of a good monarch loved by the people. From Catherine's perspective, his choice denied the necessity of reconciling individual conscience with legitimate authority.[60]

On the late eighteenth-century Russian stage, the problem of rebellion against tyranny masked the problem of authority, and in the Vadim controversy the mask was torn away. The more difficult problem—the problem that playwrights could not answer adequately—was how to reconcile the authority of the monarch not only with individual desire, which caused tyranny, but more importantly with individual conscience, which allowed subjects to judge God-given monarchical authority. On the face of it, late eighteenth-century playwrights appeared to square the circle. They came to terms with the failings of Russian monarchy in the same manner that they came to terms with the inequities and injustices of patriarchy, social hierarchy, and legal-administrative power—by attempting to light the way toward personal perfectibility. By emphasizing individual moral virtue as the solution to social and political problems, playwrights depicted a bureaucratic authority that relied on charismatic authority to achieve rational results.

In July 1787 the future emperor Alexander I and his brother Constantine Pavlovich attended a drama with ballet performed by students at the Tver

Noble School. The published version of the drama, titled *Appreciation of Good Works* (1790) and attributed to I. A. de Teil's, is an unequivocal glorification of Catherine II, who appears as both the goddess Minerva and the spiritual successor to Peter the Great.[61] At the end of the drama, Peter himself bestows the laurel given to him by the Russians on the head of the goddess, a bust of Catherine, and declares that her greatness now exceeds his own. Appropriate to the school setting of the drama's composition and performance, the bust of the goddess resides in the Temple of True Enlightenment, and Catherine's educational reforms figure prominently in the paeans of praise and adulation. Indeed, Peter recognizes in Catherine's policies the realization of his own plans: what the great reformer could only think or imagine, Catherine has brought to pass. Obey her blindly, Peter tells the Russians, for as he had done in his own time, she strives to bring them happiness. Catherine's noble intentions—all that she does is designed to benefit her subjects—provide the basis for her authority, and it is her personal virtue that makes possible the goodness of her subjects. Thus, a retired serviceman and Tver landlord tells his children the story of a virtuous noble criminal who assumed responsibility and suffered punishment for a crime committed by his maternal grandfather in order to save the latter from exile and loss of rank. "Such superior acts come into being solely during the reign of wise and magnanimous Sovereigns." In the virtuous monarch the virtuous subject found the mirror image of his own moral being, thereby achieving complete identification with constituted authority.

Still, at the same time that reliance on the virtue of individuals to solve social and political problems facilitated reconciliation with constituted authority, it also validated individual conscience, which in turn heralded the ability of subjects to judge the goodness of monarchs. In spotlighting individual conscience, late eighteenth-century Russian playwrights moved beyond the medieval right to resist tyranny and suggested that in society and polity, the individual subject had an independent role to play.[62] In Ia. B. Kniazhnin's tragedy *Rosslav* (1784), the hero not only adheres to duty through his willingness to forgo personal happiness and die for society; he also shows that duty does not invariably require obedience to authority.[63] Rosslav, a Russian conqueror and prisoner of Khristiern, tyrant of Denmark and Sweden, possesses an understanding of personal honor that impels him to oppose both an evil tyrant and a good tsar. The Russian monarch has offered to return the cities taken from Khristiern if Rosslav is set free, but the hero adamantly rejects the proposal. The monarch has no right to sacrifice society's happiness for him. On the contrary, it is Rosslav's fate to sacrifice personal happiness for society. Rosslav seeks reward only in virtue, and when Khristiern condemns him to death, he displays the tranquility of a man destined to die for glory. Khristiern may have power over the prisoner's life and freedom—but not over the feelings of his soul. For Rosslav duty is defined by personal honor, which represents the only legitimate basis for either obedience or freedom.

In *Rosslav,* the individual hero's commitment to the common good leads him to oppose the wishes of a well-intentioned monarch. Rosslav refuses to define duty simply in terms of obedience to legitimate authority—in this case a ruler who wants to buy his freedom—but only because he values the needs of society over his own personal happiness. Nearly two decades later, in a less rarified setting, a similar sense of personal honor produced a quite different result: the elevation of the individual and his family over the needs of society. In the dramatic anecdote *A Father Returned to His Children* by an unidentified author, Dobroserdov (Good-Hearted), father of Cheston (Honorable) and Sof'ia, has suffered imprisonment due to defamation by his enemies.[64] Published in 1801, the anecdote may represent an elite perception that the arbitrariness of the emperor Paul has been superseded by the magnanimity of Alexander I (ruled 1801–1825). An equally plausible interpretation, however, is that attitudes elevating family relationships and responsibilities over service to sovereign and fatherland have come to the fore. Away on campaign at the time of Dobroserdov's arrest, Cheston quickly responds to his sister's entreaties to return home and once there ignores the expiration of his leave because she lies ill. Cheston does try to rejoin his regiment after Sof'ia recovers but is refused appointment. Although cognizant of the shame associated with dismissal from the service, he accepts the inevitable consequences of military discipline. Cheston has no regrets about having put the needs of his sister before his regiment. On the contrary, his actions show that the marker of virtue has changed from absolute personal sacrifice for the good of the fatherland to the sacrifice of career advancement for the good of one's family.

When the monarch who had imprisoned Dobroserdov dies, Cheston journeys to the capital to plead his father's case before the new sovereign. There he learns that an amnesty has been announced and Dobroserdov is free. (Alexander I also announced an amnesty at his ascension.) Overcome with joy, Cheston weeps at the feet of the monarch. Dobroserdov shows greater reserve but still urges his children to pray to God that the sovereign enjoy a long reign. The responses of both men reveal a personal identification with the monarch. Clearly, however, the expressions of gratitude are secondary to the images of family happiness. Happiness, Dobroserdov declares, comes not from "the splendor of honors"—not, that is, from recognition by the monarch, who can make mistakes—but from a pure conscience. In the characters of Dobroserdov and Cheston, the reliance on individual moral virtue to ensure rightful order produces a visible distinction between the subject's conscience and the monarch's gaze, regardless of whether or not tyranny plays a role. Thus while the monarch continues to represent the font of earthly justice and God-given authority, the limits of the royal gaze mean that right also can be embodied in individual conscience. Armed with conscience, subjects possess the right, indeed the duty, not only to rebel against tyranny but also to judge the rightfulness of a good monarch's actions.

THE INDIVIDUAL
IN SOCIETY AND POLITY

• By the middle of the eighteenth century, Europeanized service classes had formed in Russia, and this relatively small
grouping of educated, predominantly noble individuals not
only patronized but also actively participated in the creation
of Russian literature and theater. Determined that in the realm
of European culture the empire would attain the greatness it
already had achieved on the field of battle and in international relations, Russia's educated service classes functioned
more as a circle of personal acquaintances, friends, and relatives than as an impersonal audience or public. Catherine II's
extensive involvement in theater and journalism; her direct
encouragement of poets, playwrights, and publishers; and finally, the absolutist power she wielded in repressing what she
did not want to hear—all testified to the personal relationships driving the development of Russian Enlightenment culture. In the manner of a grand *salonnière*, Catherine cultivated
polite conversation and sociability among her educated subjects even though as empress she also unabashedly destroyed
the public personhood of anyone who overtly or inadvertently challenged her orchestration.

One reason for the duality of Catherine's cultural policies—
and of Enlightenment thinking in general—was the as yet incomplete transition from a small-scale to a large-scale society
and politics. The transition could be glimpsed in eighteenth-
century Russia as important features of European modernity—
centralized bureaucracy, a standing army, technical education,
and professionally trained service classes—became established.
Even though throughout the eighteenth century the vast majority of the empire's population continued to live in isolated
agricultural villages, in the capitals and provincial towns ser-

vice in the army and bureaucracy together with participation in the new print culture, the new sites of public sociability, and the reformed civic institutions (schools, courts, noble assemblies, and boards of social welfare) encouraged the educated and economically privileged elite to identify themselves with membership in a larger social collective. By the end of Catherine's reign, they could join an educated society *(obshchestvo)* or public *(publika)* structured around Enlightenment culture and civic engagement. For the moment at least, this educated society remained synonymous with the educated service classes and, in terms of ideology and cultural product, was barely distinguishable from the court. Political and personal differences notwithstanding, educated Russians articulated a relatively uniform brand of Enlightenment thinking derived from common ideological categories.

In terms of social composition, Russian educated society also appeared strikingly homogeneous, coming primarily from the Orthodox nobility. Even so, when commentators invoked the concept of educated society for rhetorical purposes, they also had in mind a prepolitical literary public sphere that transcended established hierarchies of birth, age, and gender.[1] Theoretically at least, membership in educated society in no way hinged upon lineage or rank, but rather derived from participation in and knowledge of European Enlightenment culture. Like much of the social vocabulary of the eighteenth century, the concept of educated society represented both historical reality and polemical device. Educated society could be honorable or corrupt, it could constitute an inclusive or exclusive social community, and it could refer to a concrete audience or abstract sociological entity. In the prepolitical literary public sphere, educated society enjoyed the status of a "court" exercising independent, if not always good, judgment. Regardless of how commentators defined educated society, they counted among its members people of diverse origins and status, who temporarily came together to communicate and reflect on their shared social experiences. In contrast to the authority of the church and the monarchy, which emanated from God, and in contrast to the authority of military commanders, state officials, judges, and seigniors, which emanated from the monarch, the authority of educated society was socially constituted in itself. This structural autonomy did not yet add up to political power in the form of self-conscious public opinion, but it did encourage public discussion of significant social questions.

Eighteenth-century playwrights actively participated in the conversation about Russian society, a society in which—as poets and servicemen—they had acquired the capacity to see the world from the perspective of both individual subject and government official. Irrespective of any literary contribution, the plays they wrote offered a complex and sometimes heart-wrenching portrait of conflicts and tensions in the relationship of individuals and social groups to the government and to institutions such as the patriarchal household and serfdom. Their images of Russian society

could be highly critical though by and large, among playwrights and educated Russians more generally, an acute awareness of the social strains led
not to revolt but to reconciliation—not to a desire to overthrow flawed institutions but to live within them, despite a recognition of their costs. That
in the eighteenth century the social thinking of the educated service classes
almost always produced reconciliation is well known, and in the case of
playwrights, literary convention also required dramatic resolution. But how
was the reconciliation achieved in cognitive moral and philosophical
terms? As the preceding chapters have shown, it was not only the dilemmas of power and powerlessness that playwrights put on display, but those
of duty and desire, of obligation and freedom.

Indeed, the evidence from the eighteenth-century plays reveals a charac-
teristically Enlightenment tension in the way educated Russians thought
about social relationships. The more long-standing attitude assumed the
existence of a transcendent natural order created by God (in classical literature also represented by the gods and fate) and protected on earth by
church and monarch. This natural order, which—absent the laws of physics
and modern scientific knowledge—was fully consistent with the God-given
Christian universe, represented right and justice. It became manifest in human history, so that concrete relationships and events were understood to
be the unfolding of providential or divine laws. The providential view of
social relationships did not allow for open-ended linear change, but neither
was it static, immutable, or exclusively religious. Through rational inquiry
and the scientific discovery of nature's physical laws, human beings acquired the ability not only to discern but also to act upon the God-given
order. Thus justice and legitimate social relationships corresponded to the
natural order, whereas injustice and social conflict signaled its violation.
Because the natural order remained fully knowable only to God, the justice
of God's vicar on earth, the sovereign monarch, provided a divinely sanctioned though as yet imperfect framework for regulating social relationships. Transgressions and abuses inevitably occurred, but the path to justice
and legitimacy lay in the restoration and rediscovery of the God-given natural order—change being circular—rather than in the open-ended linear
transformation of established social relationships.

Alongside the traditional understanding of social relationships, a relatively modern way of thinking, associated throughout eighteenth-century
Europe with the Enlightenment belief in secular progress, embraced the
possibility of open-ended transformation through human agency.[2] In this
conception, there was no assumption of a preexisting rightful order that
necessarily had to be preserved or, when violated, restored. Instead, history
and concrete experience provided the standard by which to measure
earthly well-being. Human beings, armed with rational thought and free
will, possessed the capacity to improve not only their own selves but also
the societies in which they lived. Human judgment replaced the God-given
natural order as the basis for evaluating social relationships. The individ-

ual's social identity—how he defined himself and was defined by others in social terms—no longer was divided between transcendent idea and historical reality. Instead, reform-minded people assumed that idea and reality should over time achieve correspondence. Given that complete correspondence could only be imagined—what people thought they were or wanted to be often was at odds with what historical conditions allowed them to be—cognitive reconciliation with concrete relationships became increasingly difficult to achieve. Consequently, the molding of social relationships to promote justice and virtue became an end in itself rather than an expression of the transcendent natural order. The possibility of infinite change became joined to the exercise of free will within the God-given universe.[3]

In Russia, the combined languages of the Enlightenment and absolute monarchy encouraged not political contestation, as in France, but moral deliberation that for decades could be successfully reconciled with established hierarchy and authority.[4] Still, a contradiction arose between the goals of absolute monarchy, which by actively pursuing resource mobilization fostered ideas of social transformation and progress, and the social thinking of policymakers and the educated service classes, which by overcoming the tension between Enlightenment ideas and historical realities consistently upheld the hierarchy and authority of God-given order. Throughout the eighteenth century and even into the nineteenth, the reformist policies of the government and the social thinking of the educated classes remained sufficiently elastic to permit a reconciliation of the two. Binary categories of opposition and rebellion were muted, and in neither government nor educated society was there significant awareness of a need for fundamental change. Even if an enlightened monarch such as Catherine II (ruled 1762–1796) believed that the abolition of serfdom was in principle necessary, she certainly did not think it was immediately possible or desirable. Similarly, political reformers might seek to alter the institutional projection of monarchical authority but not its essential nature. Educated Russians, in official and unofficial capacities, subordinated their belief in progress and human freedom to the assumed rightness of the God-given natural order.

It was precisely the ability of socially aware and morally self-conscious individuals to come to terms with imperfection and inconsistency that ensured the Russian reconciliation with hierarchy and authority. Throughout the eighteenth century, the crucial dynamic in the imperial government's relationship with the educated service classes was not the emergence of a civil society in opposition to the state, but rather the effort to extend legal-administrative authority by institutionalizing civic engagement—an effort most fully elaborated in the Catherinean provincial reforms and "constitutional" charters. In a society in which property rights carried no judicial or administrative authority beyond the family estate, the development of an educated populace capable of employing reason to make independent judgments produced an abstract philosophical form of politics, concerned more with moral principles than with the routine functioning of institutions. Unable to identify viable alternatives to existing social and political arrangements, Russia's educated service classes assimilated the moralistic dimension of European Enlightenment culture but not its understanding of political rights. In western and central Europe, the very success of absolute monarchy in excluding morality from politics and in asserting the primacy of the state interest allowed privatized morality to become a source of rebellion.[5] In eighteenth-century Russia, by contrast, absolute monarchy effectively coopted morality into politics, so that morality could serve as an instrument of reconciliation.

Court coups and succession crises, fear of aristocratic oligarchy, distrust of the common people as a result of the Pugachev rebellion, regicide and terror in the aftermath of the French Revolution—memories such as these encouraged the perception among educated Russians that only through reconciliation with existing institutions could the good society be achieved. Even so, reconciliation carried its own sources of cognitive dissonance to which the idealized situations of the late eighteenth-century Russian plays also gave public expression. When playwrights pinpointed the social and political problems of their time—problems such as parental abuse, serfdom, conscription, noble insecurity, judicial corruption, and tyranny, they implicitly, if not explicitly, justified social and political resistance. Whether playwrights were fully aware of the outcomes their plots made imaginable, they nonetheless participated in an Enlightenment transformation of Europe that by placing people in the larger arenas of "the public" and "society" brought them out of "familism," localism, and parochialism.[6] Enlightenment Russia may not have produced a canonical philosopher or philosophe of pan-European stature, but "enlightened cultural practices" clearly influenced the thinking and sociability of the educated classes. Christian principles of human equality and individual dignity acquired secular meanings that pointed directly toward identification with the public as judge and with society (not the monarchy) as the common good.

To identify society with the common good set the stage for the emergence of a self-conscious society in opposition to the state. But in conditions of censorship and political absolutism, the very power of the social critique resulted from the inability of participants in the Russian Enlightenment conversation to recognize its revolutionary potentialities.[7] Although by the time of the Decembrist uprising in 1825 Enlightenment ideas would produce elite political opposition—and by 1905 mass revolution—in the eighteenth century Russia bore witness neither to political transformation nor to politically organized civil society. The practices or lived experience of the Enlightenment (that some historians equate with civil society or the Habermasian public sphere) encouraged the cultivation of individual moral virtue, which in turn required adherence to duty within a framework defined by patriarchy, social hierarchy, and absolute monarchy. To identify abuses and invoke human rationality as the means to improve society did not necessarily lead to a desire for institutional change. Rather, the belief in progress sounded the call to employ reason in the service of goodness and virtue. Because this call could be answered by enlightened individuals, it reinforced a form of politics rooted in the personal relationships of the educated service classes, including their relationship to a personal monarch.

Thus in the late eighteenth century, Russian playwrights assumed that the individual—the individual constructed on a moral rather than a legal or political basis—held the key to *social* progress. By reconciling the satisfaction of personal desire with adherence to duty, the individual attained freedom *(vol'nost')* and became integrated into society and polity. The ideal site for the realization of freedom—the place where desire and duty became reconciled most effectively—was the patriarchal household. In late eighteenth-century depictions of the patriarchal household, playwrights identified the principles, concepts, and categories of thought and feeling needed to guide the individual in his or her dealings with the outside world. The virtuous individual, imbued with belief in duty, would carry the altruism of family relations into the arena of civic society. Personal perfectibility, personal responsibility, personal service, personal sacrifice, and personal monarchy—these were the building blocks of the good society, which in turn would preserve the rightful order created by God and embodied in social hierarchy and political authority. Historians who see in the eighteenth-century Enlightenment the utopian roots of twentieth-century authoritarianism do not consider that the Russian understanding of human progress hinged more upon the cultivation of personal perfectibility and less upon the remaking of social relationships and institutions.[8] Perfectibility was as much an Orthodox Christian as a modern rationalistic concept, and while institutions might encourage the cultivation of virtue, without virtuous individuals, institutions easily became a source of injustice rather than rightful order.

The idea that social progress depended on the moral reformation of the individual pervaded the Russian Enlightenment in all its intellectual, political, and social manifestations. But the agreed-upon goal of personal perfectibility also could lead to moral rebellion. Indeed, individual moral rebellion, rather than social alienation or a new way of thinking, became the characteristic quality of the Russian intelligentsia after "the parting of ways" between the government and the educated classes in the early nineteenth century.[9] Historians have long connected a growing awareness of individuality in the eighteenth century, frequently expressed in literature, with alienation and incipient opposition. The evidence for alienation consists of critical remarks about the monarch, court, and bureaucracy; complaints about service appointments and rewards; a desire to escape the storms of civic life; and, eventually, participation in secret organizations and radical intellectual circles. Less obvious, though more forcefully elucidated in the fictional relationships displayed on the late eighteenth-century stage, was the capacity of educated Russians to accommodate themselves to the demands of the monarchy. Playwrights regularly articulated social criticism while affirming their identification with constituted authority. The social thinking expressed in eighteenth-century plays illustrates how the heightened awareness of individuality produced not only disaffection but also reconciliation with official ideology. Playwrights confronted the abuses and inequities threatening rightful order, yet found in the Enlightenment (and Christian) goal of personal perfectibility a satisfactory solution to injustice and social conflict.

The eighteenth-century emphasis on inner virtue was fully consistent with classical stoicism, civic humanism, and the religious sense of individuality. But as a consequence of the Enlightenment belief in earthly progress, the individual's constitution as a moral being became as much a secular as a religious concern, and the cultivation of individual virtue emerged as a solution to civic problems. Ironically, because reliance on personal virtue to ameliorate the consequences of social hierarchy, moral corruption, and abuse of power aimed to preserve rightful order, rather than achieve fundamental change, it also signaled acceptance of an intractable gap between idea and reality. To premise good order on individual moral virtue (as opposed, for example, to technical juristic formulas) required reciprocity, achieved either through the actions of other equally virtuous persons or through identification with the shared well-being of the common good. In the realm of the common good, or similarly the fatherland and later the nation, the worthy individual looked beyond immediate civic relationships, in which reciprocal virtue could *not* be guaranteed, to the higher authority of the sovereign. In relation to the monarch, who was inseparable from the common good, the individual subject could find the reciprocity in virtue that made reconciliation with society possible.

Still, the individual's relationship to society appeared problematic: on the one hand, moral virtue became manifest through usefulness to and hence action in civic society, but on the other hand, the preservation of virtue and hence good order depended on the individual's ability to remain free of the corruption so prevalent in civic society. The solution to this conundrum was found in the monarch, at once an abstract principle and a personal ruler who righted specific wrongs. It was the monarch who provided the basis for the individual subject's identification with the imperial polity, though here too instability loomed. The heroism and justice of transcendent monarchy inevitably clashed with the reality of organized institutional life, in which intrigue and deception frequently were decisive. The subject's relationship to the monarch, realized concretely through service, judicial practice, and acts of mercy, was filled with moral and political ambiguity. In administrative settings ambiguity arose because although members of the elite enjoyed a personal relationship to the monarch, the rewards of service did not necessarily go to persons of merit. Nor did the deserving always receive judicial satisfaction. The tension between rightful expectations and social organization on a large scale highlighted a central dynamic of integration (and disintegration) in the Russian imperial polity. Understood in terms of an ideological framework that sought to resolve social and political conflict on moral grounds, political authority combined the charismatic principle represented by the sovereign (monarch) with the bureaucratic principle represented by the fatherland (state).[10] By depicting sovereign and fatherland as inseparable, playwrights perpetuated a personalized understanding of monarchy despite significant bureaucratization begun in the seventeenth century.

Precisely because the sovereign authority remained personal, it could be coupled with or decoupled from the actual exercise of power. The movement of authority between the monarch and the state in turn allowed service to the state to become bureaucratized, depersonalized, and disjoined from the rules of everyday morality. By extension, social identification also could move beyond personal relationships into the realms of civic society and the nation. When the sovereign embodied the fatherland—as opposed to the fatherland being the patrimony of the sovereign—or when the sovereign became the abstract principle of monarchy, the person of the sovereign became conceptually separated from the actual functioning of government. At the same time, because the sovereign also was personally responsible for administration and ultimately held accountable for the failings of government, he or she could be removed from power without undermining authority and bringing harm to the country. In the eighteenth century, transcendent monarchy took precedence over the person of the sovereign and effectively bolstered monarchical authority. Direct experience of the gap between the idea of what the monarch should be and the reality of legal-administrative authority on the ground focused attention on the human failings of the individual sovereign without, however, destroying the transcendent principle of monarchy. In contrast to France where prior to the revolution of 1789 the monarch lost his sacred bearing and became the object of public ridicule, in Russia the monarchy remained sacred even though the monarch became concretized as a morally responsible individual. The Russian application of Enlightenment morality and individual conscience to politics led not to revolution but to reconciliation.

Appendix
BIOGRAPHIES OF AUTHORS

- The 260 plays examined in this study represent the work of 78 known authors; 45 of the plays remain without authorial attribution. For authorial attributions—many plays were published anonymously or pseudonymously—I relied on published anthologies and the *Svodnyi katalog russkoi knigi grazhdanskoi pechati XVIII veka 1725–1800* (hereafter *SK*). Together with scholarly monographs and anthologies, the main sources for the biographical data include *Entsiklopedicheskii slovar'* (hereafter *ES*); *Dictionary of Literary Biography.* Vol. 150, *Early Modern Russian Writers, Late Seventeenth and Eighteenth Centuries* (hereafter *DLB*), ed. Marcus C. Levitt; *Slovar' russkikh pisatelei XVIII veka* (hereafter *SRP*); *Russkii biograficheskii slovar'* (hereafter *RBS*); *Russkie pisateli, 1800–1917: Biograficheskii slovar'* (hereafter *RP 1800–1917*); *Russkie pisateli XIX vek: Biograficheskii slovar'* (hereafter *RP XIX vek*), ed. P. A. Nikolaev.

Ablesimov, A. O. (1742–1783). Born the son of a modest service noble in Kostroma province, Ablesimov was educated at home. In 1751 he was registered in military service and attached to the Office of the Master of the Heraldry. In 1756, at the request of A. P. Sumarokov, Ablesimov became a copyist for the new Russian Theater. Ablemisov entered active military service as an artillery soldier in 1758, became a sub-ensign *(podpraporshchik)* in 1759, and participated in the Seven Years' War as a sergeant in 1760–1762. After becoming a driver *(furmeister)* in 1765, Ablesimov retired with the rank of ensign in 1766. In 1767 he was appointed to the Legislative Commission, and in 1770 he returned to military service. As adjutant to Major General A. N. Sukhotin, Ablesimov participated in campaigns against the Turks in Georgia and at the siege of Poti. After retiring from the military in 1772 with the rank of captain, he joined the Moscow city police *(uprava blagochiniia)* as an administrator *(ekzekutor)*. *DLB*, 150:3–7; *SRP*, 1:18–19.

Baibakov, A. D. (Apollos) (1737–1801). Originally from a poor non-noble family, Baibakov was educated at the Moscow Slavonic-Greek-Latin Academy (1757–1767) and the Philosophy Faculty of Moscow University (1768–1770). At Moscow University he studied jurisprudence, mathematics, and modern languages and in 1770–1771 worked as a proofreader at the university's press. In 1772 Baibakov became a teacher of rhetoric and poetics at the Slavonic-Greek-Latin Academy and in 1774 took monastic vows. As monk Apollos, he served as rector of the Trinity Seminary (from April 1775), assistant *(namestnik)* to the superior of the Trinity-Sergius Monastery *(Troitse-Sergieva lavra)* in 1782–1783, archimandrite of the Zaikonospasskii Monastery (from December 1783), and rector of the Slavonic-Greek-Latin Academy in 1783–1785. In December 1785, Platon Levshin appointed Apollos to perform divine services and hear confession at court for a year, and from there he became superior *(nastoiatel')* of the Voskresenskii (New Jerusalem) Monastery. In 1788 Apollos was ordained a bishop and appointed Bishop of Sevsk and Orel (1788–1798). In 1798 he was transferred to Arkhangel'sk, where he finished his service career, and in 1801 he became a member of the Russian Academy. *SRP*, 1:48–52; *ES*, 2:908.

Baturin, P. S. (1740/1–1803). Born into an old and poor noble family, Baturin began service in the Guards Cavalry Regiment in 1754. In 1756 he was appointed lieutenant in the Active Army, and after a period of imprisonment in Prussia, he retired with the rank of captain. In retirement Baturin traveled around Europe, returning to service in 1770 to fight in the First Turkish War. After suffering wounds in combat, he was promoted to second major *(sekund-maior)* and in 1776–1777 served in the Apsheronskii Infantry Regiment. Following additional transfers and promotions, in 1781 Baturin retired from military service with the rank of lieutenant-colonel. In civilian life, he pursued literary activities and a career in state service. In 1783 Baturin accepted an offer from his patron, the Kaluga governor-general *(namestnik)* M. N. Krechetnikov, to serve as councilor of the Kaluga Civil Chamber. At the same time, Krechetnikov placed him in charge of the Kaluga theater and printing press. Baturin also served as councilor of the Kaluga Provincial Administration before moving to Tula with Krechetnikov, who appointed him councilor of the Criminal Chamber in 1778. In 1790 Baturin again followed Krechetnikov to a new location, this time Kiev, where he became director of economy at the Kiev Treasury Chamber. In 1793, with the rank of collegial councilor, Baturin became president of the Criminal Chamber of the newly formed Iziaslav governor-generalship *(namestnichestvo)*. With the creation of the Zhitomir governor-generalship, he became president of the Criminal Chamber of Volhynia province. Promoted to state councilor in 1796, Baturin's service career was briefly interrupted but then resumed in 1798 with his appointment as the president of the Second Department of the Voronezh Chamber of the Court and Court for State Peasants *(palata suda i raspravy)*. *SRP,* 1:68–70.

Belosel'skii-Belozerskii, A. M. (1752–1809). Belosel'skii-Belozerskii, member of an old princely clan, began service in the guards cavalry in 1759 and subsequently reached the rank of second lieutenant in the Izmailovskii Guards Regiment. Between 1768 and 1778, Belosel'skii-Belozerskii's very good home education was supplemented by study and travel in London, Berlin, France, and Italy. In 1773 he received his first court rank as gentleman of the bedchamber *(kamer-iunker)*, and in 1779–1793 held diplomatic posts in Dresden, in Vienna, and at the court of Sardinia. Recalled from Sardinia because his reports on the French Revolution displeased Catherine II, he subsequently claimed that the empress tried to close her eyes to events he had foreseen. At the ascension of Paul, Belosel'skii-Belozerskii was appointed to the Senate but soon requested release from service. Alexander I granted him the rank of actual privy councilor in 1801 and one of the highest court ranks *(ober-shenk)* in 1808. *SRP,* 1:79–81.

Berkh, G. I. (no dates). Johann von Berg, a teacher in the Land Forces Noble Cadet Corps, reached the rank of major in 1790. *SRP,* 1:84.

Blagodarov, Ia. I. (1764–1833). Blagodarov came from the Polish nobility and graduated from Moscow University in 1788. He reached the rank of state councilor, remaining in service until his death. Blagodarov's service assignments included translator and proofreader at the university press, land-surveyor in Tambov province, bursar *(kaznachei)* in Mozhaisk, and postmaster in V'iazma and Pereiaslavl. Influenced by Freemasonry, Blagodarov's literary activities began as a student and continued until 1803. His publications included translations from French and German as well as original works. During the period he served in the Tambov Surveying Office (1791–1801), Blagodarov also worked as a proofreader for the publishing firm of I. G. Rakhmaninov. *SRP,* 1:92–94.

Blank, B. K. (1769–1825). The son of a St. Petersburg architect and nobleman, Blank served in guards regiments until retiring with the rank of lieutenant-colonel in 1797. In retirement he served as a deputy to the Mozhaisk Noble Assembly in 1803–1807 and as marshal of the nobility of Mozhaisk district (Moscow province) in 1807–1810. *SRP,* 1:94–95.

Bogdanovich, I. F. (1743–1803). Known for his literary, historical, and editorial accomplishments, Bogdanovich (1743–1803) was born to a noble family of Poltava province and received his early education at home. In 1754 he was appointed a junker in the Moscow College of Justice and began to study at the Mathematical School of the Senate Office. Under the patronage of M. M. Kheraskov, his education continued at the gymnasium of Moscow University and then at the university itself. Appointed ensign in the Navaginskii Regiment in 1761, Bogdanovich also served as supervisor of classes at Moscow University. In 1762, in connection with the coronation of Catherine II, Bogdanovich served on the Commission for the Construction of Ceremonial Gates. In 1763 he became a translator in the War College, attached to the staff of P. I. Panin, and moved to St. Petersburg, where in 1764 he joined the College of Foreign Affairs and became a member of the Free Economic Society. In 1766–1769 Bogdanovich served as secretary in the Russian embassy in Saxony, but then returned to his St. Petersburg post as translator in the College of Foreign Affairs. In 1779 Bogdanovich was transferred to the Heraldry Office without salary, which led to temporary retirement. He returned to service in 1780 with appointment to the newly established St. Petersburg Archive and in 1783 was elected a member of the Russian Academy. In 1784 Bogdanovich was promoted to court councilor *(nadvornyi sovetnik),* and in 1788 he became chairman *(predsedatel')* of the St. Petersburg Archive. His involvement in literary activities declined thereafter, and in 1789 he retired from service. *SRP,* 1:104–9; *ES,* 7:158–59.

Bolotov, A. T. (1738–1833). Bolotov came from modest noble origins, the son of a colonel with significant combat experience. Bolotov did not receive a systematic education but did learn reading and writing, drawing, and foreign languages. He was appointed to the Arkhangelogorod Infantry Regiment in 1748 and began active service as a sergeant in 1755. After serving as an officer in the Seven Years' War from 1757 to 1758, Bolotov became a clerk and translator in the chancery of N. A. Korf, Russian governor-general of Prussia. While serving in Königsberg he also participated in an amateur theater organized by G. G. Orlov. In 1760 Bolotov was promoted to lieutenant, and in 1762 he became aide-de-camp to Korf, who had been appointed general chief of police in St. Petersburg. When Peter III emancipated the nobility from compulsory service in June of that year, Bolotov retired to his Tula estate. While residing in Tula province, Bolotov managed estates belonging to Catherine II from 1774 and crown estates from 1776. In connection with this last assignment he lived in Bogoroditsk for 20 years. Following the death of Catherine II, Bolotov, a member of the Free Economic Society since 1766, left service with the rank of collegial assessor, which he had acquired in 1783. *SRP,* 1:114–17; *ES,* 7:318–19.

Bukharskii, A. I. (1767–1833). Bukharskii was born to a poor noble family in Kursk province and received a home education. In 1775 he registered in the Preobrazhenskii Guards Regiment and in 1787 transferred to the Nevskii Infantry Regiment with the rank of captain. Bukharskii retired from military service with the rank of major in 1788. Beginning in 1796 he occupied state administrative posts in the St. Petersburg grain magazines, the state accounting department, the chancery of the main director of the Postal Department (from 1801), and the Vil'no Postal Department where he became director in 1811. *SRP,* 1:137.

Catherine II, Empress (1729–1796). Born Sophie Friederike Auguste, princess of Anhalt-Zerbst, Catherine arrived in St. Petersburg in 1744, the bride of the heir to the Russian throne, the future Peter III. That same year she converted to Orthodoxy under the name of Catherine Alekseevna and in 1745 married Peter. Following a court coup, Catherine ascended the throne in 1762 and reigned until her death. *SRP,* 1:291–302.

Cherniavskoi, Osip (no dates). No biographical information is available. *RBS,* 22:335.

Damskii, K. F. (no dates). A ward of the St. Petersburg Foundling Home from 1768 until 1798, Kupriian [Kipriian] Damskii is easily confused with a Moscow ward of the same name (Kipriian Iakovlevich Damskii). K. F. Damskii worked as a prompter *(sufler)* for the troupe of the Free Russian Theater, and from September 1783 until August 1784 served in the Directorate of Imperial Theaters. In 1800 he operated a book store at the Anichkov bridge on Nevskii Prospect. *SRP,* 1:237; *ADIT,* I, 3:27–28.

Dashkova, E. R. (1743/4–1810). Dashkova (née Voronstova) belonged to an aristocratic family with direct ties to the imperial family. Educated in the home of an uncle, she was widowed at a young age but traveled extensively in Europe. Today Dashkova is best remembered for her political memoirs, which claim close friendship with Catherine II and active participation in the palace coup that brought the empress to power. From 1783 until 1794, Dashkova served as director of the Academy of Sciences and president of the Russian Academy, where she oversaw the compilation and publication of the *Dictionary of the Russian Academy* (1789–1794). During her service career she edited and supervised the publication of various journals and literary collections, including the *Complete Collection of All Russian Theatrical Works (RF)* (1786–1794), a major source for this book. Banished from court by Paul, Dashkova was invited to return to service in 1801 but chose to remain on her estate. *SRP,* 1:243–47.

Dolgorukov (Dolgorukii), I. M. (1764–1823). Grandson of I. A. Dolgorukii (favorite of Peter II), Dolgorukov received a home education, later attended Moscow University but did not graduate, and in 1789 began service as a lowly ensign in the First Moscow Infantry Regiment. After serving as an orderly to V. M. Dolgorukov-Krymskii, Dolgorukov transferred to the Semenovskii Guards Regiment in St. Petersburg, where he belonged to the private circle of Tsarevich Paul. Following the Finnish campaign of 1789–1790, Dolgorukov retired from military service with the rank of brigadier and in 1791 became vice governor in Penza. There he continued his literary activities, begun while at Moscow University, and organized an amateur theater that folded soon after his departure. Due to accusations of corruption, in

1812 Dolgorukov retired from the governorship in Vladimir, a post he had held since 1802. His interest in amateur theater continued throughout his life, and after returning to Moscow in 1814, he built a home theater with 100 seats, which housed winter performances from 1816 until the early 1820s. *SRP,* 1:279–83; *ES,* 20:924.

Efim'ev, D. V. (1768–1804). The son of a modest landowner and army officer from Novgorod province, Efim'ev studied at the Artillery and Engineering Corps at state expense and in 1789 joined the field artillery as a *shtyk-iunker* (rank 13). Efim'ev rose rapidly in military service, becoming a second lieutenant *(podporuchik)* by 1792 and a colonel *(polkovnik)* and battalion commander by 1800. *SRP,* 1:312–13; *ES,* 22:692.

El'chaninov, B. E. (1744–1770). El'chaninov came from an old noble family and studied philosophy at the Kiev Academy. From there he entered military service, joined the Noble Land Forces Corps with the rank of captain, and died a colonel in the First Turkish War. As a playwright, El'chaninov was associated with the circle of I. P. Elagin, who emphasized the pedagogical uses of theater and the need to adapt foreign plays to Russian mores. *SRP,* 1:310; *ES,* 22:628.

Emin, N. F. (d. 1814). Educated in the St. Petersburg Mining School, Emin served in the administration of the Petrozavodsk governor-generalship under G. R. Derzhavin and then briefly in the Academy of Sciences before becoming governor of Vyborg. *ES,* 80:763.

Fedorov, V. M. (no dates). Virtually nothing is known about Fedorov's biography. He published nine plays in the period 1803–1823 and served in civil administration in Moscow and St. Petersburg. *RBS,* 21:30–31; *ES,* 82:883.

Fonvizin, D. I. (1744/5–1792). One of the great writers of eighteenth-century Russia, Fonvizin (Von Vizin) was born in Moscow, most likely in 1745, the descendant of a German knight captured during the reign of Ivan the Terrible. His father was a modest landowner whose career encompassed military and civil service. In 1755 Fonvizin enrolled in the Moscow University gymnasium and briefly attended the university in 1762. Assigned to the Semenovskii Guards Regiment in 1754, he became a sergeant in 1760 and a translator in the College of Foreign Affairs in 1762. After moving to St. Petersburg in 1763, he worked as a secretary to Ivan Elagin, a position he found intolerable by 1768. In 1769 Fonvizin became secretary to Nikita Panin, head of the College of Foreign Affairs, and continued his diplomatic career. While in service Fonvizin received additional lands and serfs, and also benefited financially from his marriage to the daughter of a merchant. In 1781 he began work in the Postal Department, retiring from service in 1783. *DLB,* 150:98–109.

Golitsyn, Prince A. I. (1765–1807). Golitsyn served in the Izmailovskii Guards Regiment from 1779, participated in the Second Turkish War, and retired a lieutenant-colonel *(podpolkovnik)*. *SRP,* 1:209–10. *ES* (17:52) identifies Golitsyn as a colonel at retirement.

Gorchakov, D. P. (1758–1824). Born into the modest Kostroma branch of an ancient princely family, Gorchakov received a home education and was enrolled as a sergeant-major *(vakhmistr)* in the Viatka Carabineer Regiment in 1768. The following year he served as adjutant to P. S. Gagarin during the taking of Khotin and was promoted to ensign *(praporshchik)*. In 1774–1780 Gorchakov repeatedly served in combat, including service in the Kuban and Crimea in the corps of A. V. Suvorov. In 1782 he left service with the rank of second major to live in Moscow as well as on his Tula and Kostroma estates. In 1790 Gorchakov returned to service as a volunteer and participated in the storming of Izmail; he was wounded in action and subsequently decorated. In 1793 Gorchakov also served as president of the Tula Upper Court for State Peasants *(verkhniaia rasprava)* but did not return to permanent service until the reign of Alexander I. Between 1807 and 1816 he occupied a variety of posts: Pskov provincial procurator (1807), procurator in Tauride province (1807–1810), supervisor of the Simferopol district school (1807), official in the Ministry of Popular Education in St. Petersburg (1811), head of the chancery of M. I. Golenishchev-Kutuzov in the Danubian Army (1811), official in the War Ministry, vice governor of Kostroma province (1813), and finally, governor of Kostroma province (1815). In 1816 Gorchakov retired from service and settled in Moscow. *SRP,* 1:223–26.

Gorodchaninov, G. N. (1772–1852). G. N. Gorodchaninov was born into a merchant family and received his education at the Nizhnii Novgorod Seminary and Moscow University. In 1799 he began service in the Postal Department in St. Petersburg, became a junior assistant *(ad"iunkt)* of Russian literature at Kazan University in 1806, served as librarian at the Medical Surgical Academy in Moscow from 1808, and finally returned to Kazan as professor of Russian literature in 1810. After retiring in 1829, Gorodchaninov participated episodically in literary and journalistic activities. *ES,* 17:320–21; *RP 1800–1917,* 1:641–42.

Iukin, Ivan. No biographical information is available.

Ivanov, L. M. (d. before 1793). Little is known about the life of Ivanov. The dedication to the opera *Serdtseplena* (1793) indicates that Ivanov served under Prince G. P. Gagarin in the Sixth Department of the Senate and possessed the rank of titular councilor (rank 9). *SRP,* 1:349–50.

Kapnist, V. V. (1758–1823). Born in Ukraine, and educated at home, Kapnist was the son of a Greek immigrant and brigadier. At age 13 he entered the military school of the Izmailovskii Guards Regiment and two years later joined the Preobrazhenskii Guards Regiment. After leaving military service in 1775, Kapnist devoted himself to literary activities. In 1783 he left a position in the St. Petersburg Postal Department to live in his Ukrainian village, and in 1785 he was elected marshal of the nobility for Kiev province. From 1799 to 1801, Kapnist served in the Directorate of Imperial Theaters, where, ironically, his duties included the examination and correction of plays. During the period 1802–1822 he held judicial and administrative posts in Poltava province. *DLB,* 150:129–34; *SRP,* 2:21–28.

Karamzin, N. M. (1766–1826). A towering cultural figure, Karamzin is noted for perfecting Russian sentimentalism, encouraging the development of gothic and pre-romantic literary themes, and earnestly addressing himself to the Russian woman reader. Descended from a noble family that served Ivan III and from the Tatar prince Kara-Murza, Karamzin was the son of a retired army captain and Simbirsk landowner. He received his early education at home and at a Simbirsk boarding school, followed by instruction at a Moscow boarding school and lectures at Moscow University. In 1774 Karamzin enrolled in the army and in 1781 transferred to the Preobrazhenkii Guards Regiment in St. Petersburg with the rank of sub-ensign. After retiring with the rank of lieutenant in 1784, he became involved in masonic lodges in Simbirsk and Moscow. His literary career took off in Moscow where he participated in the publishing ventures of N. I. Novikov. Karamzin's 1803 appointment as court historian brought the rank of court councilor in 1804, followed by promotion to state councilor in 1816. *DLB,* 150:135–50; *SRP,* 2:32–43.

Kheraskov M. M. (1733–1807). The son of a Wallachian emigré, Kheraskov was educated at the Land Forces Noble Cadet Corps in St. Petersburg and became one of the most important literary figures of the eighteenth century. In 1755 he left the military to help found Moscow University, where he spent most of his service career. In 1770–1775, Kheraskov again served in St. Petersburg as vice president of the College of Mines. Following several years of disgrace brought on by masonic activities, Kheraskov returned to service in the late 1770s as rector of Moscow University. *DLB,* 150:156–72.

Khvostov, D. I. (1757–1835). Khvostov, member of an old noble family dating back to the thirteenth century, was educated at home, in a private boarding school, and at Moscow University. He began service as a private in the Preobrazhenkii Guards Regiment in 1772, became a provisioning official *(ober-proviantmeister)* in 1779, and served in the Senate under the procurator-general from 1783. In 1787 Khvostov left service and went to Moscow. In 1790 he became a lieutenant-colonel of the Chernigov Infantry Regiment attached to the person of A. V. Suvorov, one of his closest friends. In 1799, at the request of Suvorov, the king of Sardinia granted Khvostov the title of count, which from 1802 he also was permitted to use in Russia. In 1797 Khvostov reached the rank of actual state councilor and was appointed ober-procurator of the Senate; in 1799 he was assigned to the same post in the Synod. In 1802, with the rank of privy councilor (obtained in 1800), Khvostov again left service. In 1807 he became a senator and in 1818 a member of the State Council and judge of the St. Petersburg Conscience Court *(Sovestnyi sud).* He retired from service in 1831 with the rank of actual privy councilor. Although Khvostov's literary activities were ridiculed by contemporaries, he published and distributed his writings at personal expense and in 1791 was elected a member of the Russian Academy. *RBS,* 21:297–300; *RP XIX vek,* 2:367–69; *ES,* 73:142.

Kireevskii, V. I. (1773–1812). The Kireevskiis traced their lineage back to the service gentry of the early seventeenth century. Vasilii Ivanovich, father of the noted Slavophiles Ivan and Peter, possessed a broad European-style education and served in the guards before retiring with the rank of second-major in the reign of Paul. Known for his interest in science and medicine, Kireevskii also was reputed to be a benevolent serf master. During the War of 1812, after establishing a hospital to treat the sick and wounded near Orel, Kireevskii caught typhoid and died. *RP 1800–1917,* 2:534; Abbott Gleason, *European and Muscovite: Ivan Kireevsky and the Origins of Slavophilism* (Cambridge, Mass.: Harvard University Press, 1972), 7–18.

Kliucharev, F. P. (1751–1822). Kliucharev was born to a noble family and began service in 1766 as a copyist in the Moscow office of the College of Mines. In 1767 he was promoted to junior chancery clerk *(podkantseliarist)* and in 1776 to chancery clerk with transfer to Mogilev province. In Mogilev, Kliucharev became secretary of the chancery of the Belarusian governor-general, reaching the rank of titular councilor in 1780. He also reportedly participated in amateur theatrical productions. In 1782 Kliucharev obtained a position as procurator in the Moscow Provincial Magistracy and simultaneously enrolled in Moscow University. In Moscow, he became an active mason and close friend of N. I. Novikov. In 1783–1784 he served as procurator in the Viatka Upper Land Court before retiring and returning to Moscow. Kliucharev returned to service in 1785 as secretary to the vice president of the Admiralty College, retired again in 1792 with the rank of court councilor, and returned to service in the Moscow Postal Department in 1795. That same year he was appointed Astrakhan postal director and in 1797 reached the rank of collegial councilor. In 1799 Kliucharev was promoted to state councilor and sent to Tambov as postal director. Then in 1801–1812 he occupied the post of Moscow postal director with the rank of actual state councilor from 1802. Accused of treason by Moscow Governor-General F. V. Rostopchin, Kliucharev was exiled to Voronezh in 1812 but later exonerated and paid back-salary in 1814. In 1816, Alexander I granted him the rank of privy councilor and appointed him a senator. Kliucharev died in poverty, financially ruined by the deaths of five children, all of whom left orphans in his care. *SRP*, 2:67–70.

Klushin, A. I. (1763–1804). Klushin belonged to a modest service family that had attained noble status in the reign of Peter I. His father served as a junior chancery clerk *(podkantseliarist)* in the town of Livny (Orel province), and in 1793 his mother owned ten serfs. Klushin attended a local school and began his service career in the Orel Provincial Chancery *(provintsial'naia kantseliariia)* in 1778. Next he received assignment in the chancery of Governor-General N. V. Repnin. Klushin began military service in 1780; he participated in the Polish campaign of 1783–1784 and left service for health reasons as a second lieutenant *(podporuchik)* in 1786. From 1788 he served on the Commission for the Construction of Roads in St. Petersburg. In 1793 Klushin was released from service to study and travel, returning in 1799 to serve as censor of Russian plays for the Directorate of Imperial Theaters. From May 1800 he also served as inspector (director) of the Russian troupe. Klushin retired from service with the rank of court councilor in 1803. *SRP*, 2:62–67.

Kniazhnin, Ia. B. (1740–1791). A major literary figure of the eighteenth century, Kniazhnin was born into the Pskov nobility and educated at the gymnasium of the Academy of Sciences in St. Petersburg. He began civil service in 1755 and from 1762 served as secretary to high-level military officers. In 1773 Kniazhnin was convicted of gambling away over 5,000 rubles of public funds. Deprived of noble status, the rank of captain, and his estate, he was sentenced to death by hanging. He then received a pardon from Catherine II, became a private in the St. Petersburg garrison, and supported his family from translations and tutoring. In 1777 he regained the rank of captain and reentered civil service. From 1778 until his death, he worked as secretary to I. I. Betskoi, head of the Chancellery for the Construction of Houses and Parks. *DLB*, 150:173–81.

Kokoshkin, I. A. (1765–1835). Identified as the first cousin of F. F. Kokoshkin (1773–1838)—a prominent actor, Moscow theater director, and writer—I. A. Kokoshkin was from a noble family and in 1816 became a member of the Free Society of Lovers of Russian Literature. *ES*, 30:630–31; *SRP*, 2:103–4.

Kolychev, V. P. (1736–1794). Kolychev was born to aristocratic parents—his father was from an ancient boyar family and his mother was E. B. Sheremeteva. He received his early education at home and then entered the Land Forces Noble Cadet Corps in 1752. After serving in the Vyborg Infantry Regiment and the Seven Years' War, he left military service with the rank of lieutenant. Kolychev then entered civil service in Moscow, which allowed him to spend summers on his Tula estate. Until his death he remained an active estate manager. *SRP*, 2:109–10.

Konstantinov, T. V. (1765– after 1798). Son of a senior officer, Konstantinov began service in the administration of the Tula governor-general in 1777. During the years 1780–1787, he served first as a junior chancery clerk *(podkantseliarist)* in the Tula Upper Court for State Peasants *(verkhniaia rasprava)* and the Tula Criminal Chamber, and then as a chancery clerk in the Tula Upper Land Court for Nobles. While serving in Tula, Konstantinov also performed in the theater attached to the governor-generalship. In 1787–1791 he studied acting with the St. Petersburg Russian troupe, then served in the theater of the Kazan governor-generalship, and in 1793 returned to the court stage as a back-up for P. A. Plavil'shchikov, who had begun to perform in Moscow. In 1795 Konstantinov was appointed collegial actuary *(aktuarius)* in the administration of the Khar'kov governor-general. He also became impresario of the Khar'kov theater, which he transformed from a troupe of male amateurs into a well-regarded troupe of six actors and three actresses, including several St. Petersburg actors. The Khar'kov theater benefited from the support of the provincial authorities and nobility but closed in 1796 to observe a period of mourning for Catherine II. Earlier that year Konstantinov had requested release from his administrative post in order to seek another position, and when the theater closed he moved his theatrical activities to Smolensk. *SRP*, 2:121.

Kop'ev, A. D. (1767–1846). Kop'ev was the son of the Penza vice-governor D. S. Kop'ev. Registered in the guards in 1775, he was promoted to sergeant in the Izmailovskii Guards Regiment in 1778. Sometime after 1791, as a member of the favorite P. A. Zubov's staff *(shtat)*, Kop'ev quickly attained the rank of army lieutenant-colonel *(podpolkovnik)*. In 1794 he participated in the taking of Warsaw and the subsequent suppression of the Polish insurgency. In 1797 Paul I sentenced Kop'ev to four months of arrest and service in an army regiment for "bad behavior." Entertaining anecdotes suggest that buffoonery aroused Paul's ire, but the archival record reveals only that two months earlier Kop'ev had petitioned the emperor for leave from the Pskov Dragoon Regiment in connection with the death of his father. In 1802, under Alexander I, Kop'ev returned to St. Petersburg, received the rank of major-general, and continued service. In 1808–1810 he served on a commission investigating Finnish affairs and in 1827 was elected to the Shlissel'burg district commission responsible for the compilation of noble genealogical books. A colorful literary figure, and active in business, Kop'ev bought and sold estates in the St. Petersburg area, participated in trade, and fulfilled state contracts. *SRP*, 2:123–26; *ES*, 31:184.

Kozel'skii, F. Ia. (1734–after 1799). Kozel'skii's family came from the Cossack host. He studied at the Kiev Academy in 1751–1755 and ended his formal education at the Academy of Sciences gymnasium in St. Petersburg (1755–1758). During the 1760s he served in the army, which brought promotion to captain in 1769 and transfer to the Senate as a protocolist. In 1772 Kozel'skii briefly retired but then returned to service in the College of Foreign Affairs, where he reached the rank of collegial assessor in 1774. He continued service in the college throughout the 1790s and is last mentioned in the calendar of 1799. *SRP,* 2:88–91.

Kozodavlev, O. P. (1754–1819). The son of a captain *(rotmistr)* in the Guards Cavalry Regiment, at age eight Kozodavlev became a page enrolled in service. In 1769–1774 he studied at Leipzig University, and after returning to Russia, served as a protocolist in the Senate with the rank of army captain. Three years later Kozodavlev became an administrator *(ekzekutor)* with the rank of colonel, in December 1780 he became a councilor of the St. Petersburg Civil Chamber, and in January 1783 councilor to the director of the Academy of Sciences, E. R. Dashkova. In 1783 Kozodavlev was chosen to be a member of the Russian Academy and the following year he joined the Commission on Popular Schools. He served as an assistant and then director of the Main Popular School in St. Petersburg and in 1786–1788 inspected the popular schools of ten provinces. In 1793 Kozodavlev was appointed chief-procurator *(ober-prokuror)* of the Third Department of the Senate, becoming a senator in 1799 and serving as director of the Heraldry Office in 1800. In 1801, Kozodavlev was chosen to be a member of the Commission on the Examination of Criminal Cases, and in 1810 he became Minister of Internal Affairs. As minister, he was responsible for preparing the law on free farmers, an effort to encourage the emancipation of serfs on a voluntary basis. *SRP,* 2:100–102.

Kropotov, P. A. (1736/7–1790). Son of the governor *(voevoda)* of Riazan district, Kropotov entered the Land Forces Noble Corps in 1750 and began service as an ensign in the Koporskii Infantry Regiment in 1756. A few months later the Senate appointed him a surveyor *(mezhevshchik)* in Moscow district, and in 1757–1759 he served as administrator in the Moscow Surveying Office. In 1761 Kropotov retired with the rank of lieutenant and in 1764 entered state service. From 1775 until January 1778 he served as assistant to the inspector of the Stone Chancery and for the rest of 1778 as judge in the Tula Court for Free Peasants. From December 1778, Kropotov occupied the same post in Riazan, before becoming chairman of the Riazan Upper Court for State Peasants *(verkhniaia rasprava)* in 1782. Promotion to titular councilor came in 1780, followed by appointment as collegial assessor in 1782. Kropotov retired from service in 1785, due to illness, and spent the rest of his life on his estate in Riazan district. *SRP,* 2:155–56.

Krutitskii, A. M. (1754–1803). The son of a garrison sergeant, Krutitskii, at age six, entered the Moscow Foundling Home where he acquired an elementary education. Beginning in 1778 he also performed leading roles in the theatrical troupe of the home. In 1779 Krutitskii joined the troupe of the St. Petersburg Free Russian Theater managed by K. Knipper. There he completed his training under I. A. Dmitrevskii, who took over management of the theater at the end of 1782. In 1783 the Free Theater and its troupe came under the Directorate of Imperial Theaters, and Krutitskii became a court actor. Recognized for his comic roles, Krutitskii also served as inspector of the Russian theatrical troupe in 1793–1800. *SRP,* 2:156–57; *ES,* 32:858.

Krylov, I. A. (1769–1844). A world-renowned fabulist, giant of modern Russian literature, and professional card player, Krylov came from the social category of "senior officers' children." His father was a military officer who rose from soldier rank and settled his family in Tver after the Pugachev rebellion. After his father died in 1778, Krylov's family struggled economically. His mother, reportedly forced to work as a servant in rich households, nonetheless managed to provide irregular education for her son. Some sources say he attended school in Tver. Krylov's service career began in 1777, before his father's death, when he was registered as a junior chancery clerk *(podkantseliarist)* at the Lower Land Court in Kaliazin. After his father died, he began active service as a copyist *(pisets)* for the Tver Magistracy and also took lessons with the children of the L'vov family. In 1782 he moved to St. Petersburg with F. P. L'vov and in 1783 became a chancery clerk in the Treasury Chamber *(kazennaia palata)*. Soon thereafter he reached the rank of provincial secretary *(provintsial'nyi sekretar')*, followed by an appointment in the Department of Mines in 1787. In 1788 Krylov left service to pursue a full-time literary career. After a series of journalistic endeavors, he moved to Moscow in 1794 and in 1797 became secretary to Prince S. F. Golitsyn. When Golitsyn fell from favor and was exiled to his estates in Saratov province and Ukraine, Krylov went along as the family tutor. From 1801 to 1803 he administered the chancery of Golitsyn, who had been appointed military governor-general in Riga, and he reached the rank of provincial secretary *(gubernskii sekretar')* before again leaving service. From Riga, Krylov went to live with his brother in Serpukhov. In 1805 he was living in Moscow, and in 1806 he returned to St. Petersburg. During this time he began to write the fables that secured his literary reputation and brought him lasting fame. In 1808–1810, Krylov served in the Minting Department with the rank of titular councilor, in 1811 he was elected a member of the Russian Academy, and in 1812 he obtained a position at the new Imperial Public Library, along with a lifetime pension. In 1830, Krylov reached the rank of state councilor after being exempted from educational and examination requirements for promotion. He retired from service in 1841. *DLB*, 150:197–207; *RP 1800–1917*, 3:177–83; *RP XIX vek*, 1:388–92.

Kugushev, N. M. (1777–1825). Born to an old but poor princely family, Kugushev became a sergeant in the Preobrazhenskii Guards Regiment in 1794 and an army ensign in 1797. In 1799 he fought in Galicia and Austria, participated in Suvorov's Italian campaign, and after suffering serious wounds, retired with the rank of lieutenant. In 1801–1802, Kugushev served as chief of police in Tambov, a post he left for health reasons. In 1822 he occupied two administrative posts: supervisor of a district school and member of the estate administration of M. M. Speranskii. *SRP*, 2:163–65; *ES*, 32:927.

Levshin, V. A. (1746–1826). Born in Tula province, the son of a modest landowner and army officer who reached the rank of colonel, Levshin joined the Novotroitsk Cuirassier Regiment in 1765 and served in the Russo-Turkish War of 1768–1774. Due to illness he left service in 1772, with the rank of lieutenant, and returned to the family estate. In 1779 Levshin was elected to a four-year term as district judge and in 1803 became special official to State Secretary A. A. Vitovtov in St. Petersburg. Levshin retired from state service with the rank of state councilor in 1818. Throughout his career Levshin's activities as author, translator, and compiler supplemented his salary and the meager income from his estate. *SRP*, 2:198–201.

Lomonosov, M. V. (1711–1765). One of the leading cultural figures of eighteenth-century Russia, Lomonosov is renowned as a scientist, poet, linguist, grammarian, historian, and mosaic artist. A state peasant by birth, his father was a wealthy shipowner and fisherman active in the White and Berents Seas. After learning to read and write from a church sacristan, Lomonosov entered the Moscow Slavonic-Greek-Latin Academy in 1731. To gain admission Lomonosov lied about his social origins, but by the time the authorities discovered his peasant status in 1734, he had been recognized as a gifted student and was allowed to continue his studies. He spent 1734 at the Kiev Academy and from there entered the gymnasium attached to the Academy of Sciences in St. Petersburg. In 1736–1740 Lomonosov studied science in Germany, and after returning to Russia and the academy in 1741, he was appointed professor of chemistry in 1745. Together with V. K. Trediakovskii, professor of Latin and Russian eloquence, he became one of only two Russian professors at the academy. During the 1750s, Lomonosov became active in academy administration, and in 1754 he authored the plan that led to the creation of Moscow University. Despite bitter conflict with literary and scientific rivals, Lomonosov continued to garner recognition at home and abroad. In 1753 Empress Elizabeth granted him an estate of 200 souls. In state service he reached the rank of state councilor (class 5) and acquired honorary membership in both the Swedish and Bologna Academies. *DLB*, 150:208–21; *SRP*, 2:212–26.

Lopukhin, I. V. (1756–1816). Known for his memoirs, masonic writings, and other religious and mystical compositions, Lopukhin belonged to the Novikov-Schwarz circle of Moscow masons. He began military service in 1775 as an ensign in the Preobrazhenskii Guards Regiment, and from 1782 until his retirement in 1785 with the rank of state councilor, he served as senior councilor and later chairman of the Moscow Criminal Chamber. In retirement Lopukhin devoted himself to literary and philanthropic activities before being called back to service at the ascension of Paul. After brief service in St. Petersburg as a state secretary with the rank of actual state councilor, he returned to Moscow as a senator with the rank of titular councilor. There he reviewed judicial cases in the Fifth (criminal) Department of the Senate in Moscow and was sent out to conduct inspections in various provinces. In 1802, Lopukhin became a judge of the Moscow Conscience Court and headed a commission to settle disputes and apportion state obligations in Crimea. He continued service in the Moscow departments of the Senate in 1805–1812, organized militias in several provinces in 1806, and attained the rank of actual privy councilor in 1807. Lopukhin left Moscow for his Orel estate in 1812 and married the daughter of a Moscow merchant the following year. *SRP*, 2:229–35; *ES*, 35:9; I. V. Lopukhin, *Masonskie trudy: Dukhovnyi rytsar'. Nekotorye cherty o vnutrennei tserkvi* (Moscow: Alteina, 1997).

Lukin, V. I. (1737–1794). The son of a court lackey, or stoker, who attained noble status in 1761, Lukin was self-educated, owned no villages, and lived off his salary. He began service in 1752 as a copyist in the Heraldry Office, and from 1756 he performed the same function as a sergeant in the Preobrazhenskii Guards Regiment. Promoted to second lieutenant *(podporuchik)* in 1759, he served with the Guards Corps in Prussia in 1760–1761 and in 1762 became secretary to K. G. Razumovskii. Lukin's success as a translator led to his appointment as secretary in I. P. Elagin's chancellery, attached to the empress's Cabinet, a post he occupied in 1764–1774. From 1774 until his death, Lukin served in the Main Court Chancery where he reached the rank of active state councilor (rank 4). His close association with Elagin also included extensive masonic activities. *SRP*, 2:236–40.

L'vov, N. A. (1751–1803). Best known as an architect but also a recognized literary figure, L'vov was born into the nobility of Tver province and began service in the Preobrazhenskii Guards Regiment at the age of 18. In 1775 he retired from the military with the rank of captain and in 1776 entered service in the College of Foreign Affairs. In 1782–1797 L'vov served in the Postal Department and from 1797 until his death maintained a concession for processing and marketing coal. *DLB*, 150:222–27; *ES*, 35:136–37.

Maikov, A. A. (1761–1838). Born to a noble family, Maikov served in the guards as a young man and began his administrative career in the Directorate of Imperial Theaters in 1802. Maikov held positions within the directorate in both Moscow and St. Petersburg; he left his post as director of the St. Petersburg imperial theaters (1821–1825) when the position became subordinate to the Committee on Theatrical Affairs. In 1821–1828 he served in the Moscow armory. *SRP*, 2:257; *ES*, 35:371.

Maikov, V. I. (1730–1778). A renowned literary figure and active mason, Maikov was born to a landowning guards officer from Iaroslav province in 1728 or 1730. He began formal studies at the Academy of Sciences gymnasium in 1740, enrolled in the Semenovskii Guards Regiment in 1742, and returned to the family estate to complete his education in 1743. His career in active military service began in 1747 and continued until 1761 when he retired with the rank of captain. Maikov then settled in Moscow where in 1766–1768 he occupied the post of assistant to the Moscow governor. In 1768 he was appointed secretary of the Directorate Committee of the Legislative Commission and moved to St. Petersburg. From March 1770, Maikov served as procurator of the War College, a post he combined with membership in the Free Economic Society and with an unsuccessful manufacturing venture. The rise of G. A. Potemkin led to the removal of Maikov's patron, Z. G. Chernyshev, and to the poet's own retirement from the War College. In 1775 Maikov returned to Moscow where he was elected to the Free Russian Assembly of Moscow University. Later that year an imperial ukase granted him the rank of brigadier and a post in the Office of the Armory *(Kontora Masterskoi i Oruzheinoi Palaty)*. Maikov died in 1778 soon after being recalled to St. Petersburg to serve as master of the Heraldry Office *(gerol'dmeister)*. *DLB*, 150:228–32; *SRP*, 2:258–61.

Matinskii, M. A. (1750–ca 1820). Matinskii was born in Moscow province, the serf of Count S. P. Iaguzhinskii. Iaguzhinskii sent him to study in the gymnasium for non-nobles at Moscow University and further supported his education with travel to Italy in 1783. In 1785 Matinskii, his mother, and his wife received their freedom. The following year Matinskii became a translator for the Commission on Popular Schools, with the rank of titular councilor (rank 9), in 1797 became secretary of the commission, and in 1815 received the rank of court councilor (rank 7). From 1785, Matinskii also served as teacher of mathematics, history, and geography at the Corps of Pages, and in 1797–1802 at the Smol'nyi Institute for Noble Girls. *SRP*, 2:276–78; *ES*, 36:803–4.

Matveev, Filiter. No biographical information is available.

Mikhailov, Ivan (no dates). In *SK*, Mikhailov is called a teacher and is distinguished from another Ivan Mikhailov (no dates), who in 1791 called himself a student of philosophy, probably at the Moscow Slavonic-Greek-Latin Academy, and in 1800 a second lieutenant. In 1826 a reviewer also described the latter Ivan Mikhailov as an author who wrote for the simple people. *SRP,* 2:293–94.

Narezhnyi, V. T. (1780–1825). Of Polish origins, Narezhnyi was the son of a sergeant-major *(vakhmistr)* of the Chernigov Carabineer Regiment who retired in 1786 with the rank of cornet and personal nobility. Until age 11, Narezhnyi was educated at home in Ustivits where his father owned land but no serfs. In 1792 Narezhnyi began to study in the noble gymnasium at Moscow University; in 1798 he became a student and in 1799 transferred to the Philosophy Faculty. In 1801, Narezhnyi left the university, and in 1802–1803 he served in various administrative posts in Georgia. Narezhnyi soon returned to St. Petersburg where he served in the salt and mining administrations from 1803 until 1813. In 1813 he married and retired from service with the rank of collegial assessor. Narezhnyi returned to service in the Inspectors Department of the War Ministry in 1815 and was promoted to court councilor in 1818. In 1821 he again retired from service. *RP 1800–1917,* 4:230–33.

Nekhachin, I. V. (1771–1811). Of unspecified non-noble origins, Nekhachin (Nakhachin, Nekhochin) called himself "a servitor *(sluzhitel')* of Mrs. Naryshkina" and may have worked as a private tutor. *SRP,* 2:345–47.

Nikolev, N. P. (1758–1815). Educated under the supervision of his relative, Princess E. R. Dashkova, Nikolev was the son of a guards major-general; his mother was of merchant origins. At age 15 he began military service in the guards; in 1778 poor eyesight forced him to retire with the rank of major. After leaving service Nikolev made his name as a poet and playwright. *DLB,* 150:244–48; *SRP,* 2:350–56.

Ozerov, V. A. (1769–1816). Born to a noble family from Tver province, Ozerov studied at the Land Forces Noble Cadet Corps in 1776–1787 and began administrative service as a lieutenant in the chancery of the governor-general of Orel and Kursk. After serving with the governor-general in the Southern Army in 1789, during the Second Turkish War, Ozerov was appointed to the Treasury Chamber of the Kursk governor-generalship. In 1792 he returned to the cadet corps as an instructor and adjutant to the commander, and in 1794 went back into state service with the rank of captain. His service assignments included positions in the chancery of the general-procurator of the Senate, in the Department of State Economy (as collegial assessor in 1797 and as collegial councilor in 1798), and in the Forestry Department (1799). In 1800 Ozerov continued his forestry appointment in military service with the rank of major-general. After a temporary retirement in 1801–1803, he returned to the Forestry Department of the Ministry of Finance and in 1804 became an actual state councilor. Ozerov retired from service in 1808. Literary historians describe Ozerov's tragedies as the culmination of the Russian neoclassical tradition, but his work is best understood in the context of the early nineteenth century when romanticism and an autonomous public theater culture became established in Russia. *RP 1800–1917,* 4:405–8.

Parpura, M. O. (1763–1828). Parpura was a Ukrainian noble educated at the Kiev Seminary. In 1783 he began service as a chancery clerk *(kantseliarist)* in the St. Petersburg Assignat Bank, while also pursuing medical studies. From 1785 he taught midwifery at the St. Petersburg Foundling Home, and from 1787 he was teacher of German and Russian at the St. Petersburg Surgical School as well as translator in the Medical College. At the turn of the century, Parpura became director of medical institutions on Vasil'evskii island and general supervisor of the printing press of the Medical College. In 1800 he was promoted to court councilor. *SRP*, 2:411–12.

Pavlov, Vasilii (no dates). Believed to be from an administrative family, Pavlov studied at Moscow University in the early 1780s. *SRP*, 2:397.

Perepechin, N. I. (1749–1799). Born into a modest noble family, Perepechin and his brother A. I. Perepechin together owned 375 souls in Kostroma province in 1798. In 1762 Perepechin enrolled simultaneously in the guards and in the Moscow University gymnasium. In 1782 he began service in the St. Petersburg Treasury Chamber and in 1789 became a director of the St. Petersburg Assignat Bank. Perepechin served in this position until his death, having reached the rank of privy councilor. *SRP*, 2:419; *RBS*, 13:516–17.

Plavil'shchikov, P. A. (1760–1812). Plavil'shchikov was born into a merchant family with close ties to Moscow University. From 1768 he attended the gymnasium at the university and in 1776–1779 studied in the Philosophy Faculty. After completing the university, Plavil'shchikov became a professional actor, quickly found a position in the Directorate of Imperial Theaters, and also taught Russian literature at both the Academy of Arts and the Mining Corps. In addition to acting and writing, Plavil'shchikov served as inspector of the imperial troupe (from 1787) and director (from 1791) before returning to Moscow in 1793. In Moscow he continued to act on the public stage, taught history at a military school and declamation at the Moscow Noble Boarding School, and directed several domestic theaters. Plavil'shchikov remained in Moscow until the city was occupied by the French in 1812, also the year of his death. *SRP*, 2:438–41.

Popov, M. I. (1742–1790). Active as a translator and author, Popov was the son of a Iaroslavl merchant and an early member of F. G. Volkov's theater troupe. His association with the court theater is documented from 1764. In 1765 Popov moved to Moscow to attend lectures at the university and in 1767 became assistant to the secretary of the Legislative Commission. In 1769 he received the rank of collegial registrar *(kollezhskii registrator)* and returned to St. Petersburg. By 1776, Popov achieved the rank of provincial secretary *(gubernskii sekretar')*, and in 1780 he still was serving in the Legislative Commission (renamed the Commission for the Composition of the Laws). *DLB*, 150:308–12; *SRP*, 2:469–72.

Potemkin, P. S. (1743–1796). Count P. S. Potemkin, a relative of Prince G. A. Potemkin, probably studied at Moscow University before beginning military service in the Semenovskii Guards Regiment in 1756. He served in the Active Army during the Russo-Turkish War of 1769–1774, reaching the rank of captain in 1772 and brigadier in 1774. Potemkin then commanded troops in Kazan at the time of the Pugachev rebellion; his role in suppressing and investigating the rebellion brought him promotion to lieutenant general in 1782 and appointment as commander of the two Caucasian corps. In 1784 Potemkin was appointed governor-general of Saratov province and the Caucasus; he returned to active military service in 1787 during the Second Turkish War and distinguished himself at the storming of Izmail in 1790. In

1794 Potemkin fought with Suvorov against the Poles, which brought him the rank of *general en chef* and the title of count. At the time of his death Potemkin was under investigation in connection with the murder of the Gilian khan Gedaet. *SRP,* 2:484–86; *ES,* 48:730.

Prokudin-Gorskii, M. I. / Prakudin, Mikhail (1744–1813). Prokudin-Gorskii came from a noble family of Vladimir province. He received a home education, including six years of instruction in mathematics, and as a child was enrolled in the Iz-mailovskii Guards Regiment with the rank of corporal. In 1753 Prokudin-Gorskii obtained a patent for the rank of second lieutenant in the field artillery and transferred to the Semenovskii Guards Regiment. In 1759–1760 he participated in a diplomatic mission to Constantinople and upon returning to Russia began active service as a sergeant in the Preobrazhenskii Guards Regiment. Prokudin-Gorskii retired from military service with the rank of guards ensign, and following the Moscow plague of 1770–1772, he served as an assessor in the Civil Chamber of the Vladimir governor-generalship until 1781 and as a marshal of the nobility in 1778–1781. *SRP,* 2:498–99; *RBS,* 15:47–48.

Rzhevskii, A. A. (1737–1804). An active mason and noted man of letters, Rzhevskii was born into an old noble family and began his service career in the Semenovskii Guards Regiment in 1749. In 1767–1768 he represented the city of Vorotynsk (Moscow province) at the Legislative Commission. From 1768 until his retirement in 1800, Rzhevskii occupied a range of posts in the civil service: councilor of the Administration of Banks, vice-director and then director of the Academy of Sciences, president of the Medical College, and elected judge of the Conscience Court. In 1783 Rzhevskii became a senator with the rank of privy councilor and was promoted to actual privy councilor in 1797. *ES,* 52:670–71; *RBS,* 16:149–51.

Seliavin, N. I. (1770s–1833). A highly decorated veteran of the Napoleonic Wars, Seliavin was born a noble of Moscow province and in 1790 began service as a sergeant in the Ekaterinoslav Grenadier Regiment. Four years later he was appointed adjutant at the headquarters of Major General Prince Volkonskii. In 1797 Seliavin became a second lieutenant in the Azov Musketeer Regiment, in which he reached the rank of captain in 1803. During this period, Seliavin participated in the Italian and Swiss campaigns of Suvorov and was decorated for excellence. After returning to his regiment from French imprisonment, in early 1803 Seliavin was transferred to the Suite of His Imperial Majesty where he served as adjutant inspector under Quartermaster General Count Sukhtelen. In 1806 he was promoted to major and transferred to the Second Sapper Regiment, two years later he returned to his previous position on the staff of Count Sukhtelen, and during the Finnish War he served at general headquarters of the Active Army. In 1809, Seliavin reached the rank of lieutenant colonel, and two years later he became a colonel. In 1812–1814 he served as general on duty *(dezhurnyi general)* to Adjutant General Prince Volkonskii, again received decorations for excellence, and was promoted to major general. In 1814–1817, Seliavin served in the quartermaster's administration of Prince Volkonskii and then became a member of the Council of the War Ministry, a position he held for nine years. During this time, he also reached the rank of lieutenant general and received additional decorations. From 1826 until just before his death, Seliavin served as vice president of His Majesty's Cabinet. *RBS,* 18:294.

Sokolov, I. Ia. (b. 1739). A brief biographical entry identifies three additional come-dies by court actor Ivan Sokolov: *Vydumannyi klad* (1782), *Vliublennyi slepets* (1784), and *Sibiriak* (1807). No date of death is provided. *ES*, 60:731.

Sudovshchikov, N. R. (1770/1–1812). Very little is known about the biography of Sudovshchikov: his father was a major general in the artillery, and he himself may have served in the military before becoming a civil servant in the St. Petersburg and Kazan offices of the Appanage Administration *(udel'noe vedomstvo)*. He also served in the imperial theaters in St. Petersburg. *RBS*, 20: 104–5. See also A. A. Gozenpud, ed., *Stikhotvornaia komediia, komicheskaia opera, vodevil' kontsa XVIII–nachala XIX veka*, 2 vols. (Leningrad: Sovetskii pisatel', 1990), 1:542, 683.

Sumarokov, A. P. (1717–1777). Sumarokov was born into a prominent noble family and received an elite education at the Noble Cadet Corps. After serving as adjutant to Counts M. G. Golovkin and A. G. Razumovskii, he became the first director of the Russian Imperial Theater, a post he retained until 1761. A major figure in the devel-opment of modern Russian literature, Sumarokov enjoyed the patronage of Em-presses Elizabeth and Catherine II, which allowed him in effect to become a full-time professional author. *DLB*, 150:370–81.

Teil's, I. A. de (1744–1815). A privy councilor and senator, de Teil's may have worked on the composition of a new law code as a member of the Directorate of the Legislative Commission. His known service appointments include: administrator *(ekzekutor)* in the First Department of the Senate, from 1786 chairman of the Tver Criminal Chamber un-der the court of the Tver governor-general *(namestnik)* and director of the local school, vice-governor and later governor of Tver province, and from 1807 commander of the newly acquired regions of Belostok and Tarnopol. *RBS*, 20:438–39.

Titov, P. N. (d. 1845). Little is known about the life of Titov—only that he held the rank of court councilor, authored several plays, and did some translations. *RBS*, 20:567.

Trediakovskii, V. K. (1703–1769). A major literary figure of the mid-eighteenth cen-tury, Trediakovskii was born in Astrakhan, the son and grandson of priests. He re-ceived his early education in a school run by Italian Capuchins, entered the Moscow Slavonic-Greek-Latin Academy in 1723, and in 1726–1730 studied at the Hague and in Paris and Hamburg. When Trediakovskii returned to St. Petersburg, he became a student at the Academy of Sciences, where subsequently he worked as a translator in 1732 and a secretary in 1733. Trediakovskii's academy duties included the writing of ceremonial poems, translating, and the preparation of a Russian grammar and dic-tionary. In 1745 he was appointed professor of Latin and Russian eloquence, joining professor of chemistry M. V. Lomonosov as the first Russian professors in the Ger-man-dominated academy. Ironically, literary battles with Lomonosov and Sumarokov led to isolation at the academy, and in 1757 Trediakovskii stopped at-tending; dismissal with the rank of court councilor (class 8) followed in 1759. After leaving service, Trediakovskii gave private lessons and continued his work as a trans-lator and poet. He died in poverty and isolation. *DLB*, 150:382–93.

Verevkin, M. I. (1732–1795). Verevkin belonged to a poor noble family from Moscow province, attended the Naval Cadet Corps, and served in the navy until

1755, when he became assessor at Moscow University. From 1759 he served as director of the Kazan Gymnasium, where he organized a successful theatrical troupe of students, and from 1760 he also served as assistant to the Kazan governor. After asking the parents of gymnasium students to provide supplies for the underfunded school, Verevkin was released from the post of director in 1761 but continued to serve in the Kazan Provincial Chancery. In 1762 he received the rank of court councilor; in 1763 he retired from service in disgrace with the rank of collegial councilor but also became a translator attached to the empress's Cabinet *(kabinet)*. Eventually exonerated, Verevkin returned to service at the time of the Pugachev rebellion (1773) as director of P. I. Panin's military chancery. His subsequent posts included an appointment in the Novgorod Provincial Chancery, councilor of the Tver Provincial Administration, councilor of the Novgorod Provincial Administration, and chairman of the Tver Civil Chamber, which brought him the rank of state councilor. In 1782 Verevkin became corresponding member of the Academy of Sciences and in 1792 a member of the Free Economic Society. He retired from service in 1785 with the rank of actual state councilor. *SRP,* 1:148–50; *ES,* 11:20.

Viazemskii, V. S. (d. 1823). Viazemskii was the son of a Kostroma landowner with princely title, and he himself was the master of several villages in Kostroma province. *SRP,* 1:183.

Viazmitinov, S. K. (1749/44–1819). A self-educated serviceman, Viazmitinov enjoyed an illustrious military and administrative career under Catherine II, Paul, and Alexander I. Born to a modest noble family from Kursk province, he began service in 1759 as a noncommissioned officer in the Observation Corps. In 1761 he was appointed ensign *(praporshchik)* in the Corps of the Ukrainian Land Forces, and in 1762 he was transferred to the Manège Company. From 1768, Viazmitinov served as aide-de-camp to Count Z. G. Chernyshev and from 1770 administered his campaign chancery as adjutant-general. In the 1780s and 1790s, Viazmitinov commanded several regiments and corps, and participated in key battles. He also occupied important military administrative posts: throughout the 1790s he served as military governor and governor-general in different localities. In 1797 Viazmitinov was commandant of the St. Petersburg Fortress and commander of the Commissariat Department. After being promoted to general of the infantry in 1798, he was briefly released from service in 1799. In 1802–1808 he served as Russia's first minister of land forces, and in 1805–1898 and 1812–1818 as governor-general of St. Petersburg. In 1812–1816, Viazmitinov headed the Ministry of Police. Viazmitinov received the title of count in 1818. *SRP,* 1:183–85; *ES,* 14:723.

Volkov, A. A. (1736–1788). Translator of European plays and author of three comedies, Volkov's literary activities did not extend beyond the 1760s. He was born into an hereditary noble family of Iaroslav province and enrolled in the Semenovskii Guards Regiment as a child. At 18, Volkov had reached the rank of captain. In 1765 he left military service with the rank of colonel and entered state service where he reached the rank of state councilor in 1773 and actual state councilor in 1779. Before retiring from service in 1783, his administrative assignments included posts in the Heraldry Office and in the Chancery for the Construction of State Roads, deputy to the Legislative Commission, assignment to fight heresy in Orel and Tambov, director of the Imperial Porcelain Factory, and master of heraldry in the Heraldry Office attached to the Senate. *SRP,* 1:167–68.

Volkov, D. V. (1727–1785). Volkov, the son of an administrative clerk *(pod'iachii)* who achieved personal nobility in 1731, received his early education at home and in 1742 became a student in the College of Foreign Affairs. In 1745 he became junker with the rank of ensign *(praporshchik)* and a noble; in 1747 he served as a translator and in 1749 was appointed secretary of the College of Foreign Affairs. In 1754 Volkov moved to St. Petersburg where under the patronage of Count P. I. Shuvalov he occupied the post of secretary of the Ministerial Conference. In 1761–1762 he was personal secretary to Peter III. Briefly arrested after the coup that elevated Catherine II to the throne, Volkov became vice governor in Orenburg in July 1762. In 1764 he returned to the capital as president of the College of Manufactures, and from 1768 he was a privy councilor and senator. In 1771 he was sent to Moscow to assist in the struggle against the cholera epidemic and in 1772 helped to organize the restoration of the Moscow theater. In 1776 Volkov became governor-general *(namestnik)* in Smolensk while remaining a senator and president of the College of Manufactures. In 1778 he returned to St. Petersburg as general policemaster *(general-politseimeister)*, a post he retained until 1780. Volkov retired in 1782 and spent the last years of his life on his estate in Vitebsk province. *SRP*, 1:169–70; *ES*, 13:36-37.

Zheltov, Andrei (no dates). In 1790 Zheltov was an actor in the home theater of N. V. Kolychev. *SRP*, 1:316.

ABBREVIATIONS

ADIT   *Arkhiv direktsii imperatorskikh teatrov*

DLB   *Dictionary of Literary Biography*

DS   *Dramaticheskie sochineniia*

EIT   *Ezhegodnik imperatorskikh teatrov*

ES   *Entsiklopedicheskii slovar'*

FOG   *Forschungen zur osteuropäischen Geschichte*

HUS   *Harvard Ukrainian Studies*

IRDT   *Istoriia russkogo dramaticheskogo teatra*

JGO   *Jahrbücher für Geschichte Osteuropas*

JMH   *Journal of Modern History*

MP   *Muzykal'nyi Peterburg: Entsiklopedicheskii slovar'*

OCD   *Oxford Classical Dictionary*

PKNO   *Pamiatniki kul'tury: Novye otkrytiia*

PSVS   *Polnoe sobranie vsekh sochinenii v stikhakh i proze*

PSZ   *Polnoe sobranie zakonov Rossiiskoi imperii*

RBS   *Russkii biograficheskii slovar'*

RF   *Rossiiskii featr, ili Polnoe sobranie vsekh Rossiiskikh teatral'nykh sochinenii*

RGADA   Rossiiskii gosudarstvenyi arkhiv drevnikh aktov

RP 1800–1917   *Russkie pisateli 1800–1917*

RP XIX vek   *Russkie pisateli XIX vek*

RR   *Russian Review*

SEEJ   *Slavic and East European Journal*

SEER   *Slavonic and East European Review*

SIPVL   *Sochineniia i perevody Vladimera Lukina*

SK   *Svodnyi katalog russkoi knigi grazhdanskoi pechati XVIII veka 1725–1800*

SR   *Slavic Review*

SRP   *Slovar' russkikh pisatelei XVIII veka*

TLS   *The Times Literary Supplement*

NOTES

1: THEATER AND SOCIETY

1. The most recent historical research clearly documents the fundamental nature of the Petrine reforms. See James Cracraft, *The Petrine Revolution in Russian Imagery* (Chicago: University of Chicago Press, 1997); Lindsey Hughes, *Russia in the Age of Peter the Great* (New Haven: Yale University Press, 1998). On the Petrine myth, see Nicholas V. Riasanovsky, *The Image of Peter the Great in Russian History and Thought* (New York: Oxford University Press, 1985).

2. On the opposition to Peter and his policies, see Paul Bushkovitch, *Peter the Great: The Struggle for Power, 1671–1725* (Cambridge, Eng.: Cambridge University Press, 2001); James Cracraft, "Opposition to Peter the Great," in *Imperial Russia, 1700–1917: State, Society, Opposition,* ed. Ezra Mendelsohn and Marshall S. Shatz (DeKalb: Northern Illinois University Press, 1988), 22–36.

3. Keith Michael Baker, *Inventing the French Revolution: Essays on French Political Culture in the Eighteenth Century* (New York: Cambridge University Press, 1990), 4–7.

4. A. Arkhangel'skii, *Teatr do-Petrovskoi Rusi. Publichnaia lektsiia* (Kazan: Tipografiia gubernskogo pravleniia, 1884), 9–21; P. O. Morozov, *Istoriia russkogo teatra,* vol. 1, *Do poloviny XVIII stoletiia* (St. Petersburg: Tipografiia V. Demakova, 1889), 5–24, 30–41; Bertha Malnick, "The Origin and Early History of the Theatre in Russia," *SEER* 19 (1940): 203–5; V. N. Vsevolodskii-Gerngross, *Istoriia russkogo dramaticheskogo teatra,* vol. 1, *Ot istokov do kontsa XVIII veka* (Moscow: Iskusstvo, 1977), 25–38, 41–55; A. F. Nekrylova, *Russkie narodnye gorodskie prazdniki, uveseleniia, i zrelishcha, konets XVIII–nachalo XX veka* (Leningrad: Iskusstvo, 1988).

5. Historians also give 1689 and 1694 as dates for the collegium's elevation.

6. Arkhangel'skii, *Teatr do-Petrovskoi Rusi,* 21–31; Morozov, *Istoriia russkogo teatra,* 1:41–122, 360–91; Malnick, "Origin and Early History," 208; Paulina Lewin, "Early Ukrainian Theater and Drama," *Nationalities Papers* 8 (1980): 219–32; idem, "The Staging of Plays at the Kiev Mohyla Academy in the Seventeenth and Eighteenth Centuries," *HUS* 5 (1981): 320–34. According to Lewin, the languages of the Ukrainian drama were western Church Slavonic, colloquial Ukrainian, and Polish.

7. Paulina Lewin, "The Ukrainian Popular Religious Stage of the Seventeenth and Eighteenth Centuries on the Territory of the Polish Commonwealth," *HUS* 1 (1977): 308–29; idem, "Early Ukrainian Theater," 226–28.

8. A. S. Dëmin, "Evoliutsiia moskovskoi shkol'noi dramaturgii," in *Ranniaia russkaia dramaturgiia (XVII–pervaia polovina XVIII v.). P'esy shkol'nykh teatrov Moskvy* (Moscow: Nauka, 1974), 7–48; I. M. Badalich and V. D. Kuz'mina, eds., *Pamiatniki russkoi shkol'noi dramy XVIII veka (po zagrebskim spiskam)* (Moscow: Nauka, 1968), 3–121; L. M. Starikova, *Teatral'naia zhizn' starinnoi Moskvy: Epokha. Byt. Nravy* (Moscow: Iskusstvo, 1988), chap. 4; Morozov, *Istoriia russkogo teatra,* 1:294–360.

9. Dmitrii Rostovskii studied at the Kiev brotherhood school attached to the Theophany Monastery. Established in 1615, the school was absorbed into Petro Mohyla's Kiev Collegium. O. A. Derzhavina, "Russkii teatr 70-90-kh godov XVII v. i

nachala XVIII v.," in *Ranniaia russkaia dramaturgiia (XVII–pervaia polovina XVIII v.)*. *Russkaia dramaturgiia poslednei chetverti XVII i nachala XVIII v.* (Moscow: Nauka, 1972), 44–51; Malnick, "Origin and Early History," 206; Victor Terras, ed., *Handbook of Russian Literature* (New Haven: Yale University Press, 1985), 225; *Russkie sviatye: Tysiacha let russkoi sviatosti. Zhitiia sobrala monakhinia Taisiia* (St. Petersburg: Izdatel'stvo Azbuka, 2000), 564–65.

10. Other centers of church-sponsored school drama included Irkutsk (first half of the eighteenth century), Pskov (first half of the eighteenth century), Smolensk (1750s), Tver (1740s), Novgorod (1740s), the Trinity-Sergius Monastery (1740s), and possibly St. Petersburg (1720s) in connection with the activities of Feofan Prokopovich. The dates given indicate the period for which there is documentation. V. P. Andrianova, "Iz istorii teatra v Tveri v XVIII veke," in *Starinnyi teatr v Rossii XVII–XVIII vv.*, ed. V. N. Peretts (Petersburg: Academia, 1923), 93–142; A. S. Eleonskaia, "Tvorcheskie vzaimosviazi shkol'nogo i pridvornogo teatrov v Rossii," in *Ranniaia russkaia dramaturgiia (XVII–pervaia polovina XVIII v.). P'esy stolichnykh i provintsial'nykh teatrov pervoi poloviny XVIII v.* (Moscow: Nauka, 1975), 7–46, esp. 7–12; A. B. Kosterina-Azarian, *Teatral'naia starina Urala* (Ekaterinburg: Demidovskii institut, 1998), 102–9; Derzhavina, "Russkii teatr 70-90-kh godov," 45; Badalich and Kuz'mina, *Pamiatniki*, 56–93, 120–22; Vsevolodskii-Gerngross, *Istoriia russkogo dramaticheskogo teatra*, 429–30; R. M. Lazarchuk, "Iz istorii provintsial'nogo teatra (teatral'naia zhizn' Vologdy 1780-kh gg.)," *XVIII vek* 15 (1986): 52–69; V. I. Fedorov, ed., *Russkaia literatura XVIII veka: Slovar'-spravochnik* (Moscow: MGPU, 1997), 118–20.

11. In the late sixteenth and early seventeenth centuries, troupes of English actors began to tour the European continent and became especially popular in Germany. A collection of English plays from their repertoire was published in 1620, with a second collection of mainly German titles appearing in 1630. *Concise Oxford Companion to the Theatre*, 2nd ed., 146; N. Tikhonravov, ed., *Russkiia dramaticheskiia proizvedeniia 1672–1725 godov. K 200–letnemu iubileiu russkago teatra.* (St. Petersburg: Izdatel'stvo D. E. Kozhanchikova, 1874), 1:xii–xxiv; Kurt Günther, "Neue deutsche Quellen zum ersten russischen Theater," *Zeitschrift für Slawistik* 8 (5) (1963): 664–75; Starikova, *Teatral'naia zhizn'*, chap. 1; O. A. Derzhavina, A. S. Dëmin, A. N. Robinson, "Poiavlenie teatra i dramaturgii v Rossii v XVII v.," in *Ranniaia russkaia dramaturgiia (XVII–pervaia polovina XVIII v.). Pervye p'esy russkogo teatra* (Moscow: Nauka, 1972), 7–98; Arkhangel'skii, *Teatr do-Petrovskoi Rusi*, 32–37; Morozov, *Istoriia russkogo teatra*, 1:122–93; Vsevolodskii-Gerngross, *Istoriia russkogo dramaticheskogo teatra*, 62–75; Malnick, "Origin and Early History," 212–16.

12. Lindsey Hughes, *Sophia, Regent of Russia, 1657–1704* (New Haven: Yale University Press, 1990), 172–75; Morozov, *Istoriia russkogo teatra*, 1:192–98; Arkhangel'skii, *Teatr do-Petrovskoi Rusi*, 38–42.

13. Polotskii settled in Moscow in 1664, becoming a teacher at the Latin school of the Zaikonospasskii Monastery (from 1687 the Slavonic-Greek-Latin Academy) and tutor to the tsar's children. In the early 1670s, he also authored the play *On Tsar Nebuchadnezzar, the Golden Statue, and the Three Youths Not Consumed in the Fiery Furnace*, a variation on the liturgical *Furnace Play*. It is important to emphasize, however, that while historians connect Polotskii's plays to the court theater of Aleksei Mikhailovich, they also note the absence of information on performances. See *Dictionary of Literary Biography*, vol. 150, *Early Modern Russian Writers, Late Seventeenth and Eighteenth Centuries* (hereafter *DLB*), ed. Marcus C. Levitt (Detroit: Gale Research, 1995), 291–307;

Derzhavina, Dëmin, and Robinson, "Poiavlenie teatra," 13; Derzhavina, "Russkii teatr 70-90-kh godov," 33–44; Starikova, *Teatral'naia zhizn'*, chap. 2.

14. Because the court moved back to St. Petersburg in 1732, the comedy house built on Red Square at the beginning of Anna's reign never operated; a fire destroyed the structure in 1737. L. M. Starikova, "Russkii teatr petrovskogo vremeni, komedial'-naia khramina, i domashnie komedii Tsarevny Natal'i Alekseevny," in *Pamiatniki kul'tury: Novye otkrytiia 1990* (hereafter *PKNO*) (Moscow: Krug, 1992), 137–47; idem, *Teatr v Rossii XVIII veka: Opyt dokumental'nogo issledovaniia* (Moscow: GTsTM im. A. A. Bakhrushina, 1997), 9–16; idem, ed., *Teatral'naia zhizn' Rossii v epokhu Anny Ioan-novny* (Moscow: Radiks, 1995), 68–69; idem, *Teatral'naia zhizn'*, chaps. 5–6; P. Moro-zov, "Russkii teatr pri Petre Velikom," *Ezhegodnik imperatorskikh teatrov* (hereafter *EIT*), god 4, sezon 1893–1894, *Prilozheniia*, kn. 1 (1894): 52–80; Morozov, *Istoriia russkogo teatra*, 1:198–294.

15. Natal'ia died in 1716, but because Peter was abroad her burial took place only in 1717. Thus her theatrical staff received salaries in 1717.

16. I. F. Petrovskaia and V. V. Somina, *Teatral'nyi Peterburg nachalo XVIII veka–oktiabr' 1917 goda. Obozrenie-putevoditel'* (St. Petersburg: Rossiiskii institut istorii iskusstv, 1994), 15–18; Starikova, "Russkii teatr petrovskogo vremeni," 147–56; idem, *Teatr v Rossii*, 16–19.

17. Eleonskaia, "Tvorcheskie vzaimosviazi," 12–14.

18. The court had moved to Moscow at the beginning of 1728 in connection with Peter II's coronation.

19. L. M. Starikova, "Novye dokumenty o deiatel'nosti ital'ianskoi truppy v Rossii v 30-e gody XVIII v. i russkom liubitel'skom teatre etogo vremeni," *PKNO 1988* (Moscow: Nauka, 1989), 67–95; idem, *Teatral'naia zhizn' Rossii*, 15–31; idem, *Teatr v Rossii*, 23–28; idem, *Teatral'naia zhizn'*, 126–44; Petrovskaia and Somina, *Teatral'nyi Peterburg*, 27–32.

20. The comedies were published in the form of detailed summaries, and the intermezzos as dialogues for two voices. The relevant titles and publication information are available in *Svodnyi katalog russkoi knigi grazhdanskoi pechati XVIII veka, 1725–1800* (hereafter *SK*), 5 vols. (Moscow: Kniga, 1963–1967). For the surviving texts, see also V. N. Peretts, ed., *Italianskiia komedii i intermedii predstavlennyia pri dvore imperatritsy Anny Ioannovny v 1733–1735 gg. Teksty.* (Petrograd: n.p., 1917); idem, "Italianskaia intermediia 1730-kh godov v stikhotvornom russkom perevode," in Peretts, *Starinnyi teatr*, 143–79.

21. AVPRI, *f.* 94, *op.* 1, *d.* 6, *ll.* 306–11; *Polnoe sobranie zakonov Rossiiskoi imperii,* 1st series, 1649–1825, 46 vols. (hereafter *PSZ*) (St. Petersburg: Tipografiia 2. otdeleniia sobstvennoi E. I. V. kantseliarii, 1830), 17:12759, 12760; *Arkhiv direktsii impera-torskikh teatrov* (hereafter *ADIT*), ed. V. P. Pogozhev, A. E. Molchanov, and K. A. Petrov, vypusk 1 (1746–1801 gg.), otdel 3 (St. Petersburg: Direktsiia imperatorskikh teatrov, 1892), 178–220; Starikova, *Teatral'naia zhizn' Rossii*, 31–32, 60.

22. Eleonskaia, "Tvorcheskie vzaimosviazi," 14–16; Starikova, *Teatral'naia zhizn' Rossii*, 32–55, 387–405; idem, *Teatral'naia zhizn'*, 144–47; Petrovskaia and Som-ina, *Teatral'nyi Peterburg*, 32–33.

23. Until the late eighteenth century, the term "comedy" not only referred to the dramatic genre but also could designate a theater building or a play in general, whether or not it was comical. Starikova, *Teatr v Rossii*, 37–40; Petrovskaia and Som-ina, *Teatral'nyi Peterburg*, 13, 25–27. Alongside comedy, foreign puppet theater also became established. See L. M. Starikova, "Inostrannye kukol'niki v Rossii v pervoi

polovine XVIII v.," in *PKNO 1995* (Moscow: Nauka, 1996), 135–58; idem, *Teatr v Rossii,* 43–45; idem, *Teatral'naia zhizn' Rossii,* 61–64.

24. Starikova, *Teatr v Rossii,* 37–47; idem, *Teatral'naia zhizn' Rossii,* 55–64; Petrovskaia and Somina, *Teatral'nyi Peterburg,* 91–93. Other foreign impresarios are mentioned in G. Z. Mordison, *Istoriia teatral'nogo dela v Rossii: Osnovanie i razvitie gosudarstvennogo teatra v Rossii (XVI–XVIII veka),* 2 vols. (St. Petersburg: Sankt-Peterburgskaia gosudarstvennaia akademiia teatral'nogo iskusstva, 1994).

25. L. M. Starikova, "Teatral'no-zrelishchnaia zhizn' Moskvy v seredine XVIII v.," in *PKNO 1986* (Leningrad: Nauka, 1987), 133–36, 143–48; idem, *Teatr v Rossii,* 43–47.

26. Michael Stewart performed in St. Petersburg and Moscow in 1756–1757, Michael Maddox (of whom more later) followed in 1767, and a Mr. Sanders performed in the capitals and provincial towns between 1772 and 1790. Anthony Cross, *"By the Banks of the Neva": Chapters from the Lives and Careers of the British in Eighteenth-Century Russia* (Cambridge, Eng.: Cambridge University Press, 1997), 39.

27. Of course, these remarks do not apply to German theater in Baltic cities such as Reval, Riga, Mitau, Vyborg, and Kronstadt.

28. Scolari also had collaborated with Hilferding. *PSZ* 15:11483; *ADIT,* vypusk 1, otdel 2:83; Petrovskaia and Somina, *Teatral'nyi Peterburg,* 92–93.

29. Rundthaler's troupe had performed in the Academy of Arts theater in 1798. S. I. Mel'nikova, "K istorii Nemetskogo teatra v Rossii," *Istoricheskii arkhiv* no. 1 (1998): 159–65; idem, "Das Deutsche Theater in Sankt Petersburg am Anfang des 19. Jahrhunderts," *JGO* 44 (1996): 523–36; Petrovskaia and Somina, *Teatral'nyi Peterburg,* 89–90, 93.

30. RGADA, *f.* 248, *op.* 1, *d.* 3178, *ll.* 546–554ob.; *f.* 10, *op.* 1, *d.* 589. See also Starikova, *Teatral'naia zhizn',* 190–93; A. L. Porfir'eva, ed., *Muzykal'nyi Peterburg: Entsiklopedicheskii slovar', XVIII vek* (hereafter *MP*), 3 vols. (St. Petersburg: Izdatel'stvo Kompozitor, 1996–1999), 2:141–45.

31. *PSZ* 19:13477.

32. Petrovskaia and Somina, *Teatral'nyi Peterburg,* 40; Mordison, *Istoriia teatral'nogo dela,* 2:320–22.

33. A. G. Cross, "Mr. Fisher's Company of English Actors in Eighteenth-Century Petersburg," *Newsletter. Study Group on Eighteenth-Century Russia* 4 (1976): 49–56; idem, *"By the Banks of the Neva,"* 36–39.

34. The discussion of Russian impresarios is based on Starikova, "Teatral'no-zrelishchnaia," 137–42; idem, *Teatr v Rossii,* 51–69; Petrovskaia and Somina, *Teatral'nyi Peterburg,* 19–20..

35. The theater of the imperial grooms may have been active already in the 1720s; definitely, it existed in the 1760s.

36. Petrovskaia and Somina, *Teatral'nyi Peterburg,* 32–33, 36–40, 89–91.

37. Baron N. Drizen, "Liubitel'skii teatr pri Ekaterine II (1761–1796 gg.)," *EIT,* god 6, sezon 1895–1896, *Prilozheniia,* kn. 2 (1897): 100–101.

38. Discussion of audience behavior and crowd control follows in this chapter.

39. Starikova's data are based on the number of permissions requested; consequently, a single manager could be counted repeatedly. Starikova, "Teatral'no-zrelishchnaia," 137–42; idem, *Teatr v Rossii,* 51–69. Comparable documentation is lacking, but theater historians believe that Russian impresarios also operated in St. Petersburg. Petrovskaia and Somina, *Teatral'nyi Peterburg,* 19–20.

40. O. A. Derzhavina, A. S. Dëmin, and A. N. Robinson, "Rukopisnaia dramaturgiia i teatral'naia zhizn' pervoi poloviny XVIII v.," in *Ranniaia russkaia dramaturgiia (XVII–pervaia polovina XVIII v.). P'esy liubitel'skikh teatrov* (Moscow: Nauka, 1976), 7–52.

41. Cultural historians of early modern Europe, citing the work of Jürgen Habermas, regularly invoke the category of the "bourgeois public sphere" situated between the private sphere of the household and the sphere of public authority represented by the state. In the "bourgeois public sphere," so termed because of its roots in the capitalist market economy, the freedom and openness of relationships within the private household extend into the arena of public authority. Through the development of autonomous civic organizations, the commercialization of print culture, the assertiveness ("new politics") of constituted bodies, and the formation of communities structured around sites of sociability, the "bourgeois public sphere" eventually limits the absolutist power of the state to the point where public authority becomes the common domain of society and government. Prior to the moment of political actualization, the "bourgeois public sphere" can be thought of as a "prepolitical literary public sphere." Jürgen Habermas, *The Structural Transformation of the Public Sphere: An Inquiry into a Category of Bourgeois Society*, trans. Thomas Burger with Frederick Lawrence (Cambridge, Mass.: MIT Press, 1989). For a recent application of the concept of the public to historical analysis, see James Van Horn Melton, *The Rise of the Public in Enlightenment Europe* (Cambridge, Eng.: Cambridge University Press, 2001). On the emergence of a "new politics" of open contestation within the institutions of the old regime, see Baker, *Inventing the French Revolution*.

42. The practice applied in St. Petersburg no later than 1770 and continued throughout the century. A decree of 1798 reduced the proportion of the admission receipts assigned to the orphanages from a quarter to a tenth. *PSZ* 16:11908; 25:18394.

43. Generally regarded as the first Russian tragedy, *Khorev* had been published in 1747 and was followed by *Sinav and Truvor* in 1751.

44. L. M. Starikova's work on Volkov is not extensive, but the archival material she presents clearly shows that existing accounts of his career are generally unreliable. F. G. *Volkov i russkii teatr ego vremeni: Sbornik materialov*, ed. Iu. A. Dmitriev (Moscow: Izdatel'stvo akademii nauk SSSR, 1953); *PSZ* 14:10599; Starikova, *Teatr v Rossii*, 81–130.

45. *ADIT*, vypusk 1, otdel 2:57.

46. Mordison, *Istoriia teatral'nogo dela*, 1:210–11.

47. The masquerade was performed on January 30–February 2, 1763.

48. The archival record extends from 1769 to 1771.

49. Starikova, *Teatr v Rossii*, 69–77; idem, "Teatral'no-zrelishchnaia zhizn'," 140–42, 176–83.

50. V. I. Lukin, "Pis'mo k gospodinu El'chaninovu," in *Sochineniia i perevody Vladimera Lukina* (hereafter *SIPVL*), 3 vols. (St. Petersburg: n.p., 1765), 2:145–61.

51. Lukin called the theater on Brumberg Square "the theater on the vacant plot of land behind Malaia Morskaia [Street]." I employ the name preferred by present-day historians of eighteenth-century Russian theater. Starikova, *Teatr v Rossii*, 69–77; idem, "Teatral'no-zrelishchnaia zhizn'," 140–42, 176–83; Petrovskaia and Somina, *Teatral'nyi Peterburg*, 23–24; Lukin, "Pis'mo k gospodinu El'chaninovu," in *SIPVL*, 2:145–61.

53. See chap. 2.

53. The theater subsequently was replaced by the Stone Theater, built in 1775–1783. *PSZ* 19:13993; Petrovskaia and Somina, *Teatral'nyi Peterburg*, 25, 81–82.

54. In 1775, Catherine II again assisted Titov by paying his debt to the Moscow city authorities.

55. RGADA, *f.* 17, *op.* 1, *d.* 325; *f.* 10, *op.* 1, *d.* 546.

56. RGADA, *f.* 16, *d.* 575, *ch.* 2, *ll.* 141–143ob.; N. Selivanov, "Teatr v tsarstvo-vanie Imperatritsy Ekateriny II," *EIT,* god 6, sezon 1895–1896, *Prilozheniia,* kn. 3 (1897): 86–117; Starikova, *Teatr v Rossii,* 133–41; idem, *Teatral'naia zhizn',* 194–201.

57. RGADA, *f.* 16, *d.* 575, *ch.* 2, *ll.* 141–143ob.; Selivanov, "Teatr v tsarstvo-vanie Imperatritsy Ekateriny II," kn. 3:103–12; Starikova, *Teatral'naia zhizn',* 249–57, 299–306. On Maddox's debts, see RGADA, *f.* 16, *op.* 1, *d.* 576, *ll.* 156–157ob.; *f.* 1263, *op.* 1, *d.* 6783.

58. The most noteworthy exception—the Free Russian Theater established in 1779 by the St. Petersburg merchant and German native K. P. Knipper—became a state theater just a few years later. Petrovskaia and Somina, *Teatral'nyi Peterburg,* 11–12, 65–70.

59. *PSZ* 17:12759, 12760.

60. For the effort to bring order to the administration of the imperial theaters, see RGADA, *f.* 17, *d.* 322; *f.* 1239, *op.* 3, *ch.* 3, *dd.* 56399, 56400, 56405, 56381, 56383, 56389, 56392; *f.* 1392, *op.* 1, *d.* 88.

61. At the very end of 1782 court actor I. A. Dmitrevskii took over Knipper's Free Russian Theater, which in 1783 became the Wooden Theater. The last perfor-mance in the Wooden Theater took place in November 1796, and by June 1797 it no longer existed.

62. *PSZ* 21:15783; Selivanov, "Teatr v tsarstvovanie Imperatritsy Ekateriny II," kn. 2:28–75.

63. *ADIT,* vypusk 1, otdel 3:365–78.

64. See the Preface for use of the term "civic society."

65. D. Malinin, *Nachalo teatra v Kaluge. K istorii kaluzhskogo teatra v XVIII veke* (Kaluga: Gubernskaia tipo-litografiia, 1912). One historian characterizes the Kaluga theater as a serf troupe. See Tat'iana Dynnik, *Krepostnoi teatr* (Leningrad: Academia, 1933), 243.

66. Research on the Tobol'sk theater has uncovered evidence of a comparable institution in Perm: in a 1793 letter to A. A. Volkov, governor-general *(general-guber-nator)* of Perm, Aliab'ev requested that the actor and director Vigant be sent to To-bol'sk. Kosterina-Azarian, *Teatral'naia starina Urala,* 109–15, 186–88.

67. The performances continued into January 1787 and resumed again in June. Mel'gunov's primary residence in Iaroslavl housed a domestic theater.

68. R. M. Lazarchuk, "Iz istorii provintsial'nogo teatra (Vologodskii publichnyi teatr kontsa XVIII–nachala XIX v.)," *XVIII vek* 18 (1993): 156–71; idem, "Iz istorii provintsial'nogo teatra (teatral'naia zhizn' Vologdy 1780-kh gg.)."

69. *Sanktpeterburgskie vedomosti,* no. 9 (29 January 1787): 115–16.

70. I. P. Popov, E. S. Stepanova, E. G. Tarabrin, and Iu. V. Fulin, *Dva veka ria-zanskoi istorii (XVIII v.–mart 1917 g.)* (Riazan: Riazanskoe otdelenie sovetskogo fonda kul'tury, 1991), 18–19.

71. The theater ceased operations at Chertkov's death in 1793 and upon re-opening in 1798 remained a noble theater. The title of the official in question, *gen-eral-gubernator,* also is rendered in English as governor-general. Z. Ia. Anchipolovskii, *Staryi teatr Voronezh, 1787–1917* (Voronezh: Izdatel'sko-poligraficheskii tsentr cher-nozem'e, 1996), 7–34.

72. On the drama performed in Tver, see chap. 6. Writing in 1896, Drizen gives governor-general *(namestnik)* F. I. Kamenskii credit for the organization of the Khar'kov theater. Drizen, "Liubitel'skii teatr," 112–14. See also, Anchipolovskii, *Staryi teatr,* 21–22, 33–34.

73. The well-known serf theater of G. V. and V. G. Gladkov opened in 1806

and continued to operate until 1829. Even though its actors were serfs, the Gladkov theater was a commercial operation that charged admission. M. P. Molebnov, *Penzenskii krepostnoi teatr Gladkovykh* (Penza: Penzenskoe knizhnoe izdatel'stvo, 1955).

74. E. P. Privalova, "A. T. Bolotov i teatr dlia detei," *XVIII vek* 3 (1958): 247–50.

75. The families represented include Belosel'skii, Chernyshev, Istlen'ev, Khovanskii, Shcherbatov, Sol'm, and Stroganov.

76. On the Sheremetev productions, see RGADA, *f.* 1287, *op.* 1, *d.* 3739a; N. A. Elizarova, *Teatry Sheremetevykh* (Moscow: Ostankinskii dvorets-muzei, 1944), 18–19; "Varvara Golovina 1766–1822: Freilina Vysochaishego dvora," in *Tainy tsarskogo dvora (iz zapisok freilin): Sbornik*, ed. I. V. Eremina (Moscow: Znachenie, 1997), 66; Drizen, "Liubitel'skii teatr," 86–88.

77. Drizen, "Liubitel'skii teatr," 77–86, 106–7.

78. Indeed, in the 1880s members of the Trubetskoi family traveled significant distances to participate in theatricals staged in the dining room of the Osorgins' manor house in Kaluga province. The theatricals continued after the family fled to France in the wake of the 1917 revolution. In 1940–1941, Schmemanns and Osorgins in Paris staged a musical play with a libretto by S. N. Trubetskoi. Serge Schmemann, *Echoes of a Native Land: Two Centuries of a Russian Village* (New York: Alfred A. Knopf, 1997), 111.

79. The memoirist provides no specific information on the identity of Countess Golovkina. E. F. Komarovskii, *Zapiski grafa E. F. Komarovskogo* (Moscow: Vneshtorgizdat, 1990), 30–32.

80. L. Lepskaia, *Repertuar krepostnogo teatra Sheremetevykh: Katalog p'es* (Moscow: GTsTM im. A. A. Bakhrushina, 1996); L. M. Starikova, "K istorii domashnikh krepostnykh teatrov i orkestrov v Rossii kontsa XVII–XVIII vv.," *PKNO 1991* (Moscow: Nauka, 1997), 53–65; Bertha Malnick, "Russian Serf Theatres," *SEER* 30 (1952): 393–411; Dynnik, *Krepostnoi teatr*, 243–55; Elizarova, *Teatry Sheremetevykh*; Molebnov, *Penzenskii krepostnoi teatr Gladkovykh*.

81. Lepskaia, *Repertuar*.

82. The actors then were required to stay with the theater for ten years in return for a salary and housing. A. S. Gatsiskii, *Nizhegorodskii teatr (1798–1867)* (Nizhnii Novgorod: Tipografiia nizhegorodskogo gubernskogo pravleniia, 1867), 1–23; B. N. Beliakov, *Letopis' Nizhegorodskogo-Gor'kovskogo Teatra, 1798–1960*, ed. Iu. Volchek (Gor'kii: Volgo-Viatskoe knizhnoe izdatel'stvo, 1967), 11–25.

83. Melton, *Rise of the Public*, 166–67; Jeffrey S. Ravel, *The Contested Parterre: Public Theater and French Political Culture, 1680–1791* (Ithaca, N.Y.: Cornell University Press, 1999), 67.

84. For a more comprehensive overview of the developments traced above, see Mordison, *Istoriia teatral'nogo dela*.

85. I have only scattered information on the size of eighteenth-century theaters. The Danish clergyman and theologian Peder von Haven (1715–1757), who spent several months in St. Petersburg in 1736–1737, wrote that the opera/comedy house in the Winter Palace contained places for about 1,000 spectators. Peder fon Khaven, "Puteshestvie v Rossiiu," in *Peterburg Anny Ioannovny v inostrannykh opisaniiakh*, ed. Iu. N. Bespiatykh (St. Petersburg: Blits, 1997), 22–28, 325–26. G. Z. Mordison gives a figure of 450 places in the Theater of Comedy and Opera in the New Winter (Wooden) Theater for the years 1734–1742. In addition, the Opera House on Nevskii Prospekt that functioned in 1743–1749 had places for 1,000 spectators, and the New Opera House in the New (Stone) Winter Palace for 3,000.

Mordison, *Istoriia teatral'nogo dela,* 1:129–30. In 1796 the monthly periodical *Muza* reported that the Moscow Opera House (also known as the Golovin Opera House) built for Elizabeth's coronation accommodated 5,000 spectators; however, historians do not confirm this figure. *Muza. Ezhemesiachnoe izdanie,* ch. 1 (1796): 193–94.

86. A. P. Sumarokov, *Dmitrii Samozvanets. Tragediia,* in *Polnoe sobranie vsekh sochinenii v stikhakh i proze* (hereafter *PSVS*), 6 vols. (Moscow: Universitetskaia tipografiia u N. Novikova, 1781), 4:62–64.

87. James H. Johnson, *Listening in Paris: A Cultural History* (Berkeley: University of California Press, 1995); Ravel, *The Contested Parterre;* James Van Horn Melton, "School, Stage, Salon: Musical Cultures in Haydn's Vienna" (unpublished paper, Department of History, Emory University, 2001); David Bromwich, "The Great Fidget: David Garrick's 'Uncanny Mobility' both On and Off the Stage," *TLS,* no. 5118 (May 4, 2001), 3–4.

88. Melton, "School, Stage, Salon."

89. For Sumarokov's idea of the public, see chap. 2.

90. Lukin, "Pis'mo k gospodinu El'chaninovu," in *SIPVL,* 2:148–52, 158–59.

91. V. I. Lukin, "Predislovie k *Motu liuboviiu ispravlennomu,*" in *SIPVL,* 1:xxii–xxviii.

92. For discussion of authors' motivations and the social functions of theater, see chap. 2. On Russian theater audiences in general, see D. Dmitriev, "Russkaia teatral'naia publika vo vremena Sumarokova," *Drevniaia i novaia Rossiia* 3 (1875): 313–16; Malcolm Burgess, "Russian Public Theatre Audiences of the Eighteenth and Nineteenth Centuries," *SEER* 38 (1958): 160–83.

93. *Vsiakaia vsiachina,* no. 154 (1770): 420–24.

94. *Vechera, ezhenedel'noe izdanie na 1772 god,* 2 vols., 2d. ed. (Moscow: Tipografiia kompanii tipograficheskoi, 1788), 2:67–69. Almost two decades later, I. A. Krylov reported similar behavior among theater spectators, who instead of paying attention to the performance, gossiped and showed themselves. See *Pochta dukhov,* ch. 1 (April 1789), letter 19.

95. Starikova, "Teatral'no-zrelishchnaia zhizn'," 138, 150–76, 183.

96. Ibid.,164–65, 167–72.

97. See chap. 2.

98. On the notion of "social censorship," see Sophia Rosenfeld, "Writing the History of Censorship in the Age of Enlightenment," in *Postmodernism and the Enlightenment: New Perspectives in Eighteenth-Century French Intellectual History,* ed. Daniel Gordon (New York: Routledge, 2001), 117–45.

99. Censorship is a subject in need of detailed research. The brief account provided here is based on G. V. Zhirkov, *Istoriia tsenzury v Rossii XIX–XX vv.: Uchebnoe posobie* (Moscow: Aspekt-Press, 2001), 7–33; Gary Marker, *Publishing, Printing, and the Origins of Intellectual Life in Russia, 1700–1800* (Princeton: Princeton University Press, 1985), chap. 8; John P. LeDonne, *Ruling Russia: Politics and Administration in the Age of Absolutism, 1762–1796* (Princeton: Princeton University Press, 1984), 109–12; Charles A. Ruud, *Fighting Words: Imperial Censorship and the Russian Press, 1804–1906* (Toronto: University of Toronto Press, 1982), 1–23; S. P. Luppov, *Kniga v Rossii v poslepetrovskoe vremia, 1725–1740* (Leningrad: Nauka, 1976), 36–107; K. A. Papmehl, *Freedom of Expression in Eighteenth-Century Russia* (The Hague: Martinus Nijhoff, 1971); D. D. Shamrai, "Tsenzurnyi nadzor nad tipografiei sukhoputnogo shliakhetnogo kadetskogo korpusa," *XVIII vek* 2 (1940):

293–329; idem, "K istorii tsenzurnogo rezhima Ekateriny II," *XVIII vek* 3 (1958): 187–206; N. V. Drizen, "Ocherki teatral'noi tsenzury v Rossii v XVIII v.," *Russkaia starina* 90 (April–June 1897): 539–68.

100. The Moscow Printing Office published secular books until 1727.

101. The press at the Senate continued to publish governmental decrees and orders.

102. Similar criteria applied in France, where publications that undermined "the authority of the king, the Church, or conventional morality" were deemed illegal. Robert Darnton, *The Forbidden Best-Sellers of Pre-Revolutionary France* (New York: W. W. Norton, 1996), 3–6.

103. Shamrai, "K istorii tsenzurnogo rezhima," 191–92.

104. How censorship worked in practice requires further study. In Moscow at least, two church and two state censors appointed by the governor-general performed these duties beginning in 1785.

105. G. V. Zhirkov, "Vek ofitsial'noi tsenzury," in *Ocherki russkoi kul'tury XIX veka*, vol. 2, *Vlast' i kul'tura* (Moscow: Izdatel'stvo moskovskogo universiteta, 2000), 167–68; D. G. Korolev, *Ocherki iz istorii izdaniia i rasprostraneniia teatral'noi knigi v Rossii XIX-nachala XX vekov* (St. Petersburg: Rossiiskaia natsional'naia biblioteka, 1999), 10–12, 28–29.

106. The law of 1763 required booksellers to submit to the Academy of Sciences and Moscow University annual registers of the books they intended to order. Zhirkov, *Istorii tsenzury*, 23–25.

107. Papmehl, *Freedom of Expression*, 121–22; Zhirkov, "Vek ofitsial'noi tsenzury," 167.

108. Papmehl, *Freedom of Expression*, 137–45; Zhirkov, "Vek ofitsial'noi tsenzury," 168; Korolev, *Ocherki iz istorii izdaniia*, 10–12; Marker, *Publishing*, chap. 8.

109. From 1766 to 1779, I. P. Elagin (1725–1793) served as director of the newly centralized administration of imperial theaters. Papmehl, *Freedom of Expression*, 102; Drizen, "Ocherki teatral'noi tsenzury"; Mordison, *Istoriia teatral'nogo dela*, chap. 3.

110. Korolev, *Ocherki iz istorii izdaniia*, 12; *ADIT*, vypusk 1, otdel 2:514, 578–80, 586–87, 592–93, 617.

111. *Vsiakaia vsiachina*, no. 15 (1769): 43–46.

112. Gary Marker, "The Creation of Journals and the Profession of Letters in the Eighteenth Century," in *Literary Journals in Imperial Russia*, ed. Deborah A. Martinsen (New York: Cambridge University Press, 1997), 11–33; Faith Wigzell, *Reading Russian Fortunes: Print Culture, Gender, and Divination in Russia from 1765* (Cambridge, Eng.: Cambridge University Press, 1998); A. Iu. Samarin, *Chitatel' v Rossii vo vtoroi polovine XVIII veka (po spiskam podpischikov)* (Moscow: Izdatel'stvo MGUP, 2000). According to Richard Hellie, it is impossible to speak of any consumer society or culture in Russia before the reign of Peter I. See Richard Hellie, *The Economy and Material Culture of Russia, 1600–1725* (Chicago: University of Chicago Press, 1999). Using retrospective forecasting, Boris Mironov has arrived at the following literacy rates for inhabitants of European Russia over the age of nine in 1797: urban males—28.6 percent, urban females—12 percent, urban population as a whole—21 percent, entire population—6.9 percent. See B. N. Mironov, "Gramotnost' v Rossii 1797–1917 godov: Poluchenie novoi istoricheskoi informatsii s pomoshch'iu metodov retrospektivnogo prognozirovaniia," *Istoriia SSSR*, no. 4 (1985): 137–53, esp. 149.

2: THE SOCIAL MEANING OF PLAYS

1. Recent studies stress the "parting of ways" that increasingly divided the educated classes from the monarchy and state. See Nicholas V. Riasanovsky, *A Parting of Ways: Government and the Educated Public in Russia, 1801–1855* (Oxford: Clarendon Press, 1976); I. F. Khudushina, *Tsar'. Bog. Rossiia. Samosoznanie russkogo dvorianstva (konets XVIII–pervaia tret' XIX vv.)* (Moscow: IFRAN, 1995); E. N. Marasinova, "Obraz imperatora v soznanii elity rossiiskogo dvorianstva poslednei treti XVIII veka (po materialam epistoliarnykh istochnikov)," in *Tsar' i tsartsvo v russkom obshchestvennom soznanii*, ed. A. A. Gorskii (Moscow: Institut rossiiskoi istorii RAN, 1999), 141–77; idem, *Psikhologiia elity rossiiskogo dvorianstva poslednei treti XVIII veka (Po materialam perepiski)* (Moscow: ROSSPEN, 1999).

2. For more detailed discussion, see K. A. Smolina, *Russkaia tragediia. XVIII vek. Evoliutsiia zhanra* (Moscow: Nasledie, 2001).

3. I use the term "neoclassical" to distinguish eighteenth-century classicism from the classical models of antiquity and to make clear that classical precedents existed for most of the neoclassical features discussed here. Russian scholars generally prefer the label "classicist"; however, in European scholarship as whole, one finds classical, classicist, and neoclassical used interchangeably.

4. M. M. Kheraskov, *Venetsianskaia monakhinia. Tragediia v trekh deistviiakh*, in *Russkaia literatura. Vek XVIII. Tragediia*, ed. Iu. V. Stennik (Moscow: Khudozhestvennaia literatura, 1991), 315–62. On Kheraskov's literary innovations in *The Nun of Venice*, see Michael Green, "Italian Scandal as Russian Tragedy: Kheraskov's *Venetsianskaia Monakhinia*," in *Russia and the World of the Eighteenth Century*, ed. R. P. Bartlett, A. G. Cross, and Karen Rasmussen (Columbus, Ohio: Slavica Publishers, 1988), 388–99.

5. Indeed, my sources do not list any performances of *Milozor and Prelesta*. Throughout this book, the information on performances comes primarily from the first two volumes of *Istoriia russkogo dramaticheskogo teatra* (hereafter *IRDT*), ed. E. G. Kholodov, 7 vols. (Moscow: Iskusstvo, 1977–1987).

6. V. L., *Milozor i Prelesta. Opera komicheskaia* (Moscow: Universitetskaia tipografiia u N. Novikova, 1787). See also E. D. Kukushkina, "Komediografiia V. A. Levshina," *XVIII vek* 19 (1995): 86–101.

7. Catherine II, *Podrazhanie Shakespiru. Istoricheskoe predstavlenie bez sokhraneniia obyknovennykh featral'nykh pravil iz zhizni Riurika*, in *Rossiiskii featr, ili Polnoe sobranie vsekh Rossiiskikh teatral'nykh sochinenii* (hereafter *RF*), 43 vols. (St. Petersburg: Imperatorskaia akademiia nauk, 1786–1794), 14:107–66; idem, *Nachal'noe upravlenie Olega. Podrazhanie Shakespiru. Bez sokhraneniia featral'nykh obyknovennykh pravil*, in *RF*, 14:167–248. See also Ernest J. Simmons, "Catherine the Great and Shakespeare," *PMLA* 47 (1932): 790–806, esp. 801–5.

8. On French "happy tragedy," see Oscar Mandel, *A Definition of Tragedy* (New York: New York University Press, 1961), 28–30, 71.

9. Patrice Pavis, *Dictionary of the Theatre: Terms, Concepts, and Analysis*, trans. Christine Shantz (Toronto: University of Toronto Press, 1998), 415.

10. On Diderot as the model for Russian drama, see "to the reader" from translator Ivan Iakovlev in *Pobochnyi syn, ili Ispytaniia dobrodeteli. Drama v piati deistviiakh. Perevedena s Frantsuzskogo iazyka I. Ia.* (Moscow: Senatskaia tipografiia u soderzhatelia V. O., 1788). See also the translation by E. S. Kharlamov with accompanying preface, published in St. Petersburg no later than 1764 (*SK* 1861). A second edition appeared as

Pobochnyi syn, ili Iskusheniia dobrodeteli. Komediia v piati deistviiakh i prostoiu rech'iu pisan-naia. Sochinenie G. Diderota (Moscow: Universitetskaia tipografiia u N. Novikova, 1788).

11. Sidney D. Braun, ed., *Dictionary of French Literature* (New York: Philosophical Library, 1958), 59–62, 87–97, 339–41; Michael Green, "Diderot and Kheraskov: Sentimentalism in its Classicist Stage," in *Russia and the West in the Eighteenth Century,* ed. A. G. Cross (Newtonville, Mass.: Oriental Research Partners, 1983), 206–13.

12. David Wallace, "Bourgeois Tragedy or Sentimental Melodrama? The Significance of George Lillo's *The London Merchant," Eighteenth-Century Studies* 25 (Winter 1991–1992): 123–43. Historians now question the notion that a distinctive middle-class domesticity arose in eighteenth-century England. Instead, they stress the mingling of provincial gentry and middle groups in a genteel society imbued with a "domestic ideology" already known in classical and humanist thought. Amanda Vickery, "Golden Age to Separate Spheres? A Review of the Categories and Chronology of English Women's History," *The Historical Journal* 36 (1993): 383–414; idem, *The Gentleman's Daughter: Women's Lives in Georgian England* (New Haven: Yale University Press, 1998).

13. *Pobochnyi syn, ili Ispytaniia dobrodeteli,* vii–viii.

14. V. L., *Milozor i Prelesta.*

15. N. P. Nikolev, *Rozana i Liubim. Dramma s golosami v chetyrekh deistviiakh. Sochinena v Moskve* (Moscow: Universitetskaia tipografiia u N. Novikova, 1781).

16. V. L., *Milozor i Prelesta.*

17. D. I. Fonvizin, *Nedorosl'. Komediia v piati deistviiakh,* in *Ot russkogo klassitsizma k realizmu: D. I. Fonvizin, A. S. Griboedov,* ed. E. Rogachevskaia (Moscow: Shkola-Press, 1995).

18. D. V. Volkov, *Vospitanie* (Moscow: Imperatorskii moskovskii universitet, 1774).

19. David Wiles, "Theatre in Roman and Christian Europe," in *The Oxford Illustrated History of Theatre,* ed. John Russell Brown (New York: Oxford University Press, 1995), 50–56; Erich Segal, "Introduction," in Plautus, *Four Comedies,* trans. Erich Segal (New York: Oxford University Press, 1998), xi–xl; idem, "Pay Attention, Folks," *TLS,* no. 5017 (May 28, 1999): 4; Maya Slater, "Meant to Be Played: Molière's Mystery, Panache and Love of the Stage," *TLS,* no. 5004 (February 26, 1999): 4–5.

20. In 1793 reviews of A. I. Klushin's comedies *Laughter and Sorrow* and *The Alchemist,* I. A. Krylov criticized excessive use of the joke as unnatural, though he himself made use of the technique in *Mischievous People.* I. A. Krylov, "Primechanie na komediiu *Smekh i gore," Sankt-Peterburgskii merkurii,* ch. 1 (1793): 104–30; idem, "Teatr," *Sankt-Petersburgskii merkurii,* ch.2 (1793): 213–22; idem, *Prokazniki. Komediia,* in *RF,* 40:153–329. On Klushin's *Laughter and Sorrow,* see chap. 4. Plays that employ the joke but are not discussed in the chapters to follow include: *Liubovnik koldun. Opera komicheskaia v odnom deistvii,* in *RF,* 18:214–65; *Opasnaia shutka. Komicheskaia opera v odnom deistvii* (incomplete), in *RF,* 39:75–112; N. F. Emin, *Mnimyi mudrets. Komediia v piati deistviiakh,* in *RF,* 29:189–272; D. P. Gorchakov, *Kalif na chas. Komicheskaia opera v chetyrekh deistviiakh,* in *RF,* 26:67–146; Ivan Iukin, *Koldun, vorozheia i svakha. Komicheskaia opera v trekh deistviiakh,* in *RF,* 37:247–311; A. I. Klushin, *Alkhimist. Komediia v odnom deistvii,* in *Russkaia komediia i komicheskaia opera,* ed. P. N. Berkov (Moscow and Leningrad: Iskusstvo, 1950), 465–83; O. P. Kozodavlev, *Persten'. Komediia v odnom deistvii* (St. Petersburg: Vol'naia tipografiia Veitbrekhta i Shnora, 1780); idem, *Nashla kosa na kamen'. Komediia v odnom deistvii* (St. Petersburg: Izhdivenie avtora u Shnora, 1781); V. A. Levshin, *Mnimye vdovtsy. Opera komicheskaia.*

V trekh deistviiakh, in *RF*, 43:5–104; idem, *Molodye poskoree starykh mogut obmanut'*. *Komediia liricheskaia v odnom deistvii*, in *Trudy Vasiliia Levshina* (Moscow: Universitet-skaia tipografiia, 1796), 1:3–34; N. P. Nikolev, *Samoliubivyi stikhotvorets*. *Komediia v piati deistviiakh*, in *RF*, 15:3–148; idem, *Opekunprofessor, ili Liubov' khitree kras-norechiia. Shutlivaia opera. Sochinena v 1782 godu*, in *RF*, 24:3–62; idem, *Popytka ne shutka, ili Udachnyi opyt. Komediia v trekh deistviiakh*, in *RF*, 35:105–82; V. Pavlov, *Tri sunduka, ili Khitrost' zhenshchiny. Komediia v trekh deistviiakh*, in *RF*, 38:241–351; A. P. Sumarokov, *Vzdorshchitsa. Komediia*, in *Dramaticheskie sochineniia*, ed. Iu. V. Stennik (hereafter *DS*) (Leningrad: Iskusstvo, 1990), 412–33; idem, *Pridanoe obmanom. Komediia*, in *DS*, 346–61; A. A. Volkov, *Chadoliubie. Komediia v odnom deistvii* (Moscow: Universitetskaia tipografiia u N. Novikova, 1788).

21. Thomas Newlin, "Rural Ruses: Illusional Anxiety on the Russian Estate," *SR* 57 (1998): 295–319.

22. Segal, "Introduction"; idem, "Pay attention."

23. See chap. 3.

24. James C. Scott, *Weapons of the Weak: Everyday Forms of Peasant Resistance* (New Haven: Yale University Press, 1985).

25. *Igrok shchaslivoi. Opera v odnom deistvii. Sochinenie Rossiiskoe* (St. Petersburg: n.p., 1783). In *The Lucky Gambler* both deceiver and deceived sacrifice the happiness of a young woman to their love of money, and as a result the deception fails to bring about a rightful outcome. There is no record of the opera being performed.

26. Krylov, "Primechanie na komediiu *Smekh i gore*," 116–17, 122–24.

27. Pavis, *Dictionary of the Theatre*, 431.

28. On the artificial reproduction of peasant, merchant, and regional speech, see K. Iu. Lappo-Danilevskii, "Komicheskaia opera N. A. L'vova 'Iamshchiki na pod-stave,'" *XVIII vek* 18 (1993): 93–112, esp. 104–7; Nikolev, *Rozana i Liubim*.

29. On death, see Philippe Ariès, *Western Attitudes toward Death from the Middle Ages to the Present*, trans. Patricia M. Ranum (Baltimore: Johns Hopkins University Press, 1974).

30. V. O. Kliuchevskii, "Nedorosl' Fonvizina (Opyt istoricheskogo ob"iasneniia uchebnoi p'esy)" (1896), in *O nravstvennosti i russkoi kul'ture*, ed. R. A. Kireeva (Moscow: Institut rossiiskoi istorii RAN, 1998), 171–98, esp. 177–78.

31. Lukin, "Predislovie k *Motu liuboviiu ispravlennomu*," in *SIPVL*, 1:xv–xviii. Lukin's *Spendthrift* is an adaptation of Philippe Néricault Destouches's *Le Dissipateur* (1736), which reached Russia via a Polish adaptation, *Marnotrawca*, by Franciszek Bo-homolec (1720–1784). Iu. D. Levin, ed., *Istoriia russkoi perevodnoi khudozhestvennoi lit-eratury. Drevniaia Rus'. XVIII vek*, 2 vols. (St. Petersburg: Dmitrii Bulanin, 1995–1996), 2:30.

32. On the upbringing of noble girls, see Jessica Tovrov, *The Russian Noble Family: Structure and Change* (Ph.D diss., University of Chicago, 1980; reprint, New York: Garland, 1987); Catriona Kelly, "Educating Tat'yana: Manners, Motherhood, and Moral Education *(Vospitanie)*, 1760–1840," in *Gender in Russian History and Cul-ture*, ed. Linda Edmondson (Houndmills, New York: Palgrave, 2001), 1–28.

33. Performance history allows scholars to show the meaningfulness of literary formulas in specific, chronologically discrete historical settings. See Wendy Gris-wold's analysis of why Renaissance revenge tragedy appealed to British audiences from the late 1950s through the 1970s. Wendy Griswold, *Renaissance Revivals: City Comedy and Revenge Tragedy in the London Theatre, 1576–1980* (Chicago: University of Chicago Press, 1986).

34. *Sanktpeterburgskii vestnik,* ch. 3 (March 1779): 234.

35. The comedy was published anonymously as *Neudachnoe upriamstvo. Komediia v odnom deistvii* (St. Petersburg: n.p., 1779). According to *IRDT,* it was performed twice in St. Petersburg in 1764 and once in 1765.

36. A. G. Cross, "The Eighteenth-Century Russian Theatre through British Eyes," in *Studies on Voltaire and the Eighteenth Century,* vol. 219 (Oxford: Voltaire Foundation, 1983), 225–40.

37. Joseph Brodsky, "A Hidden Duet: The Intimate Connection Between the 'Magdalene' Poems of Boris Pasternak and Marina Tsvetaeva," *TLS,* no. 5030 (August 27, 1999): 13–16.

38. On the small size and narrow social parameters of the reading public, see Marker, "The Creation of Journals and the Profession of Letters in the Eighteenth Century," 11–33.

39. In *The Imaginary Sage,* N. F. Emin followed Catherine's lead and drew specific parallels to her comedy *The Deceiver. The Deceiver* was first published in 1785 and performed 6 times in St. Petersburg and 7 times in Moscow in 1786–1787. *The Imaginary Sage* was performed once in St. Petersburg in 1785 and published there the following year. See Catherine II, *Two Comedies by Catherine the Great, Empress of Russia: Oh, These Times! and The Siberian Shaman,* trans. and ed. Lurana Donnels O'Malley (Amsterdam: Harwood Academic Publishers, 1998), xiv–xxxi; idem, "The Monarch and the Mystic: Catherine the Great's Strategy of Audience Enlightenment in *The Siberian Shaman,*" *SEEJ* 41 (1997): 224–42; Douglas Smith, *Working the Rough Stone: Freemasonry and Society in Eighteenth-Century Russia* (DeKalb: Northern Illinois University Press, 1999), 145–52; Emin, *Mnimyi mudrets.*

40. Dashkova, E. R., *The Memoirs of Princess Dashkova,* trans. and ed. Kyril Fitzlyon (1958; reprint, Durham: Duke University Press, 1995), 235–36.

41. See, for example, the dedication by court actor T. V. Konstantinov to Princess E. P. Dolgorukaia (née Bakunina) in *Blagovremennoe vspomozhenie. Original'-naia drama v trekh deistviiakh* (St. Petersburg: n.p., 1794); B. K. Blank's dedication to P. A. Dolgov in *Krasavitsa i prividenie. Opera v odnom deistvii. Perevod s Arabskogo* (Moscow: Universitetskaia tipografiia u A. Svetushkina, 1789). See also V. P. Kolychev's pastoral opera written for the Kuskovo theater of Count P. B. Sheremetev: V. K., *Tshchetnaia revnost', ili Perevozchik kuskovskoi. Pastush'ia opera v dvukh deistviiakh* (Moscow: n.p., 1781).

42. On Catherine's pedagogical plays, written for her grandsons, see chap. 6.

43. Bolotov's third play, *Virtue Rewarded (Nagrazhdennaia dobrodetel'),* written in 1781, has been lost. A. T. Bolotov, *Zhizn' i prikliucheniia Andreia Bolotova, opisannye samim im dlia svoikh potomkov,* 3 vols. (1871–1873; reprint, Moscow: Terra, 1993), 3:282–313; A. K. Demikhovskii, "A. T. Bolotov—dramaturg," in A. T. Bolotov, *Izbrannoe* (Pskov: POIPKRO, 1993), 5–23; Privalova, "A. T. Bolotov i teatr dlia detei," 242–61.

44. See Volkov's comedy *Upbringing* discussed in chap. 5.

45. I. V. Lopukhin, *Torzhestvo pravosudiia i dobrodeteli, ili Dobroi sud'ia. Dramma v piati deistviiakh* (Moscow: Vol'naia tipografiia Ponomareva, 1794).

46. The text of Dashkova's second play, *Fabian's Wedding, or The Greed for Wealth Punished (Svad'ba Fabiana, ili Alchnost' k bogatstvu nakazannaia),* has not survived. In 1798, Kotzebue's *Armuth und Edelsinn* appeared in a Russian translation as *Bednost' i blagorodstvo dushi;* that same year it was performed 7 times in Moscow and another 4 times in 1799. In Kotzebue's play the conceited fool Fabian is rejected as

suitor, and the honorable lover Cederström wins the hand of Louise Rose (Josephine Plum). Dashkova reportedly viewed a performance of the play in her brother's serf theater. F. Gepfert, "O dramaturgii E. R. Dashkovoi," in *Ekaterina Romanovna Dashkova: Issledovaniia i materialy,* ed. A. I. Vorontsov-Dashkov (St. Petersburg: Dmitrii Bulanin, 1996), 147–51; Albert William Holzmann, *Family Relationships in the Dramas of August von Kotzebue* (Princeton: Princeton University Press, 1935), 27, 38, 60–61.

47. *Elizaveta. Dramaticheskoi otryvok. Sochinitelem Kodra* (Moscow: Universitet-skaia tipografiia u Ridigera i Klaudiia, 1800).

48. On amateur theatricals, see Fedor Dostoevsky, *Memoirs from the House of the Dead,* trans. Jessie Coulson, ed. Ronald Hingley (New York: Oxford University Press, 1983); Gary Thurston, *The Popular Theatre Movement in Russia, 1862–1919* (Evanston, Ill.: Northwestern University Press, 1998); Reginald E. Zelnik, "*Weber* into *Tkachi:* On a Russian Reading of Gerhart Hauptmann's Play *The Weavers,"* in *Self and Story in Russian History,* ed. Laura Engelstein and Stephanie Sandler (Ithaca, N.Y.: Cornell University Press, 2000), 217–41. On the Soviet period, see Lynn Mally, *Revolutionary Acts: Amateur Theater and the Soviet State, 1917–1938* (Ithaca, N.Y.: Cornell University Press, 2000).

49. Lukin, "Pis'mo k gospodinu El'chaninovu," in *SIPVL,* 2:145–61; idem, "Predislovie k *Shchepetil'niku,"* in *SIPVL,* 2:162–7; Simon Karlinsky, *Russian Drama from Its Beginnings to the Age of Pushkin* (Berkeley: University of California Press, 1985), 97–98.

50. A Russian translation from the English by Aleksandr Krasovskii appeared in 1799. See *SK.*

51. Marcus C. Levitt, "The Illegal Staging of Sumarokov's *Sinav i Truvor* in 1770 and the Problem of Authorial Status in Eighteenth-Century Russia," *SEEJ* 43 (1999): 299–323. Sumarokov's stature at home and abroad is evident from the story of his life and career published soon after his death: "Sokrashchennaia povest' o zhizni i pisaniiakh gospodina statskago deistvitelnago sovetnika i Sviatyia Anny kavalera, Aleksandra Petrovicha Sumarokova," *Sanktpeterburgskii vestnik,* ch. 1 (January 1778): 39–49. For repeated references to Sumarokov as "the father of Russian theater," see "Teatr," *Zritel': Ezhemesiachnoe izdanie,* ch. 2 (June 1792): 121–45, (August 1792): 251–77; ch. 3 (September 1792): 25–39, (October 1792): 113–37, (December 1792): 249–55.

52. The situation was not that different further to the west, where in Britain, France, and Italy, authors began to subsist from literary activities only late in the eighteenth century. See Roger Chartier, "The Man of Letters," in *Enlightenment Portraits,* ed. Michel Vovelle, trans. Lydia G. Cochrane (Chicago: University of Chicago Press, 1997), 173–75.

53. On the literary polemics and accusations surrounding Lukin, see A. N. Pypin, "V. I. Lukin," in *Sochineniia i perevody Vladimira Ignat'evicha Lukina i Bogdana Egorovicha El'chaninova,* ed. P. A. Efremov (St. Petersburg: Ivana Il'ich Glazunov, 1868), i–lxxii. For contemporary examples, see *Truten'* (19 May 1769), list 4; (29 September 1769), list 23; (13 October 1769), list 25. All reprinted in P. N. Berkov, ed., *Satiricheskie zhurnaly N. I. Novikova* (Moscow and Leningrad: Akademiia nauk SSSR, 1951), 54–5, 133, 137–39.

54. Lukin, *SIPVL,* vol. 1.

55. Lukin, "Predislovie k *Motu liuboviiu ispravlennomu,"* in *SIPVL,* 1:i–xxxi.

56. Ibid., ii–iii.

57. Ibid., xxx–xxxi.

58. Marker, *Publishing;* Martinsen, *Literary Journals;* V. M. Zhivov, *Iazyk i kul'-tura v Rossii XVIII veka* (Moscow: Shkola iazyki russkoi kul'tury, 1996).

59. Examples include Pypin, "V. I. Lukin"; I. Z. Serman, "Iz istorii literaturnoi bor'by 60-kh godov XVIII veka (Neizdannaia komediia Fedora Emina 'Uchenaia shaika')," *XVIII vek* 3 (1958): 207–25; Iu. V. Stennik, "Rol' komedii v polemike 1750–1760-kh godov," *XVIII vek* 17 (1991): 28–46; T. V. Mal'tseva, "'Prazdnichnyi' komponent v opisanii protsessa tvorchestva v komediiakh XVIII–nachala XIX vekov na literaturnuiu temu," in *Prazdnik v russkoi kul'ture, fol'klore, i literature. Sbornik statei Pushkinskikh chtenii-97,* ed. T. V. Mal'tseva (St. Petersburg: Leningrad-skii gosudarstvennyi oblastnoi universitet, 1998), 16–23; M. S. Grinberg and B. A. Uspenskii, *Literaturnaia voina Trediakovskogo i Sumarokova v 1740-kh-nachale 1750-kh godov* (Moscow: Rossiiskii gosudarstvennyi gumanitarnyi universitet, 2001). Examples of eighteenth-century plays that incorporate literary polemics include A. P. Sumarokov, *Iadovityi. Komediia,* in *PSVS,* 6:155–96; idem, *Nartsiss. Komediia,* in *PSVS,* 6:197–238; idem, *Tresotinius. Komediia* (directed against V. K. Trediakovskii), in *DS,* 294–308; N. P. Nikolev, *Samoliubivyi stikhotvorets* (directed against A. P. Sumarokov), in *RF,* 15:3–148; Dmitrii Khvostov, *Mnimyi schastlivets, ili Pustaia revnost'. Komediia v odnom deistvii,* in *RF,* 31:319–66. On the problem of bad writers, see Novikov's *Truten'* (11 August 1769), list 16; (18 August 1769), list 17; (25 August 1769), list 18. *Truten'* is reprinted in Berkov, *Satiricheskie zhurnaly,* 103–4, 110–11, 113.

60. Andreas Schönle, "The Scare of the Self: Sentimentalism, Privacy, and Private Life in Russian Culture, 1780–1820," *SR* 57 (1998): 743.

61. On the French models in Russia, see Kelly Herold, "Russian Autobiographical Literature in French: Recovering a Memoiristic Tradition (1770–1830)" (Ph.D. diss., University of California at Los Angeles, 1998).

62. V. I. Lukin, "Predislovie k *Nagrazhdennomu postoianstvu,*" in *SIPVL,* 2:i–xxvii.

63. The author of Sumarokov's life story agreed that his comedies were not a great success. "Povest'," 40–41.

64. Philippe Néricault Destouches (1680–1754), Jean-François Regnard (1655–1709), Louis de Boissy (1694–1758).

65. *Constancy Rewarded* is an adaptation to Russian mores of *L'Amante amant* (1684) by Jean Galbert de Campistron (1656–1723).

66. *Persten'. Komediia v odnom deistvii* (St. Petersburg: Vol'naia tipografiia Veit-brekhta i Shnora, 1780). The explanatory introduction is reprinted in *Sanktpeter-burgskii vestnik,* ch. 7 (January 1781): 47–48. Neither publication identifies Kozo-davlev by name.

67. V. I. Lukin, "Predislovie k *Pustomele,*" in *SIPVL,* 1:151–56. For acerbic depiction of bad writers, including one who steals the work of others, see Krylov, *Prokazniki,* in *RF,* 49:153–329.

68. *Vybor po razumu. Komediia v trekh deistviiakh* (St. Petersburg: n.p., 1773).

69. Nikolev, *Rozana i Liubim.*

70. Serman, "Iz istorii literaturnoi bor'by."

71. The Russian title is *Svoia nosha ne tianet.* See *Trudy Vasiliia Levshina i Ivana Fr. Kertseliia na 1793 god* (Kaluga: n.p., 1793).

72. Matinskii's authorized version appeared anonymously as *Tak pozhivesh', tak i proslyvesh'. Zabavnoe zrelishche s pesniami v trekh deistviiakh* (St. Petersburg: Tipografiia F. Breitkopfa, 1792). The unauthorized version, also published anonymously, appeared

as *Opera komicheskaia*. *Sanktpeterburgskii gostinoi dvor v trekh deistviiakh* (Moscow: Vol'-naia tipografiia A. Reshetnikova, 1791).

73. "Teatr," *Zritel'*, ch. 2–3 (June-December 1792), esp. 2 (August 1792): 254, 260–62; 3 (October 1792): 123–29. On Plavil'shchikov's authorship, see *Slovar' russkikh pisatelei XVIII veka*, vols. 1–2 (hereafter *SRP*) (Leningrad/St. Petersburg: Nauka, 1988, 1999–), 2:440.

74. *Pustomelia* (July 1770); *Zhivopisets*, ch. 1 (1772), list 21. Both reprinted in Berkov, *Satiricheskie zhurnaly*, 278–79, 357–58.

75. The reference to "the creative spirit" appears in the dedication of A. I. Klushin, *Khudo byt' blizorukim. Komediia v odnom deistvii, v proze* (St. Petersburg: Gubernskoe pravlenie, 1800).

76. Lukin had in mind the good servant Vasilei, who, critics claimed, could not exist in Russia. Lukin, "Predislovie k *Motu liuboviiu ispravlennomu*," in *SIPVL*, 1:xv–xx.

77. V. K., *Tshchetnaia revnost'*; Volkov, *Vospitanie*; Lopukhin, *Torzhestvo pravosudiia*. See the translation by Ivan Iakovlev of Denis Diderot's *Le Fils naturel* (1757): *Pobochnyi syn, ili Ispytaniia dobrodeteli*. The 1766 translation by Sergei Glebov also assumes the play will be read: *Pobochnyi syn, ili Opyt dobrodeteli. Komediia v piati deistviiakh G. Diderota* (St. Petersburg: n.p., 1766). S. I. Glebov (1736–1786) belonged to an old noble family. During the course of a distinguished military career, he reached the rank of major general before retiring because of poor health. His literary activities were limited to translations from French. *SRP*, 1:197–98. Lukin's dedication to Elagin in his *Works* and the introductions to his plays offer additional examples: Lukin, *SIPVL*, vol. 1; idem, "Predislovie k *Pustomele*," in *SIPVL*, 1:151–56; idem, "Predislovie k *Shchepetil'niku*," in *SIPVL*, 2:166.

78. On actors, see Lukin, "Predislovie k *Motu liuboviiu ispravlennomu*," in *SIPVL*, 1:xxvi–xxviii; idem, "Predislovie k *Pustomele*," in *SIPVL*, 1:151–56; B. E. El'chaninov, *Nakazannaia vertoprashka. Komediia v odnom deistvii* (St. Petersburg: n.p., 1767).

79. Lukin, *SIPVL*, vol. 1.

80. Lukin, "Predislovie k *Motu liuboviiu ispravlennomu*," in *SIPVL*, 1:xiii–xiv; idem, "Predislovie k *Nagrazhdennomu postoianstvu*," in *SIPVL*, 2:iv–viii, xix, xxii.

81. James Van Horn Melton, "From Image to Word: Cultural Reform and the Rise of Literate Culture in Eighteenth-Century Austria," *JMH* 58 (1986): 95–124; Malcolm Burgess, "Fairs and Entertainers in Eighteenth-Century Russia," *SEER* 38 (1959): 95–113. Early Russian minstrels *(skomorokhi)* faced persecution at the hands of princes, churchmen, and landlords: see Russell Zguta, *Russian Minstrels: A History of the Skomorokhi* (Philadelphia: University of Pennsylvania Press, 1978).

82. On February 10, 1783, Mr. Spinakuta, an impresario in St. Petersburg, advertised the performance of "an entertaining Pantomime with many alterations, in which Harlequin will dance with Mr. Pierrot." *Sanktpeterburgskie vedomosti*, no. 12 (10 February 1783). Harlequin and Pierrot are characters from the commedia dell'arte.

83. Sumarokov's comments, which are undated and untitled, introduce a 1769 letter from Voltaire. Sumarokov, *PSVS*, 4:61–68. A Russian translation of *Eugénie*, called a comedy, was published in St. Petersburg in 1770. There were 9 performances of *Eugénie* in St. Petersburg in 1774–1799 and 17 in Moscow in 1770–1798.

84. Nikolev, *Rozana i Liubim*. That Nikolev took offense at personal criticism did not prevent him from satirizing Sumarokov in *The Vain Poet*. See Karlinsky, *Russian Drama*, 146. Written in 1775 and published in St. Petersburg in 1787, *The Vain Poet* was performed 10 times in the capital between 1781 and 1800.

85. In 1781, Nikolev could not have anticipated the success of *Rozana and Liubim*, which received 34 Moscow performances in the years 1778 to 1800. *Sinav and Truvor*, a tragedy by A. P. Sumarokov, was staged in 1750 and published in 1751. A reworked version appeared in 1768.

86. Ia. I. Blagodarov, *Smeshnoe sborishche, ili Meshchanskaia komediia v trekh deistviiakh*, in *RF*, 36:147–289. First published in 1787, *A Funny Assemblage* is not listed in *IRDT*.

87. D. P. Gorchakov, *Shchastlivaia tonia. Komicheskaia opera* (Moscow: n.p., 1786). *A Lucky Haul of Fish* was performed 37 times in Moscow in 1786–1800, with music by M. Stabinger.

88. Klushin, *Khudo byt' blizorukim.*

89. Klushin also claimed to be carrying out the command of his superior, A. L. Naryshkin, who wanted to give the public a new Russian opera. I. A. Krylov, *Amerikantsy. Opera komicheskaia v dvukh deistviiakh* (St. Petersburg: Gubernskoe pravlenie, 1800). For further discussion, see chap. 4.

90. Krylov had criticized Klushin's comedies *Laughter and Sorrow* and *The Alchemist* on artistic grounds in reviews published in the *St. Petersburg Mercury* in 1793. I. A. Krylov, "P. A. Soimonovu," in *Sochineniia v dvukh tomakh*, 2 vols. (Moscow: Izdatel'stvo Pravda, 1956), 2:341–48, 380–81. For an earlier critique of authorial self-love, see Novikov's *Zhivopisets*, ch. 1 (1772), list 2; reprinted in Berkov, *Satiricheskie zhurnaly*, 284–88.

91. On the prepolitical literary public sphere, see chap. 1, n. 41.

92. On literature as a form of knowledge, see Ia. B. Kniazhnin, *Rosslav. Tragediia v stikhakh v piati deistviiakh*, in *RF*, 6:145–240. On theatrical works as moralistic literature, see Sergei Glebov's introduction to *Chadoliubivoi otets. Komediia v piat' deistvii. Sochinenie G. Diderota. Perevedena s Frantsuzskogo* (St. Petersburg: n.p., 1765).

93. See the preface to F. Ia. Kozel'skii, *Velesana. Tragediia*, in *Sochineniia Fedora Kozel'skogo*, 2 vols., 2d ed. (St. Petersburg: Imperatorskaia akademiia nauk, 1778), 2:66–133.

94. *RF*, 1: "Preuvedomlenie."

95. *Sanktpeterburgskie vedomosti*, no. 9 (29 January 1787): 115–16.

96. *Dramaticheskoi slovar', ili Pokazaniia po alfavitu vsekh Rossiiskikh teatral'nykh sochinenii i perevodov, s oznacheniem imen izvestnykh sochinitelei, perevodchikov, i slagatelei muzyki, kotoryia kogda byli predstavleny na teatrakh, i gde, i v kotoroe vremia napechatany. V pol'zu liubiashchikh teatral'nyia predstavleniia* (Moscow: Tipografiia A. A., 1787), "Preuvedomlenie."

97. Priscilla Roosevelt, *Life on the Russian Country Estate: A Social and Cultural History* (New Haven: Yale University Press, 1995), 122–25.

98. Rousseau penned his critique of theater in 1758. Jean-Jacques Rousseau, *Politics and the Arts: Letter to M. D'Alembert on the Theatre*, trans. Allan Bloom (1960; reprint, Ithaca, N.Y.: Cornell University Press, 1993); Benjamin R. Barber, "Rousseau and the Paradoxes of the Dramatic Imagination," *Daedalus* (Summer 1978): 79–92.

99. Prince M. M. Shcherbatov, *On the Corruption of Morals in Russia*, ed. and trans. A. Lentin (Cambridge, Eng.: Cambridge University Press, 1969), 225–27, 243–45, 253. The Smol'nyi Institute in St. Petersburg began to educate noble girls in 1764; a section for non-nobles opened in 1765.

100. A fictional debate along these lines appeared in [M. Prokudin-Gorskii], *Sud'ba derevenskaia. Komediia sochinennaia v nravakh derevenskikh zhitelei. V trekh deistviiakh*, in *RF*, 29:93–132.

101. Mikhail Kheraskov, *Nenavistnik. Komediia v trekh deistviiakh*, in *RF*, 10:37–120.

102. V. I. Lukin, *Nagrazhdennoe postoianstvo. Komediia v piati deistviiakh*, in *RF*, 36:5–146.

103. Ravel, *The Contested Parterre*, 54–63.

104. The relevant articles are reprinted in L. M. Starikova, ed., *Teatral'naia zhizn' Rossii v epokhu Anny Ioannovny*. Vypusk 1, *Dokumental'naia khronika 1730–1740* (Moscow: Radiks, 1995), 577–84. I. A. Krylov recognized that audiences preferred novelty to instruction, but he also blamed bad plays for the failure to correct morals. See *Pochta dukhov*, ch. 2 (August 1789), letters 41 and 44.

105. Ivan Sokolov, "Komedii, i tragedii, i vse drammaticheskiia sochineniia ili sluzhat k ispravleniiu nravov chelovecheskikh, ili bol'she ikh razvrashchaiut," *Poleznoe uveselenie*, no. 12 (March 1760): 121–26. For biographical details, see *Entsiklopedicheskii slovar'*, 43 vols. in 86 pts. (St. Petersburg: F. A. Brokgauz–I. A. Efron, 1890–1907) (hereafter *ES*), 60:731.

106. Sokolov briefly extended his argument to tragedy, which reformed morals by depicting the sad consequences of vice and the reward of virtue. For Catherine II's views on this point, see Novikov's *Zhivopisets*, ch. 1 (1772), listy 2 and 7; reprinted in Berkov, *Satiricheskie zhurnaly*, 283–84, 301–2.

107. Lukin, "Predislovie k *Pustomele*," in *SIPVL*, 1:151–56.

108. *Podrazhatel'. Komediia v odnom deistvii. Sochinena v Dmitrove* (Moscow: Tipografiia imperatorskogo moskovskogo universiteta, 1779). *The Imitator* was performed once in Moscow in 1783 and possibly once in St. Petersburg in 1794. According to *IRDT*, its author may have been either M. D. Chulkov or M. I. Verevkin.

109. *Baba Iaga. Komicheskaia opera v trekh deistviiakh i s baletom* (Kaluga: n.p., 1788). Published anonymously, *Baba Iaga* was performed in Moscow with music by M. Stabinger 17 times in 1786–1797, once in 1801, and once again in 1812.

110. On Baba Iaga, see W. F. Ryan, *The Bathhouse at Midnight: An Historical Survey of Magic and Divination in Russia* (University Park: Pennsylvania State University Press, 1999), 78–79, 421.

111. Lukin, "Predislovie k *Motu liuboviiu ispravlennomu*," in *SIPVL*, 1:v–xviii.

112. For a later exposé of the dangers posed by card games, see [P. S. Baturin], *Zgovor. Komediia v trekh desitviiakh*, in *RF*, 29:5–92. First published in St. Petersburg in 1783, *The Betrothal* was performed once at the Free Russian Theater in 1792 under the title *The Gamblers (Igroki)*.

113. *Narodnoe igrishche. Komediia v odnom deistvii* (1774), reprinted in Berkov, *Satiricheskie zhurnaly*, 495–504, 589–90.

114. *Igrishche o sviatkakh* (St. Petersburg: n.p., 1774).

115. V. K., *Dvorianiushcheisia kupets. Komediia v trekh deistviiakh*, in *Teatr V. K.*, vol. 1 (Moscow: Senatskaia tipografiia u F. Gippiusa, 1781), 107–65.

116. On the power of theater to reform good people who fall into ruin, see also Novikov's *Pustomelia* (June 1770), reprinted in Berkov, *Satiricheskie zhurnaly*, 257–62.

117. V. L., *Milozor i Prelesta*.

118. For recent appraisal of scholarship on the Enlightenment, see Michael Sonescher, "Enlightenment and Revolution," *JMH* 70 (1998): 371–83; Keith Michael Baker and Peter Hanns Reill, eds., *What's Left of the Enlightenment? A Postmodern Question* (Stanford: Stanford University Press, 2001); Gordon, *Postmodernism and the Enlightenment*.

119. On the "new politics," see chap. 1, n. 41.

120. Georg August Griesinger, *Biographical Notes Concerning Joseph Haydn*, in *Haydn: Two Contemporary Portraits*, trans. Vernon Gotwals (Madison: University of Wisconsin Press, 1968), 31.

121. Quoted in Daniel Roche, *A History of Everyday Things: The Birth of Consumption in France, 1600–1800*, trans. Brian Pearce (New York: Cambridge University Press, 2000), 117–18.

122. A classic statement of this thinking is Immanuel Kant's essay "What Is Enlightenment?" See Immanuel Kant, *Foundations of the Metaphysics of Morals and What Is Enlightenment?*, trans. Lewis White Beck, 2d ed. (Upper Saddle River, N.J.: Prentice Hall, 1995). See also the discussion in Leonard Krieger, *An Essay on the Theory of Enlightened Despotism* (Chicago: University of Chicago Press, 1975). The universal civil or human rights enshrined by the American and French Revolutions, though not realized in practice before the twentieth century, should not be confused with the civic or legal rights granted to subjects of the Russian Empire. Not only were Russian "civic rights" privileges rather than natural rights, they varied based on the individual's inherited social status. Nor was there any effort before the twentieth century to make these rights universal, in the sense of equal, across society. For further discussion, see chap. 5, n. 22.

3: THE PATRIARCHAL HOUSEHOLD

1. On the Muscovite household, see Carolyn Johnston Pouncy, ed. and trans., *The Domostroi: Rules for Russian Households in the Time of Ivan the Terrible* (Ithaca, N.Y.: Cornell University Press, 1994).

2. The abuses suffered by Anna Labzina are legendary, as are the sacrifices endured by Princess Natal'ia Dolgorukaia while in exile with her husband. Gary Marker, "The Enlightenment of Anna Labzina: Gender, Faith, and Public Life in Catherinian and Alexandrian Russia," *SR* 59 (2000): 369–90; "Svoeruchnye zapiski kniagini Natal'i Borisovny Dolgorukoi, docheri g. fel'dmarshala grafa Borisa Petrovicha Sheremeteva," in E. Anisimov, ed., *Bezvremen'e i vremenshchiki: Vospominaniia ob "epokhe dvortsovykh perevorotov" (1720e–1760e gody)* (Leningrad: Khudozhestvennaia literatura, 1991), 255–79.

3. See Valerie A. Kivelson, *Autocracy in the Provinces: The Muscovite Gentry and Political Culture in the Seventeenth Century* (Stanford: Stanford University Press, 1996); Lee A. Farrow, "Peter the Great's Law of Single Inheritance: State Imperatives and Noble Resistance," *RR* 55 (1996): 430–47; Michelle Lamarche Marrese, *A Woman's Kingdom: Noblewomen and the Control of Property in Russia, 1700–1861* (Ithaca, N.Y.: Cornell University Press, 2002); William G. Wagner, *Marriage, Property, and Law in Late Imperial Russia* (New York: Oxford University Press, 1994).

4. Steven Ozment, *When Fathers Ruled: Family Life in Reformation Europe* (Cambridge, Mass.: Harvard University Press, 1983), chaps. 1–2; Vickery, "Golden Age to Separate Spheres?"

5. Fear of love is the theme of *Ptitselov. Pastush'ia opera v odnom deistvii*, in *RF*, 28:5–38. The opera was published anonymously in 1789 and is not listed in *IRDT*. The need to become independent of parental authority in order to find happiness through love is represented by N. A. L'vov (1751–1803) in the pastoral comedy *Milet and Mileta;* written in 1794, it depicts the courtship and marriage of the poet G. R. Derzhavin and D. A. D'iakova. N. P. Iakhontov (1764–1840) composed music

for the play, though there is no record of performance in *IRDT*. See N. A. L'vov, *Milet i Mileta. Pastush'ia shutka dlia dvukh lits i v odnom deistvii s pesniami*, in *Izbrannye sochineniia*, ed. K. Iu. Lappo-Danilevskii (reprint, St. Petersburg: Akropol', 1994), 275–83.

6. V. M., *Pigmalion, ili Sila liubvi. Drama s muzykoiu v odnom deistvii*, in *RF*, 18:173–214. *Pygmalion* was first published and performed in Moscow in 1779 with music by N. G. Pomorskii (1747–1804).

7. Maikov reproduces Ovid's story that celebrates love through Pygmalion's ardor for the ideal woman he has created. Betty Radice, *Who's Who in the Ancient World* (New York: Penguin Books, 1973), 207–8; *Oxford Classical Dictionary*, 3d ed. (hereafter *OCD*), 1281.

8. *Dobrodetel'noi volshebnik. Drammaticheskaia opera v piati deistviiakh* (Moscow: Tipografiia A. A., 1787). Although I have no evidence regarding actual performances, the text of the opera calls for a chorus and ballet.

9. Prince I. M. Dolgorukov, *Liubovnoe volshebstvo. Opera v trekh deistviiakh* (Moscow: Gubernskaia tipografiia u A. Reshetnikova, 1799). The opera is not listed in *IRDT* but reportedly was performed in Nizhnii Novgorod.

10. On church and state policies, see L. N. Semenova, *Ocherki istorii byta i kul'turnoi zhizni Rossii. Pervaia polovina XVIII v.* (Leningrad: Nauka, 1982), 19–26. For preliminary evidence that serf owners did not interfere in peasant marriages, see John Bushnell, "Did Serf Owners Control Serf Marriage? Orlov Serfs and Their Neighbors, 1773–1861," *SR* 52 (1993): 419–45.

11. *Razluka, ili Ot"ezd psovoi okhoty iz Kuskova. Komicheskaia opera, v dvukh deistviiakh s eia posledovaniem v odnom deistvii* (Moscow: Vol'naia tipografiia Ponomareva, 1785). The opera is not listed in *IRDT* but was performed on the Kuskovo estate of Count P. B. Sheremetev in 1785. An especially popular play of the late eighteenth and early nineteenth centuries that roundly condemned forced marriage with reference to both masters and peasants is P. A. Plavil'shchikov, *Bobyl'. Komediia v piati deistviiakh*, in *Russkaia komediia*, Berkov, 407–64. *The Landless Peasant* was first published in St. Petersburg in 1792; between 1790 and 1800 it was performed 14 times in St. Petersburg and 22 times in Moscow. In 1802–1822, the comedy received 13 performances in St. Petersburg and 24 in Moscow.

12. *Olin'ka, ili Pervonachal'naia liubov'. Selo Iasnoe. 1796* (Moscow: Tipografiia A. Reshetnikova, 1796). Reportedly performed by serf actors in the Moscow home of A. A. Stolypin, the published play is an altered version of the scandalous original. *IRDT* lists 2 Moscow performances in 1801. A. M. Belosel'skii-Belozerskii also composed the accompanying music.

13. For a riveting popular history of marriage arrangements at court, see Evgenii Anisimov, *Zhenshchiny na rossiiskom prestole* (St. Petersburg: Norint, 1997).

14. Ia. B. Kniazhnin, *Sofonisba. Tragediia v piati deistviiakh*, in *RF*, 34:109–204. First published in St. Petersburg in 1787, *Sophonisba* was performed there twice in 1789–1790 and once in 1807; in Moscow there was one known performance, in 1808. The historical Sophonisba (Saphanba'al) was married to Syphax, king of Numidia, who in the late third century B.C. suffered defeat at the hands of the Numidian prince Masinissa, an ally of Rome. According to Livy, Sophonisba took poison sent to her by Masinissa, because he could not save her from Roman capitivity. *OCD*, 398, 668, 934, 1425, 1463.

15. V. I. Maikov, *Femist i Ieronima. Tragediia*, in *Russkaia literatura*, Stennik, 267–314, 702–3. First published in Moscow in 1775, *Femist and Ieronima* is not listed in *IRDT*.

16. A. P. Sumarokov, *Sinav i Truvor. Tragediia*, in *DS*, 83–133, 458–60. First published in St. Petersburg in 1751, the reworked version of *Sinav and Truvor* appeared in 1768. The original version also appeared in French translation and was reviewed in *Journal étranger* in 1755. In St. Petersburg there were 33 performances in 1750–1799 and 5 in 1807–1816; in Moscow there were 16 performances in 1760–1800, followed by single performances in 1801 and 1815.

17. Mikhail Kheraskov, *Marteziia i Falestra. Tragediia*, in *RF*, 4:85–164. Although first published in Moscow in 1767, *Marteziia and Falestra* was not performed until 1802. *IRDT* lists 2 Moscow performances for that year.

18. V. K., *Bedstvo proizvedennoe strast'iu, ili Sal'vinii i Adel'son. Tragediia grazhdanskaia v piati deistviiakh*, in *Teatr V. K.*, vol. 1 (Moscow: Senatskaia tipografiia u F. Gippiusa, 1781), 1–106. The tragedy is not listed in *IRDT*.

19. Vsl. Lvshn., *Garstlei i Florinichi. Meshchanskaia tragediia* (Moscow: Universitetskaia tipografiia u N. Novikova, 1787). The tragedy is not listed in *IRDT*.

20. Mikhail Kheraskov, *Plamena. Tragediia*, in *RF*, 4:3–84. First published in Moscow in 1765, *Plamena* was performed once in Moscow prior to 1772.

21. P. S. Potemkin, *Torzhestvo druzhby. Drama*, in *RF*, 8:97–176. Dedicated to Paul, heir to the Russian throne, *Celebration of Friendship* was first published in Moscow in 1773. It was performed once at court in St. Petersburg in 1773 and once in Moscow in 1778.

22. *Vybor po razumu. A Reasonable Choice* is not listed in *IRDT*, and its French model is not identified.

23. Resolution occurs because at age 21, Liubima is old enough to claim her inheritance through the courts. Ia. B. Kniazhnin, *Skupoi. Opera komicheskaia v odnom deistvii*, in *RF*, 30:171–244. First published in St. Petersburg in 1787, *The Miser* was performed with music by V. A. Pashkevich (1749–1797); there was one performance in St. Petersburg in 1782 and 18 performances in Moscow in 1782–1799.

24. *Pis'mo, ili Bogataia nevesta. Komediia v dvukh deistviiakh*, in *RF*, 33:295–339. First published in Moscow in 1788, the comedy is not listed in *IRDT*.

25. Only one voice of dissension is heard—that of Sirova, a poor orphan taken in by Liumilova's mother. Sirova tries to dissuade Liumilova from pursuing Den'gov: women, she argues, are weak and filled with pride, and too easily they assume men love them. A man looks at a woman, says a few insignificant words, and instantly she regards him as a passionate lover. Ignored by the self-serving bride and groom, both of whom know they are being used, Sirova resolves to avoid marriage and instead devote herself to Liumilova's mother.

26. *Otgadai i ne skazhu. Komediia v odnom deistvii. 1772*, in *RF*, 21:5–56. The comedy is not listed in *IRDT*.

27. Love and economic need also are reconciled in A. P. Sumarokov's comedy *Cuckold by Fancy*—written about 1772, first published in Moscow in 1781, and performed once there in 1782. A. P. Sumarokov, *Rogonets po voobrazheniiu. Komediia*, in *DS*, 387–411, 474.

28. P. A. Kropotov, *Fomushka—babushkin vnuchek. Komediia*, in *Russkaia komediia*, Berkov, 369–405, 697. Berkov dates the opera from 1785; it was published in 1790 and is not listed in *IRDT*.

29. From the reign of Peter I until the abolition of serfdom in 1861, the primary measurement of noble wealth was the number of male peasants or "souls" owned by a seignior.

30. Dobrovidov himself frequently helps his peasants by giving them free

grain, paying their poll taxes, and providing monies for recruits.

31. In accordance with inheritance law, Chistoserdov notes that the village is not part of his family patrimony but property he acquired and can therefore give away.

32. Vasil'i Levshin, *Kto staroe pomianet, tomu glaz von. Komediia liricheskaia v trekh deistviiakh* (Moscow: Tipografiia pri teatre u Khr. Klaudiia, 1791). The lyric comedy is not listed in *IRDT* but was performed in 1791 with music by Kesler at the Petrovskoe theater of Prince V. I. Shcherbatov.

33. See below for discussion of the tension between deception and the preservation of patriarchal authority.

34. *Zhenikh dovolen. Komediia v trekh deistviiakh, vol'nymi stikhami* (Moscow: n.p., 1795). The comedy is not listed in *IRDT*.

35. P. A. Plavil'shchikov, *Sgovor Kuteikina. Komediia v odnom deistvii*, 2d ed. (St. Petersburg: V. Plavil'shchikov, 1821). First published in St. Petersburg in 1799, *The Betrothal of Kuteikin* was performed there once in 1789 and once in 1807; in Moscow there was one performance in 1800.

36. Full reconciliation then is achieved because Pimen repays Preslep's debt to the father of Pravdin, the official who in Fonvizin's comedy was responsible for placing the Prostakov estate under guardianship.

37. Fonvizin, *Nedorosl'*, 82–148. Written in 1781 and published anonymously in 1783, *The Minor* was performed in St. Petersburg 23 times in 1782–1800 and 50 times in 1802–1825, in Moscow 27 times in 1783–1800 and 26 times in 1801–1824.

38. *Nakazannaia vertoprashka. Komediia v odnom deistvii* (St. Petersburg: n.p., 1767). *The Giddypate Punished* was performed once in St. Petersburg in 1767.

39. Another coquette, eventually abandoned by all her lovers, appears in Ivan Krylov, *Sochinitel' v prikhozhei. Komediia v trekh deistviiakh*, in *RF*, 41:149–228.

40. *Toisiokov. Komediia v piati deistviiakh*, in *RF*, 19:239–317. First published in St. Petersburg in 1786, *Mr. This-and-That* was performed once at court in 1786 and once in Moscow that same year.

41. Dashkova, *Memoirs*, 235.

42. Euripides, *Three Plays: Alcestis, Hippolytus, Iphigenia in Tauris*, trans. Philip Vellacott, revised ed. (London: Penguin, 1974). A. P. Sumarokov, *Al'tsesta. Opera*, in *PSVS*, 4:221–46. First published in St. Petersburg in 1759, *Alcestis* is not listed in *IRDT*. Both Francesco Araija (1709–1775) and Hermann Friedrich Raupach (1728–1778) wrote music to Sumarokov's libretto. Raupach's opus was performed in 1758 and 1759. See *MP*, 1:60.

43. A. A. Rzhevskii, *Podlozhnyi Smerdii. Tragediia*, in *Russkaia literatura*, Stennik, 213–66, 700–701. *The False Smerdis* was performed once in St. Petersburg in 1769 but not published until 1956.

44. See chap. 6 for discussion of tyranny.

45. N. N., *Ispytannoe postoianstvo. Komediia v odnom deistvii*, in *RF*, 23:3–68. Written in 1775 and first published in Moscow in 1776, *Constancy Tested* also was performed that year by the noble society *(blagorodnoe obshchestvo)* at the home of Prince P. M. Volkonskii. *IRDT* lists one performance in Moscow in 1783 and 2 in St. Petersburg in 1801–1804.

46. *Toch' v toch'. Komediia v trekh deistviiakh. Sochinennaia v Simbirske*, in *RF*, 33:133–74. First published in St. Petersburg in 1785, the comedy is not listed in *IRDT*.

47. The Russian Orthodox Church allowed divorce under tightly controlled conditions. Gregory L. Freeze, "Bringing Order to the Russian Family: Marriage and

Divorce in Imperial Russia, 1760–1860," *JMH* 62 (1990): 709–46. Already in Kievan and Muscovite times the punishment of rape was seen as a means to restore the victim's lost honor. See Nancy Shields Kollmann, *By Honor Bound: State and Society in Early Modern Russia* (Ithaca, N.Y.: Cornell University Press, 1999), 35, 43, 72–75.

48. Research on the social condition of Russian women in the eighteenth century is particularly sparse, but honor suits from the Muscovite period support this interpretation. See Kollmann, *By Honor Bound,* chap. 2.

49. *Pritvornaia nevernost'. Komediia v odnom deistvii. Prelozhennaia na zdeshnie nravy vol'nym perevodom s sochineniia G. Barte* (St. Petersburg: n.p., 1772). *IRDT* lists 5 Moscow performances in 1779–1785 and one in 1803.

50. *Obmena shliap, ili Blagorazumiem unichtozhennoe pokushenie* (St. Petersburg: Vol'naia tipografiia u Shnora, 1782). *Exchange of Hats* was performed once in St. Petersburg in 1782.

51. N. M. Kugushev, *Liubovnaia shutka. Original'naia komediia v odnom deistvii* (Smolensk: Gubernskaia tipografiia, 1800). *Love Joke* was performed once in Moscow in 1808.

52. Citing nineteenth-century literature, Iu. M. Lotman describes the role of assemblies, balls, and masquerades in structuring social intercourse while also allowing romantic communication, including illicit communication, between men and women. Iu. M. Lotman, *Besedy o russkoi kul'ture. Byt i traditsii russkogo dvorianstva (XVIII–nachalo XIX veka)* (St. Petersburg: Izdatel'stvo Iskusstvo-SPB, 1994), 90–102.

53. N. M., *Mshchenie za nevernost'. Komediia v odnom desitvii* (Moscow: Universitetskaia tipografiia u N. Novikova, 1781). The comedy is not listed in *IRDT.*

54. *Nevernost' zhenskaia. Komediia v odnom deistvii* (Moscow: Universitetskaia tipografiia u N. Novikova, 1788). The comedy is not listed in *IRDT.*

55. Ivan Mikhailov, *Komediia Odno na drugoe pokhozhe, v chetyrekh deistviiakh* (Moscow: Tipografiia pri teatre u Khr. Klaudiia, 1788). The comedy is not listed in *IRDT.*

56. Although comedy represented the most common vehicle for depicting adultery, a melodramatic treatment ending in madness, murder, and suicide can be found in Nikolai Karamzin, *Sofiia. Dramaticheskoi otryvok,* in *Moi bezdelki,* 2d ed., 2 vols. (Moscow: Universitetskaia tipografiia u Ridigera i Klaudiia, 1797), 1:109–61.

57. The most famous articulation of this thinking appears in Shcherbatov, *On the Corruption of Morals in Russia.*

58. See chap. 4 for discussion of attitudes toward fashionable sociability.

59. Mikhail Prakudin (M. I. Prokudin-Gorskii), *Dobrodetel' uvenchannaia vernost-'iu. Komediia,* in *RF,* 25:83–144. First published in Moscow in 1774, the comedy is not listed in *IRDT.*

60. A. P. Sumarokov, *Pustaia ssora. Komediia,* in *DS,* 334–45, 472. Composed in 1750, the comedy was reworked in the 1760s and published in Sumarokov's collected works (1781). *IRDT* lists one performance in St. Petersburg in 1757 and one in Moscow in 1782. Stennik adds a second Moscow performance in 1751.

61. Ia. B. Kniazhnin, *Neudachnyi primiritel', ili Bez obedu domoi poedu. Komediia v trekh deistviiakh prozoiu,* in *RF,* 33:195–294. First published in St. Petersburg in 1787, the comedy is not listed in *IRDT.*

62. *Ieffai. Sviashchennaia tragediia koeia soderzhanie v bibleiskikh knigakh sudei glava 11 k kontsu,* in *RF,* 6:241–72. First published in Moscow in 1778, *Jephthah* is not listed in *IRDT.*

63. P. A. Plavil'shchikov, *Riurik,* in *Russkaia literatura,* Stennik, 592–642, 715.

Created in the early 1790s and performed in St. Petersburg in 1791 under the title *Vseslav, Riurik* in its present form was prepared by the author in 1812 and published in St. Petersburg in 1816. *IRDT* lists the St. Petersburg performance of 1791 as well as 2 Moscow performances in 1794 and 2 in 1803.

64. See chap. 6.

65. John Locke, *Some Thoughts Concerning Education, and Of the Conduct of the Understanding*, ed. Ruth W. Grant and Nathan Tarcov (Indianapolis: Hackett Publishing Company, 1996), 152. *Some Thoughts Concerning Education* was first published in 1706. According to *SK*, a Russian translation from the French appeared in 1759. On Rousseau, see Peter Gay's introduction to Jean-Jacques Rousseau, *The Basic Political Writings*, trans. Donald A. Cress (Indianapolis: Hackett Publishing Company, 1987).

66. Mikhail Kheraskov, *Bezbozhnik. Geroicheskaia komediia*, in *RF*, 10:5–36. First published in Moscow in 1761, *The Godless One* was performed in Moscow that same year. A. T. Bolotov reports that in 1779 the children's theater he directed in Bogoroditsk performed a play called *The Godless One*, presumably Kheraskov's comedy.

67. *Troe lenivykh. Opera v odnom deistvii*, in *RF*, 37:5–30. The opera is not listed in *IRDT*.

68. G. G., *Kukla Lizan'ke, ili Nagrazhdennoe prilezhanie. Detskaia dramma* (St. Petersburg: I. Sytin, 1799). The drama is not listed in *IRDT*.

69. Bolotov, *Zhizn' i prikliucheniia Andreia Bolotova*, 3:288. The comedy was published for the first time as *Chestokhval. Komediia detskaia v trekh deistviiakh, sochinennaia v gorode Bogoroditske 1779 goda*, in Bolotov, *Izbrannoe*, 35–81.

70. A. A. Maikov, *Neudachnoi zgovor, ili Pomolvil da ne zhenilsia. Komediia v odnom deistvii* (St. Petersburg: Tipografiia korpusa chuzhestrannykh edinovertsov, 1794). *The Unsuccessful Betrothal* was performed 3 times in St. Petersburg in 1794, including a performance at the Hermitage Theater in the presence of the empress.

71. *Neshchastnyia siroty. Dramma v trekh deistviiakh. Sochinena v Bogoroditske, v 1780 gode* (Moscow: Universitetskaia tipografiia u N. Novikova, 1781). D. I. Fonvizin's *The Minor* was written in 1781, first performed in 1782, and first published in 1783.

72. Iakov Kniazhnin, *Zbiten'shchik. Komicheskaia opera v trekh deistviiakh*, in *RF*, 30:5–156. First published in 1787, *Zbiten'shchik* was performed frequently, with music by Anton Bullandt (d. 1821): there were 19 performances in St. Petersburg in 1784–1800 and 34 in 1802–1825; in Moscow there were 33 performances in 1787–1800 and 26 in 1803–1822.

73. Iakov Kniazhnin, *Komicheskaia opera pritvorno sumashedshaia, v dvukh deistviiakh*, in *Sobranie sochinenii Iakova Kniazhnina*, 4 vols. (St. Petersburg: Tipografiia gornogo uchilishcha, 1787), 4:91–153. *The Sham Madwoman* was performed with music by Gennaro Astarita (b. between 1745 and 1749, d. after 1803), once in St. Petersburg in 1789 and 7 times in Moscow in 1795–1800.

74. *Pobeda nevinnosti, ili Liubov' khitree ostorozhnosti. Komediia v odnom deistvii*, in *RF*, 25:5–82. The comedy is not listed in *IRDT*.

75. V. S. Viazemskii, *Pustynnik. Dramma v trekh deistviiakh* (Moscow: Gubernskaia tipografiia u A. Reshetnikova, 1800). Described as an imitation of M. M. Kheraskov's *The Persecuted* (1775), *The Hermit* is not listed in *IRDT*.

76. A. P. Sumarokov, *Likhoimets. Komediia*, in *PSVS*, 5:55–122. First published in St. Petersburg in 1768, *The Usurer* was performed in St. Petersburg once in 1769, twice in 1781, and once in 1782; in Moscow there was one performance in 1769.

77. I. F. B., *Komediia nechaiannaia zhenidba, ili Obmanutoi starik*, 2d ed.

(Moscow: Tipografiia kompanii tipograficheskoi, 1788). First published in St. Petersburg in 1766, the comedy is not listed in *IRDT.*

78. M. V., *Imianinniki. Komediia v piati deistviiakh,* in *RF,* 21:187–306. First published in Moscow in 1774, the comedy is not listed in *IRDT.*

79. *Dobronrav. Komediia v odnom deistvii,* in *RF,* 38:5–36. First published in Moscow in 1789, *Dobronrav* is not listed in *IRDT.*

80. *Nevesta pod fatoiu, ili Meshchanskaia svad'ba. Komicheskaia opera, bez nabliudeniia teatral'nykh i stikhotvorcheskikh pravil* (Moscow: Universitetskaia tipografiia u V. Okorokova, 1790). The comic opera is not listed in *IRDT.*

81. Nik. Sel., *Osmeiannoi vertoprakh. Original'naia komediia v trekh deistviiakh, v stikhakh* (Moscow: Tipografiia A. Reshetnikova, 1796). The comedy is not listed in *IRDT.*

82. Kn. Aleksei Golitsyn, *Otets nevidimka, ili Svatalsia na materi, zhenilsia na docheri. Komediia v trekh deistviiakh* (Moscow: Universitetskaia tipografiia, 1799). The comedy is not listed in *IRDT.*

83. As seen in chap. 6. An explicit statement can be found in the anonymous *Zloumnyi. Komediia v piati deistviiakh,* in *RF,* 23:69–271.

84. David J. Welsh, *Russian Comedy, 1765–1823* (The Hague and Paris: Mouton, 1966), 80–86.

85. *Domashniia nesoglasiia. Komediia v piati deistviiakh,* in *RF,* 12:205–390. The comedy is not listed in *IRDT.*

86. On the transition from moral to political economy, see Roche, *History of Everyday Things.* The moral economy of scarcity offered a twofold justification for wealth: wealth would be redistributed in charity, and consumption provided work for the poor. Because a just economy promoted the circulation of goods, hoarding and its derivative, usury, elicited condemnation. Roche, *History of Everday Things,* 72–78.

87. Kheraskov, *Venetsianskaia monakhinia,* 315–62. First published in Moscow in 1758, *The Nun of Venice* was republished in 1793 in an updated and expanded version. Stennik reproduces the 1798 version of the tragedy. The tragedy is not listed in *IRDT* but may have been performed at Moscow University in 1758–1759.

4: CIVIC SOCIETY

1. Our modern conception of civil society implies the separation of an autonomous society from the state. That conception has its origins in Hegel's definition of civil society as the realm of free market relations beyond the family and distinct from government. Prior to Hegel, theorists such as John Locke, Adam Ferguson, Adam Smith, and various French Enlightenment figures concerned with the problem of making society more civil used "civil society" as a synonym for the political state. For an overview, see Manfred Riedel, "Gesellschaft, bürgerliche," in *Geschichtliche Grundbegriffe: Historisches Lexikon zur politisch-sozialen Sprache in Deutschland,* 8 vols., ed. Otto Brunner, Werner Conze, and Reinhart Koselleck (Stuttgart: Ernst Klett, 1972–1997), 2:719–800. On Russia, see Roger Bartlett, "Aufklärung, Adel, und Gesellschaft in Russland," in *Europa in der Frühen Neuzeit: Festschrift für Günter Mühlpfordt,* Band 5, *Aufklärung in Europa,* ed. Erich Donnert (Cologne: Böhlau, 1999), 521–30; idem, "The Free Economic Society: The Foundation Years and the Prize Essay Competition of 1766 on Peasant Property," in *Russland zur Zeit Katharinas II. Absolutismus—*

Aufklärung—Pragmatismus, ed. Eckhard Hübner, Jan Kusber, and Peter Nitsche (Cologne: Böhlau, 1998), 181–214; Adele Lindenmeyr, *Poverty Is Not a Vice: Charity, Society, and the State in Imperial Russia* (Princeton: Princeton University Press, 1996); Smith, *Working the Rough Stone.*

2. For synthesis of the scholarship covering imperial social categories, see Elise Kimerling Wirtschafter, *Social Identity in Imperial Russia* (DeKalb: Northern Illinois University Press, 1997); B. N. Mironov, *Sotsial'naia istoriia Rossii perioda imperii (XVIII–nachalo XX v.) Genezis lichnosti, demokraticheskoi sem'i, grazhdanskogo obshchestva, i pravovogo gosudarstva,* 2 vols. (St. Petersburg: Dmitrii Bulanin, 1999).

3. Muscovite sources provide little evidence of Russians self-consciously imagining themselves as a social collective. Nancy Kollmann notes that "Muscovites did not reflect self-consciously on the collective body in which they lived." Similarly, "Muscovites did not have a collective vision, even a collective noun, for their society as an entity. They saw society in multiplicity, not unity." See Kollmann, *By Honor Bound,* 59.

4. *Slovar' Akademii rossiiskoi,* 6 vols. (St. Petersburg: Imperatorskaia akademiia nauk, 1789–1794; 2d ed., 1806–22).

5. Marc Raeff, "Transfiguration and Modernization: The Paradoxes of Social Disciplining, Paedagogical Leadership, and the Enlightenment in Eighteenth-Century Russia," in *Alteuropa—Ancien Régime—Frühe Neuzeit: Probleme und Methoden der Forschung,* ed. Hans Erich Bödeker and Ernst Hinrichs (Stuttgart and Bad Cannstatt: Fromann-Holzboog, 1991), 109; Anthony G. Netting, "Russian Liberalism: The Years of Promise," (Ph.D. diss., Columbia University, 1967), 20.

6. Raeff, "Transfiguration and Modernization," 108–110.

7. V. M. Zhivov, "Gosudarstvennyi mif v epokhu prosveshcheniia i ego razrushenie v Rossii kontsa XVIII veka," in *Iz istorii russkoi kul'tury,* vol. 4 *(XVIII–nachalo XIX veka)* (Moscow: Shkola iazyki russkoi kul'tury, 1996), 670.

8. Tzvetan Todorov, *The Morals of History,* trans. Alyson Waters (Minneapolis: University of Minnesota Press, 1995), 192.

9. Note also that neither the charters nor local historical practice incorporated the principle of proprietary claims to public authority. Marc Raeff, *The Well-Ordered Police State: Social and Institutional Change through Law in the Germanies and Russia, 1600–1800* (New Haven: Yale University Press, 1983); David Griffiths, "Introduction: Of Estates, Charters, and Constitutions," in *Catherine II's Charters of 1785 to the Nobility and the Towns,* ed. and trans. David Griffiths and George E. Munro (Bakersfield, Calif.: Charles Schlacks, Jr., 1991), xvii–lxix.

10. Daniel Roche, *France in the Enlightenment,* trans. Arthur Goldhammer (Cambridge, Mass.: Harvard University Press, 1998), 247.

11. V. M., *Derevenskii prazdnik, ili Uvenchannaia dobrodetel'. Pastusheskaia drama s muzykoiu v dvukh deistviiakh,* in *RF,* 18:135–72. I. F. Kertselli composed the music for *Village Holiday.* The drama was first published and performed (once) in Moscow in 1777.

12. *Prikashchik. Drammaticheskaia pustel'ga s golosami, v odnom deistvii* (Moscow: Universitetskaia tipografiia u N. Novikova, 1781). Written in 1777 and published anonymously, *The Bailiff,* with music by F. Zh. Darsi, received 12 performances in Moscow in 1778–1793. For historical evidence of the abuses committed by bailiffs and other peasant officials, see Edgar Melton, "Household Economies and Communal Conflicts on a Russian Serf Estate, 1800–1817," *Journal of Social History* 26 (1993): 559–85; idem, "Enlightened Seigniorialism and Its Dilemmas in Serf Rus-

sia, 1750–1830," *JMH* 62 (1990): 675–708; Steven L. Hoch, *Serfdom and Social Control in Russia: Petrovskoe, a Village in Tambov* (Chicago: University of Chicago Press, 1986).

13. V. L., *Milozor i Prelesta. IRDT* does not list this play.

14. Yet another abusive bailiff eventually removed by a good master appears in [Prokudin-Gorskii], *Sud'ba derevenskaia*, in *RF*, 29:93–132. First published in Moscow in 1782, *Village Fate* is not listed in *IRDT*.

15. Ivan Nekhachin, *Neudachlivoi v liubvi pod'iachii. Komicheskaia opera v dvukh deistviiakh* (Moscow: Tipografiia A. Reshetnikova, 1795). *IRDT* does not list this play.

16. Elise Kimerling Wirtschafter, "Legal Identity and the Possession of Serfs in Imperial Russia," *JMH* 70 (1998): 561–87; idem, *Social Identity*, 118–23.

17. M. I. Popov, *Aniuta. Komicheskaia opera v odnom deistvii*, in *RF*, 28:145–84. Based on the work of Charles Simon Favart (1710–1792), *Annette et Lubin* (1762), Popov's text was first published and received one court performance in St. Petersburg in 1772.

18. Nikolev, *Rozana i Liubim*. Written in 1776, published anonymously, and set to music by I. F. Kertselli, *Rozana and Liubim* was performed 34 times in Moscow in 1778–1800 and 4 times in St. Petersburg in 1780–1782.

19. See chap. 3, n. 37.

20. Kliuchevskii, "Nedorosl' Fonvizina," 183–88.

21. For recent treatment of these debates, see Roger Bartlett, "Russische und baltische Publizistik gegen die Leibeigenschaft: Aleksandr Radiščevs *Reise von St. Petersburg nach Moskau* und Garlieb Merkels *Die Letten* und *Rükkehr ins Vaterland*," in *"Ich werde gewiss grosse Energie zeigen." Garlieb Merkel (1769–1850) als Kämpfer, Kritiker und Projektemacher in Berlin und Riga*, ed. Jörg Drews (Bielefeld: Aisthesis, 2000), 27–40; idem, "Defences of Serfdom in Eighteenth-Century Russia," *A Window on Russia: Papers from the Fifth International Conference of the Study Group on Eighteenth-Century Russia, Gargnano, 1994*, ed. Maria Di Salvo and Lindsey Hughes (Rome: La Fenice Edizioni, 1996), 67–74; Paola Ferretti, "'Razdelenie Zemel': A Proposal Against the Servile System by V. F. Malinovskii," *A Window on Russia*, 107–13.

22. *Vecherinki, ili Gadai gadai devitsa otgadyvai krasnaia. Opera komicheskaia* (St. Petersburg: n.p., 1788).

23. On these issues, and on the sequestration of estates, see Wirtschafter, *Social Identity*, 118–23.

24. Various ethnic minorities enjoyed exemptions from conscription. Merchants made monetary payments until 1807, when they became fully exempt, and although clergy also were exempt, the government carried out periodic levies of their "excess" offspring.

25. Elise Kimerling Wirtschafter, *From Serf to Russian Soldier* (Princeton: Princeton University Press, 1990), chap. 1.

26. Ia. B. Kniazhnin, *Neschast'e ot karety. Komicheskaia opera v dvukh deistviiakh*, in *Russkaia komediia*, Berkov, 247–62. First published in 1779, *Misfortune from a Carriage*, with music by V. A. Pashkevich, was performed 8 times in St. Petersburg in 1779–1791, 44 times in Moscow in 1780–1800, and twice again in Moscow in 1810.

27. N. A. L'vov, *Iamshchiki na podstave. Igrishche nevznachai*, in *Izbrannye sochineniia*, Lappo-Danilevskii, 253–74. First published in Tambov in 1788 and corrected by the author in the late 1790s, *Coachmen at the Relay Station* was performed once in St. Petersburg in 1787 with music by E. I. Fomin. On the different versions of the opera, see Lappo-Danilevskii, "Komicheskaia opera N. A. L'vova 'Iamshchiki na podstave,'"

93-112. L'vov's coachmen appear to be state peasants who provide drivers and horses at official relay stations. Hence they also remain subject to conscription and to the decisions of the peasant community *(mir)*. True *iamshchiki* were exempt from the capitation and conscription. Elise Kimerling Wirtschafter, *Structures of Society: Imperial Russia's "People of Various Ranks"* (DeKalb: Northern Illinois University Press, 1994), 165, n. 3.

28. On the social condition of soldiers and their families, see Wirtschafter, *From Serf to Russian Soldier;* idem, "Soldiers' Children, 1719-1856: A Study of Social Engineering in Imperial Russia," *FOG* 30 (1982): 61-136. There is evidence that soldiers' wives were disproportionately represented among persons investigated by Moscow criminal courts in the eighteenth century. See Christoph Schmidt, *Sozialkontrolle in Moskau: Justiz, Kriminalität, und Leibeigenschaft, 1649-1785* (Stuttgart: Steiner, 1996), 250-56.

29. M. D. Chulkov, *Prigozhaia povarikha, ili Pokhozhdenie razvratnoi zhenshchiny,* in *Khrestomatiia po russkoi literature XVIII veka,* 4th ed., ed. A. V. Kokorev (Moscow: Prosveshchenie, 1965), 586-607.

30. A. Ablesimov, *Shchastie po zhereb'iu. Komicheskaia opera v odnom deistvii* (Moscow: Universitetskaia tipografiia, 1780). *IRDT* does not list *Happiness by Lot,* which was written in 1779.

31. *Matrosskiia shutki. Opera komicheskaia,* in *RF,* 24:137-94. *Sailors' Jokes,* with music by Sebastian George, was performed once in Moscow in 1780, also the year of its first publication, and once in St. Petersburg before 1787. For the possibility that the author of *Sailors' Jokes* is Pavel Ivanovich Fonvizin (1744-1803), brother of Denis Fonvizin, see I. M. Badalich and P. N. Berkov, "Komicheskaia opera 'Matrosskie shutki' i ee avtor," *XVIII vek* 4 (1959): 422-25.

32. Krasana's mother and the bailiff actually know that Provor has returned, but they stage a joke to test the feelings of the young lovers.

33. *Novoe semeistvo. Komicheskaia opera v odnom deistvii,* in *RF,* 24:233-79. Published anonymously in 1781, *New Family,* with music by Freilikh, was performed in Moscow 60 times in 1782-1800 and 17 times in 1804-1811; in St. Petersburg, there were 17 performances in 1808-1814.

34. M. M. Kheraskov, *Dobrye soldaty. Komicheskaia opera v trekh deistviiakh sochinennaia na Rossiiskom iazyke,* in *RF,* 28:185-262. First published in 1779, *Good Soldiers,* with music by Hermann Friedrich Raupach (1728-1778), was performed 5 times in St. Petersburg in 1780-1784, 36 times in Moscow in 1779-1800, and once again in Moscow in 1810.

35. Written in 1782, *March from Stationary Quarters* was performed 8 times in Moscow in 1782-1785 with music by M. Ekkel'. The opera was published only in 1956, without the third act, which has been lost. P. N. Berkov, ed., "Komicheskaia opera A. O. Ablesimova 'Pokhod s nepremennykh kvartir'," *Teatral'noe nasledstvo* (Moscow: Iskusstvo, 1956), 189-224. Ablesimov himself participated in military campaigns during the Seven Years' War and in the Caucasus in 1770-1772.

36. *Pokhod pod Shveda. Komediia v trekh deistviiakh s khorami i baletom* (St. Petersburg: n.p., 1790). The comedy was performed once in St. Petersburg in 1790, though according to *ES,* it played frequently in Catherine II's Hermitage Theater. Following the outbreak of war between Russia and Turkey in 1787, Sweden unsuccessfully attempted to reassert its position in the Baltic. Land and naval operations began in the summer of 1788 and ended in the summer of 1790 with the Treaty of Verelä. A. A. Kersnovskii, *Istoriia russkoi armii v chetyrëkh tomakh,* vol. 1, *Ot Narvy do Parizha, 1700-1814* (reprint, Moscow: Golos, 1992), 156-58.

37. The prototype of the useless and poorly educated young noble who does not want to serve appears in Fonvizin's *The Minor*. In addition to G. N. Gorodchaninov's Mitrofanushka (see chap. 5) and Kokoshkin's Falalei Mitrofanovich, P. A. Kropotov's Fomushka, in *Fomushka—Grandma's Boy*, also represents a variation on Fonvizin's character. See Kropotov, *Fomushka—babushkin vnuchek*, 369–405, 697. *Fomushka* was first published in *RF* in 1790, and according to Berkov, written in 1785; it is not listed in *IRDT*, and I have no additional information regarding possible performances.

38. Elise Kimerling Wirtschafter, "Social Misfits: Veterans and Soldiers' Families in Servile Russia," *Journal of Military History* 59 (1995): 215–35.

39. V. M. Fedorov, *Russkoi soldat, ili Khorosho byt' dobrym gospodinom. Original'-naia dramma v dvukh deistviiakh* (St. Petersburg: Gubernskoe pravlenie, 1803). In 1802–1810, *Russian Soldier* was performed 20 times in St. Petersburg; in 1803–1811, there were 10 performances in Moscow.

40. Note here the emphasis on morality and sin, manifested in the failure to distinguish looting in war from the crime of theft or robbery.

41. Vasil'i Levshin, *Torzhestvo liubvi. Dramma. V trekh deistviiakh* (Moscow: Universitetskaia tipografiia u N. Novikova, 1787). *Celebration of Love* received one performance in Moscow in 1782. In the comic opera version of the play discussed above, the love of Milozor and Prelesta also triumphs.

42. Mikhail Kheraskov, *Drug neshchastnykh. Sleznaia drama* in *RF*, 8:177–240. *Friend of the Unfortunate* was first published in St. Petersburg in 1774 and received one Moscow performance in 1778.

43. Kupriian [Fedorovich] Damskii, *Opera komicheskaia Vinetta, ili Taras v ul'e. V dvukh deistviiakh* (Petropol': n.p., 1799). *Vinetta* is not listed in *IRDT* but may have been performed with music by Anton Bullandt in the theater of the St. Petersburg Foundling Home.

44. A. O. Ablesimov, *Melnik—koldun, obmanshchik, svat. Komicheskaia opera v trekh deistviiakh*, in *Russkaia komediia*, Berkov, 217–46, 692–93. Berkov reprints the 1785 edition of *The Miller*, which originally was published in Moscow in 1779. M. M. Sokolovskii and E. I. Fomin composed the music for the opera. The performance record includes 42 performances in St. Petersburg in 1781–1800 and 81 in 1801–1825. In Moscow there were 44 performances in 1779–1800 and 47 in 1801–1824.

45. Identified in the legislation of Peter I, single householders were free landowners who retained the right to seek official recognition of their noble ancestry. While permitted to own serfs, they fulfilled tax and conscription obligations on the same basis as state peasants, though with a shorter term of service and easier terms of promotion. Wirtschafter, *Structures of Society*, 96.

46. Osip Cherniavskoi, *Kupetskaia kompaniia. Komediia v odnom deistvii*, in *RF*, 27:149–208. *In the Company of Merchants* was first published in Moscow in 1780. *IRDT* does not list any performances.

47. The landowner was in debt to another noble, and the letter of credit was supposed to allow him to pay his creditor with the money the merchant would owe for the grain. The landowner died, all his property went to settle debts owed to the treasury, and the merchant was made liable, because of the letter of credit he had signed, for paying the noble creditor, who also happened to be the father of the prospective groom.

48. For historical evidence of similar arrangements, see Wirtschafter, "Legal Identity."

49. Vasil'i Levshin, *Svad'ba g. Voldyreva. Opera komicheskaia v odnom deistvii*, in

RF, 42:109–56. Set to music by I. F. Kertselli, *The Wedding of Mr. Voldyrev* was originally published in Kaluga in 1793 and received one Moscow performance in 1803.

50. V. K., *Dvorianiushcheisia kupets. Komediia v trekh deistviiakh*, in *Teatr V. K.*, vol. 1 (Moscow: Senatskaia tipografiia u F. Gippiusa, 1781), 107–65. *Merchant Becoming a Noble* was performed once in St. Petersburg in 1780. A similar critique of "the school of merchants becoming nobles" appears in *Obman na obman, ili Neudachnoi razvod. Komediia v trekh deistviiakh*, in *RF*, 38:177–240.

51. Griffiths, "Of Estates, Charters, and Constitutions."

52. *Peremena v nravakh. Komediia v dvukh deistviiakh*, in *RF*, 38:37–128. Published in 1789, *Change of Morals* is not listed in *IRDT*.

53. To my knowledge, incarceration for debt has not been documented for eighteenth-century Russia. Normal legal-administrative practice was to confiscate the property of the debtor for sale at auction. M. V. Vorozhbitova, "Dokumenty Kantseliarii konfiskatsii kak istochnik dlia kharakteristiki byta gorozhan serediny XVIII v.," *Vestnik moskovskogo universiteta*, seriia 8, *Istoriia*, no. 1 (1999): 71–84.

54. Dena Goodman, *The Republic of Letters: A Cultural History of the Enlightenment* (Ithaca, N.Y.: Cornell University Press, 1994); Daniel Gordon, *Citizens without Sovereignty: Equality and Sociability in French Thought, 1670–1789* (Princeton: Princeton University Press, 1994).

55. The tavern *(traktir)* was a public gathering place where patrons might be instructed to "leave all ranks outside the doors and likewise all hats and especially swords." "Precedence and snobbishness or any such like thing, when they exist, are to be left at the door." Quoted from a framed broadside (located in room 171 of the State Hermitage Museum in St. Petersburg) in George E. Munro, "Food in Catherinian St. Petersburg," *Food in Russian History and Culture*, ed. Musya Glants and Joyce Toomre (Bloomington: Indiana University Press, 1997), 44–45.

56. *Sosednii prazdnik. Predstavlenie v odnom deistvii*, in *RF*, 33:179–94. First published in St. Petersburg in 1790, *Neighborly Celebration* is not listed in *IRDT*.

57. *Nagrazhdenie dobrodeteli. Drama, predstavlennaia pitomtsami Aleksandrovskogo uchilishcha zavedennogo v Sanktpeterburge izdateliami Utrenniago sveta i dlia nikh sochinennaia*, in *RF*, 9:113–78. Published anonymously in St. Petersburg in 1780, *Reward of Virtue* is not listed in *IRDT*. St. Alexander was a charity subscription school established in St. Petersburg in 1778 by the mason, philanthropist, and publisher N. I. Novikov (1744–1818) with his collaborators at the journal *Morning Light*. In 1783 the school was absorbed into the Catherinean state schools established in 1782. On Novikov, see *SRP*, 2:363–76. On the St. Alexander School, see W. Gareth Jones, "The *Morning Light* Charity Schools, 1777–1780," *SEER* 56 (1978): 47–67.

58. For allegorical treatment of this theme, see I. F. Bogdanovich, *Radost' Dushin'ki. Liricheskaia komediia posleduemaia baletom v odnom deistvii*, in *RF*, 24:101–36. First published in St. Petersburg in 1786, *The Happiness of Dushin'ka* was performed once before the empress that same year.

59. *Opyt druzhby. Drama v chetyrekh deistviiakh. Predstavlena v Voronezhe na blagorodnom teatre 1798 goda* (Voronezh: Tipografiia gubernskogo pravleniia, 1799). The drama is not listed in *IRDT*.

60. Vladimir Lukin, *Mot liubov'iu ispravlennoi. Komediia v piati deistviiakh*, in *RF*, 19:5–154. First published in St. Petersburg in 1765, *Spendthrift* was performed at the court's Russian Theater that year, and again in St. Petersburg in 1791. See chap. 2, n. 31.

61. V. K., *Razvratnost' ispravliaemaia blagomysliem. Komediia v piati deistviiakh,* in *Teatr V. K.,* 1:167–282. *Profligacy* is not listed in *IRDT.*

62. Ia. B. Kniazhnin, *Khvastun. Komediia v stikhakh, v piati deistviiakh,* in *RF,* 10:121–270. First published in 1786, *The Braggart* was performed in St. Petersburg 15 times in 1785–1800 and 10 times in 1802–1825, and in Moscow 24 times in 1786–1800 and 22 times in 1802–1822.

63. See chap. 2.

64. A. I. Golitsyn, *Novye chudaki, ili Prozhekter. Komediia v piati deistviiakh. Sochinena v Moskve (1797),* in *Drammaticheskiia sochineniia i perevody podpolkovnika kniaz' Alekseia Golitsyna, v odnom tome* (Moscow: Universitetskaia tipografiia, 1798), 1–62. *New Eccentrics* is not listed in *IRDT.* A. I. Golitsyn, *Svetskoe obrashchenie, ili Nravy veka. Komediia v trekh deistviiakh. Sochineniia G. Garrika. Perevel dva deistviia, a tretie pridelal Kniaz' Aleksei Golitsyn,* in *Sochineniia i perevody Kn. A. I. Golitsyna,* vol. 1 (Moscow: Universitetskaia tipografiia, 1800), 63–125. Composed in 1798, *Worldly Intercourse* is not listed in *IRDT.*

65. An explicit statement appears in the anonymous *Zloumnyi.*

66. Kheraskov, *Nenavistnik. The Hater* was written in 1774, first published in 1779, and performed at the Russian Imperial Theater that same year. For another story of a corrupt courtier who manipulates a foolish country noble, see L. T., *Svad'ba Gospodina Promotalova. Komediia v trekh deistviiakh,* in *RF,* 27:53–148.

67. A similar story is told by Zdravomyslov (Sensible) in a spinoff play *Mitrofanushka in Retirement* (1800), by G. N. Gorodchaninov (1772–1852). See chap. 5.

68. A. I. Klushin, *Smekh i gore. Komediia v piati deistviiakh v stikhakh,* in *Stikhotvornaia komediia, komicheskaia opera, vodevil' kontsa XVIII–nachala XIX veka,* ed. A. A. Gozenpud, 2 vols. (Leningrad: Sovetskii pisatel', 1990), 1:443–541, 681–82. First published in St. Petersburg in 1793, *Laughter and Sorrow* was performed once at the Little (Malyi) Theater that same year. In Moscow there were 16 performances in 1793–1798 and 5 in 1811–1821.

69. John Brewer, *The Pleasures of the Imagination: English Culture in the Eighteenth Century* (New York: Farrar, Straus and Giroux, 1997).

70. The 1754 legislation allowed an interest rate of 6 percent a year, reduced to 5 percent in 1786. Mironov, *Sotsial'naia istoriia,* 2:41.

71. On the economic pressures created by consumerism and the adoption of Enlightenment culture, see Arcadius Kahan, "The Costs of 'Westernization' in Russia: The Gentry and the Economy in the Eighteenth Century" (1966), reprinted in *The Structure of Russian History: Interpretive Essays,* ed. Michael Cherniavaky (New York: Random House, 1970), 224–50.

72. I. N., *Pobeg ot dolgov, ili Raskaiavshiisia mot. Komediia v odnom deistvii* (Moscow: Tipografiia A. Reshetnikova, 1792). *Flight from Debt* is not listed in *IRDT.*

73. *Kak pozhiVesh', tak i proslyvesh'. Zabavnoe zrelishche s pesniami v trekh deistviiakh* (St. Petersburg: Tipografiia F. Breitkopfa, 1792). Produced with music by V. A. Pashkevich, *As You Live* received single performances in St. Petersburg in 1782, 1792, and 1810. In Moscow there were 25 performances in 1783–1799, one in 1801, one in 1810, 4 in 1820, and one in 1821. See chap. 2, n. 72.

74. On cameralism in Russia, see Raeff, *Well-Ordered Police State.*

75. Dmitrii Efim'ev, *Prestupnik ot igry, ili Bratom prodannaia sestra. Komediia v stikhakh v piati deistviiakh* (St. Petersburg: n.p., 1790). *Criminal from Gaming* was performed in St. Petersburg 16 times in 1788–1800 and 12 times in 1801–1814, in Moscow 17 times in 1790–1797 and 17 times in 1802–1817.

76. Catherine II, *Obmanshchik*, in *Sochineniia Ekateriny II*, ed. O. N. Mikhailov (Moscow: Sovetskaia Rossiia, 1990), 270–99; idem, *Obol'shchennyi*, in *Sochineniia Ekateriny II*, Mikhailov, 300–38; idem, *Shaman sibirskii*, in *Sochineniia Ekateriny II*, Mikhailov, 339–83. *The Deceiver* was performed 6 times in St. Petersburg and 7 times in Moscow in 1786–1787. *The Deceived* was performed once in St. Petersburg and twice in Moscow in 1786. *The Siberian Shaman* was performed once in St. Petersburg in 1786 and 4 times in Moscow in 1787.

77. Catherine II, *O vremia! Komediia v trekh deistviiakh. Sochinena v Iaroslavle vo vremia chumy 1772 g.*, in *Sochineniia Ekateriny II*, Mikhailov, 240–69. First published in St. Petersburg in 1772, *Oh, These Times!* was performed in St. Petersburg 10 times in 1772–1791 and 8 times in 1804–1811, in Moscow once in 1782 and once in 1811.

78. Catherine's antiheroes often prefer the old social mores and customs. See, for example, *Gospozha Vestnikova s sem'eiu. Komediia v odnom deistvii. Sochinena v Iaroslavle*, in *RF*, 11:263–308. First published in St. Petersburg in 1774, *Mrs. Vestnikova* (Tattler) was performed in St. Petersburg 3 times in 1780–1796 and once in 1804, in Moscow once prior to 1787.

79. *Imianiny Gospozhi Vorchalkinoi. Komediia v piati deistviiakh. Sochinena v Iaroslavle*, in *RF*, 11:85–220. First published in St. Petersburg in 1774, *The Nameday of Mrs. Vorchalkina* (Grumbler) was performed once at court in 1772.

80. The superiority of rural values represented a recurring theme in treatments of social vice. See, for example, [Prokudin-Gorskii], *Sud'ba derevenskaia*.

81. For a critique of the old social mores and of ignorance masking itself as enlightenment, see the anonymous *Igrishche o sviatkakh*.

82. A. P. Sumarokov, *Pustynnik. Drama*, in *DS*, 434–50. Written in 1757, *The Hermit* was performed at the Imperial Theater that same year. A revised version of the drama was published in St. Petersburg in 1769. On the religious sources of *The Hermit*, see M. Levitt, "Drama Sumarokova 'Pustynnik'. K voprosu o zhanrovykh i ideinykh istochnikakh russkogo klassitsizma," *XVIII vek* 18 (1993): 59–74.

83. Mikhail Kheraskov, *Gonimyia. Sleznaia drama*, in *RF*, 8:241–308. *The Persecuted* was originally published and performed once in Moscow in 1775.

84. L. M. Ivanov, *Serdtseplena. Opera v trekh deistviiakh. Sochinena v Moskve Tituliarnym Sovetnikom Leont'em Ivanovym 1788 goda* (Moscow: Senatskaia tipografiia, 1793). *Serdtseplena* is not listed in *IRDT*.

85. D. I. Fonvizin, *Korion. Komediia v trekh aktakh, peredelannaia v russkuiu s frantsuzskogo iazyka*, in *Stikhotvornaia komediia*, Gozenpud, 1:59–96. Performed once in St. Petersburg in 1764 and once in Moscow in 1769, *Korion* was not published until 1835.

86. A. Kopiev [Kop'ev], *Obrashchennyi mizantrop, ili Lebedianskaia iarmonka. Komediia v piati deistviiakh* (St. Petersburg: n.p., 1794). *The Converted Misanthrope* was performed in St. Petersburg 8 times in 1794–1800 and 3 times in 1803–1804, in Moscow 7 times in 1795–1800 and 9 times in 1801–1820.

87. One *versta* equals 1.06 km.

88. I. A. Krylov, *Amerikantsy. Opera komicheskaia v dvukh deistviiakh* (St. Petersburg: Gubernskoe pravlenie, 1800). *The Americans* was performed 4 times in St. Petersburg in 1800–1803 with music by E. I. Fomin. The version of *The Americans* published in 1800 was a reworking by A. I. Klushin, inspector of the Russian troupe of the Imperial Theater. Klushin claimed that Krylov's original opera had been accepted at the theater twelve years earlier but was not performed for artistic reasons.

5: THE COMMON GOOD

1. The relevant scholarship is enormous. On the consequences of Russia's lack of constituted political bodies, see Raeff, *Well-Ordered Police State*. On eighteenth-century Russian politics in practice, see Bushkovitch, *Peter the Great;* John P. LeDonne, *Absolutism and Ruling Class: The Formation of the Russian Political Order, 1700–1825* (New York: Oxford University Press, 1991).

2. The earliest example would be the reform projects submitted by noble assemblies in the 1850s, in connection with the serf emancipation. See Terence Emmons, *The Russian Landed Gentry and the Peasant Emancipation of 1861* (London: Cambridge University Press, 1968).

3. This is evident in Peter I's hounding of courtiers who failed to attend public events and in Catherine II's inability to garner enthusiastic noble or urban participation in local legal-administrative organs.

4. Although the discussion here focuses on military service, the concept of an obligation to serve could encompass either military or civil service.

5. On the nobility, see I. V. Faisova, *"Manifest o vol'nosti" i sluzhba dvorianstva v XVIII stoletii* (Moscow: Nauka, 1999); Marasinova, *Psikhologiia*, chap. 2; Michael Confino, "À propos de la notion de service dans la noblesse russe au XVIIIe et XIXe siècles," *Cahiers du Monde russe et soviétique* 34 (1993): 47–58; Marc Raeff, *Origins of the Russian Intelligentsia: The Eighteenth-Century Nobility* (New York: Harcourt, Brace, and World, 1966). On popular attitudes, see Wirtschafter, *From Serf to Russian Soldier*, chaps. 1, 5–6.

6. This is my understanding, though the question is in need of systematic research. For a recent overview of the long-term problem of noble identification, see A. Riber [Rieber], "Sotsial'naia identifikatsiia i politicheskaia volia: Russkoe dvorianstvo ot Petra I do 1861 g.," in *P. A. Zaionchkovskii (1904–1983 gg.): Stat'i, publikatsii, i vospominaniia o nem*, ed. L. G. Zakharova, Iu. S. Kukushkin, and T. Emmons (Moscow: ROSSPEN, 1998), 273–314. For epistolary evidence that in the second half of the eighteenth century the intellectual elite of the landowning nobility continued to regard their estates as grants from the tsar for service, see E. N. Marasinova, "Votchinik ili pomeshchik? (Epistoliarnye istochniki o sotsial'noi psikhologii rossiiskogo feodala vtoroi poloviny XVIII veka)," in *Mentalitet i agrarnoe razvitie Rossii (XIX–XX vv.)*, ed. V. P. Danilov and L. V. Milov (Moscow: ROSSPEN, 1996), 135–45.

7. Wirtschafter, "Legal Identity," 561–87.

8. Data from 1834 reveal that among the 106,000 nobles with fewer than one hundred souls, 17,000 had no land at all. At the time of the tenth revision (1857–1858), about three-fourths of serf owners possessed fewer than one hundred souls and together held less than 20 percent of the serfs. Daniel Field, *The End of Serfdom: Nobility and Bureaucracy in Russia, 1855–1861* (Cambridge, Mass.: Harvard University Press, 1976), 131; Emmons, *Russian Landed Gentry*, 3–14. On the notion that the 1762 emancipation freed the state from its obligations to the nobility, see Robert E. Jones, *The Emancipation of the Russian Nobility, 1762–1785* (Princeton: Princeton University Press, 1973).

9. Volkov, *Vospitanie*. Published anonymously, *Upbringing* was performed once in Moscow in 1774.

10. I have translated *rod* as family, rather than clan or kinship group, because the meaning seems confined to direct patrilineal descent (father/guardian and grandfather) and does not imply extended family in the broad sense. This concept of

family is consistent with the findings of recent research on inheritance laws and practices, though the relationship between state laws and social attitudes requires further study. See Kivelson, *Autocracy in the Provinces;* Farrow, "Peter the Great's Law of Single Inheritance"; Marrese, *A Woman's Kingdom;* Wagner, *Marriage, Property, and Law in Late Imperial Russia.*

11. During the eighteenth century, promotion to grade 14 in military service and grade 8 in civil service brought automatic ennoblement. Grade 14 was the lowest grade in the Table of Ranks. L. E. Shepelev, *Chinovnyi mir Rossii XVIII–nachalo XX v.* (St. Petersburg: Iskusstvo-SPb, 1999), 141–42.

12. It is important to treat the generational differences metaphorically. There is no historical evidence that nobles of a particular generation were more or less likely to evade service. If anything, the most extensive evidence of resistance to service comes from the reign of Peter I, when new and harsher obligations were imposed.

13. The colonel's attitude toward service recurs in Fonvizin's *The Minor,* where Starodum (Old-Thinking) argues that as long as a noble can be useful to the fatherland, he should remain in service. Fonvizin, *Nedorosl',* 82–148.

14. Note the distinction between the abstract concept of monarchical favor and the person of the actual ruler. See chap. 6 for the distinction between the person of the ruler and the abstract principle of the fatherland (state), which nevertheless incorporated the person of the sovereign.

15. *Mitrofanushka v otstavke. Komediia v piati deistviiakh. Rossiiskoe sochinenie G. G.* (Moscow: Universitetskaia tipografiia, 1800). Published pseudonymously, *Mitrofanushka in Retirement* was performed once in Moscow in 1801 and has been described as an imitation of Fonvizin's *The Minor.*

16. This reverses the process described for seventeenth- and eighteenth-century France, where merit evolved from an innate quality of nobility to an attribute denoting effective performance in service. Jay M. Smith, *The Culture of Merit: Nobility, Royal Service, and the Making of Absolute Monarchy in France, 1600–1789* (Ann Arbor: University of Michigan Press, 1996).

17. A second officer who depends on the Domosedovs, Trusilkin, is too cowardly (as indicated by his name) to defend his honor and thus appears even more pathetic than Khrabrilkin.

18. Here Zdravomyslov's understanding of merit parallels the French pattern outlined in n. 16.

19. Epistolary evidence expresses the same attitude. See Marasinova, *Psikhologiia,* chap. 2.

20. Historians of Muscovy trace the "individualization of noble culture" to the late seventeenth century, when individual fame rather than inherited family honor (*mestnichestvo*) began to define identity among courtiers. David Das, "History Writing and the Quest for Fame in Late Muscovy: Andrei Lyzlov's *History of the Scythians,*" *RR* 51 (1992): 502–9. On the individualization of morality and virtue, see Paul Bushkovitch, *Religion and Society in Russia: The Sixteenth and Seventeenth Centuries* (New York: Oxford University Press, 1992), chaps. 6–7.

21. This continued in the nineteenth century when noble intellectuals and self-conscious members of the intelligentsia embraced a code of behavior that emphasized moral autonomy. G. M. Hamburg, *Boris Chicherin and Early Russian Liberalism, 1828–1866* (Stanford: Stanford University Press, 1992), 338.

22. Civil rights are by definition translocal and universal. Rights that are con-

fined to a particular social category constitute privileges, not civil rights. On the concept of civil rights, see Isabel de Madariaga, *Politics and Culture in Eighteenth-Century Russia: Collected Essays* (New York: Longman, 1998), 78–94.

23. The dates of Russian involvement are given here.

24. For a survey of Russia's eighteenth-century wars, see Kersnovskii, *Istoriia russkoi armii,* vol. 1.

25. On conscription, see chap. 4.

26. P. S. Potemkin, *Rossy v Arkhipelage. Drama,* in *RF,* 8:33–96. Published in 1772, *Russians in the Archipelago* may have been performed in St. Petersburg that same year.

27. Kersnovskii, *Istoriia russkoi armii,* 1:125–37; I. A. Zaichkin and I. N. Pochkaev, *Ekaterininskie orly* (Moscow: Mysl', 1996), 108–21, 168–80.

28. A. G. Orlov (1737–1808) commanded the Russian naval expedition in the archipelago. F. G. Orlov (1741–1796) served in the Mediterranean and at Chesme under Admiral G. A. Spiridov (1713–1790), also a character in the drama, and repeatedly distinguished himself during the First Turkish War. *ES,* 43:169–70, 61:223.

29. Historical figures who served at Chesme and appear as characters in the drama include Prince Iu. V. Dolgorukov (1740–1830); Captain Samuel Greig (1736–1788), who was promoted to rear admiral soon after Chesme and by 1782 became a full admiral in the Russian navy; and Rear Admiral John Elphinstone, who left Russian service in 1771. *ES,* 18:606, 20:924, 80:690; Cross, *"By the Banks of the Neva,"* 183–204.

30. *Zel'mira i Smelon, ili Vziatie Izmaila. Liricheskaia dramma* (St. Petersburg: Tipografiia korpusa chuzhestrannykh edinovertsov, 1795). Published anonymously, the drama is not listed in *IRDT,* but a performance with music by O. A. Kozlovskii (1752–1831) took place in 1795 at the Ostankino theater of N. P. Sheremetev. Lepskaia, *Repertuar,* 40–41, 91.

31. As in 1774, the terms of peace returned Izmail to Turkish rule. During the Russo-Turkish War of 1806–1812, Russian troops again captured Izmail, which from 1809 remained under Russian rule. Kersnovskii, *Istoriia russkoi armii,* 1:148–56; *ES,* 24:849–51.

32. Smelon's modest rank may represent an allusion to the belief that Suvorov was not sufficiently rewarded for his military achievements. Oleg Mikhailov, *Suvorov* (Moscow: Molodaia gvardiia, 1980), 281–83.

33. Although the Turkish commander Osman expresses political loyalty in Russian terms, the meaning conveyed clearly is not limited to the tsarist polity.

34. *Soldatskoe shchast'e. Komediia v piati deistviiakh G. Lessinga. Prelozhil s nemetskogo na Rossiiskie nravy I. Z.* (Moscow: Tipografiia imperatorskogo moskovskogo universiteta, 1779). *A Soldiers' Happiness* was performed 4 times in Moscow in 1779–1790.

35. *Pokhod pod Shveda. Komediia v trekh deistviiakh s khorami i baletom* (St. Petersburg: n.p., 1790).

36. General population censuses introduced in the reign of Peter I to determine liability for conscription and the capitation counted numbers of male serfs, referred to as souls; consequently, the number of souls also became the primary measurement of noble wealth.

37. A. P. Sumarokov, *Khorev. Tragediia*, in *DS*, 36–82. After the initial publication of *Khorev* in St. Petersburg in 1747, Sumarokov radically reworked the tragedy and republished it in 1768. *Khorev* was performed 7 times in St. Petersburg in 1750–1758 and 14 times in Moscow in 1760–1797. A single revival performance occurred in St. Petersburg in 1811. In the tragedy *Deidamia* (1750), by V. K. Trediakovskii (1703–1769), King Lycomedes of Scyros responds to Ulysses's description of the Greek attack on Troy as "just revenge" by condemning the evil, inhumanity *(neliudkost')*, and violence of war. Vasilii Trediakovskii, *Deidamiia. Tragediia*, in *RF*, 3:177–314.

38. Ia. I. Blagodarov, *Materniaia liubov'. Komediia v odnom deistvii*, in *RF*, 29:133–88. First published in Moscow in 1786, *Maternal Love* does not appear in *IRDT*.

39. On the uncertainties surrounding the "right" of serfs to seek legal redress, see Wirtschafter, *Social Identity*, 118–21.

40. Wirtschafter, *From Serf to Russian Soldier*, chaps. 4–6; idem, "Legal Identity."

41. A. P. Sumarokov, *Chudovishchi. Komediia*, in *DS*, 309–33. First published in 1781, *The Monsters* was performed once in St. Petersburg in 1750, also the year it was written, and once in Moscow in 1760.

42. A. P. Sumarokov, *Opekun. Komediia*, in *DS*, 362–86. First published in 1765, *The Guardian* is not listed in *IRDT*.

43. In Sumarokov's comedy and literary polemic *The Venomous One* (1768), an innocent noble, fraudulently deprived of his property, is saved through the intervention of a procurator *(prokuror)* who protests the original decision. The comedy was performed once in St. Petersburg in 1769. Sumarokov, *Iadovityi*, 6:155–96.

44. *Tak i dolzhno. Komediia v piati deistviiakh*, in *RF*, 19:155–238. Dedicated to Prince P. I. Repnin, *As It Should Be* was first published in 1773 without authorial attribution. It was performed 7 times in St. Petersburg in 1777–1799 and 3 times in Moscow in 1780–1783.

45. The reported abuses include neglect of bridges, roads, and transport, as well as irregularities in administering trade, conscription, and the capitation. In addition, the clerk has been accused of illegally purchasing disputed lands and is supposed to be brought under guard to the provincial government.

46. On judicial abuses prior to the Catherinean reforms, see Schmidt, *Sozialkontrolle in Moskau*. For the post-reform situation, see Wirtschafter, "Legal Identity"; Jörg Baberowski, *Autokratie und Justiz: Zum Verhältnis von Rechtsstaatlichkeit und Rückständigkeit im ausgehenden Zarenreich, 1864–1914* (Frankfurt on Main: Vittorio Klostermann, 1996), chap. 1; Richard S. Wortman, *The Development of a Russian Legal Consciousness* (Chicago: University of Chicago Press, 1976).

47. I. S., *Sudeiskie imenini. Komediia v trekh deistviiakh*, in *RF*, 35:3–104. First published in 1781, *The Judge's Nameday* was performed 5 times in St. Petersburg in 1780–1788 and 4 times in Moscow in 1782–1785.

48. To avoid detection, Bedniakov will sign a letter indicating that he has borrowed money from Khamkin.

49. When a noble who had given him a mortgage deed as collateral for a loan repaid the debt, Khamkin kept the security and later was able to claim that the loan had not been redeemed.

50. V. V. Kapnist, *Iabeda. Komediia v piati deistviiakh*, in *Sobranie sochinenii v dvukh tomakh*, vol. 2, *Stikhotvoreniia, p'esy*, ed. D. S. Babkin (Moscow and Leningrad: Akademiia nauk SSSR, 1960), 285–402, 746–51. *Chicanery* was performed 36 times in

St. Petersburg in 1805–1825 and 28 times in Moscow in 1808–1825. Kapnist began writing *Chicanery* in 1791; the version discussed here was prepared by the author after February 1798, with almost all the censored passages restored.

51. The provincial judicial chambers created in the reign of Catherine II consisted of appointed members, whereas the reformed civil chambers of 1801 included appointed and elected judges—two judges elected by nobles and two by merchants. N. N. Evremova, *Sudostroistvo Rossii v XVIII–pervoi polovine XIX vv. (istoriko-pravovoe issledovanie)* (Moscow: Nauka, 1993), 130, 153.

52. The genealogical record identifies the son of the deceased Priamikov as Fedot (his church name) rather than Bogdan (the colloquial name he goes by).

53. The neighbors of one petitioner have stolen his land and burned down his house, a landowner has enserfed poor nobles by registering them in the capitation rolls, and another landowner has intimidated and physically abused his opponent in a property dispute. Similarly, a secretary has taken the hereditary house of a cornet, and a major is trying unsuccessfully to collect on a promissory note given to him by the procurator.

54. For cases of disputed social identity, see Wirtschafter, "Legal Identity"; idem, *Social Identity;* idem, *Structures of Society.* On chronic property litigation among noble landowners, see Robert D. Givens, "To Measure and to Encroach: The Nobility and the Land Survey," in *Russia and the World of the Eighteenth Century,* Bartlett, Cross, and Rasmussen, 533–47; Marrese, *A Woman's Kingdom;* Kivelson, *Autocracy in the Provinces;* idem, "Cartography, Autocracy, and State Powerlessness: The Uses of Maps in Early Modern Russia," *Imago Mundi* 51 (1999): 83–105. Noble memoirs are filled with accounts of property disputes. See, for example, F. F. Vigel', *Zapiski,* 2 vols. (1928; reprint, Cambridge, Mass.: Oriental Research Partners, 1974); Bolotov, *Zhizn' i prikliucheniia Andreia Bolotova.*

55. For historical accounts of the various courts described in *Chicanery,* see Mironov, *Sotsial'naia istoriia* 2:46–54; Evremova, *Sudostroistvo Rossii;* LeDonne, *Ruling Russia;* Janet M. Hartley, "Catherine's Conscience Court—An English Equity Court?" *Russia and the West in the Eighteenth Century,* Cross, 306–18.

56. N. R. Sudovshchikov, *Neslykhannoe divo, ili Chestnyi sekretar'. Komediia v trekh deistviiakh v stikhakh,* in *Stikhotvornaia komediia kontsa XVIII–nachala XIX v.,* ed. M. O. Ianovskii (Moscow and Leningrad: Sovetskii pisatel', 1964), 177–270. The first published version (1802) of *Unheard-of Wonder* is discussed here; however, the play probably was written in the early 1790s. The comedy was performed 16 times in St. Petersburg in 1809–1822 and 10 times in Moscow in 1814–1819.

57. In reality he intends to force Milena to marry a stupid, arbitrary, and drunken police official.

58. [Lopukhin], *Torzhestvo pravosudiia. Celebration of Justice* was published anonymously, though it did include a dedication to F. G. Orlov. The drama is not listed in *IRDT.* On Lopukhin's masonic activities, see Smith, *Working the Rough Stone.*

59. In the case of one man condemned to exile, Pravdoliubov and a friend give money to the convict's wife, so that she can accompany her husband, and even agree to raise their children.

60. Volkov, *Neudachnoe upriamstvo.* Published anonymously, *Unsuccessful Stubbornness* received 3 performances in St. Petersburg in 1764–1765.

61. For concrete examples, see Wirtschafter, *From Serf to Russian Soldier,* chaps. 4–6; idem, "Legal Identity," 584–85.

62. Decades later the distinction between justice and formal legality still figured

prominently in Slavophile thought. In an essay published in 1852, I. V. Kireevskii decried "the formalistic tendency of European jurisprudence" that, like Roman law, concentrates on "wording at the expense of true justice." Kireevskii attributed to Roman laws an "amazing logical perfection of form and an equally amazing absence of essential justice." By contrast, Russian laws preferred "evident genuine justice to literal formal meaning." Ivan Vasil'evich Kireevski, "On the Nature of European Culture and its Relation to the Culture of Russia. Letter to Count E. E. Komarovskii," in *Russian Intellectual History: An Anthology*, ed. Marc Raeff (1966; reprint, New York: Humanity Books, 1999), 174–207, esp. 183–84, 187, 197–98.

63. A Russian philosophy of jurisprudence did not begin to develop before the late eighteenth century, the first professor of Russian law was appointed only in 1768, and there were no lawyers or independent judges in Russia before 1864.

64. The term "Russianness" is my selection.

65. Hans Rogger, *National Consciousness in Eighteenth-Century Russia* (Cambridge, Mass.: Harvard University Press, 1960); Mark Bassin, "Russia between Europe and Asia: The Ideological Construction of Geography," *SR* 50 (1991): 1–17; Liah Greenfeld, *Nationalism: Five Roads to Modernity* (Cambridge, Mass.: Harvard University Press, 1992); Yuri Slezkine, "Naturalists versus Nations: Eighteenth-Century Russian Scholars Confront Ethnic Diversity," *Representations* 47 (1994): 170–95. On the creation of a national theater, see "Teatr," *Zritel'*.

66. Rogger, *National Consciousness*; Greenfeld, *Nationalism*.

67. D. I. Fonvizin, *Brigadir. Komediia v piati deistviiakh*, in *Ot russkogo klassitsizma k realizmu*, Rogachevskaia, 25–81. Scholars variously identify the earliest publication date for *The Brigadier* as 1783, 1786, and 1792. *SK* argues for 1792. The comedy was performed in St. Petersburg 22 times in 1772–1800 and 39 times in 1804–1824, in Moscow 14 times in 1784–1800 and 27 times in 1805–1822.

68. In A. P. Sumarokov's comedy *Mother in Place of Daughter*, a husband cannot understand his wife who uses French words to express feelings and describe human behavior. A. P. Sumarokov, *Mat' sovmestnitsa docheri. Komediia*, in *PSVS*, 6:57–106. The comedy is not listed in *IRDT*.

69. D. I. Khvostov, *Ruskoi parizhanets. Komediia v trekh deistviiakh*, in *RF*, 15:149–260. Written in 1783, *The Russian Parisian* in not listed in *IRDT*.

70. Mark Bassin, "Inventing Siberia: Visions of the Russian East in the Early Nineteenth Century," *American Historical Review* 96 (1991): 763–75.

71. Maksim Parpura, *Neshchastie ot Ochakova, ili Torzhestvuiushchee kovarstvo v Tsar'grade. Teatral'noe zrelishche* (St. Petersburg: n.p., 1789). The play is not listed in *IRDT*.

72. Thomas Kaiser, "The Evil Empire? The Debate on Turkish Despotism in Eighteenth-Century French Political Culture," *JMH* 72 (2000): 6–34.

73. Kropotov, *Fomushka—babushkin vnuchek*, 369–405, 697.

74. See chap. 6.

75. Quoted in William B. Edgerton, "Ambivalence as the Key to Kniazhnin's Tragedy *Vadim Novgorodskii*," in *Russia and the World of the Eighteenth Century*, Bartlett, Cross, and Rasmussen, 307–8. On Brius's career, see V. N. Baliazin, *Moskovskie gradonachal'niki* (Moscow: TERRA, 1997), 163–70. Nikolev's *Sorena and Zamir* was first performed at a Moscow theater in 1785.

76. *Blagodeianii priobretaiut serdtsa. Dramma v odnom deistvii* (St. Petersburg: n.p., 1770). The drama is not listed in *IRDT*. The editors of *SK* regard the drama as an original work, though it also has been identified as a translation. In either case, the

drama is fully Russified and articulates a Russian perspective.

77. William C. Fuller, Jr. *Strategy and Power in Russia, 1600–1914* (New York: Free Press, 1992), 169–70.

78. Slezkine, "Naturalists versus Nations."

79. On the association of moral corruption with French culture in eighteenth-century England, see Brewer, *The Pleasures of the Imagination,* chap. 2.

80. Slezkine, "Naturalists versus Nations," 183, 188.

81. Ippolit Bogdanovich, *Slaviane. Drama v trekh deistviiakh s khorom i baletom v kontse predstavleniia,* in *RF,* 9:219–307. *The Slavs* is not listed in *IRDT.*

82. M. M. Kheraskov, *Osvobozhdennaia Moskva,* in *Russkaia literatura,* Stennik, 363–430. First published in Moscow in 1798, *Moscow Liberated* was performed there twice in 1798 and once in 1799, 1801, and 1816; in St. Petersburg, 7 times in 1806 and twice in 1812.

83. The campaign was led by Prince D. M. Pozharskii (1578–1642), Prince D. T. Trubetskoi (d. 1625), and the Nizhnii Novgorod merchant Kuz'ma Minin (d. before mid-1616). For brief treatment of these events, see Robert O. Crummey, *The Formation of Muscovy, 1304–1613* (New York: Longman, 1987), 223–32.

84. On Rousseau's ambivalence toward the "civilizing imagination," see Barber, "Rousseau and the Paradoxes of the Dramatic Imagination."

85. Hans Rogger, "Nationalism and the State: A Russian Dilemma," *Comparative Studies in Society and History* 4 (1961–1962): 253–64; idem, "The Skobelev Phenomenon: The Hero and His Worship," *Oxford Slavonic Papers* 9 (1976): 46–78.

6: MORAL MONARCHY

1. On the absence of elite resistance leading to "constitutional change," see Richard Hellie, "Thoughts on the Absence of Elite Resistance in Muscovy," *Kritika: Explorations in Russian and Eurasian History* 1 (2000): 5–20; Valerie A. Kivelson, "Kinship Politics/Autocratic Politics: A Reconsideration of Early-Eighteenth-Century Political Culture," in *Imperial Russia: New Histories for the Empire,* ed. Jane Burbank and David L. Ransel (Bloomington: Indiana University Press, 1998), 5–31.

2. Dashkova, *Memoirs,* 60, 63, 69, 72, 81, 252, 275, 279.

3. Stephen Lessing Baehr, *The Paradise Myth in Eighteenth-Century Russia: Utopian Patterns in Early Secular Russian Literature and Culture* (Stanford: Stanford University Press, 1991); Richard S. Wortman, *Scenarios of Power: Myth and Ceremony in Russian Monarchy,* vol. 1, *From Peter the Great to the Death of Nicholas I* (Princeton: Princeton University Press, 1995); Madariaga, *Politics and Culture in Eighteenth-Century Russia,* 15–39.

4. The classical idiom of rulership dominated until the reign of Nicholas I (ruled 1825–1855), when images of family life portrayed the emperor as a father to his people. See Wortman, *Scenarios of Power,* vol. 1.

5. Sumarokov, *Khorev.*

6. A. P. Sumarokov, *Gamlet. Tragediia,* in *PSVS,* 3:59–119. First published in St. Petersburg in 1748, *Hamlet* was performed 6 times in 1750–1758 and once in Moscow in 1760.

7. A. P. Sumarokov, *Semira. Tragediia,* in *DS,* 189–246, 461–62; idem, *Vysheslav. Tragediia* in *PSVS,* 4:1–56. Written and performed at court in 1751, *Semira* was reworked for publication in 1768. The tragedy also appeared in German (1762) and

French (1770). *Semira* was performed in St. Petersburg 11 times in 1751–1798 and 12 times in 1807–1812, in Moscow 4 times in 1763–1798. *Vysheslav* was first published and performed in St. Petersburg in 1768; in Moscow it was performed twice in 1769–1770. The *Primary Chronicle* describes Askold and Dir as boyars—not of Riurik's clan—who ruled in Kiev in 866–882. When Riurik, who ruled in Novgorod, died in 879, Oleg exercised power on behalf of the infant Igor. Oleg is said to have lured Askold and Dir to their deaths in 882 and then ruled in Kiev. The *Chronicle* story is not established as historically accurate and seems to represent an effort to fill chronological gaps for which there are no sources. Thus Igor is known to have been in his prime while ruling the Rus in the mid-tenth century and therefore could not have played a leading political role in the late ninth century. For these and other details of early Rus history, I rely on Simon Franklin and Jonathan Shepard, *The Emergence of Rus, 750–1200* (New York: Longman, 1996), 57–58, 115–19.

8. Iskorest probably refers to the principal town of the Derevlians, Iskorosten (modern Korosten), located 150 kilometers from Kiev. Iskorosten is mentioned in Franklin and Shepard, *Emergence of Rus,* 117.

9. On eighteenth-century Russian tragedy as an effort to imitate God's actions on earth in order to assert the reality of a divinely rational utopia, see Marcus Levitt, "Sumarokov's Russianized 'Hamlet': Texts and Contexts," *SEEJ* 38 (1994): 319–41.

10. Trediakovskii, *Deidamiia.* Composed in 1750 by order of Empress Elizabeth, *Deidamia* was first published in Moscow in 1775; there is no record of any performance.

11. Trediakovskii based his plot on *Achille in Sciro* (1737) by Pietro Metastasio (1698–1782). *DLB,* 150:388–89. Greek legend recounts that because Achilles's mother feared her son's death in the Trojan War, she sent him to live at the court of King Lycomedes of Scyros disguised as a girl. There he fell in love with the king's daughter Deidamia, who bore him a son. Odysseus (called Ulysses in Trediakovskii's tragedy) then came searching for Achilles, tricked him into revealing his identity, and led the hero off to war. Except for the detail of the child, Trediakovskii incorporates the basic elements of the Greek story, which his introduction describes as material suitable for heroic comedy.

12. K., *Kodr. Drammaticheskoi otryvok* (Moscow: Universitetskaia tipografiia u Ridigera i Klaudiia, 1799). Written at Dolbino, the Kireevskii family estate in Kaluga province, *Codrus* is not listed in *IRDT.*

13. *OCD,* 355.

14. A. P. Sumarokov, *Artistona. Tragediia,* in *DS,* 134–88, 460–62. First published in St. Petersburg in 1751, *Artistona* was not reworked in 1768. The only known performance, by the troupe of the Noble Cadet Corps, took place in the imperial rooms of the Winter Palace in October 1750.

15. Vasilii Maikov, *Agriopa. Tragediia,* in *RF,* 5:5–74. First published in Moscow in 1775, *Agriopa* was Maikov's first tragedy. It was performed at the court theater in St. Petersburg in October 1769.

16. Praporshchik [Ensign] V. L., *Traian i Lida. Tragediia v piati deistviiakh,* in *RF,* 7:175–240. Identified by the author as an initial effort, *Trajan and Lida* was first published in St. Petersburg in 1780 and does not appear in *IRDT.*

17. Of course, from our present-day perspective Lida appears justified in her refusal to marry Pertinax, whereas her father appears tyrannical.

18. Nikolai Nikolev, *Pal'mira. Tragediia,* in *RF,* 5:147–234. Written in 1781, *Pal'mira* was performed in Moscow 9 times in 1783–1794 and in St. Petersburg 7 times in 1801–1806.

19. Sumarokov, *Iaropolk i Dimiza*, in *PSVS*, 3:331–96. Written in 1758 under the title *Dimiza* and then revised for publication in 1768, the tragedy was performed in St. Petersburg once in 1758 and once in 1764.

20. Sumarokov, *Dmitrii Samozvanets. Tragediia*, in *DS*, 247–92. Written in Moscow in 1769–1770, *Dmitrii the Pretender* was first published in St. Petersburg in 1771. In St. Petersburg there were 9 performances in 1771–1797, and in Moscow 35 performances in 1782–1800 and 3 in 1801–1802. In an entry for 1807 the memoirist S. P. Zhikharev reports that among soldiers of the Izmailovskii Guards Regiment, who regularly performed tragedies during Christmastide *(sviatki)* and Shrovetide *(maslenitsa)*, *Dmitrii the Pretender* was the most popular. S. P. Zhikharev, *Zapiski sovremennika. Vospominaniia starogo teatrala*, 2 vols. (Leningrad: Iskusstvo, 1989), 2:272. The historical Dmitrii was the first False Dmitrii (the runaway monk Grigorii from the Chudov Monastery in Moscow, and before tonsure the petty noble Iurii Otrep'ev), who ruled in Moscow in 1605–1606, claiming to be the son of Ivan IV.

21. Rzhevskii, *Podlozhnyi Smerdii*, 213–66, 700–701. Not published until 1956, *The False Smerdis* was performed once in St. Petersburg in 1769.

22. The historical Vasilii Shuiskii behaved similarly: after initially supporting the first False Dmitrii, he helped to assassinate the pretender and emerged as the new tsar. Shuiskii ruled amidst violence, instability, social rebellion, and foreign intervention until a Moscow crowd forced him to abdicate and be tonsured a monk in 1610. Crummey, *Formation of Muscovy*, 216–25.

23. Cf. the political literature of pre-revolutionary France, in which the theme of despotism, understood as systemic, had superseded the traditional theme of tyranny, understood as individual. See Darnton, *The Forbidden Best-Sellers of Pre-Revolutionary France*, 198–231; Kaiser, "The Evil Empire?," 6–34. For appreciation of the variability and ambiguity in the eighteenth-century understanding of "despotism," see Krieger, *An Essay on the Theory of Enlightened Despotism*.

24. A. P. Sumarokov, *Mstislav. Tragediia*, in *PSVS*, 4:127–79. *Mstislav* was first published and performed in St. Petersburg in 1774 and received one Moscow performance in 1785.

25. When Mstislav died without a living son, Iaroslav took over his domains. Franklin and Shepard, *Emergence of Rus*, 186–88.

26. Mstislav and Iaroslav were indeed the sons of Vladimir, probably by Rogneda, but the Olga of Sumarokov's tragedy was not an historical personage.

27. Mikhail Kheraskov, *Borislav. Tragediia*, in *RF*, 4:165–222. First published in St. Petersburg in 1774, *Borislav* was performed once in 1772 at the Imperial Theater.

28. V. A. Ozerov, *Iaropolk i Oleg. Tragediia v piati deistviiakh, v stikhakh*, in *Tragediia. Stikhotvoreniia*, ed. I. N. Medvedeva (Leningrad: Sovetskii pisatel', 1960), 75–126. *Iaropolk and Oleg* was performed in St. Petersburg 5 times in 1798 and once in 1805; it was first published in 1828. The historical sons of Sviatoslav (d. 972), Iaropolk (d. 978) and Oleg (d. 977), clashed openly after Oleg had the son of Iaropolk's servitor, Sveneld, put to death for trespassing. Although Iaropolk attacked and defeated his brother, he also buried and mourned him after Oleg died in the crush of fleeing fighters. Iaropolk then returned to Kiev, where he met his death at the hands of Vladimir (d. 1015), Sviatoslav's third son and the subsequent Christianizer of Russia. According to the *Primary Chronicle*, this murder followed from Vladimir's desire to marry Rogneda of Polotsk, whose father rebuffed Vladimir in favor of a match with Iaropolk. In response, Vladimir devastated Polotsk, abducted Rogneda, and took Kiev by treachery. Iaropolk then was persuaded by threats of

popular rebellion to leave the city, and when he returned to negotiate with Vladimir, he was killed. See Franklin and Shepard, *Emergence of Rus,* 151–54. Ozerov's Iaropolk and Oleg combine the historical Iaropolk, Oleg, and Vladimir.

29. F. Ia. Kozel'skii, *Velesana. Tragediia,* in *Sochineniia Fedora Kozel'skogo,* 2d ed., 2 vols. (St. Petersburg: Imperatorskaia akademiia nauk, 1778), 2:66–133. *Velesana* is not listed in *IRDT.*

30. Franklin and Shepard, *Emergence of Rus,* 300–303.

31. F. Kliucharev, *Vladimir Velikii. Tragediia,* in *RF,* 6:81–144. First published in Moscow in 1779, *Vladimir the Great* is not listed in *IRDT.* S. N. Glinka reports, however, that at age 7 his brother enjoyed reading aloud from the tragedy. S. N. Glinka, *Zapiski,* in *Zolotoi vek Ekateriny Velikoi. Vospominaniia,* ed. V. M. Bokova and N. I. Tsimbaev (Moscow: Izdatel'stvo moskovskogo universiteta, 1996), 137.

32. Mikhail Kheraskov, *Idolopoklonniki, ili Gorislava. Tragediia,* in *RF,* 4:223–303. *The Idolators* was first published in Moscow in 1782 and performed there 5 times in 1782–1784.

33. Vladimir had several wives, and the parentage of Sviatopolk remains uncertain. Possibly, he was the son of a Byzantine nun abducted by Vladimir and Iaropolk. On Sviatopolk's birth and the alleged plot against Vladimir, see Franklin and Shepard, *Emergence of Rus,* 184–85, 190–91.

34. *Podrazhanie Shakespiru. Istoricheskoe predstavlenie bez sokhraneniia obyknovennykh featral'nykh pravil iz zhizni Riurika,* in *RF,* 14:107–66.

35. *Dobrodetel' priobretennaia v uchilishche. Predstavlenie v odnom deistvii* (St. Petersburg: Morskoi shliakhetnyi kadetskii korpus, 1775). The anonymous author claims both amateur status and indifference to glory. In an "introduction to the reader," he describes *Virtue Acquired at School* as his first literary composition, written solely for the cadets to perform, but persons knowledgeable about literature urged him to publish it. The play is not listed in *IRDT.*

36. Although memoirs and histories paint a much harsher view of conditions in military schools, they did indeed perform an effective welfare function. Wirtschafter, "Soldiers' Children"; John L. H. Keep, *Soldiers of the Tsar: Army and Society in Russia, 1462–1874* (New York: Oxford University Press, 1985), 242–49; S. V. Volkov, *Russkii ofitserskii korpus* (Moscow: Voenizdat, 1993), 99–110, 126–44.

37. Filiter Matveev, *Drama. Dobrodetel'naia prestupnitsa, ili Prestupnik ot liubvi, v trekh deistviiakh* (Moscow: Vol'naia tipografiia A. Reshetnikova, 1792). The drama is not listed in *IRDT.*

38. Rossiiskii pridvornyi akter T. V. Konstantinov, *Blagovremennoe vspomozhenie. Original'naia drama v trekh deistviiakh,* in *RF,* 43:105–90. The drama was first published in 1794 and is not listed in *IRDT.*

39. Ia. B. Knaizhnin, *Titovo miloserdie. Tragediia v piati deistviiakh,* in *RF,* 32:3–92. Written in free verse with choruses and ballet, *The Mercy of Titus* received one performance in St. Petersburg in 1785 and 12 in 1802–1813; in Moscow there were 29 performances in 1786–1800 and 5 in 1802–1806.

40. *Geroistvo liubvi. Drama v piati deistviiakh,* in *RF,* 43:191–289. The drama is not listed in *IRDT.*

41. Catherine II, *Peredniaia znatnogo boiarina. Komediia v odnom deistvii,* in *RF,* 11:221–62. The comedy was written and performed once at court in 1772.

42. A characteristic historical figure of Enlightenment Europe, the "projector" or "project-maker" became an object of literary satire and public debate. Although in 1767 Catherine had brought Le Mercier de la Rivière to court, he quickly fell from fa-

vor because of grandiose schemes to re-create Russia. In a 1774 letter to Voltaire, Catherine wrote that the projector intended "to raise us onto our hind legs." Roger Bartlett, *Projects and Peasants: Russia's Eighteenth Century.* Occasional Paper No. 44 (London: School of Slavonic and East European Studies, 2000).

43. Catherine II, *Khlor Tsarevich, ili Roza bez shipov, kotoraia ne koletsia. Inoskazatel'noe zrelishche v trekh deistviiakh. 1786 goda,* in *RF,* 24:195–232. *IRDT* does not list any performances of *Tsarevich Khlor.*

44. Catherine II, *Opera komicheskaia Fevei, sostavlena iz slov skaski, pesnei ruskikh, i inykh sochinenii,* in *RF,* 2:4–54. First published in St. Petersburg in 1786, *Fevei* was performed in the capital with music by V. A. Pashkevich 19 times in 1786–1795 and twice in 1803–1804. *Skazka o Gorebogatyre Kosometoviche i opera komicheskaia iz slov skaski sostavlennaia* (St. Petersburg: Tipografiia gornogo uchilishcha, 1789). *Woeful Hero Kosometovich* was performed in St. Petersburg 6 times in 1789 with music by Vincente Martín y Soler (1754–1806).

45. Russia was at war with Sweden in 1788–1790. On the parody of Gustav, see Lurana Donnels O'Malley, "Catherine the Great's *Woeful Knight:* A Slanted Parody," *Theatre History Studies* 21 (2001): 11–26.

46. Vasil'i Levshin, *Korol' na okhote. Opera komicheskaia v trekh deistviiakh,* in *RF,* 42:1–108. *The King on a Hunt* is an adaptation of the work by Michel-Jean Sedaine (1719–1797), *Le Roi et le Fermier.* I. F. Kertselli composed music for the opera, which was first published in Kaluga in 1793. It is not listed in *IRDT.*

47. I. A. Krylov, *Podshchipa. Shuto-tragediia v dvukh deistviiakh v stikhakh,* in *Sochineniia v dvukh tomakh,* 2 vols. (Moscow: Izdatel'stvo Pravda, 1956), 1:265–96. *Podshchipa* is not listed in *IRDT.*

48. Krylov had offered a critique of eighteenth-century Russian tragedy as early as 1789, after writing tragedy in the neoclassical style just a few years earlier. *Pochta dukhov,* ch. 2 (August 1789), letter 46. I. A. Krylov, *Filomela. Tragediia,* in *RF,* 39:197–286. First published in St. Petersburg in 1793, *Filomela* has not been performed. The tragedy is reprinted in Ivan Andreevich Krylov, *Polnoe sobranie dramaticheskikh sochinenii,* ed. L. N. Kiseleva (St. Petersbrug: Giperion, 2001), 47–107.

49. For brief discussion of the language and literary polemics of *Podshchipa,* see M. Gordin and Ia. Gordin, *Teatr Ivana Krylova* (Leningrad: Iskusstvo, 1983), 102–8.

50. For summary of the various interpretations of the Vadim episode, see Smolina, *Russkaia tragediia,* 64–76.

51. Catherine II, *Iz zhizni Riurika.* Published anonymously, the play first appeared in St. Petersburg in 1786 and is not listed in *IRDT.*

52. The second and third editions of Catherine's play, published in St. Petersburg in 1792 and 1793, include extensive historical commentary by Major-General I. [N.] Boltin (1735–1792). On Boltin, see *SRP,* 1:118–19; *ES,* 7:320–21. Modern histories, including the classic accounts by S. M. Solov'ev and V. O. Kliuchevskii, treat the calling of the Varangians and Vadim's rebellion as legendary.

53. Catherine's only genealogical claim to the throne derived from her status as the wife of Peter III and the mother of his son, Tsarevich Paul. Peter III (b. 1725) was the son of Peter I's daughter, Anna, Duchess of Holstein. At age 11 he was brought to the Russian court by his aunt, Empress Elizabeth (ruled 1741–1761), and in 1742 was received into the Orthodox Church and proclaimed heir to the throne.

54. In *The Beginning of Oleg's Reign,* Catherine recounts campaigns against Constantinople, led by Oskol'd (Askold) and later Oleg, that led to favorable treaty terms for Russia. Catherine also depicts Oskol'd's removal from power as an action

taken at the request of the Kievan people, who lost confidence in his ability to rule. *Nachal'noe upravlenie Olega*. Classified by historians as an opera, *The Beginning of Oleg's Reign* was performed in St. Petersburg 7 times in 1790–1795 with music by Carlo Canobbio (1741–1822), V. A. Pashkevich (1740–1820), and Giuseppe Sarti (1729–1802). For discussion of the opera as political spectacle designed to represent the Greek project and associate Russia with Byzantine power and Greek culture, see Lurana Donnels O'Malley, "Catherine the Great's Operatic Splendor at Court: *The Beginning of Oleg's Reign*," *Essays in Theatre* 17 (1998): 33–51. For historical details regarding the campaigns against Constantinople and the terms of the Rus-Byzantine treaties, see Franklin and Shepard, *Emergence of Rus*, 51, 97, 103–8, 112–24.

55. Ia. Kniazhnin, *Vadim Novgorodskii. Tragediia v stikhakh, v piati deistviiakh* (St. Petersburg: Imperatorskaia akademiia nauk, 1793). Written in 1788–1789, published and banned in 1793, *Vadim the Novgorodian* does not appear in *IRDT*.

56. P. A. Plavil'shchikov also depicted a fully repentant Vadim, who accepted Riurik's right to rule based on moral superiority. Initially an evil avenger eager to sacrifice his daughter's life in order to overthrow Riurik, Vadim is transformed by Riurik's willingness to forgive subjects who act against him. First performed in St. Petersburg in 1791 under the title *Vseslav*, Plavil'shchikov's *Riurik* was not published until 1816. In addition to the 1791 performance, there were two performances in Moscow in 1794 and two in 1803. Plavil'shchikov, *Riurik*, 592–642, 715.

57. On the classical model of a tragic "opposition between man and a higher moral or religious principle," see Pavis, *Dictionary of the Theatre*, 414–18.

58. Dashkova, *Memoirs*, 237–40.

59. Knaizhnin, *Titovo miloserdie*.

60. In the comic opera *The Novgorodian Hero Boeslaevich*, Catherine portrays another Novgorodian rebellion, but this time it is directed against an heir to the throne who misbehaves and offends the people. Even so, the rebels repent after Boeslaevich defeats them by force of arms and begins to show evidence of self-control. Clearly, the rebellion is wrong even though the future ruler behaved poorly. *Novgorodskoi bogatyr' Boeslaevich'. Opera komicheskaia, sostavlena iz skazki, pesnei russkikh, i inykh sochinenii*, in *RF*, 20:55–100. *The Novgorodian Hero* was first published and performed once, with music by E. I. Fomin, in St. Petersburg in 1786.

61. *Chuvstvovanie blagotvorenii. Dramma s baletom*, in *RF*, 34:205–40. The drama is not listed in *IRDT*.

62. Vladimir Val'denberg, *Drevnerusskiia ucheniia o predelakh tsarskoi vlasti: Ocherki russkoi politicheskoi literatury ot Vladimira Sviatogo do kontsa XVII veka* (1916; reprint, The Hague: Europe Printing, 1966); Fritz Kern, *Kingship and Law in the Middle Ages: I. The Divine Right of Kings and the Right of Resistance in the Early Middle Ages. II. Law and Constitution in the Middle Ages. Studies by Fritz Kern*, trans. and with an introduction by S. B. Chrimes (Oxford: B. Blackwell, 1939).

63. Iakov Kniazhnin, *Rosslav. Tragediia v stikhakh v piati deistviiakh*, in *RF*, 6:145–240. First published and performed in St. Petersburg in 1784, *Rosslav* also was performed 13 times in 1805–1820. In Moscow there were 6 performances in 1806–1816.

64. M. V., *Otets vozvrashchennyi detiam. Drammaticheskii anekdot. V dvukh deistviiakh* (Moscow: Gubernskaia tipografiia u A. Reshetnikova, 1801). The play is not listed in *IRDT*.

CONCLUSION: THE INDIVIDUAL IN SOCIETY AND POLITY

1. On the prepolitical literary public sphere, see Habermas, *Structural Transformation of the Public Sphere*. For my use of the concept, see chap. 1, n. 41.

2. For analysis of parallel changes in political thought, see Krieger, *An Essay on the Theory of Enlightened Despotism*, chap. 2.

3. Ernst Kantorowicz traces the belief in infinite progress to a concept of earthly time as eternal rather than transitory, which has it roots in the thirteenth-century reception of Aristotle's idea of the eternity/continuity of the world. Ernst H. Kantorowicz, *The King's Two Bodies: A Study in Mediaeval Political Theology* (Princeton: Princeton University Press, 1957), 273–84.

4. On the political contestation that resulted from interaction "between the political languages of the Enlightenment and those of the Old Regime," see Baker, *Inventing the French Revolution*, 150.

5. Reinhart Koselleck, *Critique and Crisis: Enlightenment and the Pathogenesis of Modern Society* (Cambridge, Mass.: MIT Press, 1988).

6. Margaret C. Jacob, "The Mental Landscape of the Public Sphere: A European Perspective," *Eighteenth-Century Studies* 28 (1994): 95–113, esp. 96; idem, "The Enlightenment Redefined: The Formation of Civil Society," *Social Research* 58 (1991): 475–95.

7. In the context of the eighteenth century, "absolutism" refers not to the "absolute" power of a centralized state but to a set of political institutions and relationships presided over by a monarch whose authority was assumed to be God-given and hence "absolute." Recent scholarly critiques of the vocabulary of absolutism overlook the subtle theoretical distinctions and dynamic political relationships highlighted in the works of Fritz Kern, Leonard Krieger, Marc Raeff, and others.

8. Modern utopianism was born when belief in reason as the guide to truth was joined with Rousseauian and romantic notions regarding the goodness of human nature in its natural state prior to civilization.

9. Raeff, *Origins of the Russian Intelligentsia;* Riasanovsky, *A Parting of Ways;* Khudushina, *Tsar';* Marasinova, "Obraz imperatora v soznanii elity rossiiskogo dvorianstva," 141–77; idem, *Psikhologiia.*

10. Similarly, in the reign of Peter I "the idea of the state *(gosudarstvo)* was personified in the person of the monarch." O. G. Ageeva, "Imperskii status Rossii: K istorii politicheskogo mentaliteta russkogo obshchestva nachala XVIII veka," in *Tsar' i tsarstvo v russkom obshchestvennom soznanii,* ed. A. A. Gorskii (Moscow: Institut rossiiskoi istorii RAN, 1999), 121.

BIBLIOGRAPHY

ARCHIVES

Arkhiv vneshnei politiki Rossiiskoi imperii (AVPRI), Moscow
  f. 94 Parizhskaia missiia
Rossiiskii gosudarstvennyi arkhiv drevnikh aktov (RGADA), Moscow
  f. 10 (Razriad X) Kabinet Ekateriny II i ego prodolzhenie
  f. 16 (Razriad XVI) Vnutrennee upravlenie
  f. 17 (Razriad XVII) Nauka, literatura, iskusstvo
  f. 40 Snosheniia Rossii s Vengriei
  f. 141 Prikaznye dela starykh let
  f. 197 Portfeli A. F. Malinovskogo
  f. 233 Pechatnyi prikaz
  f. 248 Senat i ego uchrezhdeniia
  f. 931 Moskovskaia politsmeisterskaia kantseliariia
  f. 1239 Dvortsovyi otdel
  f. 1261 Vorontsovy, gr., kn.
  f. 1263 Golitsyny, kn.
  f. 1287 Sheremetevy, gr.
  f. 1392 Cheremisinovy
  f. 1272 Naryshkiny
  f. 1290 Iusupovy, kn.

EIGHTEENTH-CENTURY PERIODICALS

Koshelek (1774)
Moskovskie vedomosti (1756–1780)
Moskovskii zhurnal (1791–1792)
Moskovskoe ezhemesiachnoe izdanie (1781)
Muza. Ezhemesiachnoe izdanie (1796)
Poleznoe uveselenie (1760–1762)
Pustomelia (1770)
Rossiiskii magazin (1792–1794)
Sankt-Peterburgskie vedomosti (1743–1812)
Sankt-Peterburgskii merkurii (1793–1794)
Sankt-Peterburgskii vestnik (1778–1781)
Trudoliubivaia pchela (1759)
Truten' (1769–1770)
Utrenii svet. Ezhemesiachnoe izdanie (1777–1780)
Vechera. Ezhenedel'noe izdanie na 1772 god (1772)
Vsiakaia vsiachina (1769–1770, 1772)
Zhivopisets (1772–1773)
Zritel'. Ezhemesiachnoe izdanie (1792)

PRINTED PRIMARY AND SECONDARY SOURCES

Ablesimov, A. O. *Melnik—koldun, obmanshchik, svat. Komicheskaia opera v trekh deistvi-iakh.* In *Russkaia komediia i komicheskaia opera XVIII veka,* edited by P. N. Berkov. Moscow and Leningrad: Iskusstvo, 1950.

———. *Shchastie po zhereb'iu. Komicheskaia opera v odnom deistvii.* Moscow: Universitetskaia tipografiia, 1780.

Adariukov, V. Ia. *Bibliograficheskii ukazatel' knig, broshiur, zhurnal'nykh statei, i zametok po istorii russkogo teatra.* St. Petersburg: Tipografiia E. Arngol'da, 1904.

Afanas'eva, I. N. "A. P. Sumarokov i ital'ianskaia 'komediia masok.'" In *Problemy izucheniia russkoi literatury XVIII veka, ot klassitsizma k romantizmu,* edited by V. A. Zapadov. Vypusk 5. Leningrad: Gosudarstvennyi pedagogicheskii institut im. A. I. Gertsena, 1983.

Ageeva, O. G. "Imperskii status Rossii: K istorii politicheskogo mentaliteta russkogo obshchestva nachala XVIII veka." In *Tsar' i tsarstvo v russkom obshchestvennom soznanii,* edited by A. A. Gorskii. Moscow: Institut rossiiskoi istorii RAN, 1999.

Al'tshuller, A. Ia. "Spektakl' v kontekste istorii." In *Spektakl' v kontekste istorii,* edited by L. S. Danilova. Leningrad: LGITMiK, 1990.

———, ed. *Ocherki istorii russkoi teatral'noi kritiki.* 3 vols. Leningrad: Iskusstvo, 1975–1979.

Anchipolovskii, Z. Ia. *Staryi teatr Voronezh, 1787–1917.* Voronezh: Izdatel'sko-poligraficheskii tsentr chernozem'e, 1996.

Andrushchenko, E. A. "Materialy k stsenicheskoi istorii komedii D. I. Fonvizina 'Nedorosl'." *XVIII vek* 19 (1995): 276–93.

Anisimov, Evgenii Viktorovich. *Elizaveta Petrovna.* Moscow: Molodaia gvardiia, 1999.

———. *Zhenshchiny na rossiiskom prestole.* St. Petersburg: Norint, 1997.

———, ed. *Bezvremen'e i vremenshchiki. Vospominaniia ob "epokhe dvortsovykh perevorotov" (1720-e–1760-e gody).* Leningrad: Khudozhestvennaia literatura, 1991.

Arapov, Pimen. *Letopis' russkogo teatra.* St. Petersburg: Tipografiia N. Tiblena i komp., 1861.

Ariès, Philippe. *Western Attitudes toward Death from the Middle Ages to the Present.* Translated by Patricia M. Ranum. Baltimore: Johns Hopkins University Press, 1974.

Aristotle. *Poetics.* Translated by and with an introduction and notes by Malcolm Heath. New York: Penguin, 1996.

Arkad'ev, E. I. *Teatral'nyi slovar'.* Syzran': Tipografiia E. M. Siniavskogo, 1900.

Arkhangel'skii, A. *Teatr do-Petrovskoi Rusi. Publichnaia lektsiia.* Kazan: Tipografiia gubernskogo pravleniia, 1884.

Arkhiv direktsii imperatorskikh teatrov. Edited by V. P. Pogozhev, A. E. Molchanov, and K. A. Petrov. Vypusk 1 (1746–1801 gg.), otdel 1–3. St. Petersburg: Direktsiia imperatorskikh teatrov, 1892.

Artakserksovo deistvo: Pervaia p'esa russkogo teatra XVII v. Edited by I. M. Kudriavtsev. Moscow and Leningrad: Akademiia nauk SSSR, 1957.

Aurova, N. N. "Idei prosveshcheniia v 1–m kadetskom korpuse (konets XVIII–pervaia chetvert' XIX v.)." *Vestnik moskovskogo universiteta,* seriia 8, *Istoriia,* no. 1 (1996): 34–42.

Baberowski, Jörg. *Autokratie und Justiz: Zum Verhältnis von Rechtsstaatlichkeit und Rückständigkeit im ausgehenden Zarenreich 1864–1914.* Frankfurt on Main: Vittorio Klostermann, 1996.

Badalich, I. M., and P. N. Berkov, "Komicheskaia opera 'Matrosskie shutki' i ee avtor." *XVIII vek* 4 (1959): 422–25.

Badalich, I. M., and V. D. Kuz'mina, eds. *Pamiatniki russkoi shkol'noi dramy XVIII veka (po zagrebskim spiskam)*. Moscow: Nauka, 1968.

Baehr, Stephen Lessing. *The Paradise Myth in Eighteenth-Century Russia: Utopian Patterns in Early Secular Russian Literature and Culture*. Stanford: Stanford University Press, 1991.

Baibakov, A. D. (Apollos) *Ieffai. Sviashchennaia tragediia koeia soderzhanie v bibleiskikh knigakh sudei glava 11 k kontsu*. In *Rossiiskii featr*. 6:241–72.

Baker, Keith Michael. *Inventing the French Revolution: Essays on French Political Culture in the Eighteenth Century*. New York: Cambridge University Press, 1990.

———. "Transformations of Classical Republicanism in Eighteenth-Century France." *Journal of Modern History* 73 (2001): 32–53.

Baker, Keith Michael, and Peter Hanns Reill, eds. *What's Left of the Enlightenment? A Postmodern Question*. Stanford: Stanford University Press, 2001.

Bakhtin, Mikhail. *Rabelais and His World*. Translated by Hélène Iswolsky. Bloomington: Indiana University Press, 1984.

Baliazin, V. N. *Moskovskie gradonachal'niki*. Moscow: TERRA, 1997.

Banham, Martin, ed. *The Cambridge Guide to World Theatre*. Cambridge, Eng.: Cambridge University Press, 1988.

Barber, Benjamin R. "Rousseau and the Paradoxes of the Dramatic Imagination." *Daedalus* (Summer 1978): 79–92.

Bartlett, Roger. "Aufklärung, Adel, und Gesellschaft in Russland." In *Europa in der Frühen Neuzeit: Festschrift für Günter Mühlpfordt*. Band 5, *Aufklärung in Europa*, edited by Erich Donnert. Cologne: Böhlau, 1999.

———. "Defences of Serfdom in Eighteenth-Century Russia." In *A Window on Russia: Papers from the Fifth International Conference of the Study Group on Eighteenth-Century Russia, Gargnano, 1994*, edited by Maria Di Salvo and Lindsey Hughes. Rome: La Fenice Edizioni, 1996.

———. "The Free Economic Society: The Foundation Years and the Prize Essay Competition of 1766 on Peasant Property." In *Russland zur zeit Katharinas II. Absolutismus—Aufklärung—Pragmatismus*, edited by Eckhard Hübner, Jan Kusber, and Peter Nitsche. Cologne: Böhlau, 1998.

———. *Projects and Peasants: Russia's Eighteenth Century*. Occasional Paper No. 44. London: School of Slavonic and East European Studies, 2000.

———. "Russische und baltische Publizistik gegen die Leibeigenschaft: Aleksandr Radiščevs *Reise von St. Petersburg nach Moskau* und Garlieb Merkels *Die Letten* und *Rükkehr ins Vaterland*." In *"Ich werde gewiss grosse Energie zeigen." Garlieb Merkel (1769–1850) als Kämpfer, Kritiker und Projektemacher in Berlin und Riga*, edited by Jörg Drews. Bielefeld: Aisthesis, 2000.

Bartlett, R. P., A. G. Cross, and Karen Rasmussen, eds. *Russia and the World of the Eighteenth Century*. Columbus, Ohio: Slavica Publishers, 1988.

Bassin, Mark. "Inventing Siberia: Visions of the Russian East in the Early Nineteenth Century." *American Historical Review* 96 (1991): 763–75.

———. "Russia between Europe and Asia: The Ideological Construction of Geography." *Slavic Review* 50 (1991): 1–17.

Baturin, P. S. *Zgovor. Komediia v trekh deistviiakh*. In *Rossiiskii featr*. 29:5–92.

Becker, Carl L. *The Heavenly City of the Eighteenth-Century Philosophers*. New Haven: Yale University Press, 1932.

Begunov, Iu. K. "Teatr Tsarevny Natal'i Alekseevny i drama 'Strel'tsy' na peter-burgskom stsene." In *Russkaia dramaturgiia i literaturnyi protsess: Sbornik nauch-nykh trudov*, edited by V. A. Bochkarev. St. Petersburg: Institut russkoi literatury (Pushkinskii dom), 1991.

Beliakov, B. N. *Letopis' Nizhegorodskogo-Gor'kovskogo Teatra, 1798–1960*. Edited by Iu. Volchek and L. Farber. Gor'kii: Volgo-Viatskoe knizhnoe izdatel'stvo, 1967.

Bell, David A. "The Unbearable Lightness of Being French: Law, Republicanism, and National Identity at the End of the Old Regime." *American Historical Review* 106 (2001): 1215–35.

Belosel'skii-Belozerskii, A. M. *Olin'ka, ili Pervonachal'naia liubov'. Selo Iasnoe. 1796.* Moscow: Tipografiia A. Reshetnikova, 1796.

Berelowitch, Wladimir. "Les 'discours sur les lois' de Fonvizin: Une éthique subver-sive." *Cahiers du Monde russe et soviétique* 30 (1989): 193–206.

Berg, Johann von [G. I. Berkh]. *Komediia nechaiannaia zhenidba, ili Obmanutoi starik.* 2d ed. Moscow: Tipografiia kompanii tipograficheskoi, 1788.

Berkov, P. N. *Istoriia russkoi komedii XVIII v.* Leningrad: Nauka, 1977.

——. "Iz istorii russkoi teatral'noi terminologii XVII–XVIII vekov." *Trudy otdela drevnerusskoi literatury instituta russkoi literatury akademii nauk SSSR* 11 (1955): 280–99.

——, ed. "Komicheskaia opera A. O. Ablesimova 'Pokhod s nepremennykh kvar-tir'." *Teatral'noe nasledstvo.* Moscow: Iskusstvo, 1956.

——, ed. *Russkaia komediia i komicheskaia opera XVIII veka.* Moscow and Leningrad: Iskusstvo, 1950.

——, ed. *Satiricheskie zhurnaly N. I. Novikova.* Moscow and Leningrad: Akademiia nauk SSSR, 1951.

Bespiatykh, Iu. N., ed. *Peterburg Anny Ioannovny v inostrannykh opisaniiakh.* St. Peters-burg: Blits, 1997.

Bien, David D. "The Army in the French Enlightenment: Reform, Reaction, and Rev-olution." *Past and Present* 85 (1979): 68–98.

Blagoi, D. D. *Istoriia russkoi literatury XVIII veka.* 4th ed. Moscow: Gosudarstvennoe uchebno-pedagogicheskoe izdatel'stvo, 1960.

Blagodarov, Ia. I. *Materniaia liubov'. Komediia v odnom deistvii.* In *Rossiiskii featr.* 29:133–88.

——. *Smeshnoe sborishche, ili Meshchanskaia komediia v trekh deistviiakh.* In *Rossiiskii featr.* 36:147–289.

Blagodeianii priobretaiut serdtsa. Dramma v odnom deistvii. St. Petersburg: n.p., 1770.

Blank, B. K. *Krasavitsa i prividenie. Opera v odnom deistvii. Perevod s Arabskogo.* Moscow: Universitetskaia tipografiia u A. Svetushkina, 1789.

Bochkarev, V. A. *Russkaia istoricheskaia dramaturgiia XVII–XVIII vv.* Moscow: Prosveshchenie, 1988.

——, ed. *Stikhotvornaia tragediia kontsa XVIII–nachala XIX v.* Moscow and Leningrad: Sovetskii pisatel', 1964.

Bogdanovich, I. F. *Radost' Dushin'ki. Liricheskaia komediia posleduemaia baletom v odnom deistvii.* In *Rossiiskii featr.* 24:101–36.

——. *Slaviane. Drama v trekh deistviiakh s khorom i baletom v kontse predstavleniia.* In *Rossiiskii featr.* 9:219–307.

Bokova, V. M., and N. I. Tsimbaev, eds. *Zolotoi Vek Ekateriny Velikoi: Vospominaniia.* Moscow: Izdatel'stvo moskovskogo universiteta, 1996.

Bolotov, A. T. *Chestokhval. Komediia detskaia v trekh deistviiakh, sochinennaia v gorode*

Bogoroditske 1779 goda. In *Izbrannoe.* Pskov: Izdatel'stvo POIPKRO, 1993.

———. *Neshchastnyia siroty. Dramma v trekh deistviiakh. Sochinena v Bogoroditske, v 1780 gode.* Moscow: Universitetskaia tipografiia u N. Novikova, 1781.

———. *Virtue Rewarded (Nagrazhdennaia dobrodetel').*

———. *Zhizn' i prikliucheniia Andreia Bolotova: Opisannye samim im dlia svoikh potomkov.* 3 vols. 1871–1873. Reprint, Moscow: TERRA, 1993.

Bonnell, Victoria E., and Lynn Hunt, eds. *Beyond the Cultural Turn: New Directions in the Study of Society and Culture.* Berkeley: University of California Press, 1999.

Braun, Sidney D., ed. *Dictionary of French Literature.* New York: Philosophical Library, 1958.

Brenner, Clarence D. *A Bibliographic List of Plays in the French Language, 1700–1789.* Berkeley: n.p., 1947.

Brewer, John. *The Pleasures of the Imagination: English Culture in the Eighteenth Century.* New York: Farrar, Straus and Giroux, 1997.

Brodsky, Joseph. "A Hidden Duet: The Intimate Connection Between the 'Magdalene' Poems of Boris Pasternak and Marina Tsvetaeva." *The Times Literary Supplement,* no. 5030 (August 27, 1999): 13–16.

Bromwich, David. "The Great Fidget: David Garrick's 'Uncanny Mobility' both On and Off the Stage." *The Times Literary Supplement,* no. 5118 (May 4, 2001): 3–4.

Brooks, Peter. *The Melodramatic Imagination: Balzac, Henry James, Melodrama, and the Mode of Excess.* New Haven: Yale University Press, 1995.

Brown, Michael Hamrick. "Native Song and National Consciousness in Nineteenth-Century Russian Music." In *Art and Culture in Nineteenth-Century Russia,* edited by Theofanis George Stavrou. Bloomington: Indiana University Press, 1983.

Brown, William Edward. *A History of Eighteenth-Century Russian Literature.* Ann Arbor: Ardis, 1980.

Brunner, Otto. "Das 'Ganze Haus' und die aleuropäische 'Ökonomik.'" In *Neue Wege Der Verfassungs- und Sozialgeschichte.* 3d ed. Göttingen: Vandenhoeck and Ruprecht, 1980.

———. "Europäisches und russisches Bürgertum." In *Neue Wege Der Verfassungs- und Sozialgeschichte.* 3d ed. Göttingen: Vandenhoeck and Ruprecht, 1980.

Buckler, Julie A. *The Literary Lorgnette: Attending Opera in Imperial Russia.* Stanford: Stanford University Press, 2000.

Bukharskii, A. I. *Nedokonchannaia kartina. Komediia v odnom deistvii.* St. Petersburg: Teatral'naia tipografiia, 1805.

Burbank, Jane, and David Ransel, eds. *Imperial Russia: New Histories for the Empire.* Bloomington: Indiana University Press, 1998.

Burgess, Malcolm. "Fairs and Entertainers in Eighteenth-Century Russia." *Slavonic and East European Review* 38 (1959): 95–113.

———. "Russian Public Theatre Audiences of the Eighteenth and Early Nineteenth Centuries." *Slavonic and East European Review* 38 (1958): 160–83.

Burgess, M. A. S. "The Early Theatre." In *An Introduction to Russian Language and Literature,* edited by Robert Auty and Dimitri Obolensky. New York: Cambridge University Press, 1977.

———. "The First Russian Actor-Manager and the Rise of Repertory in Russia During the Reign of the Empress Elizabeth Petrovna." In *Gorski vijenats: A Garland of Essays Offered to Professor Elizabeth Mary Hill,* edited by R. Auty, L. R. Lewitter, and A. P. Vlasto. Cambridge, Eng.: Modern Humanities Research Association, 1970.

———. "The Nineteenth- and Early Twentieth-Century Theatre." In *An Introduction to*

Russian Language and Literature, edited by Robert Auty and Dimitri Obolensky. New York: Cambridge University Press, 1977.

Burke, Peter. *Varieties of Cultural History.* Ithaca, N.Y.: Cornell University Press, 1997.

Bushkovitch, Paul. "Aristocratic Faction and the Opposition to Peter the Great: The 1690's." *Forschungen zur osteuropäischen Geschichte* (1995): 80–120.

——. *Peter the Great: The Struggle for Power, 1671–1725.* Cambridge, Eng.: Cambridge University Press, 2001.

——. *Religion and Society in Russia: The Sixteenth and Seventeenth Centuries.* New York: Oxford University Press, 1992.

Bushnell, John. "Did Serf Owners Control Serf Marriage? Orlov Serfs and Their Neighbors, 1773–1861." *Slavic Review* 52 (1993): 419–45.

Bychkova, M. E. "Idei vlasti i poddanstva v genealogicheskoi literature XV–XVI vv." *Istoricheskaia genealogiia,* no. 2 (1993): 4–9.

Calhoun, Craig, ed. *Habermas and the Public Sphere.* Cambridge, Mass.: MIT Press, 1992.

Cassiday, Julie A. "Northern Poetry for a Northern People: Text and Context in Ozerov's *Fingal.*" *Slavonic and East European Review* 78 (2000): 240–66.

Catherine II. *Gospozha Vestnikova s sem'eiu. Komediia v odnom deistvii. Sochinena v Iaroslavle.* In *Rossiiskii featr.* 11:263–308.

——. *Imianiny Gospozhi Vorchalkinoi. Komediia v piati deistviiakh. Sochinena v Iaroslavle.* In *Rossiiskii featr.* 11:85–220.

——. *Khlor Tsarevich, ili Roza bez shipov, kotoraia ne koletsia. Inoskazatel'noe zrelishche v trekh deistviiakh. 1786 goda.* In *Rossiiskii featr.* 24:195–232.

——. *Nachal'noe upravlenie Olega. Podrazhanie Shakespiru. Bez sokhraneniia featral'nykh obyknovennykh pravil.* In *Rossiiskii featr.* 14:167–248.

——. *Nedorazumeniia. Komediia v piati deistviiakh.* In *Rossiiskii featr.* 31:153–318.

——. *Novogorodskoi bogatyr' Boeslaevich'. Opera komicheskaia, sostavlena iz skazki, pesnei ruskikh, i inykh sochinenii.* In *Rossiiskii featr.* 20:55–100.

——. *Obmanshchik.* In *Sochineniia Ekateriny II,* edited by O. N. Mikhailov. Moscow: Sovetskaia Rossiia, 1990.

——. *Obol'shchennyi.* In *Sochineniia Ekateriny II,* edited by O. N. Mikhailov. Moscow: Sovetskaia Rossiia, 1990.

——. *Opera komicheskaia Fevei, sostavlena iz slov skaski, pesnei Ruskikh, i inykh sochinenii.* In *Rossiiskii featr.* 2:4–54.

——. *Opera komicheskaia khraboi i smeloi vitiaz' Akhrideich'.* In *Rossiiskii featr.* 20:101–51.

——. *O vremia! Komediia v trekh deistviiakh. Sochinena v Iaroslavle vo vremia chumy 1772 g.* In *Sochineniia Ekateriny II,* edited by O. N. Mikhailov. Moscow: Sovetskaia Rossiia, 1990.

——. *Peredniaia znatnogo boiarina. Komediia v odnom deistvii.* In *Rossiiskii featr.* 11:221–62.

——. *Podrazhanie Shakespiru. Istoricheskoe predstavlenie bez sokhraneniia obyknovennykh featral'nykh pravil iz zhizni Riurika.* In *Rossiiskii featr.* 14:107–66.

——. *Shaman sibirskii.* In *Sochineniia Ekateriny II,* edited by O. N. Mikhailov. Moscow: Sovetskaia Rossiia, 1990.

——. *Skazka o Gorebogatyre Kosometoviche i Opera komicheskaia iz slov skaski sostavlennaia.* St. Petersburg: Tipografiia gornogo uchilishcha, 1789.

——. *Two Comedies by Catherine the Great, Empress of Russia: Oh, These Times! and The Siberian Shaman.* Translated and edited by Lurana Donnels O'Malley. Amsterdam: Harwood Academic Publishers, 1998.

Ch., K. P. *Sestry sopernitsy. Dramma v piati deistviiakh*. In *Rossiiskii featr*. 9:5–112.

Chartier, Roger. *The Cultural Origins of the French Revolution*. Translated by Lydia G. Cochrane. 1958. Reprint, Durham, N.C.: Duke University Press, 1991.

———. "The Man of Letters." In *Enlightenment Portraits*, edited by Michel Vovelle, translated by Lydia G. Cochrane. Chicago: University of Chicago Press, 1997.

Chernaia, L. A. "'Chest': Predstavleniia o chesti i bezchestii v russkoi literature XI–XVII vv." In *Drevnerusskaia literatura. Izobrazhenie obshchestva*, edited by A. S. Dëmin. Moscow: Nauka, 1991.

Cherniavskoi, Osip. *Kupetskaia kompaniia. Komediia v odnom deistvii*. In *Rossiiskii featr*. 27:149–208.

Chulkov, M. D. *Prigozhaia povarikha, ili Pokhozhdenie razvratnoi zhenshchiny*. In *Khrestomatiia po russkoi literature XVIII veka*, edited by A. V. Kokorev. 4th ed. Moscow: Prosveshchenie, 1965.

Cioranescu, Alexandre. *Bibliographie de la littérature française du dix-huitième siècle*. 3 vols. Paris: Centre National de la Recherche scientifique, 1969.

Confino, Michael. "À propos de la notion de service dans la noblesse russe au XVIIIe et XIXe siècles." *Cahiers du Monde russe et soviétique* 34 (1993): 47–58.

Cracraft, James. "Opposition to Peter the Great." In *Imperial Russia, 1700–1917: State, Society, Opposition*, edited by Ezra Mendelsohn and Marshall S. Shatz. DeKalb: Northern Illinois University Press, 1988.

———. *The Petrine Revolution in Russian Imagery*. Chicago: University of Chicago Press, 1997.

Cross, A[nthony] G. *"By the Banks of the Neva": Chapters from the Lives and Careers of the British in Eighteenth-Century Russia*. Cambridge, Eng.: Cambridge University Press, 1997.

———. "The Eighteenth-Century Russian Theater Through British Eyes." In *Studies on Voltaire and the Eighteenth Century*, vol. 219. Oxford: Voltaire Foundation, 1983.

———. "Mr. Fisher's Company of English Actors in Eighteenth-Century Petersburg." *Newsletter. Study Group on Eighteenth-Century Russia* 4 (1976): 49–56.

———. "A Royal Blue-Stocking: Catherine the Great's Early Reputation in England as an Authoress." In *Gorski vijenats: A Garland of Essays Offered to Professor Elizabeth Mary Hill*, edited by R. Auty, L. R. Lewitter, and A. P. Vlasto. Cambridge, Eng.: Modern Humanities Research Association, 1970.

———, ed. *Russia and the West in the Eighteenth Century*. Newtonville, Mass.: Oriental Research Partners, 1983.

Cross, A[nthony] G., and G. S. Smith, eds. *Literature, Lives, and Legality in Catherine's Russia*. Nottingham, Eng.: Astria Press, 1994.

Crummey, Robert O. *The Formation of Muscovy, 1304–1613*. New York: Longman, 1987.

Dal', Vladimir. *Tolkovyi slovar' velikorusskogo iazyka*. 4 vols. 2d ed. 1880–1882. Reprint, Moscow: Russkii iazyk, 1978–1980.

Damskii, Kupriian [Fedorovich]. *Opera komicheskaia Vinetta, ili Taras v ul'e. V dvukh deistviiakh*. Petropol': n.p., 1799.

Darnton, Robert. *The Forbidden Best-Sellers of Pre-Revolutionary France*. New York: W. W. Norton, 1996.

———. *The Great Cat Massacre and Other Episodes in French Cultural History*. New York: Basic Books, 1984.

———. *The Kiss of Lamourette: Reflections in Cultural History*. New York: Norton, 1990.

Das, David. "History Writing and the Quest for Fame in Late Muscovy: Andrei Lyzlov's *History of the Scythians.*" *Russian Review* 51 (1992): 502–9.

Dashkova, E. R. *The Memoirs of Princess Dashkova.* Translated and edited by Kyril Fitzlyon. 1958. Reprint, Durham, N.C.: Duke University Press, 1995.

———. *Toisiokov. Komediia v piati deistviiakh.* In *Rossiiskii featr.* 19:239–317.

Deistvie liubvi. Komediia v trekh deistviiakh. Moscow: Universitetskaia tipografiia u N. Novikova, 1783.

Dëmin, A. S. "Evoliutsiia moskovskoi shkol'noi dramaturgii." In *Ranniaia russkaia dramaturgiia (XVII–pervaia polovina XVIII v.). P'esy shkol'nykh teatrov Moskvy.* Moscow: Nauka, 1974.

———. *O khudozhestvennosti drevnerusskoi literatury.* Moscow: Iazyki russkoi kul'tury, 1998.

Derzhavina, O. A. "Russkii teatr 70–90-kh godov XVII v. i nachala XVIII v." In *Ranniaia russkaia dramaturgiia (XVII–pervaia polovina XVIII v.). Russkaia dramaturgiia poslednei chetverti XVII i nachala XVIII v.* Moscow: Nauka, 1972.

Derzhavina, O. A., A. S. Dëmin, and A. N. Robinson. "Poiavlenie teatra i dramaturgii v Rossii v XVII v." In *Ranniaia russkaia dramaturgiia (XVII–pervaia polovina XVIII v.). Pervye p'esy russkogo teatra.* Moscow: Nauka, 1972.

———. "Rukopisnaia dramaturgiia i teatral'naia zhizn' pervoi poloviny XVIII v." In *Ranniaia russkaia dramaturgiia (XVII–pervaia polovina XVIII v.). P'esy liubitel'skikh teatrov.* Moscow: Nauka, 1976.

Dictionary of Literary Biography. Vol. 150, *Early Modern Russian Writers, Late Seventeenth and Eighteenth Centuries.* Edited by Marcus C. Levitt. Detroit: Gale Research, 1995.

Diderot, Denis. *Chadoliubivoi otets. Komediia v piat' deistvii. Sochinenie G. Diderota. Perevedena s Frantsuzskogo.* Translated by Sergei Glebov. St. Petersburg: n.p., 1765.

———. *Pobochnyi syn, ili Iskusheniia dobrodeteli. Komediia v piati deistviiakh i prostoiu rech'iu pisannaia. Sochinenie G. Diderota.* Translated by E. S. Kharlamov. 2d ed. Moscow: Universitetskaia tipografiia u N. Novikova, 1788.

———. *Pobochnyi syn, ili Ispytaniia dobrodeteli. Drama v piati deistviiakh.* Translated by Ivan Iakovlev. Moscow: Senatskaia tipografiia u V. Okorokova, 1788.

———. *Pobochnyi syn, ili Ispytaniia dobrodeteli. Drama v piati deistviiakh. Perevedena s Frantsuzskogo iazyka I. Ia.* Translated by Ivan Iakovlev. Moscow: Senatskaia tipografiia u soderzhatelia V. O., 1788.

———. *Pobochnyi syn, ili Opyt dobrodeteli. Komediia v piati deistviiakh G. Diderota.* Translated by Sergei Glebov. St. Petersburg: n.p., 1766.

Di Salvo, Maria, and Lindsey Hughes, eds. *A Window on Russia: Papers from the Fifth International Conference of the Study Group on Eighteenth-Century Russia, Gargnano, 1994.* Rome: La Fenice Edizioni, 1996.

Dmitriev, D. "Russkaia teatral'naia publika vo vremena Sumarokova." *Drevniaia i novaia Rossiia* 3 (1875): 313–16.

Dmitriev, Iu. A., and T. E. Korol'kova. "Dramaturgiia balagannogo teatra." *Pamiatniki kul'tury: Novye otkrytiia 1989.* Moscow: Nauka, 1990.

Dobrodetel'noi volshebnik. Drammaticheskaia opera v piati deistviiakh. Moscow: Tipografiia A. A., 1787.

Dobrodetel' priobretennaia v uchilishche. Predstavlenie v odnom deistvii. St. Petersburg: Morskoi shliakhetnyi kadetskii korpus, 1775.

Dobronrav. Komediia v odnom deistvii. In *Rossiiskii featr.* 38:5–36.

Dolgorukov, I. M. *Kapishche moego serdtsa, ili Slovar' vsekh tekh lits, s koimi ia byl v raznykh otnosheniiakh v techenie moei zhizni.* Kovrov: BEST-V, 1997.

———. *Liubovnoe volshebstvo. Opera v trekh deistviiakh.* Moscow: Gubernskaia tipografiia u A. Reshetnikova, 1799.

Domashniia nesoglasiia. Komediia v piati deistviiakh. In *Rossiiskii featr.* 12:205–390.

Dostoevsky, Fedor. *Memoirs from the House of the Dead.* Translated by Jessie Coulson and edited by Ronald Hingley. New York: Oxford University Press, 1983.

Dramaticheskoi slovar', ili Pokazaniia po alfavitu vsekh Rossiiskikh teatral'nykh sochinenii i perevodov, s oznacheniem imen izvestnykh sochinitelei, perevodchikov, i slagatelei muzyki, kotoryia kogda byli predstavleny na teatrakh, i gde, i v kotoroe vremia napechatany. V pol'zu liubiashchikh teatral'nyia predstavleniia. Moscow: Tipografiia A. A., 1787.

Dramaticheskie sochineniia. Edited by Iu. V. Stennik. Leningrad: Iskusstvo, 1990.

Drizen, N. V. "Liubitel'skii teatr pri Ekaterine II (1761–1796 gg.)." *Ezhegodnik imperatorskikh teatrov,* god 6, sezon 1895–1896, *Prilozheniia,* kn. 2 (1897): 77–114.

———. *Materialy k istorii russkogo teatra.* 2d ed. Moscow: Izdatel'stvo A. A. Bakhrushina, 1913.

———. "Ocherki teatral'noi tsenzury v Rossii v XVIII veke." *Russkaia starina* 90 (April-May-June, 1897): 539–68.

Ducrot, Oswald, and Tzvetan Todorov. *Encyclopedic Dictionary of the Sciences of Language.* Translated by Catherine Porter. Baltimore: Johns Hopkins University Press, 1983.

Dva pluta v Gishpanii. Komediia v trekh deistviiakh. Moscow: Tipografiia Ponomareva, 1787.

Dynnik, T. *Krepostnoi teatr.* Leningrad: Academia, 1933.

Edgerton, William B. "Ambivalence as the Key to Kniazhnin's Tragedy *Vadim Novgorodskii.*" In *Russia and the World of the Eighteenth Century,* edited by R. P. Bartlett, A. G. Cross, and Karen Rasmussen. Columbus, Ohio: Slavica Publishers, 1988.

Edmondson, Linda. *Feminism in Russia, 1900–1917.* Stanford: Stanford University Press, 1984.

———, ed. *Women and Society in Russia and the Soviet Union.* New York: Cambridge University Press, 1992.

Efim'ev, Dmitrii. *Prestupnik ot igry, ili Bratom prodannaia sestra. Komediia v stikhakh v piati deistviiakh.* St. Petersburg: n.p., 1790.

Efremov, P. A., ed. *Sochineniia i perevody Vladimira Ignat'evicha Lukina i Bogdana Egorovicha El'chaninova.* St. Petersburg: Ivan Il'ich Glazunov, 1868.

El'chaninov, B. E. *Nakazannaia vertoprashka. Komediia v odnom deistvii.* St. Petersburg: n.p., 1767.

Eleonskaia, A. S. "Tvorcheskie vzaimosviazi shkol'nogo i pridvornogo teatrov v Rossii." In *Ranniaia russkaia dramaturgiia (XVII–pervaia polovina XVIII v.). P'esy stolichnykh i provintsial'nykh teatrov pervoi poloviny XVIII v.* Moscow: Nauka, 1975.

Elizarova, N. A. *Teatry Sheremetevykh.* Moscow: Ostankinskii dvorets-muzei, 1944.

Emin, N. F. *Mnimyi mudrets. Komediia v piati deistviiakh.* In *Rossiiskii featr.* 29:189–272.

Emmons, Terence. *The Russian Landed Gentry and the Peasant Emancipation of 1861.* London: Cambridge University Press, 1968.

Engel, Barbara Alpern. *Between the Fields and the City: Women, Work, and Family in Russia, 1861–1914.* New York: Cambridge University Press, 1994.

————. *Mothers and Daughters of the Intelligentsia in Nineteenth-Century Russia*. New York: Cambridge University Press, 1983.

Engel-Braunschmidt, Annelore. "Modernisierung durch Literatur: Ch. F. Gellerts 'Betschwester' und Katharinas 'O Zeit!'" In *Russland zur zeit Katharinas II. Absolutismus—Aufklärung—Pragmatismus*, edited by Eckhard Hübner, Jan Kusber, and Peter Nitsche. Cologne: Böhlau, 1998.

Engelstein, Laura, and Stephanie Sandler, eds. *Self and Story in Russian History*. Ithaca, N.Y.: Cornell University Press, 2000.

Entsiklopedicheskii slovar'. 43 vols. in 86 pts. St. Petersburg: F. A. Brokgauz–I. A. Efron, 1890–1907.

Euripides. *Three Plays: Alcestis, Hippolytus, Iphigenia in Tauris*. Translated by Philip Vellacott. Revised ed. London: Penguin, 1974.

Evremova, N. N. *Sudostroistvo Rossii v XVIII–pervoi polovine XIX vv. (istoriko-pravovoe issledovanie)*. Moscow: Nauka, 1993.

Ezhegodnik imperatorskikh teatrov. St. Petersburg, 1892–1915.

Faggionato, Rafaella. "From a Society of the Enlightened to the Enlightenment of Society: The Russian Bible Society and Rosicrucianism in the Age of Alexander I." *Slavonic and East European Review* 79 (2001): 459–87.

Faizova, I. V. *"Manifest o vol'nosti" i sluzhba dvorianstva v XVIII stoletii*. Moscow: Nauka, 1999.

Farrow, Lee A. "Peter the Great's Law of Single Inheritance: State Imperatives and Noble Resistance." *Russian Review* 55 (1996): 430–47

Fedorov, V. I., ed. *Russkaia literatura XVIII veka. Slovar'-spravochnik*. Moscow: MGPU, 1997.

Fedorov, V. M. *Russkoi soldat, ili Khorosho byt' dobrym gospodinom. Original'naia dramma v dvukh deistviiakh*. St. Petersburg: Gubernskoe pravlenie, 1803.

Feinberg, Anat. "The Representation of the Poor in Elizabethan and Stuart Drama." *Literature and History* 12 (1986): 152–63.

Fénelon, François de. *Telemachus, Son of Ulysses*. Edited and translated by Patrick Riley. Cambridge, Eng.: Cambridge University Press, 1994.

Fenichel, Otto. *The Psychoanalytic Theory of Neurosis*. With an introduction and epilogue by Leo Rangel. Fiftieth anniversary ed. New York: W. W. Norton, 1995.

Ferretti, Paola. "'Razdelenie Zemel': A Proposal Against the Servile System by V. F. Malinovskii." In *A Window on Russia: Papers from the Fifth International Conference of the Study Group on Eighteenth-Century Russia, Gargnano, 1994*, edited by Maria Di Salvo and Lindsey Hughes. Rome: La Fenice Edizioni, 1996.

F. G. Volkov i russkii teatr ego vremeni: Sbornik materialov. Edited by Iu. A. Dmitriev. Moscow: Izdatel'stvo akademii nauk SSSR, 1953.

Field, Daniel. *The End of Serfdom: Nobility and Bureaucracy in Russia, 1855–1861*. Cambridge, Mass.: Harvard University Press, 1976.

Findeisen, Nicholas. "The Earliest Russian Operas." *The Musical Quarterly* 19 (1933): 331–40.

Fleishman, Avrom. "Three Ways of Thinking about Fiction and Society." In *Russianness: Studies on a Nation's Identity, in Honor of Rufus Mathewson, 1918–1978*, edited by Robert L. Belknap. Ann Arbor: Ardis, 1990.

Fonvizin, D. I. *Brigadir. Komediia v piati deistviiakh*. In *Ot russkogo klassitsizma k realizmu: D. I. Fonvizin, A. S. Griboedov*, edited by E. Rogachevskaia. Moscow: Shkola-Press, 1995.

————. *Korion. Komediia v trekh aktakh, peredelannaia v russkuiu s frantsuzskogo iazyka*.

In *Stikhotvornaia komediia, komicheskaia opera, vodevil' kontsa XVIII–nachala XIX veka v dvukh tomakh,* edited by A. A. Gozenpud. 2 vols. Leningrad: Sovetskii pisatel', 1990.

————. *Nedorosl'. Komediia v piati deistviiakh.* In *Ot russkogo klassitsizma k realizmu: D. I. Fonvizin, A. S. Griboedov,* edited by E. Rogachevskaia. Moscow: Shkola-Press, 1995.

Frame, Murray. "Censorship and Control in the Russian Imperial Theatres during the 1905 Revolution and Its Aftermath." *Revolutionary Russia* 7 (1994): 164–91.

————. *The Saint Petersburg Imperial Theaters: Stage and State in Revolutionary Russia, 1900–1920.* Jefferson, N.C.: McFarland, 2000.

————. "Theater and Revolution in 1917: The Case of the Petrograd State Theatres." *Revolutionary Russia* 12 (1999): 84–102.

————. "Tsarist Court and Russian Culture: The Administration of the St. Petersburg Imperial Theatres, 1900–1917." *Australian Slavonic and East European Studies* 11 (1997): 117–42.

Franklin, Simon, and Jonathan Shepard. *The Emergence of Rus, 750–1200.* New York: Longman, 1996.

Freeze, Gregory L. "Bringing Order to the Russian Family: Marriage and Divorce in Imperial Russia, 1760–1860." *Journal of Modern History* 62 (1990): 709–46.

Freud, Sigmund. *Civilization and Its Discontents.* Translated and edited by James Strachey. New York: W. W. Norton, 1961.

Fuller, William C., Jr. *Strategy and Power in Russia, 1600–1914.* New York: Free Press, 1992.

Gallagher, Catherine, and Stephen Greenblatt. *Practicing New Historicism.* Chicago: University of Chicago Press, 2000.

Gatsiskii, A. S. *Nizhegorodskii teatr (1798–1867).* Nizhnii Novgorod: Tipografiia nizhegorodskogo gubernskogo pravleniia, 1867.

Geroistvo liubvi. Drama v piati deistviiakh. In *Rossiiskii Featr.* 43:191–289.

Gerth, H. H., and C. Wright Mills, eds. and trans. *From Max Weber: Essays in Sociology.* New York: Oxford University Press, 1946.

Giesemann, Gerhard. *Kotzebue in Russland.* Frankfurter Abhandlungen zur Slawistik, vol. 15. Frankfurt on Main: Athenäum, 1971.

Gil'tebrandt, Peter. "Pis'mo komedianta k Imperatritse Ekaterine I." *Drevniaia i novaia Rossiia,* no. 1 (1877): 123–24.

Givens, Robert D. "To Measure and to Encroach: The Nobility and the Land Survey." In *Russia and the World of the Eighteenth Century,* edited by R. P. Bartlett, A. G. Cross, and Karen Rasmussen. Columbus, Ohio: Slavica Publishers, 1988.

Glants, Musya, and Joyce Toomre, ed. *Food in Russian History and Culture.* Bloomington: Indiana University Press, 1997.

Gleason, Abbott. *European and Muscovite: Ivan Kireevsky and the Origins of Slavophilism.* Cambridge, Mass.: Harvard University Press, 1972.

Gleason, Walter J. *Moral Idealists, Bureaucracy, and Catherine the Great.* New Brunswick, N.J.: Rutgers University Press, 1981.

Glinka, S. N. *Zapiski.* In *Zolotoi vek Ekateriny Velikoi. Vospominaniia.* Edited by V. M. Bokova and N. I. Tsimbaev. Moscow: Izdatel'stvo moskovskogo universiteta, 1996.

Golenkova, Zinaida T. "Civil Society in Russia." *Russian Social Science Review* 40 (1999): 4–18.

————, ed. *Grazhdanskoe obshchestvo: Teoriia, istoriia, sovremennost'.* Moscow: Institut sotsiologii RAN, 1999.

Golitsyn, A. I. *Novye chudaki, ili Prozhekter. Komediia v piati deistviiakh. Sochinena v Moskve (1797)*. In *Drammaticheskiia sochineniia i perevody podpolkovnika kniaz' Alekseia Golitsyna, v odnom tome*. Moscow: Universitetskaia tipografiia, 1798.

———. *Otets nevidimka, ili Svatalsia na materi, zhenilsia na docheri. Komediia v trekh deistviiakh*. Moscow: Universitetskaia tipografiia, 1799.

———. *Svetskoe obrashchenie, ili Nravy veka. Komediia v trekh deistviiakh. Sochineniia G. Garrika. Perevel dva deistviia, a tretie pridelal Kniaz' Aleksei Golitsyn*. In *Sochineniia i perevody Kn. A. I. Golitsyna*, vol. 1. Moscow: Universitetskaia tipografiia, 1800.

Golovina, Varvara. "Varvara Golovina, 1766–1821: Freilina Vysochaishego dvora." In *Tainy tsarskogo dvora (iz zapisok freilin): Sbornik*, edited by I. V. Eremina. Moscow: Znachenie, 1997.

Goodman, Dena. "Public Sphere and Private Life: Toward a Synthesis of Current Historiographical Approaches to the Old Regime." *History and Theory* 31 (1992): 1–20.

———. *The Republic of Letters: A Cultural History of the Enlightenment*. Ithaca, N.Y.: Cornell University Press, 1994.

Goody, Jack. *The Logic of Writing and The Organization of Society*. Cambridge, Eng.: Cambridge University Press, 1986.

Gorchakov, D. P. *Baba Iaga. Komicheskaia opera v trekh deistviiakh i s baletom*. Kaluga: n.p., 1788.

———. *Kalif na chas. Komicheskaia opera v chetyrekh deistviiakh*. In *Rossiiskii featr*. 26:67–146.

———. *Shchastlivaia tonia. Komicheskaia opera*. Moscow: n.p., 1786.

Gordin, M., and Ia. Gordin. *Teatr Ivana Krylova*. Leningrad: Iskusstvo, 1983.

Gordon, Daniel. *Citizens without Sovereignty: Equality and Sociability in French Thought, 1670–1789*. Princeton: Princeton University Press, 1994.

———, ed. *Postmodernism and the Enlightenment: New Perspectives in Eighteenth-Century French Intellectual History*. New York: Routledge, 2001.

Gorodchaninov, G. N. *Kukla Lizan'ke, ili Nagrazhdennoe prilezhanie. Detskaia dramma*. St. Petersburg: I. Sytin, 1799.

———. *Mitrofanushka v otstavke. Komediia v piati deistviiakh. Rossiiskoe sochinenie G. G.* Moscow: Universitetskaia tipografiia, 1800.

Gorskaia, N. A., and E. N. Shveikovskaia, eds. *Predstavleniia o sobstvennosti v rossiiskom obshchestve XV–XVIII vv. Problemy sobstvennosti v obshchestvennom soznanii i pravovoi mysli feodal'noi epokhi*. Moscow: Institut rossiiskoi istorii RAN, 1998.

Gorskii, A. A., ed. *Tsar' i tsarstvo v russkom obshchestvennom soznanii*. Moscow: Institut rossiiskoi istorii RAN, 1999.

Gott, T. "Low Elements in the Language of Eighteenth-Century Russian Comedy." *Melbourne Slavonic Studies*, no. 11 (1976): 80–83.

Gozenpud, A. A., ed. *Stikhotvornaia komediia, komicheskaia opera, vodevil' kontsa XVIII–nachala XIX veka*. 2 vols. Leningrad: Sovetskii pisatel', 1990.

Green, Michael. "Diderot and Kheraskov: Sentimentalism in Its Classicist Stage." In *Russia and the West in the Eighteenth Century*, edited by A. G. Cross. Newtonville, Mass.: Oriental Research Partners, 1983.

———. "Italian Scandal as Russian Tragedy: Kheraskov's *Venetsianskaia Monakhinia*." In *Russia and the World of The Eighteenth Century*, edited by R. P. Bartlett, A. G. Cross, and Karen Rasmussen. Columbus, Ohio: Slavica Publishers, 1988.

———. "Kheraskov and the Christian Tragedy." In *California Slavic Studies*, vol. 9. Berkeley: University of California Press, 1976.

———. "Kheraskov's *Gonimye:* Shakespeare's Second Appearance in Russia." *Slavic Review* 35 (1976): 249–57.

———. "Kotzebue and Kheraskov: Sentimentalism in Its Pre-Romantic Stage." *Newsletter. Study Group on Eighteenth-Century Russia*, no. 10 (1982): 20–29.

———. "Mikhail Kheraskov and the Comic Opera." In *Literature, Lives, and Legality in Catherine's Russia*, edited by A. G. Cross and G. S. Smith. Nottingham, Eng.: Astria Press, 1994.

Greenfeld, Liah. *Nationalism: Five Roads to Modernity*. Cambridge, Mass.: Harvard University Press, 1992.

Griesinger, Georg August. *Biographical Notes Concerning Joseph Haydn*. In *Haydn: Two Contemporary Portraits*. Translated by Vernon Gotwals. Madison: University of Wisconsin Press, 1968.

Griffiths, David M. "In Search of Enlightenment: Recent Soviet Interpretations of Eighteenth-Century Russian Intellectual History." *Canadian-American Slavic Studies* 16 (1982): 317–56.

———. "Introduction: Of Estates, Charters, and Constitutions." In *Catherine II's Charters of 1785 to the Nobility and the Towns*, edited and translated by David Griffiths and George E. Munro. Bakersfield, Calif.: Charles Schlacks, Jr., 1991.

Grinberg, M. S., and B. A. Uspenskii. *Literaturnaia voina Trediakovskogo i Sumarokova v 1740–kh–nachale 1750–kh godov*. Moscow: Rossiiskii gosudarstvennyi gumanitarnyi universitet, 2001.

Griswold, Wendy. *Renaissance Revivals: City Comedy and Revenge Tragedy in the London Theatre, 1576–1980*. Chicago: University of Chicago Press, 1986.

Gukovskii, G. A. *Ocherki po istorii russkoi literatury XVIII veka: Dvorianskaia fronda v literature 1750–kh–1760–kh godov*. Moscow and Leningrad: Akademiia nauk, 1936.

———. *Rannie raboty po istorii russkoi poezii XVIII veka*. Edited by V. M. Zhivov. Moscow: Iazyki russkoi kul'tury, 2001.

———. *Russkaia literatura XVIII veka*. 1939. Reprint, Moscow: Aspekt Press, 1998.

Günther, Kurt. "Neue deutsche Quellen zum ersten russischen Theater. *Zeitschrift für Slawistik* 8 (5) (1963): 664–75.

Gurevich, Liubov'. *Istoriia russkogo teatral'nogo byta*. Moscow and Leningrad: Iskusstvo, 1939.

Habermas, Jürgen. *The Structural Transformation of the Public Sphere: An Inquiry into a Category of Bourgeois Society*. Translated by Thomas Burger with Frederick Lawrence. Cambridge, Mass.: MIT Press, 1989.

Hamburg, G. M. *Boris Chicherin and Early Russian Liberalism, 1828–1866*. Stanford: Stanford University Press, 1992.

Hanley, Sarah. "Social Sites of Political Practice in France: Lawsuits, Civil Rights, and the Separation of Powers in Domestic and State Government, 1500–1800." *American Historical Review* 102 (1997): 27–52.

Hartley, Janet M. "Catherine's Conscience Court—An English Equity Court?" In *Russia and the West in the Eighteenth Century*, edited by A. G. Cross. Newtonville. Mass.: Oriental Research Partners, 1983.

———. *A Social History of the Russian Empire, 1650–1825*. New York: Longman, 1999.

Havel, Václav. *Disturbing the Peace: A Conversation with Karel Hvížďala*. Translated by Paul Wilson. New York: Vintage Books, 1991.

Hellie, Richard. *The Economy and Material Culture of Russia, 1600–1725.* Chicago: University of Chicago Press, 1999.

———. "Thoughts on the Absence of Elite Resistance in Muscovy." *Kritika: Explorations in Russian and Eurasian History* 1 (2000): 5–20.

Herold, Kelly. "Russian Autobiographical Literature in French: Recovering a Memoiristic Tradition (1770–1839)." Ph.D. diss. University of California at Los Angeles, 1998.

Hiller, Peter. *D. I. Fonvizin und P. A. Plavil'ščikov: Ein Kapitel aus der russischen Theatergeschichte im 18. Jahrhundert.* Munich: Verlag Otto Sagner, 1985.

Hoch, Steven L. *Serfdom and Social Control in Russia: Petrovskoe, a Village in Tambov.* Chicago: University of Chicago Press, 1986.

Hoffman, Philip T., Gilles Postel-Vinay, and Jean-Laurent Rosenthal. "Information and Economic History: How the Credit Market in Old Regime Paris Forces Us to Rethink The Transition to Capitalism." *American Historical Review* 104 (1999): 69–94.

Holzmann, Albert William. *Family Relationships in the Dramas of August von Kotzebue.* Princeton: Princeton University Press, 1935.

Hosking, Geoffrey. "Patronage and the Russian State." *Slavonic and East European Review* 78 (2000): 301–20.

———. *People and Empire, 1552–1917.* Cambridge, Mass.: Harvard University Press, 1997.

Hübner, Eckhard, Jan Kusber, and Peter Nitsche, eds. *Russland zur zeit Katharinas II. Absolutismus—Aufklärung—Pragmatismus.* Cologne: Böhlau, 1998.

Hughes, Lindsey. *Russia in the Age of Peter the Great.* New Haven: Yale University Press, 1998.

———. *Sophia, Regent of Russia, 1657–1704.* New Haven: Yale University Press, 1990.

Huizinga, Johan. *The Autumn of the Middle Ages.* Translated by Rodney J. Payton and Ulrich Mammitzch. Chicago: University of Chicago Press, 1996.

Hunt, Lynn. *The Family Romance of the French Revolution.* Berkeley: University of California Press, 1992.

Hyart, Charles. "Le Théâtre de l'Hermitage et Catherine II." *Revue de Littérature comparée* 61 (1987): 81–103.

Ianovskii, M. O., ed. *Stikhotvornaia komediia kontsa XVIII–nachala XIX v.* Moscow and Leningrad: Sovetskii pisatel', 1964.

Igrishche o sviatkakh. St. Petersburg: n.p., 1774.

Igrok shchaslivoi. Opera v odnom deistvii. Sochinenie Rossiiskoe. St. Petersburg: n.p., 1783.

Ilyin, Eugene K. "Michael Maddox." *World Review* (February 1950): 17–22.

Istoriia russkoi dramaturgii XVII–pervaia polovina XIX veka. Leningrad: Nauka, 1982.

Iukin, Ivan. *Koldun, vorozheia i svakha. Komicheskaia opera v trekh deistviiakh.* In *Rossiiskii featr.* 37:247–311.

Ivanov, L. M. *Serdtseplena. Opera v trekh deistviiakh. Sochinena v Moskve Tituliarnym Sovetnikom Leont'em Ivanovym 1788 goda.* Moscow: Senatskaia tipografiia, 1793.

Jacob, Margaret C. "The Enlightenment Redefined: The Formation of Modern Civil Society." *Social Research* 58 (1991): 475–95.

———. "The Mental Landscape of The Public Sphere: A European Perspective." *Eighteenth-Century Studies* 28 (1994): 95–113.

Johnson, James H. *Listening in Paris: A Cultural History.* Berkeley: University of California Press, 1995.

Jones, Robert E. *The Emancipation of the Russian Nobility, 1762–1785.* Princeton: Princeton University Press, 1973.

——. "Morals and Markets: The Conflict of Traditional Values and Liberal Ideas in the Economic Thought and Policies of Catherine II." *Jahrbücher für Geschichte Osteuropas* 45 (1997): 526–40.

Jones, W. Gareth. "The *Morning Light* Charity Schools, 1777–1780." *Slavonic and East European Review* 56 (1978): 47–67.

Joukovskaia, Anna. "La naissance de l'épistolographie normative en Russie. Histoire des premiers manuels russes d'art épistolaire." *Cahiers du Monde russe* 40 (1999): 657–90.

Kahan, Arcadius. "The Costs of 'Westernization' in Russia: The Gentry and the Economy in the Eighteenth Century." 1966. Reprinted in *The Structure of Russian History: Interpretive Essays,* edited by Michael Cherniavaky. New York: Random House, 1970.

Kaiser, Daniel H. "The Seasonality of Family Life in Early Modern Russia." *Forschungen zur osteuropäischen Geschichte* 46 (1992): 21–50.

Kaiser, Thomas. "The Evil Empire? The Debate on Turkish Despotism in Eighteenth-Century French Political Culture." *Journal of Modern History* 72 (2000): 6–34.

Kalash, V. V., and N. E. Efros, eds. *Istoriia russkogo teatra.* Vol. 1. Moscow: Ob"edinenie, 1914.

Kant, Immanuel. *Foundations of the Metaphysics of Morals and What Is Enlightenment?* Translated and with an introduction by Lewis White Beck. 2d ed. Upper Saddle River, N.J.: Prentice Hall, 1995.

Kantor, Marvin. "Fonvizin and Holberg: A Comparison of *The Brigadier* and *Jean de France." Canadian-American Slavic Studies* 7 (1973): 475–84.

Kantorowicz, Ernst H. *The King's Two Bodies: A Study in Mediaeval Political Theology.* Princeton: Princeton University Press, 1957.

Kapnist, V. V. *Iabeda. Komediia v piati deistviiakh.* In *Sobranie sochinenii v dvukh tomakh.* Vol. 1, *Stikhotvoreniia, p'esy,* edited by D. S. Babkin. Moscow and Leningrad: Akademiia nauk SSSR, 1960.

——. *Izbrannye proizvedeniia.* Leningrad: Sovetskii pisatel', 1973.

——. *Klorida i Milon. Pastusheskaia opera v odnom deistvii.* In *Sobranie sochinenii v dvukh tomakh.* Vol. 1, *Stikhotvoreniia, p'esy,* edited by D. S. Babkin. Moscow and Leningrad: Akademiia nauk SSSR, 1960.

——. *Sganarev, ili Mnimaia nevernost'.* In *Sobranie sochinenii v dvukh tomakh.* Vol. 1, *Stikhotvoreniia, p'esy,* edited by D. S. Babkin. Moscow and Leningrad: Akademiia nauk SSSR, 1960.

——. *Sobranie sochinenii v dvukh tomakh.* Edited by D. S. Babkin. 2 vols. Moscow and Leningrad: Akademiia nauk, 1960.

Karamzin, N. M. *Sofiia. Dramaticheskoi otryvok.* In *Moi bezdelki,* vol. 1. 2d ed. Moscow: Universitetskaia tipografiia u Ridigera i Klaudiia, 1797.

Karlinsky, Simon. *Russian Drama from Its Beginnings to the Age of Pushkin.* Berkeley: University of California Press, 1985.

Keep, John L. H. *Soldiers of the Tsar: Army and Society in Russia, 1462–1874.* New York: Oxford University Press, 1985.

Kelly, Catriona. "Educating Tat'yana: Manners, Motherhood, and Moral Education *(Vospitanie),* 1760–1840." In *Gender in Russian History and Culture,* edited by Linda Edmondson. Houndmills, N.Y.: Palgrave, 2001.

Kern, Fritz. *Kingship and Law in the Middle Ages: I. The Divine Right of Kings and the*

Right of Resistance in the Early Middle Ages. II. Law and Constitution in the Middle Ages. Studies by Fritz Kern. Translated and with an introduction by S. B. Chrimes (Oxford: B. Blackwell, 1939).

Kersnovskii, A. A. *Istoriia russkoi armii v chetyrëkh tomakh.* Vol. 1, *Ot Narvy do Parizha, 1700–1814.* Reprint, Moscow: Golos, 1992.

Khachaturov, S. V. *Goticheskii vkus v russkoi khudozhestvennoi kul'ture XVIII veka.* Moscow: PROGRESS-Traditsiia, 1999.

Khaven, Peder fon. "Puteshestvie v Rossiiu." In *Peterburg Anny Ioannovny v inostrannykh opisaniiakh,* edited by Iu. N. Bespiatykh. St. Petersburg: Blits, 1997.

Kheraskov, M. M. *Bezbozhnik. Geroicheskaia komediia.* In *Rossiiskii featr.* 10:5–36.

———. *Borislav. Tragediia.* In *Rossiiskii featr.* 4:165–222.

———. *Dobrye soldaty. Komicheskaia opera v trekh deistviiakh sochinennaia na Rossiiskom iazyke.* In *Rossiiskii featr.* 28:185–262.

———. *Drug neshchastnykh. Sleznaia drama.* In *Rossiiskii featr.* 8:177–240.

———. *Gonimyia. Sleznaia drama.* In *Rossiiskii featr.* 8:241–308.

———. *Idolopoklonniki, ili Gorislava. Tragediia.* In *Rossiiskii featr.* 4:223–303.

———. *Marteziia i Falestra. Tragediia.* In *Rossiiskii featr.* 4:85–164.

———. *Nenavistnik. Komediia v trekh deistviiakh.* In *Rossiiskii featr.* 10:37–120.

———. *Osvobozhdennaia Moskva.* In *Russkaia literatura. Vek XVIII. Tragediia,* edited by Iu. V. Stennik. Moscow: Khudozhestvennaia literatura, 1991.

———. *Plamena. Tragediia.* In *Rossiiskii featr.* 4:3–84.

———. *Venetsianskaia monakhinia. Tragediia v trekh deistviiakh.* In *Russkaia literatura. Vek XVIII. Tragediia,* edited by Iu. V. Stennik. Moscow: Khudozhestvennaia literatura, 1991.

Kholodov, E. G., ed. *Istoriia russkogo dramaticheskogo teatra.* 7 vols. Moscow: Iskusstvo, 1977–1987.

———. *Teatr i zriteli. Stranitsy istorii russkoi teatral'noi publiki.* Moscow: Gosudarstvennyi institut iskusstvoznaniia, 2000.

Khudushina, I. F. *Tsar'. Bog. Rossiia. Samosoznanie russkogo dvorianstva (konets XVIII–pervaia tret' XIX vv.)* Moscow: IFRAN, 1995.

Khvostov, Dmitrii. *Mnimyi schastlivets, ili Pustaia revnost'. Komediia v odnom deistvii.* In *Rossiiskii featr.* 31:319–66.

———. *Ruskoi parizhanets. Komediia v trekh deistviiakh.* In *Rossiiskii featr.* 15:149–260.

Kireevski, Ivan Vasil'evich. "On the Nature of European Culture and its Relation to the Culture of Russia. Letter to Count E. E. Komarovskii." In *Russian Intellectual History: An Anthology,* edited by Marc Raeff. 1968. Reprint, New York: Humanity Books, 1999.

Kireevskii, V. I. *Elizaveta. Drammaticheskoi otryvok.* Moscow: Universitetskaia tipografiia u Ridigera i Klaudiia, 1800.

———. *Kodr. Drammaticheskoi otryvok.* Moscow: Universitetskaia tipografiia u Ridigera i Klaudiia, 1799.

Kivelson, Valerie A. *Autocracy in the Provinces: The Muscovite Gentry and Political Culture in the Seventeenth Century.* Stanford: Stanford University Press, 1996.

———. "Cartography, Autocracy, and State Powerlessness: The Uses of Maps in Early Modern Russia." *Imago Mundi* 51 (1999): 83–105.

———. "Kinship Politics/Autocratic Politics: A Reconsideration of Early-Eighteenth-Century Political Culture." In *Imperial Russia: New Histories for the Empire,* edited by Jane Burbank and David L. Ransel. Bloomington: Indiana University Press, 1998.

Klein, I. [Joachim]. "Lomonosov i Rasin ('Demofont' i 'Andromakha')." *XVIII vek* 21 (1999): 89–96

Klein, Lawrence E. "Berkeley, Shaftesbury, and the Meaning of Politeness." *Studies in Eighteenth-Century Culture* 16 (1986): 57–68.

———. "The Third Earl of Shaftesbury and The Progress of Politeness." *Eighteenth-Century Studies* 18 (Winter 1984–1985): 186–214.

Kliucharev, F. P. *Vladimir Velikii. Tragediia.* In *Rossiiskii featr.* 6:81–144.

Kliuchevskii, V. O. "Nedorosl' Fonvizina (Opyt istoricheskogo ob"iasneniia uchebnoi p'esy)." 1896. In *O nravstvennosti i russkoi kul'ture,* edited by R. A. Kireeva. Moscow: Institut rossiiskoi istorii RAN, 1998.

Klushin, A. I. *Alkhimist. Komediia v odnom deistvii.* In *Russkaia komediia i komicheskaia opera,* edited by P. N. Berkov. Moscow and Leningrad: Iskusstvo, 1950.

———. *Khudo byt' blizorukim. Komediia v odnom deistvii, v proze.* St. Petersburg: Gubernskoe pravlenie, 1800.

———. *Smekh i gore. Komediia v piati deistviiakh v stikhakh.* In *Stikhotvornaia komediia, komicheskaia opera, vodevil' kontsa XVIII–nachala XIX veka,* edited by A. A. Gozenpud. 2 vols. Leningrad: Sovetskii pisatel', 1990.

Kniazhnin, Ia. B. *Chudaki. Komediia v stikhakh v piati deistviiakh.* In *Rossiiskii featr.* 41:3–147.

———. *Didona. Tragediia v piati deistviiakh.* In *Rossiiskii featr.* 32:93–186.

———. *Khvastun. Komediia v stikhakh, v piati deistviiakh.* In *Rossiiskii featr.* 10:121–270.

———. *Komicheskaia opera pritvorno sumashedshaia, v dvukh deistviiakh.* In *Sobranie sochinenii Iakova Kniazhnina.* 4 vols. St. Petersburg: Tipografiia gornogo uchilishcha, 1787.

———. *Neschast'e ot karety. Komicheskaia opera v dvukh deistviiakh.* In *Russkaia komediia i komicheskaia opera XVIII veka,* edited by P. N. Berkov. Moscow and Leningrad: Iskusstvo, 1950.

———. *Neudachnyi primiritel', ili Bez obedu domoi poedu. Komediia v trekh deistviiakh prozoiu.* In *Rossiiskii featr.* 33:195–294.

———. *Rosslav. Tragediia v stikhakh v piati deistviiakh.* In *Rossiiskii featr.* 6:145–240.

———. *Skupoi. Opera komicheskaia v odnom deistvii.* In *Rossiiskii featr.* 30:171–244.

———. *Sofonisba. Tragediia v pitati deistviiakh.* In *Rossiiskii featr.* 34:109–204.

———. *Titovo miloserdie. Tragediia v piati deistviiakh.* In *Rossiiskii featr.* 32:3–92.

———. *Vadim Novgorodskii. Tragediia v stikhakh, v piati deistviiakh.* St. Petersburg: Imperatorskaia akademiia nauk, 1793.

———. *Vladimir i Iaropolk. Tragediia v piati deistviiakh.* In *Russkaia literatura. Vek XVIII. Tragediia,* edited by Iu. V. Stennik. Moscow: Khudozhestvennaia literatura, 1991.

———. *Vladisan. Tragediia.* In *Rossiiskii featr.* 32:187–298.

———. *Zbiten'shchik. Komicheskaia opera v trekh deistviiakh.* In *Rossiiskii featr.* 30:5–156.

Kocka, Jürgen. "Asymmetrical Historical Comparison: The Case of The German Sonderweg." *History and Theory* 38 (1999): 40–50.

Kokoshkin, I. A. *Pokhod pod Shveda. Komediia v trekh deistviiakh s khorami i baletom.* St. Petersburg: n.p., 1790.

Koliupanov, N. B. "Ocherk istorii russkogo teatra do 1812 g." *Russkaia mysl',* no. 5 (1889): 107–24, no. 6 (1889): 10–29, no. 7 (1889): 29–42.

Kollmann, Nancy Shields. *By Honor Bound: State and Society in Early Modern Russia.* Ithaca, N.Y.: Cornell University Press, 1999.

————. "Was There Honor in Kiev Rus'?" *Jahrbücher für Geschichte Osteuropas* 36 (1988): 481–92.

Kolychev, V. P. *Bedstvo proizvedennoe strast'iu, ili Sal'vini i Adel'son. Tragediia grazhdanskaia v piati deistviiakh.* In *Teatr V. K.,* vol. 1. Moscow: Senatskaia tipografiia u F. Gippiusa, 1781.

————. *Dvorianiushcheisia kupets. Komediia v trekh deistviiakh.* In *Teatr V. K.,* vol. 1. Moscow: Senatskaia tipografiia u F. Gippiusa, 1781.

————. *Razvratnost' ispravliaemaia blagomysliem. Komediia v piati deistviiakh.* In *Teatr V. K.,* vol. 1. Moscow: Senatskaia tipografiia u F. Gippiusa, 1781.

————. *Tshchetnaia revnost', ili Perevozchik kuskovskoi. Pastush'ia opera v dvukh deistviiakh.* Moscow: n.p., 1781.

Komarovskii, E. F. *Zapiski grafa E. F. Komarovskogo.* Moscow: Vneshtorgizdat, 1990.

Konechnyi, Al'bin. *Byt i zrelishchnaia kul'tura Sankt-Peterburga-Petrograda XVIII–nachalo XX veka. Materialy k bibliografii.* St. Petersburg: Rossiiskii institute istorii iskusstv, 1997.

Konstantinov, T. V. *Blagovremennoe vspomozhenie. Original'naia drama v trekh deistviiakh.* n.p., 1794; in *Rossiiskii featr.* 43:105–90.

Kopiev [Kop'ev], A. D. *Obrashchennyi mizantrop, ili Lebedianskaia iarmonka. Komediia v piati deistviiakh.* St. Petersburg: n.p., 1794.

Korolev, D. G. *Ocherki iz istorii izdaniia i rasprostraneniia teatral'noi knigi v Rossii XIX–nachala XX vekov.* St. Petersburg: Rossiiskaia natsional'naia biblioteka, 1999.

Koselleck, Reinhart. *Critique and Crisis: Enlightenment and the Pathogenesis of Modern Society.* Cambridge, Mass.: MIT Press, 1988.

Kośny, Witold. "Ein deutscher Bäcker in Petersburg, oder: Kann ein Vaudevill denn merhr als Kurzweil sein?" *Forschungen zur osteuropäischen Geschichte* 48 (1993): 93–104.

Kosterina-Azarian, A. B. *Teatral'naia starina Urala.* Ekaterinburg: Demidovskii institut, 1998.

Kozel'skii, F. Ia. *Panteia. Tragediia.* In *Rossiiskii featr.* 6:3–80.

————. *Velesana. Tragediia.* In *Sochineniia Fedora Kozel'skogo.* 2d ed. 2 vols. St. Petersburg: Imperatorskaia akademiia nauk, 1778.

Kozodavlev, O. P. *Nashla kosa na kamen'. Komediia v odnom deistvii.* St. Petersburg: Izhdivenie avtora u Shnora, 1781.

————. *Persten'. Komediia v odnom deistvii.* St. Petersburg: Vol'naia tipografiia Veitbrekhta i Shnora, 1780.

Krieger, Leonard. *An Essay on the Theory of Enlightened Despotism.* Chicago: University of Chicago Press, 1975.

Kropotov, P. A. *Fomushka—babushkin vnuchek. Komediia.* In *Russkaia komediia i komicheskaia opera XVIII veka,* edited by P. N. Berkov. Moscow and Leningrad: Iskusstvo, 1950.

Krutitskii, A. M. *Obmena shliap, ili Blagorazumiem unichtozhennoe pokushenie.* St. Petersburg: Vol'naia tipografiia u Shnora, 1782.

Krylov, I. A. *Amerikantsy. Opera komicheskaia v dvukh deistviiakh.* St. Petersburg: Gubernskoe pravlenie, 1800.

————. *Beshenaia sem'ia. Komicheskaia opera v trekh deistviiakh.* In *Rossiiskii featr.* 39:1–74.

————. *Filomela. Tragediia.* In *Rossiiskii featr.* 39:197–286.

————. *Pochta dukhov, ili Uchenaia nravstvennaia i kriticheskaia perepiska arabskogo filosofa Malikul'mul'ka s vodianymi, vozdushnymi, i podzemnymi dukhami.* St. Petersburg: n.p., 1789.

———. *Podshchipa. Shuto-tragediia v dvukh deistviiakh v stikhakh.* In *Sochineniia v dvukh tomakh.* 2 vols. Moscow: Izdatel'stvo Pravda, 1956.

———. *Polnoe sobranie dramaticheskikh sochinenii.* Edited by L. N. Kiseleva. St. Petersburg: Giperion, 2001.

———. "Primechanie na komediiu *Smekh i gore." Sankt-Peterburgskii merkurii,* ch. 1 (1793): 104–30.

———. *Prokazniki. Komediia.* In *Rossiiskii featr.* 40:153–329.

———. *Sochineniia v dvukh tomakh.* 2 vols. Moscow: Izdatel'stvo Pravda, 1956.

———. *Sochinitel' v prikhozhei. Komediia v trekh deistviiakh.* In *Rossiiskii featr.* 41:149–228.

———. "Teatr." *Sankt-Petersburgskii merkurii,* ch.2 (1793): 213–22.

Kugushev, N. M. *Liubovnaia shutka. Original'naia komediia v odnom deistvii.* Smolensk: Gubernskaia tipografiia, 1800.

Kukushkina, E. D. "Komediografiia V. A. Levshina." *XVIII vek* 19 (1995): 86–101.

Kulakova, L. I. "Problema kharaktera v russkoi komedii XVIII veka (K voprosu o genezise russkogo realizma)." In *Problemy zhanra v istorii russkoi literatury,* edited by N. N. Skatov. Leningrad: Gosudarstvennyi pedagogicheskii institut im. A. I. Gertsena, 1969.

Kulikova, K. *Rossiiskogo teatra pervye aktery.* Leningrad: Lenizdat, 1991.

Kuzmichevskii, P. "Stareishiia russkiia dramaticheskiia stseny." *Kievskaia starina* 13, no. 11 (November 1885): 371–407.

Labriolle, François de. "L'opéra-comique russe et le drame en France, 1765–1794." *Cahiers du Monde russe et soviétique* 6 (1965): 399–411.

Landes, Joan B. *Women and the Public Sphere in the Age of the French Revolution.* Ithaca, N.Y.: Cornell University Press, 1988.

Lappo-Danilevskii, K. Iu. "Komicheskaia opera N. A. L'vova 'Iamshchiki na podstave'." *XVIII vek* 18 (1993): 93–112.

———, ed. *Izbrannye sochineniia.* Reprint, St. Petersburg: Akropol', 1994.

Laskina, M. N. "Neopublikovannye dokumenty iz arkhiva direktsii imperatorskikh teatrov, kasaiushchiesia sem'i akterov Mochalovykh." *Pamiatniki kul'tury: Novye otkrytiia 1987.* Moscow: Nauka, 1988.

La Vopa, Anthony J. "Conceiving a Public: Ideas and Society in Eighteenth-Century Europe." *Journal of Modern History* 64 (1992): 79–116.

Layton, Susan. "Aleksandr Polezhaev and Remembrance of War in the Caucasus: Constructions of the Soldier as Victim." *Slavic Review* 58 (1999): 559–83.

Lazarchuk, R. M. "Iz istorii provintsial'nogo teatra (teatral'naia zhizn' Vologdy 1780-kh gg.)." *XVIII vek* 15 (1986): 52–69.

———. "Iz istorii provintsial'nogo teatra (Vologodskii publichnyi teatr kontsa XVIII–nachala XIX v.)." *XVIII vek* 18 (1993): 156–71.

Leach, Robert, and Victor Borovsky, eds. *A History of Russian Theatre.* Cambridge, Eng.: Cambridge University Press, 1999.

Lebedeva, O. B. *Russkaia vysokaia komediia XVIII veka: Genezis i poetika zhanra.* Tomsk: Izdatel'stvo tomskogo universiteta, 1996.

LeDonne, John P. *Absolutism and Ruling Class: The Formation of the Russian Political Order, 1700–1825.* New York: Oxford University Press, 1991.

———. *Ruling Russia: Politics and Administration in the Age of Absolutism, 1762–1796.* Princeton: Princeton University Press, 1984.

Lehmann, Harmut, and Melvin Richter, eds. *The Meaning of Historical Terms and Concepts: New Studies on Begriffsgeschichte.* Washington, D.C.: German Historical Institute, 1996.

Lepskaia, L. *Repertuar krepostnogo teatra Sheremetevykh. Katalog p'es.* Moscow: GTsTM im. A. A. Bakhrushina, 1996.

Lerner, Gerda. *The Creation of Feminist Consciousness from the Middle Ages to 1870.* New York: Oxford University Press, 1993.

Lessing, Gotthold. *Two Plays: Sara. Minna Von Barnhelm.* Translated by Ernest Bell and Anthony Meech. Bath, Eng.: Absolute Classics, 1990.

Levi, Peter. "Greek Drama." In *The Oxford History of Greece and the Hellenistic World,* edited by John Boardman, Jasper Griffin, and Oswyn Murray. New York: Oxford University Press, 1991.

Levin, Iu. D., ed. *Istoriia russkoi perevodnoi khudozhestvennoi literatury. Drevniaia Rus'. XVIII vek.* 2 vols. St. Petersburg: Dmitrii Bulanin, 1995–1996.

Levitt, Marcus C. "Drama Sumarokova 'Pustynnik'. K voprosu o zhanrovykh i ideinykh istochnikakh russkogo klassitsizma." *XVIII vek* 18 (1993): 59–74.

———. "The Illegal Staging of Sumarokov's *Sinav i Truvor* in 1770 and the Problem of Authorial Status in Eighteenth-Century Russia." *Slavic and East European Journal* 43 (1999): 299–323.

———. "Sumarokov's Russianized 'Hamlet': Texts and Contexts." *Slavic and East European Journal* 38 (1994): 319–41.

Levshin, Vasil'i A. [Vsl. Lvshn.] *Garstlei i Florinichi. Meshchanskaia tragediia.* Moscow: Universitetskaia tipografiia u N. Novikova, 1787.

———. *Korol' na okhote. Opera komicheskaia v trekh deistviiakh.* In *Rossiiskii featr.* 42:1–108.

———. *Kto staroe pomianet, tomu glaz von. Komediia liricheskaia v trekh deistviiakh.* Moscow: Tipografiia pri teatre u Khr. Klaudiia, 1791.

——— [V. L.]. *Milozor i Prelesta. Opera komicheskaia.* Moscow: Universitetskaia tipografiia u N. Novikova, 1787.

———. *Mnimye vdovtsy. Opera komicheskaia. V trekh deistviiakh.* In *Rossiiskii featr.* 43:5–104.

———. *Molodye poskoree starykh mogut obmanut'. Komediia liricheskaia v odnom deistvii.* In *Trudy Vasiliia Levshina,* 1:3–34. Moscow: Universitetskaia tipografiia, 1796.

———. *Svad'ba g. Voldyreva. Opera komicheskaia v odnom deistvii.* In *Rossiiskii featr.* 42:109–56.

———. *Torzhestvo liubvi. Dramma. V trekh deistviiakh.* Moscow: Universitetskaia tipografiia u N. Novikova, 1787.

———. *Traian i Lida. Tragediia v piati deistviiakh.* In *Rossiiskii featr.* 7:175–240.

———. *Trudy Vasiliia Levshina.* 2 vols. Moscow: Universitetskaia tipografiia, 1796.

———. *Trudy Vasiliia Levshina i Ivana Fr. Kertseliia na 1793 god.* Kaluga: n.p., 1793.

Lewin, Paulina. "Early Ukrainian Theater and Drama." *Nationalities Papers* 8 (1980): 219–32.

———. "The Staging of Plays at the Kiev Mohyla Academy in the Seventeenth and Eighteenth Centuries." *Harvard Ukrainian Studies* 5 (1981): 320–34.

———. "The Ukrainian Popular Religious Stage of the Seventeenth and Eighteenth Centuries on the Territory of the Polish Commonwealth." *Harvard Ukrainian Studies* 1 (1977): 308–29.

Lilla, Marc. *The Reckless Mind: Intellectuals in Politics.* New York: The New York Review of Books, 2001.

Lincoln, W. Bruce. *Between Heaven and Hell: The Story of a Thousand Years of Artistic Life in Russia*. New York: Viking, 1998.

Lindenmeyr, Adele. *Poverty Is Not a Vice: Charity, Society, and the State in Imperial Russia*. Princeton: Princeton University Press, 1996.

Liubov' i opasnost', ili Magomet. Komediia v dvukh deistviiakh. In *Rossiiskii featr.* 38:129–76.

Liubovnik koldun. Opera komicheskaia v odnom deistvii. In *Rossiiskii featr.* 18:214–65.

Livanova, T. N. *Russkaia muzykal'naia kul'tura v ee sviaziakh s literaturoi, teatrom, i bytom: Issledovaniia i materialy.* 2 vols. Moscow: Gosudarstvennoe muzykal'noe izdatel'stvo, 1952–1953.

Locke, John. *Some Thoughts Concerning Education, and Of the Conduct of the Understanding.* Edited by Ruth W. Grant and Nathan Tarcov. Indianapolis: Hackett Publishing Company, 1996.

Lojkine, A. J. "A Note on the Place of the Comic Opera of the Eighteenth Century in Russian Literature." In *Essays to Honour Nina Christesen*, edited by Judith Armstrong and Rae Slonek. Kew, Victoria-Balmain: Australia International Press and Publications, 1977.

Lomonosov, M. V. *Demofont. Tragediia.* In *Rossiiskii featr.* 1:83–158.

———. *Tamira i Selim. Tragediia.* In *Russkaia literatura. Vek XVIII. Tragediia*, edited by Iu. V. Stennik. Moscow: Khudozhestvennaia literatura, 1991.

Longinov, M. N. *Russkii teatr v Peterburge i Moskve (1749–1774).* St. Petersburg, 1873.

Lopukhin, I. V. *Masonskie trudy: Dukhovnyi rytsar'. Nekotorye cherty o vnutrennei tserkvi.* Moscow: Alteina, 1997.

———. *Torzhestvo pravosudiia i dobrodeteli, ili Dobroi sud'ia. Dramma v piati deistviiakh.* Moscow: Vol'naia tipografiia Ponomareva, 1794.

Lotareva, D. D. "Masonstvo v sisteme russkoi kul'tury vtoroi poloviny XVIII–pervoi chetverti XIX v. (Problemy kontekstnogo izucheniia istochnika)." *Vestnik moskovskogo universiteta*, seriia 8, *Istoriia*, no. 6 (November–December 1995): 37–47.

Lotman, Iu. M. *Besedy o russkoi kul'ture: Byt i traditsii russkogo dvorianstva (XVIII–nachalo XIX veka).* St. Petersburg: Iskusstvo-SPB, 1994.

———. *Izbrannye stat'i.* 3 vols. Tallinn: Aleksandra, 1992–1993.

———. "The Theater and Theatricality as Components of Early Nineteenth-Century Culture." In *The Semiotics of Russian Culture*, by Iu. M. Lotman and B. A. Uspenskii, edited by Ann Shukman. Ann Arbor: University of Michigan, 1984.

Lukin, V. I. *Mot liubov'iu ispravlennoi. Komediia v piati deistviiakh.* In *Rossiiskii featr.* 19:5–154.

———. *Nagrazhdennoe postoianstvo. Komediia v piati deistviiakh.* In *Rossiiskii featr.* 36:5–146.

———. *Sochineniia i perevody Vladimera Lukina.* 3 vols. St. Petersburg: n.p., 1765.

Luppov, S. P. *Kniga v Rossii v poslepetrovskoe vremia, 1725–1740.* Leningrad: Nauka, 1976.

L'vov, N. A. *Iamshchiki na podstave. Igrishche nevznachai.* In *Izbrannye sochineniia*, edited by K. Iu. Lappo-Danilevskii. Reprint, St. Petersburg: Akropol', 1994.

———. *Izbrannye sochineniia.* Edited by K. Iu. Lappo-Danilevskii. Reprint, St. Petersburg: Akropol', 1994.

———. *Milet i Mileta. Pastush'ia shutka dlia dvukh lits i v odnom deistvii s pesniami.* In *Izbrannye sochineniia*, edited by K. Iu. Lappo-Danilevskii. Reprint, St. Petersburg: Akropol', 1994.

———. *Sil'f, ili Mechta molodoi zhenshchiny. Komediia s pesniami v dvukh deistviiakh.* In *Izbrannye sochinenniia,* edited by K. Iu. Lappo-Danilevskii. Reprint, St. Petersburg: Akropol', 1994.

M., N. *Mshchenie za nevernost'. Komediia v odnom desitvii.* Moscow: Universitetskaia tipografiia u N. Novikova, 1781.

Madariaga, Isabel de. *Politics and Culture in Eighteenth-Century Russia: Collected Essays.* New York: Addison Wesley Longman, 1998.

Mah, Harold. "Phantasies of the Public Sphere: Rethinking the Habermas of Historians." *Journal of Modern History* 72 (2000): 153–82.

Maier, Charles S. "Consigning the Twentieth Century to History: Alternative Narratives for the Modern Era." *American Historical Review* 105 (2000): 807–31.

Maikov, A. A. *Neudachnoi zgovor, ili Pomolvil da ne zhenilsia. Komediia v odnom deistvii.* St. Petersburg: Tipografiia korpusa chuzhestrannykh edinovertsov, 1794.

Maikov, Vasilii I. *Agriopa. Tragediia.* In *Rossiiskii featr.* 5:5–74.

———. *Derevenskii prazdnik, ili Uvenchannaia dobrodetel'. Pastusheskaia drama s muzykoiu v dvukh deistviiakh.* In *Rossiiskii featr.* 18:135–72.

———. *Femist i Ieronima. Tragediia.* In *Russkaia literatura. Vek XVIII. Tragediia,* edited by Iu. V. Stennik. Moscow: Khudozhestvennaia literatura, 1991.

———. *Pigmalion, ili Sila liubvi. Drama s muzykoiu v odnom deistvii.* In *Rossiiskii featr.* 18:173–214.

———. *Sochineniia i perevody V. I. Maikova.* Edited by L. N. Maikov. St. Petersburg: I. I. Glazunov, 1867.

Makogonenko, G. P., ed. *Pis'ma russkikh pisatelei XVIII veka.* Leningrad: Nauka, 1980.

Malia, Martin. *Russia Under Western Eyes: From the Bronze Horseman to the Lenin Mausoleum.* Cambridge, Mass.: Harvard University Press, 1999.

Malinin, D. *Nachalo teatra v Kaluge. K istorii kaluzhskogo teatra v XVIII veke.* Kaluga: Gubernskaia tipo-litografiia, 1912.

Mally, Lynn. *Revolutionary Acts: Amateur Theater and the Soviet State, 1917–1938.* Ithaca, N.Y.: Cornell University Press, 2000.

Malnick, Bertha. "A. A. Shakhovskoy." *Slavonic and East European Review* 32 (1953): 29–51.

———. "The Origin and Early History of the Theatre in Russia." *Slavonic and East European Review* 19 (1940): 203–27.

———. "Russian Serf Theatres." *Slavonic and East European Review* 30 (1952): 393–411.

———. "The Theory and Practice of Russian Drama in the Early Nineteenth Century." *Slavonic and East European Review* 34 (1955): 10–33.

Mal'tseva, T. V., ed. *Prazdnik v russkoi kul'ture, fol'klore, i literature. Sbornik statei Pushkinskikh chtenii-97.* St. Petersburg: Leningradskii gosudarstvennyi oblastnoi universitet, 1998.

Manchester, Laurie. "The Secularization of the Search for Salvation: The Self-Fashioning of Orthodox Clergymen's Sons in Late Imperial Russia." *Slavic Review* 57 (1998): 50–76.

Mandel, Oscar. *A Definition of Tragedy.* New York: New York University Press, 1961.

Marasanova, V. M. "Teatral'noe delo v Iaroslavskoi gubernii v kontse XIX–nachale XX vv." *Iaroslavskii arkhiv: Istoriko-kraevedcheskii sbornik.* Moscow and St. Petersburg: Atheneum-Feniks, 1996.

Marasinova, E. N. "Obraz imperatora v soznanii elity rossiiskogo dvorianstva poslednei treti XVIII veka (po materialam epistoliarnykh istochnikov)." In *Tsar' i tsarstvo v russkom obshchestvennom soznanii,* edited by A. A. Gorskii. Moscow: Institut rossiiskoi istorii RAN, 1999.

———. *Psikhologiia elity rossiiskogo dvorianstva poslednei treti XVIII veka (Po materialam perepiski).* Moscow: ROSSPEN, 1999.

———. "Votchinik ili pomeshchik? (Epistoliarnye istochniki o sotsial'noi psikhologii rossiiskogo feodala vtoroi poloviny XVIII veka)." In *Mentalitet i agrarnoe razvitie Rossii (XIX–XX vv.),* edited by V. P. Danilov and L. V. Milov. Moscow: ROSSPEN, 1996.

Marker, Gary. "The Creation of Journals and the Profession of Letters in the Eighteenth Century." In *Literary Journals in Imperial Russia,* edited by Deborah A. Martinsen. New York: Cambridge University Press, 1997.

———. "The Enlightenment of Anna Labzina: Gender, Faith, and Public Life in Alexandrian Russia." *Slavic Review* 59 (2000): 369–90.

———. *Publishing, Printing, and the Origins of Intellectual Life in Russia, 1700–1800.* Princeton: Princeton University Press, 1985.

Marrese, Michelle Lamarche. *A Woman's Kingdom: Noblewomen and the Control of Property in Russia, 1700–1861.* Ithaca, N.Y.: Cornell University Press, 2002.

Martin, Alexander M. "The Family Model of Society and Russian National Identity in Sergei N. Glinka's *Russian Messenger* (1808–1812)." *Slavic Review* 57 (1998): 28–49.

———. *Romantics, Reformers, Reactionaries: Russian Conservative Thought and Politics in the Reign of Alexander I.* DeKalb: Northern Illinois University Press, 1997.

Martin, John. "Inventing Sincerity, Refashioning Prudence: The Discovery of the Individual in Renaissance Europe." *American Historical Review* 102 (1997): 1309–42.

Martinsen, Deborah A., ed. *Literary Journals in Imperial Russia.* Cambridge, Eng.: Cambridge University Press, 1997.

Masanov, I. F. *Slovar' psevdonimov russkikh pisatelei, uchenykh i obshchestvennykh deiatelei.* 4 vols. Moscow: Izdatel'stvo vsesoiuznoi knizhnoi palaty, 1956–1960.

Materialy k istorii teatral'noi kul'tury Rossii XVII–XX vv. Annotirovannyi katalog. Vypusk 3, *Personaliia.* 2 vols. St. Petersburg: Rossiiskaia natsional'naia biblioteka, 1992.

Matinskii, M. A. *Opera komicheskaia. Sanktpeterburgskii gostinoi dvor v trekh deistviiakh.* Moscow: Vol'naia tipografiia A. Reshetnikova, 1791.

———. *Tak pozhivesh', tak i proslyvesh'. Zabavnoe zrelishche s pesniami v trekh deistviiakh.* St. Petersburg: Tipografiia F. Breitkopfa, 1792.

Matrosskiia shutki. Opera komicheskaia. In *Rossiiskii featr.* 24:137–94.

Matveev, Filiter. *Drama. Dobrodetel'naia prestupnitsa, ili Prestupnik ot liubvi, v trekh deistviiakh.* Moscow: Vol'naia tipografiia A. Reshetnikova, 1792.

Maza, Sarah. "Luxury, Morality, and Social Change: Why There Was No Middle-Class Consciousness in Prerevolutionary France." *Journal of Modern History* 69 (1997): 199–229.

———. *Private Lives and Public Affairs: The Causes Célèbres of Prerevolutionary France.* Berkeley: University of California Press, 1993.

———. "Stories in History: Cultural Narratives in Recent Works in European History." *American Historical Review* 101 (1996): 1493–1515.

McCaffray, Susan P. "What Should Russia Be? Patriotism and Political Economy in the Thought of N. S. Mordvinov." *Slavic Review* 59 (2000): 572–96.

McKinnon, Abby A. "Duels and the Matter of Honor." In *Russia and the World of the Eighteenth Century,* edited by R. P. Bartlett, A. G. Cross, and Karen Rasmussen. Columbus, Ohio: Slavica Publishers, 1988.

McReynolds, Louise, and Joan Neuberger, eds. *Imitations of Life: Two Centuries of Melodrama in Russia*. Durham, N.C.: Duke University Press, 2002.

Mel'nikova, S. I. "Das Deutsche Theater in Sankt Petersburg am Anfang des 19. Jahrhunderts." *Jahrbücher für Geschichte Osteuropas* 44 (1996): 523–36.

———. "K istorii Nemetskogo teatra v Rossii." *Istoricheskii arkhiv*, no. 1 (1998): 159–65.

Melton, Edgar. "Enlightened Seigniorialism and Its Dilemmas in Serf Russia, 1750–1830." *Journal of Modern History* 62 (1990): 675–708.

———. "Household Economies and Communal Conflicts on a Russian Serf Estate." *Journal of Social History* 26 (1993): 559–85.

Melton, James Van Horn. "The Emergence of 'Society' in Eighteenth- and Nineteenth-century Germany." In *Language, History, and Class*, edited by Penelope J. Corfield. Oxford: Basil Blackwell, 1991.

———. "From Image to Word: Cultural Reform and the Rise of Literate Culture in Eighteenth-Century Austria." *Journal of Modern History* 58 (1986): 95–124.

———. *The Rise of the Public in Enlightenment Europe*. Cambridge, Eng.: Cambridge University Press, 2001.

———. "School, Stage, Salon: Musical Cultures in Haydn's Vienna." Unpublished paper, Department of History, Emory University, 2001.

Menut, Albert D. "Russian Courtesy Literature in the Eighteenth Century." *Symposium* 111 (1949): 78–90.

Merrick, Jeffrey. *The Desacralization of the French Monarchy in the Eighteenth Century.* Baton Rouge: Louisiana State University Press, 1990.

Mikhailov, Ivan. *Komediia Odno na drugoe pokhozhe, v chetyrekh deistviiakh*. Moscow: Tipografiia pri teatre u Khr. Klaudiia, 1788.

———. *Opera, Liubov' oprovergaet soiuz druzhestva, v piati deistviiakh*. In *Rossiiskii featr.* 28:67–144.

Mikhailov, Oleg. *Suvorov.* Moscow: Molodaia Gvardiia, 1980.

Miliukov, P. N. *Ocherki po istorii russkoi kul'tury.* 3 vols. 1937, 1964. Reprint, Moscow: Progress-Kul'tura, 1993–1995.

Mironov, B. N. "Gramotnost' v Rossii v 1797–1917 godov: Poluchenie novoi istoricheskoi informatsii s pomoshch'iu metodov retrospektivnogo prognozirovaniia." *Istoriia SSSR,* no. 4 (1985): 137–53.

———. *Sotsial'naia istoriia Rossii perioda imperii (XVIII–nachalo XX v.): Genezis lichnosti, demokraticheskoi sem'i, grazhdanskogo obshchestva, i pravovogo gosudarstva.* 2 vols. St. Petersburg: Dmitrii Bulanin, 1999.

Molebnov, M. P. *Penzenskii krepostnoi teatr Gladkovykh.* Penza: Penzenskoe knizhnoe izdatel'stvo, 1955.

Mordison, G. Z. *Istoriia teatral'nogo dela v Rossii: Osnovanie i razvitie gosudarstvennogo teatra v Rossii (XVI–XVIII veka).* 2 vols. St. Petersburg: Sankt-Peterburgskaia gosudarstvennaia akademiia teatral'nogo iskusstva, 1994.

Morozov, P. O. *Istoriia russkogo teatra.* Vol. 1, *Do poloviny XVIII stoletiia.* St. Petersburg: Tipografiia V. Demakova, 1889.

Morozov, P. "Russkii teatr pri Petre Velikom." *Ezhegodnik imperatorskikh teatrov,* god 4, sezon 1893–1894, *Prilozheniia,* kn. 1 (1894): 52–80.

Morris, Marcia. "Feofan Prokopovich's *Vladimir* as a Vehicle for the Comic View of History in Early East Slavonic Drama." *Australian Slavic and East European Studies* 10 (1996): 1–15.

Muller, Alexander V., trans. and ed. *The Spiritual Regulation of Peter the Great.* Seattle: University of Washington Press, 1972.

Muller, Jerry Z. *Adam Smith in His Time and Ours: Designing the Decent Society.* New York: The Free Press, 1993.

Munro, George E. "Food in Catherinian St. Petersburg." In *Food in Russian History and Culture,* edited by Musya Glants and Joyce Toomre. Bloomington: Indiana University Press, 1997.

Narezhnyi, V. T. *Krovavaia noch', ili Konechnoe padenie domu Kadmova.* In *Stikhotvornaia tragediia kontsa XVIII–nachala XIX v.,* edited by V. A. Bochkarev. Moscow and Leningrad: Sovetskii pisatel', 1964.

Narodnoe igrishche. Komediia v odnom deistvii. In *Satiricheskie zhurnaly N. I. Novikova,* edited by P. N. Berkov. Moscow and Leningrad: Akademiia nauk SSSR, 1951.

Neblagodarnoi. Komediia v piati deistviiakh. Moscow: Universitetskaia tipografiia u N. Novikova, 1788.

Nekhachin, Ivan V. *Neudachlivoi v liubvi pod'iachii. Komicheskaia opera v dvukh deistviiakh.* Moscow: Tipografiia A. Reshetnikova, 1795.

———. *Pobeg ot dolgov, ili Raskaiavshiisia mot. Komediia v odnom deistvii.* Moscow: Tipografiia A. Reshetnikova, 1792.

Nekrylova, A. F. *Russkie narodnye gorodskie prazdniki, uveseleniia, i zrelishcha, konets XVIII–nachalo XX veka.* Leningrad: Iskusstvo, 1988.

Nemes, Robert. "The Politics of the Dance Floor: Culture and Civil Society in Nineteenth-Century Hungary." *Slavic Review* 60 (2001): 802–23.

Netting, Anthony G. "Russian Liberalism: The Years of Promise." Ph.D. diss., Columbia University, 1967.

Nevernost' zhenskaia. Komediia v odnom deistvii. Moscow: Universitetskaia tipografiia u N. Novikova, 1788.

Nevesta pod fatoiu, ili Meshchanskaia svad'ba. Komicheskaia opera, bez nabliudeniia teatral'nykh i stikhotvorcheskikh pravil. Moscow: Universitetskaia tipografiia u V. Okorokova, 1790.

Newlin, Thomas. "Rural Ruses: Illusion and Anxiety on the Russian Estate." *Slavic Review* 57 (1998): 295–319.

Nikolev, Nikolai P. *Finiks. Drama s golosami v trekh deistviiakh. 1779.* In *Rossiiskii featr.* 22:137–218.

———. *Ispytannoe postoianstvo. Komediia v odnom deistvii.* In *Rossiiskii featr.* 23:3–68.

———. *Opekunprofessor, ili Liubov' khitree krasnorechiia. Shutlivaia opera.* In *Rossiiskii featr.* 24:3–62.

———. *Pal'mira. Tragediia.* In *Rossiiskii featr.* 5:147–234.

———. *Popytka ne shutka, ili Udachnyi opyt. Komediia v trekh deistviiakh.* Imperatorskii moskovskii universitet, 1774; in *Rossiiskii featr.* 35:105–82.

———. *Prikashchik. Drammaticheskaia pustel'ga s golosami, v odnom deistvii.* Moscow: Universitetskaia tipografiia u N. Novikova, 1781.

———. *Rozana i Liubim. Dramma s golosami v chetyrekh deistviiakh. Sochinena v Moskve.* Moscow: Universitetskaia tipografiia u N. Novikova, 1781.

———. *Samoliubivyi stikhotvorets. Komediia v piati deistviiakh.* In *Rossiiskii featr.* 15:3–148.

———. *Tochil'shchik. Opera v dvukh deistviiakh.* In *Rossiiskii featr.* 22:219–68.

Novikov, N. I. *Satiricheskie zhurnaly N. I. Novikova.* Edited by P. N. Berkov. Moscow and Leningrad: Akademiia nauk SSSR, 1951.

Obman na obman, ili Neudachnyi razvod. Komediia v trekh deistviiakh. Universitetskaia tipografiia u V. Okorokova, 1790; in *Rossiiskii featr.* 38:177–240.

O'Malley, Lurana Donnels. "Catherine the Great's Operatic Splendor at Court: *The Beginning of Oleg's Reign.*" *Essays in Theatre* 17 (1998): 33–51.

———. "Catherine the Great's *Woeful Knight:* A Slanted Parody." *Theatre History Studies* 21 (2001): 11–26.

———. "Fools in the Mirror in Catherine the Great's Imianiny Gospozhi Vorchalkinoi." *Canadian-American Slavic Studies* 34 (2000): 409–26.

———. "From Fat Falstaff to Francophile Fop: Russian Nationalism in Catherine The Great's *Merry Wives.*" *Comparative Drama* 33 (1999): 365–89.

———. "'How Great Was Catherine?': Checkpoints at the Border of Russian Theatre." *Slavic and East European Journal* 43 (1999): 33–48.

———. "Masks of the Empress: Polyphony of Personae in Catherine the Great's *Oh, These Times!*" *Comparative Drama* 31 (1997): 65–85.

———. "The Monarch and the Mystic: Catherine the Great's Strategy of Audience Enlightenment in *The Siberian Shaman.*" *Slavic and East European Journal* 41 (1997): 224–42.

Opasnaia shutka. Komicheskaia opera v odnom deistvii (incomplete). In *Rossiiskii featr.* 39:75–112.

Opera Pererozhdenie. Igrannaia na Moskovskom Rossiiskom teatre. In *Rossiiskii featr.* 28:39–66.

Opyt druzhby. Drama v chetyrekh deistviiakh. Predstavlena v Voronezhe na blagorodnom teatre 1798 goda. Voronezh: Tipografiia gubernskogo pravleniia, 1799.

Orlov, V. N., ed. *Dekabristy. Poeziia, dramaturgiia, proza, publitsistika, literaturnaia kritika.* Moscow and Leningrad: Gosduarstvennoe izdatel'stvo khudozhestvennoi literatury, 1951.

Otgadai i ne skazhu. Komediia v odnom deistvii. 1772. In *Rossiiskii featr.* 21:5–56.

The Oxford Illustrated History of Theatre. Edited by John Russell Brown. New York: Oxford University Press, 1995.

Ozerov, V. A. *Iaropolk i Oleg. Tragediia v piati deistviiakh, v stikhakh.* In *Tragediia. Stikhotvoreniia,* edited by I. N. Medvedeva. Leningrad: Sovetskii pisatel', 1960.

Ozment, Steven. *When Fathers Ruled: Family Life in Reformation Europe.* Cambridge, Mass.: Harvard University Press, 1983.

Pankratova, E. A. *Russkaia zhivopis' i teatr: Ocherki.* St. Petersburg: Izdatel'stvo SPbGTU, 1997.

Papmehl, K. A. *Freedom of Expression in Eighteenth-Century Russia.* The Hague: Martinus Nijhoff, 1971.

Pargment, Lila. "Serf Theatres and Serf Actors." *AATSEEL Journal* 14 (1956): 71–78.

Parpura, Maksim. *Neshchastie ot Ochakova, ili Torzhestvuiushchee kovarstvo v Tsar'grade. Teatral'noe zrelishche.* St. Petersburg: n.p., 1789.

Patouillet, J. *Le Théatre de Mouers russes des origines à Ostrovski (1672–1850).* Paris: Libraire ancienne Honoré Champion, 1912.

Pavis, Patrice. *Dictionary of the Theatre: Terms, Concepts, and Analysis.* Translated by Christine Shantz. Toronto: University of Toronto Press, 1998.

Pavlov, V. *Tri sunduka, ili Khitrost' zhenshchiny. Komediia v trekh deistviiakh.* In *Rossiiskii featr.* 38:241–358.

Payne, Harry C. *The Philosophes and the People.* New Haven: Yale University Press, 1976.

Pekarskii, P. *Misterii i starinnyi teatr v Rossii.* St. Petersburg: Tipografiia glavnogo shtaba Ego Imperatorskogo Velichestva po voenno-uchebnym zavedeniiam, 1857.

Peremena v nravakh. Komediia v dvukh deistviiakh. In *Rossiiskii featr.* 38:37–128.

Peretts, V. N., ed. *Italianskiia komedii i intermedii predstavlennyia pri dvore imperatritsy Anny Ioannovny v 1733–1735 gg. Teksty.* Petrograd: n.p., 1917.

———. *Pamiatniki russkoi dramy epokhi Petra Velikogo.* St. Petersburg: Imperatorskaia akademiia nauk, 1903.

———. *Starinnyi teatr v Rossii XVII–XVIII vv.* St. Petersburg: Academia, 1923.

Perkins, Etta L. "Noble Patronage, 1740s–1850." *Canadian-American Slavic Studies* 23 (1989): 429–42.

Petrovskaia, I. F. *Istochnikovedenie istorii russkogo dorevoliutsionnogo dramaticheskogo teatra.* Leningrad: Iskusstvo, 1971.

———. "K istorii opernogo teatra v Peterburge v 1801–1840 gg." *Pamiatniki kul'tury: Novye otkrytiia 1997.* Moscow: Nauka, 1998.

———, ed. *Materialy k istorii russkogo teatra v gosudarstvennykh arkhivakh SSSR. Obzory dokumentov, XVII vek–1917 g.* Moscow: Leningradskii gosudarstvennyi institut teatra muzyki i kinematografii, 1966.

Petrovskaia, I. F., and V. V. Somina. *Teatral'nyi Peterburg nachalo XVIII veka–oktiabr' 1917 goda. Obozrenie-putevoditel'.* St. Petersburg: Rossiiskii institut istorii iskusstv, 1994.

Pis'mo, ili Bogataia nevesta. Komediia v dvukh deistviiakh. In *Rossiiskii featr.* 33:295–339.

Plato. *Great Dialogues of Plato.* Translated by W. H. D. Rouse and edited by Eric H. Warmington and Philip G. Rouse. New York: New American Library, 1956.

Plavil'shchikov, P. A. *Bobyl'. Komediia v piati deistviiakh.* In *Russkaia komediia i komicheskaia opera XVIII veka,* edited by P. N. Berkov. Moscow and Leningrad: Iskusstvo, 1950.

———. *Druzhestvo. Tragediia v piati deistviiakh.* In *Rossiiskii featr.* 7:75–174.

———. *Riurik.* In *Russkaia literatura. Vek XVIII. Tragediia,* edited by Iu. V. Stennik. Moscow: Khudozhestvennaia literatura, 1991.

———. *Sgovor Kuteikina. Komediia v odnom deistvii.* 2d ed. St. Petersburg: V. Plavil'shchikov, 1821.

Pobeda nevinnosti, ili Liubov' khitree ostorozhnosti. Komedii v odnom deistvii. In *Rossiiskii featr.* 25:5–82.

Podrazhatel'. Komediia v odnom deistvii. Sochinena v Dmitrove. Moscow: Tipografiia imperatorskogo moskovskogo universiteta, 1779.

Polnoe sobranie vsekh sochinenii v stikhakh i proze. A. P. Sumarokov. 6 vols. Moscow: Universitetskaia tipografiia u N. Novikova, 1781.

Polnoe sobranie zakonov Rossiiskoi imperii. 1st series, 1649–1825. 46 vols. St. Petersburg: Tipografiia 2. otdeleniia sobstvennoi E. I. V. kantseliarii, 1830–1845.

Pomar, Mark G. "The Roots of Russian Historical Drama: School Drama and Ceremonial Spectacles." *Russian Language Journal* 35 (1981): 113–24.

Popov, I. P., E. S. Stepanova, E. G. Tarabrin, and Iu. V. Fulin. *Dva veka riazanskoi istorii (XVIII v.–mart 1917 g.).* Riazan: Riazanskoe otdelenie sovetskogo fonda kul'tury, 1991.

Popov, M. I. *Aniuta. Komicheskaia opera v odnom deistvii.* In *Rossiiskii featr.* 28:145–84.

Popov, N. "Materialy dlia istorii russkogo teatra. Vyezzhie komedianty pri Petre." *Bibliograficheskie zapiski,* no. 14 (1861): 415–17.

Porfir'eva, A. L., ed. *Muzykal'nyi Peterburg: Entsiklopedicheskii slovar', XVIII vek.* 3 vols. St. Petersburg: Izdatel'stvo Kompozitor, 1996–1999.

Porter, Roy. *The Enlightenment.* 2d ed. New York: Palgrave, 2001.

Potemkin, P. S. *Rossy v Arkhipelage. Drama.* In *Rossiiskii featr.* 8:33–96.

———. *Torzhestvo druzhby. Drama.* In *Rossiiskii featr.* 8:97–176.

———. *Zel'mira i Smelon, ili Vziatie Izmaila. Liricheskaia dramma.* St. Petersburg: Tipografiia korpusa chuzhestrannykh edinovertsov, 1795.

Pouncy, Carolyn Johnston, ed. and trans. *The Domostroi: Rules for Russian House-holds in the Time of Ivan the Terrible*. Ithaca, N.Y.: Cornell University Press, 1994.

Pritvornaia nevernost'. Komediia v odnom deistvii. Prelozhennaia na zdeshnie nravy vol'nym perevodom s sochineniia G. Barte. St. Petersburg: n.p., 1772.

Privalova, E. P. "A. T. Bolotov i teatr dlia detei." *XVIII vek* 3 (1958): 242–61.

Prokopovich, Feofan. *Vladimir. Tragedokomediia*. In *Sochineniia*, edited by I. P. Eremin. Moscow and Leningrad: Izdatel'stvo akademii nauk, 1961.

Prokudin-Gorskii, M. I. [Mikhail Prakudin]. *Dobrodetel' uvenchannaia vernost'iu. Komediia*. In *Rossiiskii featr*. 25:83–144.

———. *Sud'ba derevenskaia. Komediia sochinennaia v nravakh derevenskikh zhitelei v trekh deistviiakh*. In *Rossiiskii featr*. 29:93–132.

Pushkarev, L. N., ed. *Russkaia kul'tura poslednei treti XVIII veka—vremeni Ekateriny Vtoroi: Sbornik statei*. Moscow: Institut rossiiskoi istorii RAN, 1997.

Pushkareva, N. L. *Chastnaia zhizn' russkoi zhenshchiny: Nevesta, zhena, liubovnitsa (X–nachalo XIX v.)*. Moscow: Nauchno-izdatel'skii tsentr Ladomir, 1997.

Ptitselov. Pastush'ia opera v odnom deistvii. In *Rossiiskii featr*. 28:5–38.

Pypin, A. N. "V. I. Lukin." In *Sochineniia i perevody Vladimira Ignat'evicha Lukina i Bog-dana Egorovicha El'chaninova*. Edited by P. A. Efremov. St. Petersburg: Ivan Il'ich Glazunov, 1868.

Radice, Betty. *Who's Who in the Ancient World*. New York: Penguin Books, 1973.

Raeff, Marc. "Les Slaves, les Allemands, et les 'Lumières'" (1967). In *Politique et Culture en Russie, 18e–20e siècles*. Paris: École des Hautes Études en Sciences Sociales, 1996.

———. *Origins of the Russian Intelligentsia: The Eighteenth-Century Nobility*. New York: Harcourt, Brace, and World, 1966.

———. *Political Ideas and Institutions in Imperial Russia*. Boulder, Col.: Westview Press, 1994.

———. "Transfiguration and Modernization: The Paradoxes of Social Disciplining, Paedagogical Leadership, and the Enlightenment in Eighteenth-Century Russia." In *Alteuropa—Ancien Régime—Frühe Neuzeit: Probleme und Methoden der Forschung*, edited by Hans Erich Bödeker and Ernst Hinrichs. Stuttgart and Bad Cannstatt: Frommann-Holzboog, 1991.

———. "The Two Facets of the World of Ivan Pososhkov." *Forschungen zur osteuropäischen Geschichte* 50 (1995): 309–28.

———. *The Well-Ordered Police State: Social and Institutional Change through Law in the Germanies and Russia, 1600–1800*. New Haven: Yale University Press, 1983.

Ranniaia russkaia dramaturgiia (XVII–pervaia polovina XVIII v.). Pervye p'esy russkogo teatra. Moscow: Nauka, 1972.

Ranniaia russkaia dramaturgiia (XVII–pervaia polovina XVIII v.). P'esy liubitel'skikh teatrov. Moscow: Nauka, 1976.

Ranniaia russkaia dramaturgiia (XVII–pervaia polovina XVIII v.). P'esy shkol'nykh teatrov Moskvy. Moscow: Nauka, 1974.

Ranniaia russkaia dramaturgiia (XVII–pervaia polovina XVIII v.). P'esy stolichnykh i prov-intsial'nykh teatrov pervoi poloviny XVIII v. Moscow: Nauka, 1975.

Ranniaia russkaia dramaturgiia (XVII–pervaia polovina XVIII v.). Russkaia dramaturgiia poslednei chetverti XVII i nachala XVIII v. Moscow: Nauka, 1972.

Ransel, David L. "Character and Style of Patron-Client Relations in Russia." *Klientel-systeme im Europa der Frühen Neuzeit*, edited by Antoni Mączak. Munich: Oldenbourg, 1988.

Ravel, Jeffrey S. *The Contested Parterre: Public Theater and French Political Culture, 1680–1791.* Ithaca, N.Y.: Cornell University Press, 1999.

Razluka, ili Ot"ezd psovoi okhoty iz Kuskova. Komicheskaia opera, v dvukh deistviiakh s eia posledovaniem v odnom deistvii. Moscow: Vol'naia tipografiia Ponomareva, 1785.

Reddy, William M. "Sentimentalism and Its Erasure: The Role of Emotions in the Era of the French Revolution." *Journal of Modern History* 72 (2000): 109–52.

Reyfman, Irina. "The Emergence of the Duel in Russia: Corporal Punishment and the Honor Code." *Russian Review* 54 (1995): 26–43.

Riasanovsky, Nicholas V. *The Image of Peter the Great in Russian History and Thought.* New York: Oxford University Press, 1985.

———. *A Parting of Ways: Government and the Educated Public in Russia, 1801–1855.* Oxford: Clarendon Press, 1976.

Riber [Rieber], A. "Sotsial'naia identifikatsiia i politicheskaia volia: russkoe dvorianstvo ot Petra I do 1861 g." In *P. A. Zaionchkovskii (1904–1983 gg.): Stat'i, publikatsii, i vospominaniia o nem,* edited by L. G. Zakharova, Iu. S. Kukushkin, and T. Emmons. Moscow: ROSSPEN, 1998.

Riedel, Manfred. "Gesellschaft, bürgerliche." In *Geschichtliche Grundbegriffe: Historisches Lexikon zur politisch-sozialen Sprache in Deutschland,* edited by Otto Brunner, Werner Conze, and Reinhart Koselleck. 8 vols. Stuttgart: Ernst Klett, 1972–1997. 2:719–800.

Roche, Daniel. *France in the Enlightenment.* Translated by Arthur Goldhammer. Cambridge, Mass.: Harvard University Press, 1998.

———. *A History of Everyday Things: The Birth of Consumption in France, 1600–1800.* Translated by Brian Pearce. New York: Cambridge University Press, 2000.

Rogger, Hans. *National Consciousness in Eighteenth-Century Russia.* Cambridge, Mass.: Harvard University Press, 1960.

———. "Nationalism and the State: A Russian Dilemma." *Comparative Studies in Society and History* 4 (1961–1962): 253–64.

———. "The Skobelev Phenomenon: The Hero and His Worship." *Oxford Slavonic Papers* 9 (1976): 46–78.

Roosevelt, Priscilla. *Life on the Russian Country Estate: A Social and Cultural History.* New Haven: Yale University Press, 1995.

Rossiiskii featr, ili Polnoe sobranie vsekh Rossiiskikh teatral'nykh sochinenii. 43 vols. St. Petersburg: Imperatorskaia akademiia nauk, 1786–1794.

Rousseau, Jean-Jacques. *The Basic Political Writings.* Translated by Donald A. Cress. Indianapolis: Hackett Publishing Company, 1987.

———. *Politics and the Arts: Letter to M. D'Alembert on the Theatre.* Translated with notes and an introduction by Allan Bloom. 1960. Reprint, Ithaca, N.Y.: Cornell University Press, 1993.

Russian Primary Chronicle: Laurentian Text. Translated and edited by Samuel Hazzard Cross and Olgerd P. Sherbowitz-Wetzor. Cambridge, Mass.: The Medieval Academy of America, 1953.

"Russian Stage: From its Origin to the Reign of Catherine II, 1762." *Twentieth-Century Russia and Anglo-Russian Review* 1, no. 3 (April 1916): 169–79.

Russkie pisateli, 1800–1917: Biograficheskii slovar' (1800–1917). 4 vols. to date. Moscow: Nauchnoe izdatel'stvo Bol'shaia rossiiskaia entsiklopediia, 1992– .

Russkie pisateli XIX vek: Biograficheskii slovar'. Edited by P. A. Nikolaev. 2d ed. 2 vols. Moscow: Prosveshchenie, 1996.

Russkie sviatye: Tysiacha let russkoi sviatosti. Zhitiia sobrala monakhinia Taisiiia. St. Petersburg: Izdatel'stvo Azbuka, 2000.

Russkii biograficheskii slovar'. 25 vols. St. Petersburg: I. N. Skorokhodov, 1896–1918. Reprint, New York: Kraus Reprint Corporation, 1962–1991.

Ruud, Charles A. *Fighting Words: Imperial Censorship and the Russian Press, 1804–1906.* Toronto: University of Toronto Press, 1982.

Ryan, W. F. *The Bathhouse at Midnight: An Historical Survey of Magic and Divination in Russia.* University Park: Pennsylvania State University Press, 1999.

Rzhevskii, A. A. *Podlozhnyi Smerdii. Tragediia.* In *Russkaia literatura. Vek XVIII. Tragediia,* edited by Iu. V. Stennik. Moscow: Khudozhestvennaia literatura, 1991.

Sakmir. Tragediia v piati deistviiakh. Sochinena v Moskve. In *Rossiiskii featr.* 7:241–323.

Samarin, A. Iu. *Chitatel' v Rossii vo vtoroi polovine XVIII veka (po spiskam podpischikov).* Moscow: Izdatel'stvo MGUP, 2000.

Scharf, Claus. *Katharina II. Deutschland und die Deutschen.* Mainz: Verlag Philipp von Zabern, 1995.

Schiller, Friedrich. *Don Carlos and Mary Stuart.* Translated by Hilary Collier Sy-Quia. New York: Oxford University Press, 1996.

Schmemann, Serge. *Echoes of a Native Land: Two Centuries of a Russian Village.* New York: Alfred A. Knopf, 1997.

Schmidt, Christoph. "Aufstieg und Fall der Fortschrittsidee in Russland." *Historische Zeitschrift* 263 (1996): 1–30.

———. *Sozialkontrolle in Moskau: Justiz, Kriminalität, und Leibeigenschaft, 1649–1785.* Stuttgart: Franz Steiner Verlag, 1996.

Schönle, Andreas. "The Scare of the Self: Sentimentalism, Privacy, and Private Life in Russian Culture, 1780–1820." *Slavic Review* 57 (1998): 723–46.

Scott, James C. *Weapons of the Weak: Everyday Forms of Peasant Resistance.* New Haven: Yale University Press, 1985.

Scott, Joan W. "Deconstructing Equality-versus-Difference, or the Uses of Poststructuralist Theory for Feminism." *Feminist Studies* 14 (1988): 33–50.

Seaman, Gerald R. "Folk-song in Russian Opera of the Eighteenth Century." *Slavonic and East European Review* 41 (1962): 144–57.

———. "The National Element in Early Russian Opera, 1779–1800." *Music and Letters* 42 (1961): 252–62.

———. "Russian Folk-Song in the Eighteenth Century." *Music and Letters* 40 (1959): 253–60.

———. "Russian Opera before Glinka." In *Russia: Essays in History and Literature,* edited by Lyman H. Legters. Leiden: Brill Academic Pubishers, 1972.

Segal, Erich. "Introduction." In *Four Comedies,* by Plautus. Translated by Erich Segal. New York: Oxford University Press, 1998.

———. "Pay Attention, Folks." *The Times Literary Supplement,* no. 5017 (May 28, 1999): 4.

Seliavin, Nik. I. *Osmeiannoi vertoprakh. Original'naia komediia v trekh deistviiakh, v stikhakh.* Moscow: Tipografiia A. Reshetnikova, 1796.

Seligman, Adam B. *The Idea of Civil Society.* 1992. Reprint, Princeton: Princeton University Press 1995.

Selivanov, N. "Teatr v tsarstvovanie Imperatritsy Ekateriny II." *Ezhegodnik imperatorskikh teatrov,* god 6, sezon 1895–1896, *Prilozheniia,* kn. 2 (1897): 15–76, kn. 3 (1897): 86–117.

Semenova, L. N. *Byt i naselenie Sankt Peterburga (XVIII vek).* St. Petersburg: Blits, 1998.

——. *Ocherki istorii byta i kul'turnoi zhizni Rossii, pervaia polovina XVIII v.* Leningrad: Nauka, 1982.

Sennett, Richard. *The Fall of Public Man.* New York: W. W. Norton, 1992.

Serman, I. Z. "Iz istorii literaturnoi bor'by 60–kh godov XVIII veka (Neizdannaia komediia Fedora Emina 'Uchenaia Shaika.')." *XVIII vek* 3 (1958): 207–25.

——. *Russkii klassitsizm: Poeziia, drama, satira.* Leningrad: Nauka, 1981.

Shamrai, D. D. "K istorii tsenzurnogo rezhima Ekateriny II." *XVIII vek* 3 (1958): 187–206.

——. "Tsenzurnyi nadzor nad tipografiei sukhoputnogo shliakhetnogo kadetskogo korpusa." *XVIII vek* 2 (1940): 293–329.

Shatz, Marshall S. "The Noble Landowner in Russian Comic Operas of the Time of Catherine the Great: The Patriarchal Image." *Canadian Slavic Studies* 3 (1969): 22–38.

Shcherbakova, M. N. *Muzyka v russkoi drame 1756–pervaia polovina XIX v.* St. Petersburg: Ut, 1997.

Shcherbatov, M. M. *On the Corruption of Morals in Russia.* Edited and translated by A. Lentin. Cambridge, Eng.: Cambridge University Press, 1969.

Shepelev, L. E. *Chinovnyi mir Rossii XVIII–nachalo XX v.* St. Petersburg: Iskusstvo-SPb, 1999.

Shovlin, John. "Toward a Reinterpretation of Revolutionary Antinobilism: The Political Economy of Honor in the Old Regime." *Journal of Modern History* 72 (2000): 35–66.

Shtelin, Ia. Ia. "Kratkoe izvestie o teatral'nykh v Rossii predstavleniiakh, ot nachala ikh do 1768 goda, sochinennoe na nemetskom iazyke ego prevoskhoditel'stvom, deistvitel'nym Statskim Sovetnikom Ia. Ia. Shtelinom." *Sanktpeterburgskii vestnik,* chast' 4 (August 1779): 83–95; (September 1779): 163–74.

Simmons, Ernest J. "Catherine the Great and Shakespeare." *PMLA* 47 (1932): 790–806.

Slater, Maya. "Meant to Be Played: Molière's Mystery, Panache, and Love of the Stage." *The Times Literary Supplement,* no. 5004 (February 26, 1999): 4–5.

Slezkine, Yuri. "Naturalists versus Nations: Eighteenth-Century Russian Scholars Confront Ethnic Diversity." *Representations* 47 (1994): 170–95.

Slovar' Akademii rossiiskoi, 6 vols. St. Petersburg: Imperatorskaia akademiia nauk, 1789–1794. 2d ed., 1806–1822.

Slovar' russkikh pisatelei XVIII veka. Vols. 1–2. Leningrad/St. Petersburg: Nauka, 1988, 1999– .

Slovar' russkogo iazyka XVIII veka. Vols. 1–12. Leningrad/St. Petersburg: Nauka, 1987–2001– .

Smeliansky, Anatoly. *The Russian Theater after Stalin.* Cambridge, Eng.: Cambridge University Press, 1999.

Smith, Jay M. *The Culture of Merit: Nobility, Royal Service, and the Making of Absolute Monarchy in France, 1600–1789.* Ann Arbor: University of Michigan Press, 1996.

——. "No More Language Games: Words, Beliefs, and the Political Culture of Early Modern France." *American Historical Review* 102 (1997): 1413–40.

——. "Social Categories, the Language of Patriotism, and the Origins of the French Revolution: The Debate over *noblesse commerçante.*" *Journal of Modern History* 72 (2000): 339–74.

Smith, Douglas. *Working the Rough Stone: Freemasonry and Society in Eighteenth-Century Russia.* DeKalb: Northern Illinois University Press, 1999.

Smolina, K. A. *Russkaia tragediia. XVIII vek. Evoliutsiia zhanra.* Moscow: Nasledie, 2001.

Smuts, R. Malcolm. *Culture and Power in England, 1585–1685.* New York: St. Martin's Press, 1999.

Sokolev, I. Ia. *Komediia Vydumannoi klad.* In *Rossiiskii featr.* 27:209–66.

———. *Sudeiskie imenini. Komediia v trekh deistviiakh.* In *Rossiiskii featr.* 35:3–104.

Soldatskoe shchast'e. Komediia v piati deistviiakh G. Lessinga. Prelozhil s nemetskogo na Rossiiskie nravy I. Z. Moscow: Tipografiia imperatorskogo moskovskogo universiteta, 1779.

Somers, Margaret R. "Narrating and Naturalizing Civil Society and Citizenship Theory." *Sociological Theory* 13 (1995): 229–74.

———. "What's Political or Cultural about the Political Culture Concept? Toward an Historical Sociology of Concept Formation?" *Sociological Theory* 13 (1995): 113–44.

Sonenscher, Michael. "Enlightenment and Revolution." *Journal of Modern History* 70 (1998): 371–83.

Sosednii prazdnik. Predstavlenie v odnom deistvii. In *Rossiiskii featr.* 33:179–94.

Sperber, Jonathan. *"Bürger, Bürgertum, Bürgerlichkeit, Bürgerliche Gesellschaft:* Studies of the German (Upper) Middle Class and Its Sociocultural World." *Journal of Modern History* 69 (1997): 271–97.

Starikova, L. M. "Dinastiia kukol'nikov Iakubovskikh v Rossii v pervoi polovine XVIII v." In *Pamiatniki kul'tury: Novye otkrytiia 1989.* Moscow: Nauka, 1990.

———. "Dnevnaia zapiska 1786–1787 gg. A. V. Orlova." In *Pamiatniki kul'tury: Novye otkrytiia 1983.* Leningrad: Nauka, 1985.

———. "Dokumental'nye utochneniia k istorii teatra v Rossii Petrovskogo vremeni." In *Pamiatniki kul'tury: Novye otkrytiia 1997.* Moscow: Nauka, 1998.

———. "Dva pis'ma aktera Ivana Afanas'evicha Dmitrevskogo." In *Pamiatniki kul'tury: Novye otkrytiia 1982.* Leningrad: Nauka, 1984.

———. "Inostrannye kukol'niki v Rossii v pervoi polovine XVIII v." In *Pamiatniki kul'tury: Novye otkrytiia 1995.* Moscow: Nauka, 1996.

———. "Istoriia Moskovskoi publichnoi antreprizy vtoroi poloviny XVIII v. v dokumental'nykh podrobnostiakh." In *Pamiatniki kul'tury: Novye otkrytiia 1996.* Moscow: Nauka, 1998.

———. "K istorii domashnikh krepostnykh teatrov i orkestrov v Rossii kontsa XVII–XVIII vekov." In *Pamiatniki kul'tury: Novye otkrytiia 1991.* Moscow: Nauka, 1997.

———. *Moskva starodavniaia: Geroi, zhizn', i stseny.* Kaliningrad: Skaz, 2000.

———. "Novye dokumenty o deiatel'nosti ital'ianskoi truppy v Rossii v 30–e gody XVIII v. i russkom liubitel'skom teatre etogo vremeni." In *Pamiatniki kul'tury: Novye otkrytiia 1988.* Moscow: Nauka, 1989.

———. "Novye dokumenty o pervykh russkikh akterakh brat'iakh Fedore i Grigorii Volkovykh." In *Pamiatniki kul'tury: Novye otkrytiia 1981.* Leningrad: Nauka, 1983.

———. "Pervaia russkaia baletnaia truppa." In *Pamiatniki kul'tury: Novye otkrytiia 1985.* Moscow: Nauka, 1987.

———. "Russkii teatr petrovskogo vremeni: Komedial'naia khamina i domashnie komedii Tsarevny Natal'i Alekseevny." In *Pamiatniki kul'tury: Novye otkrytiia 1990.* Moscow: Krug, 1992.

———. "Shtrikhi k biografii pervykh russkikh aktris." In *Pamiatniki kul'tury: Novye otkrytiia 1994.* Moscow: Nauka, 1996.

———. *Teatral'naia zhizn' starinnoi Moskvy: Epokha. Byt. Nravy.* Moscow: Iskusstvo, 1988.

———. "Teatral'no-zrelishchnaia zhizn' Moskvy v seredine XVIII veka." In *Pamiatniki kul'tury: Novye otkrytiia 1986.* Leningrad: Nauka, 1987.

———. *Teatr v Rossii XVIII veka: Opyt dokumental'nogo issledovaniia.* Moscow: GTsTM im. A. A. Bakhrushina, 1997.

———. "'Zapiska o vozniknovenii i razvitii teatral'nogo iskusstva v Moskve so vremeni Alekseia Mikhailovicha po XIX vek' A. F. Malinovskogo." In *Pamiatniki kul'tury: Novye otkrytiia 1993.* Moscow: Nauka, 1995.

———, ed. *Teatral'naia zhizn' Rossii v epokhu Anny Ioannovny.* Vypusk 1, *Dokumental'naia khronika 1730–1740.* Moscow: Radiks, 1995.

Steele, Eugene, and David Welch. "The *Commedia Dell'arte* in Eighteenth-Century Poland and Russia." *Forum Italicum* 9 (1975): 409–17.

Stennik, Iu. V. "Istoriosofskie aspekty soderzhaniia russkoi dramaturgii XVIII veka. (Zhanr tragedii)." *XVIII vek* 19 (1995): 70–85.

———. "Rol' komedii v polemike 1750–1760-kh godov." *XVIII vek* 17 (1991): 28–46.

———, ed. *Dramaticheskie sochineniia.* Leningrad: Iskusstvo, 1990.

———, ed. *Russkaia literatura. Vek XVIII. Tragediia.* Moscow: Khudozhestvennaia literatura, 1991.

Stribrny, Zdenek. *Shakespeare and Eastern Europe.* New York: Oxford University Press, 2000.

Sudovshchikov, N. R. *Neslykhannoe divo, ili Chestnyi sekretar'. Komediia v trekh deistviiakh v stikhakh.* In *Stikhotvornaia komediia kontsa XVIII–nachala XIX v.,* edited by M. O. Ianovskii. Moscow and Leningrad: Sovetskii pisatel', 1964.

Sumarokov, A. P. *Al'tsesta. Opera.* In *Polnoe sobranie vsekh sochinenii v stikhakh i proze.* 4:221–46.

———. *Artistona. Tragediia.* In *Dramaticheskie sochineniia.*

———. *Chudovishchi. Komediia.* In *Dramaticheskie sochineniia.*

———. *Dmitrii Samozvanets. Tragediia.* In *Dramaticheskie sochineniia.*

———. *Dramaticheskie sochineniia.* Edited by Iu. V. Stennik. Leningrad: Iskusstvo, 1990.

———. *Gamlet. Tragediia.* In *Polnoe sobranie vsekh sochinenii v stikhakh i proze.* 3:59–119.

———. *Iadovityi. Komediia.* In *Polnoe sobranie vsekh sochinenii v stikhakh i proze.* 6:155–96.

———. *Iaropolk i Dimiza. Tragediia.* In *Polnoe sobranie vsekh sochinenii v stikhakh i proze.* 3:331–96.

———. *Izbrannye proizvedeniia.* Leningrad: Sovetskii pisatel', 1957.

———. *Khorev. Tragediia.* In *Dramaticheskie sochineniia.*

———. *Likhoimets. Komediia.* In *Polnoe sobranie vsekh sochinenii v stikhakh i proze.* 5:55–122.

———. *Mat' sovmestnitsa docheri. Komediia.* In *Polnoe sobranie vsekh sochinenii v stikhakh i proze.* 6:57–106.

———. *Mstislav. Tragediia.* In *Polnoe sobranie vsekh sochinenii v stikhakh i proze.* 4:127–79.

———. *Nartsiss. Komediia.* In *Polnoe sobranie vsekh sochinenii v stikhakh i proze.* 6:197–238.

———. *Opekun. Komediia.* In *Dramaticheskie sochineniia.*

———. *Polnoe sobranie vsekh sochinenii v stikhakh i proze.* 6 vols. Moscow: Universitetskaia tipografiia u N. Novikova, 1781.

————. *Pridanoe obmanom. Komediia.* In *Dramaticheskie sochineniia.*

————. *Pustaia ssora. Komediia.* In *Dramaticheskie sochineniia.*

————. *Pustynnik. Drama.* In *Dramaticheskie sochineniia.*

————. *Rogonets po voobrazheniiu. Komediia.* In *Dramaticheskie sochineniia.*

————. *Semira. Tragediia.* In *Dramaticheskie sochineniia.*

————. *Sinav i Truvor. Tragediia.* In *Dramaticheskie sochineniia.*

————. *Tresotinius. Komediia.* In *Dramaticheskie sochineniia.*

————. *Vysheslav. Tragediia.* In *Polnoe sobranie vsekh sochinenii v stikhakh i proze.* 4:1–56.

————. *Vzdorshchitsa. Komediia.* In *Dramaticheskie sochineniia.*

Sumarokov, P. I. "O Rossiiskom teatre, ot nachala onogo do kontsa tsarstvovaniia Ekateriny II." *Otechestvennye zapiski* 12, no. 32 (December 1822): 289–311; 13, no. 35 (March 1823): 370–99.

Svin'in, P. P. *Dostopamiatnosti Sankt-Peterburga i ego okrestnostei.* Reprint, St. Petersburg: Liga plius, 1997.

Svodnyi katalog Rossiiskikh notnykh izdanii. Vol. 1, *Vosemnadtsatyi vek.* St. Petersburg: Rossiiskaia natsional'naia biblioteka, 1996.

Svodnyi katalog russkoi knigi grazhdanskoi pechati XVIII veka, 1725–1800. 5 vols. Moscow: Kniga, 1963–1967.

Swoboda, Marina. "*The Furnace Play* and the Development of Liturgical Drama in Russia." *Russian Review* 61 (2002): 220–34.

T., L. *Svad'ba Gospodina Promotalova. Komediia v trekh deistviiakh.* In *Rossiiskii featr.* 27:53–148.

Taylor, Charles. "Modes of Civil Society." *Public Culture* 3 (1990): 95–118.

"Teatr." *Zritel': ezhemesiachnoe izdanie,* chast' 2 (June 1792): 121–45, (August 1792): 251–77; chast' 3 (September 1792): 25–39, (October 1792): 113–37, (December 1792): 249–55.

Teil's, I. A. de. *Chuvstvovanie blagotvorenii. Dramma s baletom.* In *Rossiiskii featr.* 34:205–40.

————. *Nagrazhdenie dobrodeteli. Drama, predstavlennaia pitomtsami Aleksandrovskogo uchilishcha zavedennogo v Sanktpeterburge izdateliami Utrenniago Sveta i dlia nikh sochinennaia.* In *Rossiiskii featr.* 9:113–78.

Terras, Victor, ed. *Handbook of Russian Literature.* New Haven: Yale University Press, 1985.

Thompson, Martyn P. "Reception Theory and the Interpretation of Historical Meaning." *History and Theory* 32 (1993): 248–72.

Thurston, Gary. *The Popular Theatre Movement in Russia, 1862–1919.* Evanston, Ill.: Northwestern University Press, 1998.

Tikhonravov, N., ed. *Russkiia dramaticheskiia proizvedeniia 1672–1725 godov. K 200–letnemu iubileiu russkago teatra.* 2 vols. St. Petersburg: Izdatel'stvo D. E. Kozhanchikova, 1874.

Tilly, Charles. *Durable Inequality.* Berkeley: University of California Press, 1998.

Tishkin, G. A., ed. *Feminizm i Rossiiskaia kul'tura: Sbornik trudov.* St. Petersburg: Mezhdunarodnyi institut Zhenshchina i Upravlenie, 1995.

Titov, P. N. *Nasledniki. Komediia v odnom deistvii.* St. Petersburg: Gubernskoe pravlenie, 1799.

Todorov, Tzvetan. *Genres in Discourse.* Translated by Catherine Porter. New York: Cambridge University Press, 1990.

————. *The Morals of History.* Translated by Alyson Waters. Minneapolis: University of Minnesota Press, 1995.

Torzhestvuiushchaia dobrodetel'. Drama v piati deistviiakh. In *Rossiiskii featr.* 9:179–218.

Tovrov, Jessica. *The Russian Noble Family: Structure and Change.* Ph.D. diss., University of Chicago, 1980; reprinted, New York: Garland, 1987.

Trediakovskii, V. K. *Deidamiia. Tragediia.* In *Rossiiskii featr.* 3:177–314.

Troe lenivykh. Opera v odnom deistvii. In *Rossiiskii featr.* 37:5–30.

Trudy Vasiliia Levshina i Ivana Fr. Kertseliia na 1793 god. Kaluga: n.p., 1793.

"Tsenzurnaia vedomost' 1786–1788 godov." In *Osmnadtsatyi vek.* Kniga 1. Edited by Petr Bartenev. Moscow: Tipografiia T. Ris, 1868.

Val'denberg, Vladimir. *Drevnerusskiia ucheniia o predelakh tsarskoi vlasti: Ocherki russkoi politicheskoi literatury ot Vladimira Sviatogo do kontsa XVII veka.* 1916. Reprint, The Hague: Europe Printing, 1966.

V., M. *Otets vozvrashchennyi detiam. Drammaticheskii anekdot. V dvukh deistviiakh.* Moscow: Gubernskaia tipografiia u A. Reshetnikova, 1801.

Varneke, B. *Istoriia russkogo teatra XVII–XIX vekov.* 3d ed. Moscow and Leningrad: Iskusstvo, 1939.

Vecherinki, ili Gadai gadai devitsa otgadyvai krasnaia. Opera komicheskaia. St. Petersburg: n.p., 1788.

Verevkin, M. I. *Imianinniki. Komediia v piati deistviiakh.* In *Rossiiskii featr.* 21:187–306.

———. *Tak i dolzhno. Komediia v piati deistviiakh.* In *Rossiiskii featr.* 19:155–238.

———. *Toch' v toch'. Komediia v trekh deistviiakh. Sochinennaia v Simbirske.* In *Rossiiskii featr.* 33:133–74.

Viazemskii, V. S. *Pustynnik. Dramma v trekh deistviiakh.* Moscow: Gubernskaia tipografiia u A. Reshetnikova, 1800.

Viazmitinov, S. K. *Novoe semeistvo. Komicheskaia opera v odnom deistvii.* In *Rossiiskii featr.* 24:233–79.

Vickery, Amanda. *The Gentleman's Daughter: Women's Lives in Georgian England.* New Haven: Yale University Press, 1998.

———. "Golden Age to Separate Spheres? A Review of the Categories and Chronology of English Women's History." *The Historical Journal* 36 (1993): 383–414.

Vigel', F. F. *Zapiski.* 2 vols. 1928. Reprint, Cambridge, Mass.: Oriental Research Partners, 1974.

Volkov, A. A. *Chadoliubie. Komediia v odnom deistvii.* Moscow: Universitetskaia tipografiia u N. Novikova, 1788.

———. *Neudachnoe upriamstvo. Komediia v odnom deistvii.* St. Petersburg: n.p., 1779.

Volkov, D. V. *Vospitanie.* Moscow: Imperatorskii moskovskii universitet, 1774.

Volkov, S. V. *Russkii ofitserskii korpus.* Moscow: Voenizdat, 1993.

Vorontsov-Dashkov, A. I., ed. *Ekaterina Romanovna Dashkova: Issledovaniia i materialy.* St. Petersburg: Dmitrii Bulanin, 1996.

Vorozhbitova, M. V. "Dokumenty kantseliarii konfiskatsii kak istochnik dlia kharakteristiki byta gorozhan serediny XVIII v." *Vestnik moskovskogo universiteta,* seriia 8, *Istoriia,* no. 1 (1999): 71–84.

Vovelle, Michel, ed. *Enlightenment Portraits.* Translated by Lydia G. Cochrane. Chicago: University of Chicago Press, 1997.

Vsevolodskii-Gerngross, Vsevolod N. [V. N.]. *Istoriia russkogo dramaticheskogo teatra.* Vol. 1, *Ot istokov do kontsa XVIII veka.* Moscow: Iskusstvo, 1977.

———. *Istoriia russkogo teatra.* Vol. 1. Leningrad and Moscow: Teakinopechat', 1929.

———, ed. *Khrestomatiia po istorii russkogo teatra.* Moscow: Khudozhestvennaia literatura. 1936.

Vybor po razumu. Komediia v trekh deistviiakh. St. Petersburg: n.p., 1773.

Walker, Mack. "Rights and Functions: The Social Categories of Eighteenth-Century German Jurists and Cameralists." *Journal of Modern History* 50 (1978): 234–51.

Wallace, David. "Bourgeois Tragedy or Sentimental Melodrama? The Significance of George Lillo's *The London Merchant.*" *Eighteenth-Century Studies* 25 (Winter 1991–1992): 123–43.

Wagner, William G. *Marriage, Property, and Law in Late Imperial Russia.* New York: Oxford University Press, 1994.

Ware, Timothy. *The Orthodox Church.* Revised ed. New York: Penguin Books, 1997.

Wartenweiler, David. *Civil Society and Academic Debate in Russia, 1905–1914.* New York: Oxford University Press, 1999.

Weber, William. "L'institution et son public. L'Opéra à Paris et à Londre au XVIIIe siècle." *Annales: Économies, Sociétés, Civilisations* 48 (1993): 1519–39.

Weickhardt, George G. "Music and Society in Russia, 1860s–1890s." *Canadian-American Slavic Studies* 30 (1996): 45–68.

Welsh, David J. *Russian Comedy, 1765–1823.* The Hague and Paris: Mouton, 1966.

———. "Satirical Themes in Eighteenth-Century Russian Comedies." *Slavonic and East European Review* 42 (1964): 403–14.

Whaples, Miriam Karpilow. "Eighteenth-Century Russian Opera in the Light of Soviet Scholarship." *Indiana Slavic Studies* 2 (1958): 113–34.

Wiener, Martin J. "Treating 'Historical' Sources as Literary Texts: Literary Historicism and Modern British History." *Journal of Modern History* 70 (1998): 619–38.

Wigzell, Faith. *Reading Russian Fortunes: Print Culture, Gender, and Divination in Russia from 1765.* Cambridge, Eng.: Cambridge University Press, 1998.

Williamson, George S. "What Killed August Von Kotzebue? The Temptations of Virtue and the Political Theology of German Nationalism, 1789–1819." *Journal of Modern History* 72 (2000): 890–943.

Wirtschafter, Elise Kimerling. "The Common Soldier in Eighteenth-Century Russian Drama." In *Reflections on Russia in the Eighteenth Century,* edited by Joachim Klein, Simon Dixon, and Maarten Fraanje. Cologne: Böhlau, 2001.

———. *From Serf to Russian Soldier.* Princeton: Princeton University Press, 1990.

———. "In Search of the People, in Search of Russia." *Russian Review* 60 (2001): 497–504.

———. "Legal Identity and the Possession of Serfs in Imperial Russia." *Journal of Modern History* 70 (1998): 561–87.

———. "Military Service and Social Hierarchy: The View from Eighteenth-Century Russian Theater." In *Russian Military History,* edited by Eric Lohr and Marshall Poe. Leiden: Brill Academic Publishers, 2002.

———. *Social Identity in Imperial Russia.* DeKalb: Northern Illinois University Press, 1997.

———. "Social Misfits: Veterans and Soldiers' Families in Servile Russia." *Journal of Military History* 59 (1995): 215–35.

———. "Soldiers' Children: A Study of Social Engineering in Imperial Russia." *Forschungen zur osteuropäischen Geschichte* 30 (1982): 61–136.

———. *Structures of Society: Imperial Russia's "People of Various Ranks."* DeKalb: Northern Illinois University Press, 1994.

Worobec, Christine D. *Peasant Russia: Family and Community in the Post-Emancipation Period.* Princeton: Princeton University Press, 1991.

Wortman, Richard S. *The Development of Russian Legal Consciousness.* Chicago: University of Chicago Press, 1976.

——. *Scenarios of Power: Myth and Ceremony in Russian Monarchy.* Vol. 1, *From Peter the Great to the Death of Nicholas I.* Princeton: Princeton University Press, 1995.

Zabelin, I. E. "Khronika obshchestvennoi zhizni v Moskve s poloviny XVIII stoletiia." In *Opyty izucheniia russkikh drevnostei i istorii: Izsledovaniia, opisaniia, i kriticheskiia stat'i Iv. Zabelina,* vol. 2:351–505. Moscow: Izdatel'stvo K. Soldatenkova, 1873.

Zaichkin, I. A., and I. N. Pochkaev. *Ekaterininskie orly.* Moscow: Mysl', 1996.

Zakonodatel'stvo Petra I. Moscow: Izdatel'stvo iuridicheskoi literatury, 1997.

Zelnik, Reginald E. "*Weber* into *Tkachi:* On a Russian Reading of Gerhart Hauptmann's Play *The Weavers.*" In *Self and Story in Russian History,* edited by Laura Engelstein and Stephanie Sandler. Ithaca, N.Y.: Cornell University Press, 2000.

Zguta, Russell. *Russian Minstrels: A History of the Skomorokhi.* Philadelphia: University of Pennsylvania Press, 1978.

Zheltov, Andrei. *Tri svad'by vdrug, ili Kak auknetsia tak i otklinetsia. Opera komicheskaia v dvukh deistviiakh.* Moscow: Tipografiia A. Reshetnikova, 1794.

Zhenikh dovolen. Komediia v trekh deistviiakh, vol'nymi stikhami. Moscow: n.p., 1795.

Zhikharev, S. P. *Zapiski sovremennika. Vospominaniia starogo teatrala.* 2 vols. Leningrad: Iskusstvo, 1989.

Zhirkov, G. V. *Istoriia tsenzury v Rossii XIX–XX vv.: Uchebnoe posobie.* Moscow: Aspekt-Press, 2001.

——. "Vek ofitsial'noi tsenzury." In *Ocherki russkoi kul'tury XIX veka.* Vol. 2, *Vlast' i kul'tura.* Moscow: Izdatel'stvo moskovskogo universiteta, 2000.

Zhivov, V. M. "Gosudarstvennyi mif v epokhu prosveshcheniia i ego razrushenie v Rossii kontsa XVIII veka." In *Iz istorii russkoi kul'tury.* Vol. 4 *(XVIII–nachalo XIX veka).* Moscow: Shkola iazyki russkoi kul'tury, 1996.

——. *Iazyk i kul'tura v Rossii XVIII veka.* Moscow: Shkola iazyki russkoi kul'tury, 1996.

Zloumnyi. Komediia v piati deistviiakh. In *Rossiiskii featr.* 23:69–271.

Zorin, Andrei. *Kormia dvuglavnogo orla . . . Literatura i gosudarstvennaia ideologiia v Rossii v poslednei treti XVIII–pervoi treti XIX veka.* Moscow: Novoe literaturnoe obozrenie, 2001.

INDEX

Ablesimov, A. O., 91, 93, 97, 230n
Abraham, 55, 151
absolute monarchy, 115–16, 166, 175–76, 247n
Academy of Arts, 12, 206n
Academy of Sciences, 15, 25–26, 38, 47, 211n
Achille in Sciro, 242n
Achilles, 151, 242n
actors, 43
adaptation, 36–37, 41–42. *See also* imitation; translation
Addison, Joseph, 23
Admetus, 67
adultery, 69–72. *See also* marriage
Agriopa, 152
Akulov, M. G., 16
Alcestis, 67
Alchemist, The, 213n, 219n
Aleksei Mikhailovich, Tsar, 6, 8–9, 204n
Alexander I, Emperor, 19, 27, 163, 169, 171
Alexander Nevskii Monastery, 25
Aliab'ev, A. B., 18, 208n
All Sorts of Things, 24, 28
Amante amant, L', 217n
amateur theater, 20
Amathus, 56
American Revolution, 52, 221n
Americans, The, 46, 112–13
Amsterdam, 10
Aniuta, 87
Anna Ivanovna, Empress, 7–10, 205n
Anna, Duchess of Holstein, 245n
Annette et Lubin, 229n
Ante-Room of the Eminent Boyar, The, 162–63
Apollo, 67
Apollos (A. D. Baibakov), 72
Appreciation of Good Works, 169–70
Araija, Francesco, 224n
Arbatskii Theater, 17
Aristophanes, 33
Aristotle, 144
Armuth und Edelsinn, 38, 215–16n
Arnaud, François-Thomas-Marie de Baculard d', 59
Artaxerxes Play, The, 6
artel', 19
Artemis, 67
Artillery School, 12
Artistona, 151–52
As It Should Be, 132

Askold and Dir, 242n
assemblies, 4, 70
Astarita, Gennaro, 11, 226n
As You Live, So You Are Judged, 107
Athens, 151
Attica, 151
audiences, 13, 22–25, 28, 43–47
Augustus II, 8
Austrasia, 161
authors, 36–47
autobiography, 40
Avare, L', 23

Baba Iaga, 50, 220n
Bailiff, The, 86
bailiffs, 86–89, 229n
Balkan Slavs, 125
ballet, 11, 16, 93, 128, 169
Baltic, 124, 230n
Barthe, Nicolas-Thomas, 69
Beaumarchais, Pierre-Augustin Caron de, 44–45
Beginning of Oleg's Reign, The, 31, 245–46n
Belmonti, Giovanni, 16
Belosel'skii-Belozerskii, A. M., 57, 222n
Belosel'skii family, 209n
Berg, Johann von, 77
Berger (English acrobat), 10
Betrothal of Kuteikin, The, 64–65
Betrothed, The, 220n
Betschwester, Die, 108
Bible, 5, 12
Bidloo, Nicolaas, 5
Blagodarov, Ia. I., 45, 128–29
Blank, B. K., 215n
Bogdanovich, I. F., 143–44
Bogoroditsk (Tula province), 20, 37, 226n
Bohomolec, Franciszek, 214n
Boissy, Louis de, 41, 217n
Bolotov, A. T., 20, 37, 74–75, 80, 226n
Boltin, I. N., 245n
Bon Ton, or High Life above Stairs, 104
Borislav, 155
Bourgeois Gentilhomme, Le, 50–51, 98
bourgeois public sphere. *See* public sphere
bourgeois tragedy. *See* drama
Boutique de Bijoutier, Le, 38–39
Braggart, The, 74, 104
Brigadier, The, 139–40